Once Upon A Road Trip

Angela N. Blount

Published by Artifice Press®

ISBN: 978-0-9895809-2-2

Copyright © 2013 by Angela N. Blount
Cover photography by Danielle Barnum
Cover art by Revalis
Editing by Courtney Wichtendahl

An Artifice Press book / published by arrangement with the author

ONCE UPON A ROAD TRIP

Library of Congress Control Number: 2013915506

Printed in the United States of America

Disclaimer

"This memoir is based on the author's personal experiences over a single summer. Events and conversations have been depicted to the best of my recollection; several years after the fact, and with the assistance of actual journal entries used for documentation. Some incidents and dialogue have been condensed for the ease of retelling. Names and identifying details have been changed or omitted to protect privacy. It is only my intention to tell my story, not to cause anyone harm or defamation."

For my dear husband, without whose support,
I might never have had the gall to chase my dreams.
Thank you for being my favorite adventure.

~ ~ ~ ~ ~ ~ ~

And for our children.
Because one day, I want you to know the whole story of how I met
your father.

Part 1

"How vain it is to sit down to write when you have not stood up to live."
-Henry David Thoreau

Prologue

May 14th,

     Free Spirit. Wanderlust. Soul searching. …I like to think of this as more of a pre-life crisis. What else could compel a "normal" eighteen-year-old girl from a semi-functional family in a small, Minnesota college town to get into her car and drive around the country for two months? Regardless of how bizarre that sounds, this isn't some impulsive whim. I've been planning this little venture for nearly six months now; contrary to all sound advice.

     It's my first day of owning this journal. Not that I've ever cared much for journals or diaries, but I thought it might be wise to keep a record. Although, wisdom isn't something anyone I know would equate with this little road trip I've got planned. I'm wary of it myself, but I also know it's something I need to get out of my system. I'm not driving over 6,000 miles just to sightsee and meet people. While that's part of it, I see this as a huge personal growth opportunity for me. Hopefully, I'll be using this journal to keep track of said growth.

     This will be my "Walkabout," to borrow the Australian term. Just another step in the process of me finding myself, and figuring out what I'm here for. I've been putting a lot of thought and prayer into my preparations. While part of me is afraid to go off and do all of this alone, that only confirms in my mind that it needs to be done. I don't like the idea of being afraid of anything. And so, I'm trying an approach I've come up with recently. If something scares me I'm going to charge straight into it until, a) I become so used to it that I no longer fear it, or, b) I end up unconscious. Okay, so this plan might need some tweaking. It's more of a work in progress. Just like me.

     Mom has been on edge ever since she realized how serious I am about doing this. I can't blame her for caring, but I wish she wouldn't worry. She was the one who pointed out that I was up and running at eight months old, and my very first word was "Bye-bye." Not "Ma-ma." Not "Da-da"… "Bye-bye." If that's not a sign, I don't know what is.

Of course, my second word was "donut." So maybe I'm reading too much into that…

~Ang

Chapter 1

Angie smoothed her slick palms down the seams of her scarlet graduation gown. Though dusk was falling, the loss of sunlight only took the barest edge off the early June humidity. Around her pressed hundreds of her classmates, all filed into rows in front of a portable stage that had been erected on one side of her high school football field. While she'd already endured the stifling situation for nearly an hour, the anticipation of having her name called threatened to drive her to the brink of nausea.

She distracted herself by rehearsing her steps in her mind. It was a necessity for someone who had difficulty navigating perfectly flat terrain, never mind the three steps up onto a rickety snap-together stage. For better or worse, it would all be over soon.

"Please God, don't let me fall," Angie prayed under her breath. Finally hearing her full name, Angeli, called out, she began her trek. Her anxiety peaked as the rubber of her squared heels caught along the grass, reminding her again of the Senior Prom debacle.

She'd worn these same ill-fated shoes that night. Having no success at finding a date, she'd decided to go stag along with her Somali friend, Millune. Denying her tomboy sensibilities for once, she'd spent hours in preparation for the evening — going to the trouble of coercing her long brown hair into holding curls, donning a shimmering floor-length gown, and even plunging into the foreign territory of wearing makeup. Turning prom into a girls' night out hadn't seemed like such a bad idea, up until the Grand March announcer stumbled over Millune's name and mistakenly introduced the friends as a couple.

Angie could still hear the ripples of laughter and surprised murmuring of the crowd. The error took her attention off her feet just long enough for her to trip on her way off the stage. She missed the railing, and two years of Aikido training kicked in.

Tucking her head, she converted her fall into a front roll, allowing her weight to curve along her bowed arms. Landing unhurt in a crouch on the red carpet, she sprang back to her feet, mind racing for some way of making the epic blunder look more intentional. She then clasped her hands together and raised them above her head in a triumphant gesture, and was met with a roar of applause from the photo-happy crowd. Amid the creeping burn of humiliation, determination had steeled somewhere deep within her. She wanted much more than a laughable existence in an obscure, Midwestern town.

For the last two months, Angie hadn't heard the end of that disastrous night. Her peers seemed to delight equally in poking fun at her clumsiness, as well as her supposed "outing." She had yet to decide which was worse: the mocking, or the sympathetic inquiries. If any part of her had been holding out hope of dating while she was still in high school, it died a painful and awkward death at prom.

Oh well. As far as she was concerned, the selection pool had always been shallow. Or at least, that's what she often told herself to fend off the suspicion there might be something terminally undesirable about her.

Now, in the final moments she would have to see any of these people, she was determined to maintain her dignity.

Angie pushed the past out of her mind as her foot touched the first step. With the stage squeaking under her firm stride, she crossed to the middle of the platform. Managing a smile for the school principal — a stern looking man in a gray suit — she accepted a scrolled piece of paper. This wasn't the real diploma, of course. That would be arriving in the mail the following week. She planned to be gone by then.

Continuing on to the far side of the stage, she met the second set of stairs and held her breath, counting steps on her way down. *One, two, three.* Crisis averted.

Relieved to have her feet safely on the ground, she made her way back to her original position to wait out the remainder of the ceremony. As per a new rule, no one would be allowed to throw their graduation caps at the end. Evidently, someone somewhere had put an eye out. As an alternative, her classmates readied streamers and cans of silly string while a favored English teacher took the pulpit to deliver a few final words of inspiration.

When the speaker made mention of graduation caps signifying success and knowledge, Angie's attention strayed. She didn't feel successful or knowledgeable. Having completed the requirements to pass high school, she could at least claim a sense of accomplishment. But she had come to think of it as mere survival rather than true success. In this particular rite of passage, the objective hadn't been to slay the dragon, but simply to avoid being eaten by it for four years.

While she technically knew more facts coming away from it than she had going in, she'd accumulated many more uncertainties. What career path should she take? Where would she want to live? How could she make her life count for something worthwhile? What did it feel like to be in love? These questions all seemed critical, and in no way did recalling the square root of Pi prepare her to answer any of them.

An exuberant shout from the teenage mob signaled the finale, snapping her back to reality. The crowd dispersed in all directions amid a blizzard of confetti and streamers, with the majority making their way toward the after-party in the school gymnasium. Angie wasn't interested in dragging out the goodbyes. After hugging her parents and posing for a few obligatory pictures, she wove herself through the scattering masses. Turning around to a tap on her shoulder, she found herself nose to nose with her best friend, Elsie.

At roughly the same height as Angie, just a few inches shy of six feet, Elsie was an eccentric creature in form as well as demeanor. Her eyes shone a bright and cunning shade of gray, like the surface of a pond after a freeze. Unruly russet hair fell as it pleased to frame her dusky, rounded features, which alluded to a vast and indistinct muddling of genetic heritage. For this particular occasion she'd chosen an elaborate red and gold Mandarin dress to compliment her willowy form. As she leaned in obnoxiously close to Angie's face, the contrast between her friend's elegant attire and childish demeanor was downright comical.

"Boo!"

"Ahh," Angie answered flatly.

"You look like crap." Elsie chirped out, in her usual cheerful tone.

"Thank you." Angie rolled her eyes. "So are you riding with me?"

"Yeah. The 'rents dropped me off." Elsie made a sweeping indicative motion toward the migrating horde of seniors. "Sure you don't want to stay for the shindig?"

"I'd rather thrust a sharp stick into my eye," Angie said in a glaringly unexcited tone.

Elsie tapped a slender finger to her chin as she pondered, "We could go to Walmart and I'll let you push me around in a shopping cart."

Angie shook her head. "Too risky. They almost banned us for life last time, after your little pillow-bin-diving incident."

"Killjoy." Elsie grinned. "Well...we could try an overnighter at the diner. Let's swing by my house so I can grab a sleeping bag."

As Elsie spun around to move in the direction of the parking lot, Angie saw a confrontation coming out of the corner of her eye. She shot out a hand and caught her friend's shoulder. But while a collision was avoided, the near-miss was enough to draw the attention of the passing pack of girls.

Mindy lurched to one side, as though the mere threat of contact with Elsie might result in leprosy. An average-sized girl with a fit build, her flaxen hair fell to just above her waist. Her face was set with fine features, but corrupted by the contempt she wore so readily. The exaggerated dodging movement caused her to strike shoulders with Sarah, an athletic, dark skinned beauty. They were the Beta and Alpha of their pack, respectively. Shadowing the duo were three other girls of similar social status.

"Watch it, Freak Show!" Mindy barked out, indignant.

"Oh, that was original," Elsie said, with an effortlessness that came from years of practice. "But hey, a lack of imagination ought to come in handy for that ambitious fast food career you have ahead of you."

"Easy—you just insulted the service industry everywhere." Angie murmured over her companion's shoulder, though she made no real effort to keep from being heard. She was more concerned with catching Mindy and Sarah's gaze with her hardened stare. Posturing stand-offs with this malevolent pair had been an almost daily occurrence since middle school. It was one of the many experiences she wasn't going to miss.

"You got a problem, fugly?" Sarah focused her hostility on Angie, her ample upper lip curving back into a scornful snarl. She squared her shoulders, flipping back the golden tassel of her graduation cap as she stepped forward in a blatant challenge.

Angie held her ground. "Just you," she answered, feeling too drained to scrape up a witty retort. She hoped Sarah would interpret her tone as either boredom or arrogance — neither of which could be mistaken for a sign of weakness.

To some extent, Angie knew she'd brought this kind of attention on herself. Functioning as more of a drifter than an actual part of the high school social strata, her conviction to root for the underdog had led her to befriend the most poorly-integrated of her peers. Or, as her mother liked to put it, "collect strays." Although, when it came to friends like Elsie, it was less of a collection and more of a Misfit Protection Program.

Sarah's wolfish gaze snapped aside to Elsie. "And what the hell is -that- supposed to be? Couldn't wait for Halloween?" She extended a finger to indicate Elsie's ornate dress.

Elsie, in a rare moment, seemed at a loss for words.

"That... is more culture than you'll probably ever see again." Angie cut in, mimicking Sarah's tone. "Don't you have other places to be...people to torment...small animals to sacrifice?" She leaned forward in emphasis. Her heart rate picked up tempo, readying her for a quick reaction on the off-chance the clash turned physical. Now that there was no risk of expulsion, she couldn't be sure how far beyond covert shoving and tripping the girl might go.

As their followers began edging around them in a subtle sort of urging, Mindy was the first to back down. Muttering an obscenity the blonde snorted, turned on her heel, and marched off in the direction of the gym. Sarah gave a snort and turned away.

Anticlimactic as ever, Angie mused.

"That's right—be gone! Before someone drops a house on you!" Elsie jeered, fluttering her hands in a shooing motion before Angie could prod her into moving along. Fortunately, none of their opposition seemed to understand the reference. After a few more disdainful looks and crude insults, the pack moved on as one.

Angie used her hold on Elsie's shoulder to steer the girl toward the parking lot before any more unpleasantries were exchanged. She refused to allow the minor incident to dampen her sense of relief. As far as she was concerned, she'd just walked off the set of a really bad teen movie and into the rest of her life.

"Ah," Elsie sighed with an air of refreshment. "What'll I ever do without them? My senior year is starting to look really boring."

"Good. It's not like I'm going to be around for it," Angie reminded her.

"You know you love me," Elsie said, latching onto Angie's arm in a clamorously exaggerated hug.

"Ugh. Get off." Angie gave her arm a shake, and then pried her friend from her.

Elsie relented with a cackle, only to bolt for the passenger side door of Angie's aging sedan. "Shotgun!"

Angie shook her head, lacking the energy to engage in a futile discussion about how unnecessary it was for Elsie to call shotgun when she had no competition. Any other day, she might have humored her. "I'm not up for an overnighter. I think I might need to go to the doctor tomorrow," she said as she opened her door and slid into the driver's seat.

"Still not feeling too sporty?" Elsie asked, quick to secure her seat belt. She made a show of hooking a hand through the grip bar that was secured to the ceiling just above her window, which she affectionately referred to as the "oh crap" handle. "You know, you probably got it from me. Every time I go to the doctor I test positive for all sorts of fun things. Strep, shingles, mono…malaria. But I don't actually get the symptoms—they say I'm just a carrier. Like a plague rat."

"Fan-freaking-tastic." Angie released a melancholy sigh, rapping her fingers against the steering wheel several times before starting up the car.

Elsie gave her a sugary smile. "I know. God broke the mold when He made me."

"You sure He didn't drop the mold -while- He was making you?" Angie narrowed her eyes at her friend. With a glance over her shoulder, she put the car in reverse and whipped out of the parking spot. The sudden action elicited a nervous squeak out of Elsie, effectively putting her on her best behavior for the remainder of the drive.

~ ~ ~ ~ ~ ~ ~

In this particular town there were only two places that stayed open after nine o'clock at night, aside from the bars: Wal-Mart, and Gerkin's. The latter was an all night diner which catered to a variety of patrons. It sat along the main interstate that cut through the town, making it a favorite of truckers. If one happened to be underage and preferred to be sitting down while loitering, this drab little establishment was the place to be.

Angie and Elsie claimed their usual booth in the back corner and were promptly greeted by Cliff, the night manager. Cliff was a tall, thin young man with a pasty complexion and dark hair, which he kept meticulously slicked back. His acrid sense of humor was a source of much banter for Elsie, with Angie enjoying the exchanges nearly as much. Knowing them as regulars, he had their hot teas and plate of French fries marked down before they could ask.

As a counterbalance to ordering very little and staying entirely too long, they always made a point of tipping him well. Although, whether or not he allowed Elsie to best him in their verbal sparring matches often determined whether or not his tip would be awarded to him in the form of masses of loose change.

The two spent the next few hours discussing an art show Elsie had planned for later in the summer, with a random smattering of obscure topics inserted as her attention span waned. Angie had absorbed a great deal from Elsie since they'd met in middle school, most of which resulting in her familiarity with the world of the nondescript geek. Their cache of shared interests included comic books, video games, Japanese cartoons, replica weaponry, and role play. It was a safer, less judgmental world, where the inhabitants were more sensitive and creative, if not socially impaired to varying degrees. Most of the time, the ineptitude could pass as an endearing quality. Particularly to Angie, who preferred it to the backstabbing and manipulation that seemed to be the primary teenage-girl alternative.

Graduation had cut the last tie she had to the suffocating version of reality that high school represented. She should have been giddy over her new-found freedom, but an array of unknowns continued to loom over her.

"You get any news on your Air Force guy?" Elsie deviated at last. For the most part, she shied away from any meaningful conversation. But when she did bother with it, she could be astute.

Angie peered down at her mug of tea, having lost count of how many times she'd refilled it. "It's sounding like I won't get to meet Don at the end of the trip like we were planning. They put a Stop Loss on his unit. He's supposed to let me know for sure in the next few days, but unless he can get an honorable discharge, they're going to keep him for three extra months." She was sulking now, and she allowed the fact to slip into her voice.

To anyone else, it would sound naive of her to have become attached to someone she had yet to meet in person. She'd come across Don the same way she had most of the others she intended on meeting on her fast approaching road trip: through a text-based writing community. A favored hobby from the age of fifteen, she had Elsie to thank for introducing her to the pastime. There she had been free to create and share stories. What's more, she felt closer to some of her online peers than she did to the friends she saw on a daily basis.

Don had been among these online friends, and after the September 11th attacks, she'd discovered the twenty-two-year-old was also an Air Force serviceman stationed in Germany. They began having phone conversations, and she quickly became infatuated with his soft-spoken Arkansas accent. Hopeful over the sense of connection between them, they'd made plans to meet once his service contract was up at the end of the summer. News of the Stop Loss had depressed them both and dashed her fragile hopes.

"I should have taken his offer to fly me to Germany," Angie said in lament. "Now I'll probably never get to meet him."

"Well, you know, it might be for the best." Elsie fidgeted, picking at a rip in the worn booth cushion. Offering comfort had never been one of her strong suits. "Maybe it wouldn't have worked out. You said he can be kind of moody, and you aren't exactly Little Miss Sunshine yourself. Who knows, you might hit it off with somebody while you're on your trip—"

Angie raised a hand to stop her friend's reassurances. "I'm - not- looking to start some desperate long-distance relationship. And besides, I'll have plenty of other things to worry about while I'm traveling."

"Like...staying alive?" Elsie's lips curled back in a light smirk. "I wish I could go with you. You're crazy, though—and this is coming from me." She quirked a questioning eyebrow. "I mean, I know how boring this town is, but aren't you overcompensating just a little?"

"Yeah, probably. I can't seem to talk myself out of it, though. I have to go through with it." Angie managed a tight smile. "Assuming my mom doesn't carry out her threat to sedate me before I get the chance."

Elsie giggled outright. "Can't blame her. My mom would crap a brick." She sipped at the remainder of her tea. "I mean, you've only met two of these people you're going to be staying with. Well...and one's my cousin—I guess he doesn't count. So that leaves how many?"

"Seven others," Angie answered matter-of-factly. "Yeah, I suppose it does sound pretty...out there. But I checked them all out, just to be safe. And I know I'll regret it if I don't go. I've only got one semester left before I'll have my associates degree and...then what?"

"What do you mean, 'then what?'" Elsie asked, wringing her tea bag into her cup after draining the last of its contents. "You've been taking college courses for like two years now, and you just graduated high school. I'd be grateful to be that far ahead of the game."

"I know, but I don't know what I'm supposed to do with myself. I don't know what I want—" Angie cut herself short, realizing she was starting to whine. She didn't have any right to complain, and she didn't expect her friend to comprehend the upwelling of uncertainty that seized her every time she tried to envision her future. It was all she could do not to turn and run every time someone innocently asked what her major would be. She had yet to decide if the road trip was her way of running away from destiny, or headlong into it.

Finding the hot water pot empty, Elsie reached across the table for Angie's mug.

Angie yanked her cup toward herself, sloshing a few drops of its lukewarm contents over the rim and across her knuckles. "Negative, Typhoid Mary." She leered in scolding. "You lost your sharing privileges. Flag down Cliff if you want more."

Elsie gave a dramatic sigh. "Where is that greasy weasel, anyway?" Defying common discretion, she brought two fingers to her mouth to create a shrill, beckoning whistle. It was late enough that few of the other patrons spared her a glance. Within seconds, Cliff came jogging back from behind the front counter.

"Ladies...anything else I can get you this evening?" He waggled his eyebrows at Angie and deepened his voice in jest. "My phone number, perhaps?"

"More hot water, please." Angie offered a faint smile as she held up the hotpot. All in good fun or not, flirtation had always been a concept that threw her off. She wasn't sure if she should view it as a tacky display of guile, or as a legitimate skill she simply had no knack for. Either way, she was certain her ignorance in that area had contributed to her state of perpetual singleness.

"Yeah, I bet you've got a nice bachelor pad set up in the dumpster out back." Elsie resumed her verbal jabbing. "Must be convenient, being able to walk to work."

"Oh yes, it's got plenty of glamorous perks." Cliff quipped back in his typical dry, sardonic tone. "This morning I scraped together a full breakfast -and- I found a perfectly good shoe. Jackpot." He accepted the container and swiveled on his heels before marching back toward the kitchen.

Elsie looked back toward Angie and grinned. "Too bad Cliff isn't your type. I don't think he'd need much encouragement."

Angie shifted uncomfortably. "I'm pretty sure Cliff hits on everything that moves. You just make it harder for him, what with all of the conversational castrating." She paused with her mug halfway to her lips, considering a moment before venturing to ask, "So, what exactly is my 'type?'" She wasn't sure she wanted to hear the answer, but she needed a distraction from the sense of gloom that seemed amplified by whatever was ailing her.

Elsie cleared her throat and splayed her hands across the table as though she'd prepared an important announcement. "Beefcake Philosopher," she said at last, deadpan.

Angie gauged her friend with caution. "Explain."

"See, I've actually given this some thought. Me, I like 'em smart and skinny, with minimal sun exposure. You like the big, strong, manly sort, but you won't give them a second look if they don't have brains. And those are hard to come by. Not that it's a bad thing. There have to be a few of those out there that fit the rest of your criteria. ...probably."

Angie rubbed two fingers against each temple, absently noting how warm her forehead felt to the touch. She would definitely have to get checked out in the morning. "So, you're saying I'm looking for a smart, tough-guy who can meet my standards without resenting it. Oh, and who'd actually be willing to put up with somebody like me."

"Set the bar any higher and you'd be looking for somebody with pole-vaulting credentials." Elsie gave a dour nod. "But like you said, you don't really know what you want. Give it time and some of that adorable idealism of yours might wear off."

"Thanks," Angie said in glib reply. "You should go into counseling one day. I could see you getting paid to tell people when they're being delusional."

Elsie formed the thin, crooked smile. "Or, you know, you could always settle for less and end up missing it when the right kind of guy does make an appearance."

"I take it back—you should go into politics." Angie chuckled in defeat before realizing she was no longer the focus of Elsie's attention.

Her cohort had filled the bottom of a water glass with quarters and leveled off the water at the rim. She then pressed a laminated menu to the top of the glass and, in a swift motion, flipped it upside down with her hand under the menu to maintain the seal. Steadily, she lowered the menu and maneuvered until the table took the place of her supporting hand.

Angie watched the trick with detached curiosity. "And you're doing this to him because—?"

"He's taking too long," Elsie answered without breaking her concentration. In another quick motion she slid the glass, transitioning it from the menu to the tabletop with only a small trail of water lost in the process. "Voila!"

Angie shook her head at Elsie's flair for vindictive creativity. The motion turned out to be a mistake, as it triggered a painful throbbing at her temples. "As much as I'd like to see his face when he finds that, I think I'm going to call it a night." She scooted out of the booth and made her way to the front of the diner. Elsie gave a disappointed whine, but followed without a fight.

Reaching the front counter Angie laid open her wallet, leafing out a few bills and setting them beside the cash register. A weary young busboy emerged from the back and peered over the ticket. As she waited, Don's picture grabbed her attention from its place in the transparent inner pocket of her billfold. His sandy-blonde hair was crew cut, detracting no attention away from his strong, clean-shaven jaw and keen blue eyes. Arms folded across his broad chest framed the blue AIR FORCE lettering of an otherwise gray T-shirt.

Beefcake Philosopher — Elsie was right.

Regret twisted in Angie's stomach and she snapped the wallet closed. Pining over something so unlikely was immature, she reminded herself. And this was no time to start acting her age.

June 7th,

I graduated last night, finally. It was a painfully long-winded ceremony, punctuated by an explosion of screaming and silly string. ...and nothing about it meant anything to me. I took one last look at my 370-some classmates and it was confirmed in my mind that they wouldn't miss me. At least that's mutual. But it's alright. That chapter of my life is complete. At least I made it through without embarrassing myself.

This morning I went in to the doctor and tested positive for Mono. Elsie must have given it to me when she drank from my smoothie a couple of weeks ago. In a way, it's a relief to know I'm not just lazy and out of shape. At the same time, I know it could take me weeks or months to get over it. I'll have to take it easy, especially for the first part of this trip. Hopefully I won't get anyone else sick. *Think healthy thoughts* Now, on with exploring/saving the world! Or...something.

With the Arkansas part of my trip in serious question, it looks like all I can do is pray and trust there's a reason for whatever happens. I don't know yet what I'll do if it turns out for the worst. I'll have to play this by ear and hope that Don keeps in contact with me. So far this isn't going the way I'd planned, but I'm not going to let that stop me. I need to get out of this town.

Three days left, and counting.

~Ang

Chapter 2

In the dim blueish haze of predawn, Angie perched barefooted atop the largest of the granite boulders decorating her parents' front yard, questioning her sanity one last time. An unfamiliar pairing of excitement and dread swam through the whole of her being in equal measure. It was invigorating. She guessed it to be some lesser form of the sensation skydivers must experience when stepping up to the open door of a plane before hurling themselves into a freefall.

This particular rock was her favorite spot for stargazing, and even now she felt reassured to stare up and watch as the brightly speckled veil of night was lifted. Flanked by thick forest on two sides and several acres of grassy lawn, only a handful of neighboring houses were within eyeshot. It had been a good place to grow up, being outside of town enough not to feel crowded, but not quite far enough out to be considered country.

Her father had bought the land and built their house two decades prior, when the cold war still loomed in all of its uncertainty. Some sense of precaution had convinced him to buy up additional acres that he could potentially convert into a mass garden so that, in the event of a breakdown in organized society, their family would still have a means of procuring food. While Angie understood this motivation to be somewhat paranoid, part of her had always been proud of his forethought and determination to provide for them.

Of course, the hand of the apocalypse had been stayed, and a more conservative use of the land was settled on. Five apple trees hedged the left side of the yard, each of a different variety with harvesting times varying from July through October. To the right along the tree line were beds of tomatoes and strawberries, bordered by thick loops of red raspberry bushes. She would miss most of the strawberry and raspberry season while she was gone, but the apples would still be waiting for her.

"I need you to be with me. I don't want to do this alone." She murmured the words aloud as she scanned the fading stars and settled on the brightest point of light that remained, which she absently identified as Venus. From childhood she'd been fascinated by astronomy, and on a personal level, she'd discovered that a clear night sky made it easier for her to talk to God. There was no dogma or ritualistic reasoning behind this. She found it completely natural to pray under her breath at any time as she went about her day, and often did. But there was something profound and awe-inspiring about stargazing that made her feel smaller and yet more connected at the same time.

Angie finally slid off of the rock and waded through the cool grass to her awaiting flip-flops, just beside her pale gold Geo Prism. The car had been a reward from her parents for making good enough grades to get into the Post Secondary program. She had to drive herself to her college classes, and so it made sense that she have her own vehicle.

The car's condition was too good to be called a Junker, but it was nothing fancy. And that was the way she liked it. She'd come to fondly regard it as an extension of herself, having covered the back of it with whimsical bumper stickers to suit her personality. Her car had all of the things she'd been taught to value in life: dependability, efficiency, longevity, and a Japanese engine. If it held up faithfully through her adventure, she'd vowed to drive it to the end of its life...or hers. Whichever came first.

She popped open the trunk and scanned over her inventory for the third time since she'd loaded up the previous day. Sleeping bag, road flare, flashlight, extra oil, box of non-perishable food, North America road atlas, emergency travel phone, first aid kit, duffel bag of clothes, and an eight-inch Bowie knife. She was fully prepared to sleep in her car, but given her current plans she should only need to for one night, if all went well. It wasn't the discomfort of urban camping that concerned her, it was the idea of being exposed and vulnerable. That was where the Bowie knife came in.

A quick sifting through the duffel bag produced a black baseball cap, which she donned after twisting her hair up to conceal underneath. For once, playing at gender ambiguity would be a defensive advantage rather than an oblivious social default. Her father had suggested this measure, concerned that being a lone female would make her a conspicuous target for harassment. Or worse.

"You're still too pretty to pass for a boy." The warm insistence drifted from a short distance away.

Angie smiled at the remark and all of its paternal bias. She closed the trunk and spotted her father standing a few yards off at the corner of the garage, watching her with a careworn expression.

At forty-eight, Nicolas could have passed for ten years younger. He was in the solid, trim shape that came with a highly active lifestyle, with all of his golden-brown hair still holding its color and displaying little sign of retreat. His eyes shone a clear, light blue, set with creases against skin that had hardly gone a day without seeing sun. His prominent Nordic nose was a distinguished feature that suited him well, though it was also something that Angie and her siblings were quietly grateful not to have inherited. Standing side by side, no one would have guessed him to be her father. She'd taken strongly after her mother — tall, long-limbed and dark-featured. By the time she was twelve years old she'd surpassed him in height, and now stood easily three inches taller.

Despite being vertically challenged, her father had always been an avid basketball player. What he lacked in height he made up for in speed. Being in top condition — combined with his age and the fact that his job as a postal carrier required him to walk six miles every day — made it all the more shocking when he'd suddenly had a heart attack just eight months prior. An unforeseen defect had resulted in one of the major blood vessels in his heart being far narrower than it should have been. A biological ticking time bomb.

Angie vividly remembered the night she'd gotten the news, and the distress it compounded in her just weeks after the Twin Towers had fallen. At the time, it seemed like the whole world was senselessly going to pieces.

The doctors warned of a fifty-fifty chance of stent failure in the first six months after they'd been placed to prop open the vessel in his heart. And for six months, their entire family held their collective breath. Even after that statistical hurdle had been overcome, Angie ceased to view any time spent with him as a given. Her preparations for the trip had been a welcome excuse to sit with him in the garage for hours on end as he went over the basics of car maintenance. Regardless of what happened, that was how she wanted to remember him — as a man who showed love best by working with his hands.

"I think it'll do just fine." She pressed optimism into her tone, trying to offset the unspoken worry she read in his face. He'd come to see her off. Her mother had offered her unenthusiastic farewell the night before, and Angie didn't expect her to bear witness to the start of a venture she didn't approve of in the first place.

"Here, give this to mom." Angie withdrew a folded piece of paper from her pocket and held it out. "These are all the places I'll be staying and the numbers you can reach me at. Every time I hop locations I'll call when I'm about halfway and again when I get there," she said, desperately wanting to sound responsible. Her parents had never given much reason to rebel against them — not that she'd been interested in such stereotypical teen displays of angst. This trip was the most risky life decision she'd ever made against their advice.

A calculated risk, she liked to remind herself and anyone who wanted to talk her out of it.

"I have a present for you." Nicolas slipped the list into his back pocket before holding up her keys, showing off the small canister of travel mace he'd added to the key ring. "Just be careful with it," he added. His typical fatherly disclaimer.

Angie allowed her honest delight to show in her smile as she accepted the keys and turned the device over to scan the directions. "Point and shoot. Sounds pretty straightforward." She laughed and gave him an appreciative hug. It transitioned into more of a reassuring expression when he didn't immediately release her. "I'll be alright, Dad. Jesus loves me, and I'm hard to kill." She repeated the running family joke in a light tone.

That got a low chuckle out of him. "You grew up too fast." He cupped her shoulders and held her out at arm's length.

"Thanks...for trying to understand."

"Not like I could've stopped you. You're an adult now."

Angie cringed at the title she'd long fought for, but felt she still hadn't earned. "You know what I mean. The car is still in your name, you could keep me from using it."

"Well, I don't think I have a right to hold you back." He gave a fond smile. "I did my own cross country trip by motorcycle right after I got out of the army. So really, I'm just glad you're at least using a car."

"Me too." She laughed.

"I love you." He squeezed her shoulders, voice welling with tenderness. "And I'm proud of you. I've always been proud of you."

Looking at him now, Angie marveled at how different he was since recovering from his heart attack. Both simply and profoundly put, this was not the same man she'd known while growing up. Throughout her childhood her father had been a volatile, frustrated, and unapproachable man, as his battle with his own temper seemed to leave him with no patience for his own offspring.

Like most approval-seeking children, Angie had struggled long and hard to impress him and earn his affection. Noting from an early age that quality time spent with him revolved solely around sports and outdoor activities, she'd become a tough-as-nails tomboy; in part out of the misguided impression that her father would have preferred it if she'd been a boy. Alternating between bottled emotions and aggressive outbursts, she'd spent years with undirected rage as her inheritance. She'd only recently come to realize how his angry detachment had affected her self-perception and comfort with her own femininity.

In a way, she was glad she hadn't come to understand this until after the fact. Rather than considering her father a classic excuse for her own shortcomings, she now could only see him as living proof that people can change. And she'd found an odd eloquence in the notion that it had taken a physical heart condition to remedy an intangible heart condition. As idyllic as it might have been for her to know the man he'd recently become for the first seventeen years of her life as well — she knew him now. Better late than never.

"I love you too." Angie leaned in to hug his neck again. When she let him go she turned away and walked around the front of her car. She didn't want any more second thoughts, and she knew seeing him standing there looking forlorn would make her hesitate. Taking a few moments to put on music and lay out the map of her route, she managed to pull out of the drive with only a quick wave and a glance in her rear view mirror. She was glad to have at least made it out of the driveway before her tears won out.

After twenty minutes on the road, Angie reigned in her emotions and rallied her resolve. She needed all of her focus. It would take around twelve hours of driving before she reached her first destination in Ohio. That was plenty of time for her to reflect on why she was putting herself through this.

For as long as she could remember, Angie had been slightly above-average — from her height and physical strength, to her grades, intuition, and artistic capacity. She was athletic, but lacked the innate prowess of a competitive athlete. She was bright, but not a genius. Talented, but not elite. Good, but not best. While growing up she'd entered all sorts of contests, from writing, to art, to science fairs — never achieving first or second place, but consistently given honorable mention. A pat on the head, and a "good girl, keep trying." She wasn't in the top ten percent of her graduating class, but she was in the top twenty — were that considered worthy of recognition. She managed to excel at an array of things, yet always fell short of exceptional in any one area. To her, above-average had become only a small, yet frustrating step up from the mundane. Mediocrity with benefits.

Seeing her hope of one day becoming a writer in the light of realism, she knew above-average wasn't going to cut it. If she was ever to go beyond entertaining the dream, she needed more under her belt than three years of reclusive internet storytelling — more than college English and a few creative writing courses. She would have to offer something unique and authentic.

It was this nagging conviction that had first sparked the idea of taking a road trip and experiencing more of the world first hand. If she couldn't manage to be extraordinary by nature, she reasoned the next best thing was to attempt something extraordinary. She might even come across a more practical idea for a career path along the way.

Assuming she made it back safely.

Now that she'd nearly fallen apart while taking the first step on her journey, she had to wonder if she would have the strength to see it through to the end.

June 10th,

And So It Begins.

I beat the sun heading out this morning and drove straight east into it. The sky was totally clear, so I was treated to a lovely sunrise with all of those rich shades of red. My first stop was a rest station just outside of Madison, Wisconsin. I'm holding up alright so far, but I might use my next gas stop to take a nap. I'll be more than halfway by then.

A nice old trucker was kind enough to show me where the cars are supposed to park at this rest stop. Evidently, I parked on the end where the big rigs go and he was afraid I might get run over. I must have looked like a clueless idiot. *sigh* I'll get it right next time.

I found a swallowtail butterfly in the grass, nearly dead. I gave him some water droplets and sat him on the arm rest on the passenger's side of my car. I named him Pete.

-I'm in Indiana right now. The nap helped me perk up. I've never been through this state before, but so far I'm convinced there's nothing in Indiana. My road kill count has been impressive. It's almost as though all of these animals came to the same realization about the monotony of this state, and then used the highway to end their misery. Okay, so maybe that's a little harsh. I just wasn't expecting so much of the same terrain. I don't know why...it's still the middle of the heartland, after all. The fields go on forever. If I wasn't sure I've been driving in a straight line, I could swear that's the third time I've passed the same silo.

-I made it to Brookville Ohio at 7:30pm. Now if only Alec were home so he and his mom could come and show me where they live. I'm sitting at a gas station, wondering if that was them I just saw drive by...

Status: In need of a shower, tired, but hanging in there. I think the fever is back, but the sore throat isn't as bad as it's been. Poor Pete didn't make it.

~Ang

Chapter 3

Angie followed a red Dodge sedan as it wove through open farmland for half an hour before reaching a few dozen single-level houses clustered around a lone four-way stop sign. The car ahead hung a right, and then pulled into a driveway. She parked off to one side of it and got out. Though she'd stretched her legs at the gas station while waiting for her host family, her knees still ached with stiffness.

Alec's mother, a plump woman with pleasantly rounded facial features, came spilling out of her driver's seat. They'd only exchanged greetings through their car windows before setting off, and she seemed intent on making up for it by walking around Angie's car with open arms.

"Glad you could make it back to see us!" The woman greeted. "Goodness you're brave—all by yourself this time. We'll have to have a chat later so I can instill a healthy fear of God in you!"

The maternal fussing was lighthearted, but Angie suspected the shorter woman was at least halfway serious as she stepped into the hug. "Don't worry. I've already got a healthy fear of God. It's a fear of people I probably need some work on." She laughed. "Thanks for giving me a place to crash, Claire. I don't want to impose at all."

Claire stepped back to grasp Angie's forearms, casting a sincere look over the rim of her broad, square glasses. "It's good to have the company. Charlie's away on business the next few days, so the timing worked out. I didn't feel like explaining to him where you came from, anyway."

Angie felt a twisting pang of guilt at realizing the woman had needed to omit her existence from conversations with her husband. When she'd first visited them on her test run over spring break, she'd only met Alec and his mother for lunch at a mall in a nearby town. While their meeting had been enjoyable, she'd gathered that Alec's father wouldn't be thrilled with him having internet friends — let alone meeting them in person.

"Alec can show you around while I make you up a room." Claire called over her shoulder as she headed for the side door of the house.

Alec was slower to extract himself from the passenger side of the car, standing off to one side while the women had their exchange. He looked uncertain, which Angie had come to expect. Alec had always been expressive and open online and over the phone, but in person she knew him to be painfully shy. She took the initiative of bringing the welcoming hug to him.

And there was plenty of Alec to hug. Though they stood at the same height, Angie guessed him to be at least a hundred pounds overweight. Or at least, she'd thought that if he were to lose a hundred pounds, he could be considered attractive. The thought gave her a sense of disgust with herself on one hand, and saddened her on the other. She felt hypocritical to reject the shallowness of society's expectations only to continue bowing to them in her mind. But at the same time, the health ramifications of her friend's condition seemed a valid concern. Not that she had any idea how to address it.

"Show me around the neighborhood," she said as she released him. "I could use a walk."

"Oh...okay. Sure," Alec answered in a soft mutter, falling into step with her down the short driveway. "Not much to see." He turned his head aside, looking at her through the shaggy, chestnut-brown bangs that obscured his dark gaze. "Sorry we had trouble finding you. I should have been looking at the plates, not the car color," he said, sheepish.

"Hey, you found me. That's all that matters."

They walked on past the stop sign for several blocks before the houses ended and they doubled back, turning right at the stop sign. It looked as though this would be the same sight down all four streets. That much, Angie didn't mind. The awkward silence was another matter.

"So, did you get your driver's license yet?" she asked.

"Oh, uh, no." He looked over at her, ducking his head in embarrassment. "I kinda failed the driving test...again. I was hoping to retake it the day after tomorrow."

"I failed my first driving exam," she offered in commiseration. "I'm not great at following directions under pressure.

Or at left hand turns, apparently. There goes my dream of driving for NASCAR."

"Oh," Alec picked up on the joke after a delay and chuckled. "I guess so."

"I could help you practice."

Alec brightened at the suggestion. "That'd be great. I really need to pass so I can drive myself to college this fall."

She laughed. "Yeah. Trust me, college won't be what it should be if your mother ends up dropping you off at all of your classes."

Angie smiled, trying to soften the strength of her assertion. Alec was nineteen, an only child, and had been home-schooled his entire life. She didn't have anything against home schooling, it just seemed likely to her that, in combination with being stuck in the-middle-of-nowhere-USA , his horizons could stand to be broadened. She was beginning to think she may not be nearly as sheltered and inexperienced as she'd initially thought — at least by comparison.

Alec fell quiet again through the final leg of their walk, watching the empty road in front of them until they crossed back into the gravel driveway to his front door.

"I should let a few people know that I'm still alive," Angie said. "Would anyone mind if I used your internet?"

"Oh, sure." Alec paused with his hand on the doorknob. "I think you'll be sleeping in the office anyway, so you can help yourself. It's just dial-up, so it's pretty slow," he said, apologetic. As he pushed open the door, a smoke colored tabby cat slipped past him and darted around Angie's legs.

When Alec didn't show any indication of being distressed by the feline's escape, Angie followed him inside. She found herself in a small, blandly decorated living room across from an open kitchen. A larger calico stretched itself out along the arm of a tan corduroy couch, mewling to be pet.

"All my family had was dial-up until about a year ago. I'll manage just fine." She injected a light cheeriness into her tone as she greeted the cat and surveyed her surroundings.

Short of polite conversation, Angie decided not to feign chattiness in what little was left of the evening. She would have a couple of days to coax Alec out of his shell. Now that the drive was over with, exhaustion was settling over her like a lead blanket.

~ ~ ~ ~ ~ ~ ~

"Stop! Left a little more," Angie said, peering out the passenger side window of the little red sedan. Having laid out an obstacle course of orange cones through the parking lot of Alec's church, she'd spent the last hour helping him navigate through it while his mother was occupied with choir practice.

Alec eased the car forward, narrowly missing the cone she'd warned him about. He curved with the path to the right and put the car in reverse as soon as he'd completed the course.

"Use your mirrors," she reminded him as he looked over his shoulder and then began to work his way backward through the maze.

What started out as an exercise in frustration had steadily improved once they'd realized the car mirrors needed adjusting to Alec's height rather than his mother's. Angie resolved to remain silent this time, hoping for the best, but prepared for the dull *thud* of the back wheel bowling over a hapless cone. Alec unnerved easily, and she didn't want to make things any more difficult on him.

As the car rolled to a stop, Alec shifted his gaze side to side in hopeful uncertainty. "Did I make it?"

She grinned at him and gave a thumbs-up. "Didn't even touch one."

Relief washed over Alec's face, accompanied by what she thought might be some newly acquired confidence.

"Okay, one more time. Just to make sure that wasn't a fluke," he said, eyes locked ahead in concentration.

He took the course again, relying on his mirrors without being reminded. By the end, his grip on the steering wheel caused his fingers to go white from a lack of circulation, but his effort was a marked success. Alec looked both amazed and pleased as he put the vehicle into park.

"You're pretty good at this. That was a lot easier than when my mom tries to coach me."

"That's just because she's your mom." Angie laughed.

"Now let's go do the exam, while I still remember what I'm doing," he said with an edge of nervousness.

"That's probably a good idea." Angie hopped out of the passenger seat. She then went about walking the course, collecting the orange cones into stacks. Glancing back toward the tiny church,

she spotted Claire making her way to the car — her long, floral
sundress swishing around her ankles. Offhandedly, Angie thought it
made the woman look like a walking bouquet. But then again, she
didn't consider herself any reliable judge of good fashion sense.

"Do you think he's ready?" Claire called out.

Angie nodded. "He thinks so. He wants to go now, if you're
done with practice."

Claire clasped her hands together at her bosom in what Angie
took to be a culmination of enthusiasm and anxiety. "Let's go then.
Jump in and start praying, sweetie. This is his last shot." She
confided the last part with a lowered voice before pulling open the
passenger side door.

Angie gave Claire a reassuring smile and got into the back
seat, where she listened to mother and son have a detached
conversation about Alec's weekend guitar lesson. To Claire's credit,
she seemed to make an effort not to cause him further apprehension
by bringing up any last-minute tips on driving etiquette. Judging by
the tension she noted in Alec's hunched shoulders, it wasn't working.

Fortunately, the drive to the Department of Motor Vehicles
was a short one. Angie soon found herself standing outside with
Claire at the far end of a brick building, watching Alec and the
balding examiner get into the red Dodge. Behind the DMV was an
enormous asphalt lot laid out with orange cones.

"Oh, I can't watch." Claire pressed her pallid palms to her
cheeks as she turned away. She began pacing up and down along the
front walkway.

Angie folded her arms and leaned her shoulder into the corner
of the building, gaze following Alec's car as he worked his way
through the lot. She focused, wishing she could help her friend
through sheer force of will. "Please…keep him calm. You know he
can do this," she prayed under her breath. The car left her line of
vision for several long moments as it wove through the farthest back
portion of the lot.

It seemed like very little time had passed before the Dodge
pulled back round to the front of the DMV. She couldn't decide if
that was a good or bad sign. When Alec got out of the car looking as
straight-faced as his humorless examiner, disappointment began to
prickle at the edge of her mind.

Claire managed to stay put until the man jotted something down and handed Alec a piece of paper. She then went rushing past the examiner in concern. "Alec?"

Angie pushed off from the building and trailed after her hostess, straining to read her friend's expression — or the lack thereof.

"I passed!" Alec held out the paper to his mother while breaking into a sudden, triumphant smile.

"Thank you, Jesus!" Claire squealed, throwing her arms around her son's neck. "You scamp, don't do that to me!" she scolded with her next breath.

Angie covered her mouth to hide her laughter. She waited until Claire released him before stepping up to give Alec a congratulatory pat on the shoulder. "Well, now we have to celebrate," she said, casting Claire a look of inquiry.

"Of course!" Claire agreed, the creases beside her eyes deepening with delight. "What would you like, Alec? Just name it."

Alec seemed to shrink back from their shared exuberance. He looked down and then toward the car after his mother's invitation. "How about...laser tag?"

Claire looked unimpressed. "But you've got a membership. You can play any time. Especially now that you can drive yourself—"

"I mean for both of us." Alec looked to Angie indicatively.

"Sounds like fun." Angie said, looking to his mother to weigh her approval.

"Well that's fine," Claire relented, looking pensive as she walked around to get into the car. "I just wish you'd think of something more...memorable."

"That's all I can think of, Mom. Really," Alec said, returning to the driver's seat.

The laser tag arena was a short drive into Dayton. Angie found herself oddly relieved to see large buildings, rather than endless fields. She and Alec were dropped off in front of a sizable warehouse complex and given Claire's estimate of an hour before her return.

Inside, someone had gone to great pains to make the place look futuristic. The walls and ceiling were painted black, with small LED lights embedded at random. Bright, multicolored streaks blazed in all directions from behind a set of flat-panel screens mounted to the middle of one wall. The left panel displayed a flashing countdown sequence, while the right one showed the scores of the current game. Below, a chrome reception counter was manned by two bored looking youth wearing neon yellow vests. Beyond that, the lobby was walled off and set with two unassuming doors that Angie supposed must access the arena. She could hear the deep vibration of bass and the muffled beat of dramatic music coming from the other side.

"Wow. It's…huge," she said.

"You're in for a treat." Alec cast her a sidelong smile and headed over to the counter.

Angie hung back, waiting to see what would be required of her while Alec was fitted with a vest. Behind her she overheard another set of customers.

"Aww great. Looks like they're gonna put us in there with the Michelin Man," one of them complained to the other. "This won't even be a challenge."

Angie bristled before she'd even finished processing the words, realizing they were likely in reference to Alec. She turned, fixing what she hoped was a neutral stare on the pair of young men who sat slumped on a bench.

Both were near her age, already wearing the sensor vests with Velcro attachments. One was short and scrawny, his forehead and cheeks showing the ravages of puberty — which he was only partially successful at hiding under the low bill of a black baseball cap. The other had a more burly, matured build, though his voice had a squeaky finish that told her it was still catching up to the rest of him. His corn-silk blond hair was just long enough to be unruly, and he met her stare with clear blue eyes. It occurred to her she might have found him cute, if he hadn't opened his mouth.

"What?!" The blond boy snapped at her in a dubious tone, after a long and uncomfortable moment. His voice proved him the culprit, and his posture confirmed that she'd understood his insult for what it was: malicious.

Heated indignation surged through her, and she clenched her fists to divert her energy into something physical. She barely resisted the urge to march up and kick him in the shin.

Instead she looked him up and down in one assessing sweep, curled her lip back, and then turned away in total disregard. She couldn't think of a time she'd ever purposely displayed so much nonverbal disrespect. It struck her as a stereotypical, passive-aggressive "girl" thing to do. Realizing that, part of her regretted it immediately. But she'd already done it, and crossing the room to look into her own preparations seemed like the only follow-through.

Behind her she heard the smaller of the young men make a cat-like yowling sound in commentary. The blond one answered him in a low mutter. Angie was grateful she didn't overhear anything more.

She picked out a gun with a rifle-like shape to it. Glorified piece of plastic that it was, holding it made her feel better for some reason. It also gave her something to center on while they moved to wait outside of the left arena door. Their opposition eventually stood and waited in front of the far right door, and she managed to keep from sparing them a glance.

"You look...intense." Alec sounded worried.

"Sorry, I'm just thinking." Angie smiled, attempting to defuse his concern. "Do we need a strategy or something?"

"Shoot them, and try not to get shot in the process." An amused look formed as he spoke. "First two rounds it's us against them. Third round is a free-for-all."

"Got it."

For Angie, the games were over too quickly. They won the first round, and then filed out after the second round to view the accumulative scores. She placed second in the overall, and Alec came in third. Gauging the reactions of their opponents, she guessed the one wearing the baseball cap to be in first place. That meant the blond one had come in last — which was exactly where she thought he belonged. It gave her some small sense of satisfaction to think her relentless hunting of him in the previous hour may have affected the outcome.

"Huh," Alec uttered under his breath as he looked from the score screen to Angie. "I guess I'm a little rusty. You sure you've never been to an arena before? You played like it was for keeps."

"I'm just a little competitive sometimes." She laughed, pretending not to notice when the other two young men stopped to stare at her. She imagined they thought she was strange — an overly aggressive girl with a knack for shooting games. But whatever they thought, it didn't matter. She was never going to see them again. And that knowledge was liberating.

"Now that you can drive, you should get out here a couple times a week. That was great exercise," Angie said as they made their way out of the front doors. She'd spoken before giving consideration to her choice of words. Chiding herself, she glanced over to catch Alec's reaction. His half smile told her he wasn't insulted.

"Yeah, and it's a lot less boring than a walk around the neighborhood."

Relief settle over her. He was more receptive than she'd given him credit for.

"Did you two have fun?" Claire's cheery voice carried from where she stood waiting beside the car.

"It was great!" Angie called back.

"Great for her—she scored better than I did."

"I never doubted her for a minute." Claire winked at Angie. "Well, I did some shopping while I waited…" She reached behind her to pull open the back passenger door. In doing so, she displayed the glossy black and white Fender guitar that sat propped in the seat.

Alec gaped at the instrument for a moment before moving in for a closer look. "Is it…the one we looked at last week? You bought it?!" He looked from the guitar to his mother in disbelief.

"I did good, didn't I?" Claire beamed, looking thoroughly pleased with herself. "You played with it so long, I could tell you liked it. And you needed a new one anyway. The one you practice on has duct tape holding the neck together, for heaven's sake."

Alec shifted from bewilderment to what Angie thought might be the start of a protest. "It's perfect, mom. But can we afford—"

"You let me worry about that." Claire waved a dismissive hand. "Today's a special day."

Alec smiled, shifting to give his mother a quick, grateful hug. "Thanks, mom." When he hesitated beside the car, Angie guessed he was torn over leaving the instrument in the back seat.

"Don't worry, I got it," she promised, sliding in next to the guitar. To emphasize her point, she reached over and secured the seat belt around it. "But you owe me a recital."

Alec gave an uneasy chuckle. "Alright…just don't expect much."

~ ~ ~ ~ ~ ~ ~

Back at the house, Alec took to the couch with his new guitar. Though the small amplifier box he'd plugged it into looked ancient, the sound that rumbled forth was rich and lucid. He played through the bass portion of several old hymns at his mother's request before Claire eventually migrated to the kitchen.

Angie asked Alec to play *Smoke On The Water*, which he transitioned into with ease. He'd obviously toyed with the song before. She smiled as she listened, unable to pick out any missed notes. Though Alec's fingers were thick, they moved with nimble certainty.

"See how long it takes you to guess this one." Alec glanced up at her before playing the first few chords of *Crazy Train.*

Angie placed it within a few seconds and smiled at his choice. She hummed along with the melody as it progressed.

Alec ventured into the song with a strong vocal quality that his speaking voice hadn't alluded to. Angie was both surprised and impressed. He was more musically talented than he'd let on. But the constant averting of his eyes told her he didn't know what to do with the attention that naturally accompanied the skill. When Alec broke off into incoherent mumbling in place of actual lyrics, she doubled over in laughter.

"I never remember the rest," he admitted, tapping at the side of his guitar with his thumb to elicit a light thumping sound.

"I don't either. But if you put a slurring British accent on it, I don't think most people would notice." Angie laughed, grazing her fingertips over the back of the little gray cat that had appeared in her lap.

Alec plucked through several more melodies that Angie didn't recognize. When Claire bid them goodnight, his gaze tracked her down the hallway. "So, you've got a little brother and sister, right? That must have been nice...growing up with somebody to talk to. I just have cousins, and they live a couple hours away."

Angie guessed he'd been waiting for his mother to be out of earshot before bringing this up. She detected a sadness in his voice that she immediately wanted to dispel. "It was alright. We're all pretty close together in age, so I think we competed with each other more than we kept each other company," she said. "Sometimes I think it's worse to feel alone when there -are- people around."

Alec considered before nodding. "I guess that makes sense." He continued to pluck at the strings, absently. "What about the school you went to? What was that like?"

Angie made every effort not to cringe. "Overrated. You didn't miss anything there." She tried to imagine Alec working his way through her high school, and a number of cruel scenarios came to her mind. "You know, I was almost homeschooled. My mom offered when I started junior high."

"But you decided not to?"

"Yeah." She reflected for a long moment as the cat in her lap leaned into her kneading fingers. "I think I was under the misguided impression that if I stayed in a regular school, I could make a difference. Do some good."

Alec paused to glance up at her again. "You don't think you did?"

She shook her head. "It was like...trying to swim against the current in a giant river of hormones, angst, and self-destructive tendencies. I could barely keep my own head above water, let alone help anybody else get through it. You know the old saying about the road to Hell being paved with good intentions? I actually understand that one now." She forced a small laugh.

Alec rallied a soft smile. "You never know. Maybe you had more of an effect than you think."

Angie shrugged, staring down at the blissful feline as it nuzzled her hand. "It wasn't just that. I guess I thought that if I was homeschooled, I wouldn't be as well prepared for the real world."

"That's what I'm afraid of," Alec said, his fingers stilled with his attention diverted. "For myself, I mean."

"High school isn't the real world. I figured that out when I started taking college classes," she said, hoping to reassure him. "I think you'll like college. It's a good way to meet a lot of different people. I hung out with the exchange students and learned about their cultures, joined a few clubs—"

"Meet any guys you're interested in?" Alec pressed on a teasing note.

"Well yeah, maybe," Angie answered. She hadn't expected him to ask such a bold question, but she was determined not to let that faze her candor. "But nothing mutual. It's not like I've been on the prowl or anything, but I've seen enough to know the quality of college guys beats out high school guys. And I'm pretty sure that goes both ways. So, keep your eyes open."

"Oh, well I don't really see myself ever dating…or getting married." Alec lowered his gaze to his guitar and his tone seemed to drop with it. "I'm actually okay with being alone. I'm pretty used to it."

Angie paused, wondering if his words stemmed from a genuine affinity for being a hermit, or if they were more of a resigned symptom of low self-esteem. "You never know. I think you're too young to rule anything out yet."

Alec gave a slight shrug, keeping his gaze fixed on his fingers as he resumed an idle plucking at the guitar strings. "I guess you're right. Maybe there's a chance I could meet a girl a little like you—"

Though he didn't look up at all amid his musing, Angie was unsettled by the possible implications. "The less like me, the better. Trust me. I can hardly stand myself most of the time." She laughed, trying to dispel her discomfort.

That's it, keep things light. Can't risk misleading him.

In a swift motion she scooped up her furry lap warmer and set the animal down beside her as she stood. "I should really get some sleep so I can make that drive in the morning." She diverted the topic with nonchalance, brushing a small cloud of cat hair off the front of her jeans. "How about one for the road. You know any Bon Jovi?"

Alec flashed a bemused expression before he seemed to realize what she'd asked of him. "Oh. Sure. How about this one—" His fingers flitted into position and he launched into a series of reverberating notes.

Angie paused a few steps from the hallway and listened as he played the intro to *It's My Life*. She chuckled when recognition hit her. "For some reason, I was sure you'd do *Living On a Prayer*."

"This one fits you better." Alec smiled to himself as he continued with deft precision. His voice rang clear, though he restrained his volume out of apparent courtesy to his mother.

Angie nodded with the beat and joined in at just above a whisper. She'd never given the lyrics much thought before, but now they struck her as a strangely personal narrative.

When the chorus came around for the third time, she made her way back to the spare room.

June 11th-12th,

~Heart Like An Open Highway~

I got a good 12 hours of much needed sleep the first night. Alec and I did nothing but watch movies on my first full day. I've now seen both Mission Impossible movies. And yet...I feel no more cultured. I can't complain, it was nice to have the down time to recover. I'm still getting fevers at night.

My second day here was busy. I helped Alec practice for his driving exam. Evidently in Ohio you get four attempts, and today was Alec's last chance. I guess the practice paid off, because he passed it this time. So it was a happy day.

Alec is a really sweet guy. I just think he needs to get out more. Having a driver's license can only help him, I think. He did finally open up some tonight. I was glad we at least got in a meaningful conversation before I move on to Detroit tomorrow.

Still, I'm feeling a little cowardly. I've never been all hung up on avoiding conflict. When I see a glaring problem, I usually feel compelled to examine it out loud. I'd intended on telling Alec that I'm concerned about his weight. Not just for the sake of his health, but also for the fact that some people are so shallow they won't bother looking past it to all of his remarkable traits. But try as I might, I couldn't think of a tactful way of telling someone that the elephant in the room...is them.

Maybe I just don't have the heart to risk crushing someone with such a gentle spirit. But then, there's part of me that thinks it's just as risky and uncaring to take the easy way out and not address a potentially life-threatening issue. So what's the "right" thing to do, anyway?

~Ang

Chapter 4

Driving almost due north, it took Angie less than four hours to reach Detroit.

It was late afternoon when she pulled into a middle-class suburb. The yards were large and well kept, with a generous inclusion of aging trees towering well above the houses. She pulled off in front of a two-story brick-faced home she recognized from her spring break visit. Hauling her travel bag with her to the front door, she was immediately greeted by a reddish-colored Springer Spaniel — along with his red-headed mistress.

"Angeli! Wonderful timing." Sandra spoke in a crooning voice, motioning her inside. "I was just about to go pick up Rob. He's been out all day doing his Habitat for Humanity volunteering." Average in height and full in build, the woman had a disarming softness about her appearance and demeanor. Dressed in a gray jogging suit and white sneakers, she projected the energy of someone who'd just started their day.

"Good to see you again, Sandy. Don't let me get in the way— I know I got here a little sooner than I'd told you in the email." The dog nudged his head against Angie's knee, and she bent to lay a hand between his ears.

"Nonsense—I'll just have Mark get you settled while I'm out. Mark?!" She raised her voice at the last note and directed it up the nearby staircase. "Mark, sweetie, your friend is here! Come help with her bag!" She smiled warmly to Angie again. "I hope you're hungry, I've got dinner going. It should only take a few minutes once we get back."

"Oh, I'm definitely hungry." Angie formed an easy laugh. "I'll come help you with it."

Sandra gave a dismissive wave. "No need for that. It practically makes itself."

"Peril!" Mark's exuberant voice came hurtling down the staircase ahead of him. For some reason Angie had yet to determine, the young man had always referred to her by one of her character's names from the online story-writing community. Although, when she considered some of his other tendencies, it was only a minor quirk.

"There's my favorite leprechaun!" Angie called back. Since their first meeting, she'd innately found it best to relate to Mark in the same way she would to her younger brother — which, of course, warranted a measure of teasing.

Mark planted both feet as he reached the landing, bowing curtly at the waist as he curved one arm before him. "I -have-mentioned that I'm not Irish, haven't I? Not so much as a drop." He smiled and reached for her bag. Despite his insistence, his appearance was misleading. Fiery fox-orange hair was cropped short to frame brown eyes and a pale, heavily freckled face. And in spite of being just seventeen, he sported an impressively thick beard. Combined with his slight stature and the fact that he favored clothing in limited shades of green, Angie's likening him to a mythical faerie seemed justified — at least in her mind.

"That's just what I'd expect a leprechaun to say." Angie smirked, handing him her duffel bag.

Sandra moved to the door and called back instructions over her shoulder. "Show her where she'll be staying, and get yourself ready for dinner. I'll be back in a jiffy."

Mark spun around and began tromping up the stairs. The Springer Spaniel followed close behind, with Angie bringing up the rear. At the top they veered left down a short hallway and Mark tossed the duffel bag onto the sleeper sofa in the guest room.

"What was your dog's name again?" Angie asked offhanded, peeking in to survey her quaint sleeping space. The bed took up much of the room, draped in a blue and white checkered quilt that matched the window valence. Small bouquets of dried flowers rested along eye-level display shelves, accenting with shades of blue, white, and lavender.

"His name is Godot. You know, after the French tragic comedy, *Waiting for Godot*." Mark answered cheerfully, as though the connection should be obvious to her.

Angie turned, looking at him for a moment before admitting, "No, I don't know, honestly."

Mark blinked in surprise, gaze darting about as he considered. "Oh. It's an old play. Simple and clever—you'd like it. My dad and I went to the show just before going to pick up a puppy from the breeder. We ended up sitting around waiting for the longest time while they got him ready. And I thought, 'hey, this reminds me of *Waiting for Godot*.' So I told my dad that's what we should name him," he said, all while using a small flurry of hand gestures.

Angie was reminded of his flair for conveying more excitement in storytelling than the material actually warranted. "Ah. I see."

"Of course, in the play, Godot never did arrive. So I suppose it wasn't -entirely- fitting." He gave a short shrug and waved for her to follow as he cut into a room to his left. "I actually prefer comedic opera. Come listen to my new Gilbert and Sullivan collection!"

Angie followed, thinking her friend sounded every bit as eager as a small child with a new toy. She didn't have much exposure or interest in musical theater — or any sort of theater, for that matter. But for his sake, she decided she should at least feign interest.

Mark's room was something of an eclectic monument to his childhood — which, arguably, wasn't over. The walls were plastered with everything from world maps to posters featuring an array of musicals and theater companies. Bookcases lined the walls, housing collections of figurines rather than books. Angie shuffled over to examine some of them. Set below waist level were hundreds of dinosaur statuettes, along with selections of endangered and recently-extinct animals. Closer to eye level, he'd arranged his more current fascination: a miniature army of transforming robot toys.

"Which would you like to hear first? *The Mikado? H.M.S. Pinafore? The Pirates of Penzance?*" Mark called back to her from across the room as he rifled through his CD collection.

"*Pirates of Penzance*. Definitely," Angie said, pleased that something sounded familiar to her. "Just skip ahead to the 'Modern Major General' song."

"Ah, classic!" he said. "Their most popular piece… And, it's just 'Major-General,' by the way." Mark corrected others for accuracy as naturally and often as most people breathed. Angie knew better than to be offended by the fact.

"I am the very model of a modern Major-General,
I've information vegetable, animal, and mineral,
I know the kings of England, and I quote the fights historical,
From Marathon to Waterloo, in order categorical..."

Angie kept up with the words a third of the way through
before dissolving into mumblings. Mark applauded her, clearly
delighted. Satisfied that she had contributed more than she would
have guessed herself capable, Angie returned to surveying the
figurine collection.

Mark switched CDs and belted out the lyrics to another song,
after explaining to her at length why he favored it as an auditioning
piece. He had a good voice, in Angie's opinion. Deep and
resounding. She'd often thought he would make a good announcer.
And from what she could tell, he didn't struggle to stay on key. He
played through several more songs, giving her a dissertation on the
origins of each while Angie listened as intently as she could manage.

It came as a welcome break when Mark's parents returned
home. She excused herself from his impromptu rehearsal and headed
downstairs to volunteer herself in the kitchen. Cutting through the
formal dining room, she nearly ran into Rob as he was about to take a
seat in the corner.

The short, graying man seemed older than Sandra. Although,
his build was wiry and the firmness of his greeting handshake
suggested a certain spryness.

"Hello again, young lady!" Rob greeted her. "How has your
car been holding up?"

Angie smiled. "She's doing great, so far. I haven't checked
the oil yet, but I don't expect her to burn much."

"She, hmm? So you denote a personality in your vehicle," he
said in a formal but genial tone. "Does -she- have a name?"

"Oh, well...not yet," Angie said. "But I've been thinking
about it. I had a cute Japanese name picked out at first, but then one
of my friends told me it meant 'Oh no.' I decided that wasn't the best
idea. So I'm still open to suggestions."

Rob nodded in a manner that she couldn't help but think of as
sagely. "A good vehicle is like a good pet; deserving the respect of
its own name. I'll see if I can come up with a few ideas."

"I'd appreciate the help." She dipped her head, grateful. "…and I'm sure Sandra would appreciate a little help, too. Excuse me."

"Of course. You go right ahead." Rob rumbled in amusement as he sank into the cushioned chair he'd been aiming for.

Angie found Sandra at the kitchen stove, hovering over a boiling pot of crab legs. "You see?" the woman said, after noticing she wasn't alone. "Hot water and some spices, and they're no trouble at all."

Angie peered at the steaming surface of the water. "It smells great." She'd only had crab once before in her life, for a special occasion. She silently hoped that her host family wasn't going out of their way for her. "I'll set the table," she said, scooping a stack of plates off counter and heading for the dining room before Sandra could protest.

She made two more trips, first for drinking glasses and then for the silverware. Though Mark's family made use of more pieces than she was used to, she was at least sure about the knife blades facing in toward the plate on the right side, and forks being placed on the left. She had no idea about how she should arrange the small nutcrackers and fork picks she'd been handed for the crab meat, and so she set them in the middle of each plate.

Mark appeared without being called, and carefully edged around his father's extended legs. "Well, he almost made it to dinner," he remarked with a degree of mirth, sliding out a chair for himself at the table.

Angie noticed then that Rob was slumped back, sound asleep in the corner chair. His curved, professor-like glasses had slipped down his nose, threatening to drop off his face. She recalled from her previous visit that the man suffered from a sleep disorder, which rendered him capable of falling asleep just about anywhere.

Maybe 'suffer' isn't quite the right term for it, Angie thought. He'd adapted well enough to lead a completely functional life, interspersed with frequent, impromptu naps.

"He must have had a hard day," Sandra said as she carried in a bowl of steamed vegetables in one hand and a platter of crab legs in the other. She deposited the food and then went around laying burgundy cloth napkins at each setting, which complemented the warm décor of the room.

Once the drinks had been poured, Sandra gently shook Rob awake and he joined them at the table, looking refreshed..

Angie listened as the family launched into a scholarly back-and-forth about the sights they thought she might enjoy during her stay. Mark went on for some time about the science museum, then his father steered the conversation toward his enthusiasm for the architecture on the driving tours of Detroit's historic neighborhoods. Sandra let the men go on for a time before suggesting the following day's weather would be perfect conditions for visiting the Detroit Zoo.

Angie looked up from the crab leg she'd been prying at and seized the idea while there was a rare lull in conversation. "I haven't been to a zoo in a long time. That sounds like a good way to work off my driving legs."

"Excellent!" Mark said, gathering up his silverware onto his plate as he stood. "I'd been meaning to see what they've done with the penguin enclosure. I'll look up the feeding schedule and determine an optimal departure time." Rob wasn't far behind him in excusing himself.

Sandra gave the tabletop a light pat. "Don't feel rushed, now. They're quick eaters." She chuckled airily. "I'm just about to make a pot of tea. Would you like some? I'm sure you have things to take care of—"

"Things can wait. I'd love some tea." Angie smiled, waiting until Sandra had collected dishes and gone into the kitchen before she hurriedly downed the remainder of her food.

By the time she'd cleared her place and went looking for the dishwasher, Sandra was already carrying out a ceramic tea tray, complete with an ornate kettle and matching teacups. She hurried back to the table and sat down across from the woman, accepting a cup and honey-spoon.

"I know it's summer, but I find hot tea comforting year-round," Sandra said, pouring them each a cup before easing back into her chair. Her dark eyes alighted on her guest with undivided interest. "So, where are you headed next on your grand adventure?"

Angie blew at the steam rising from her cup. "If all goes according to plan, my next stop is Toronto. Hopefully after a quick detour to see Niagara Falls. Then on to Ottawa for a few days… And then New York City."

"Oh, New York." Sandra sighed. "I hope you spend a while there. There's so much to see."

"I should have a week, so I think I can hit the highlights. I'll see what I can manage without inconveniencing my host there."

Sandra nodded. "What about those two girls you went to visit in Ohio the last time we saw you? Will you be staying with them again?"

"No, not this time." Angie shook her head in regret. "They'll be working all summer."

The older woman's brow crumpled slightly in thought. "If you don't mind my asking... Do you plan on staying with any other girls on your trip?"

Angie read the woman's tone and expression as concern, on what she guessed to be a maternal level. She took a slow sip of her tea, considering her answer. "Well, there was supposed to be Sarah in Pennsylvania, but she got the chance to visit her family in England, so I had to scratch her off of the list. Aside from her, I guess there's just Antonio's sister in Miami, but I don't really know her that well. So, yeah, it's pretty much all guys and their families hosting me." She paused. "Does that sound bad?"

"Oh, no, I wasn't trying to imply that at all—" Sandra laid a hand flat on the table top between them, seeming to grope for the right wording. "I'll admit, I'd be more worried about you staying with single men. You know how things are…it's just safer that they all still live at home. I'd hate for someone to try to take advantage of you."

Angie smiled, grateful the woman would risking offending her rather failing to voice her legitimate apprehension. "I understand. I tried to be as careful about this as I could. I know the statistics— one in four women being sexually assaulted by the age of twenty-four and all that. Most of them by someone they know. But I have no intention of becoming a statistic. I taught a few self-defense classes last semester, and I'm about to be a black belt in Aikido. I'm pretty good at taking care of myself.

"Besides, even if I were some fragile dessert flower, these guys are all computer geeks and mamma's boys. Nothing to worry about," she assured. "Plus, I've already warned everyone that I have Mono. That should discourage anyone from getting too close."

Sandra seemed to relax a bit. "Mono…isn't that the one they call the kissing disease?"

Angie winced. "Yeah. But I happened to get it from sharing a smoothie with a friend—against my will. I think I lose glamor points for that."

Sandra emitted a soft chuckle, abating her look of concern. "Tell me, why a road trip? Aren't most girls your age dreaming of touring Europe?"

"Maybe the ones with money to burn." Angie tucked her chin and laughed. "Not that I don't like the sound of it. Languages, culture, art... But my family never traveled much, so I figure there's plenty I haven't seen on the continent I actually live on. I might work my way up to Europe after I get a degree, if I can save up enough. Or maybe Japan. I might look into one of those programs where you go somewhere and teach English for a year." She shook her head, pensive. "I don't know. I'll see how this goes first."

"Oh, to be young and unattached." Sandra cast her a wistful smile. "Well, our little corner of the world may not be the most fascinating, but we'll make sure you get a good feel for it."

"I really appreciate you putting up with me. The company is a lot more important to me than the scenery," Angie stressed.

And she meant it.

~ ~ ~ ~ ~ ~ ~

By the time Angie pushed herself away from the computer in the downstairs study, it was late. She'd meant to go to bed sooner, but two things delayed her: her inability to locate her long-distance phone cards, and an unsettling email she'd received from her host in Ottawa. Zak's message came in reply to one she'd sent the day before, letting him know she was still on schedule for her original arrival date. The message was as brief as it was cryptic:

```
Umm...about that. I know what I said, but I
kinda didn't ask my mom yet. And I don't see her
taking this well, so you might want to have a
backup plan.
-Zak
```

Stunned, she'd written and re-written several replies before deleting them. She decided to call Zak the following day to sort out the issue.

This wasn't good. She was supposed to spend four nights in Ottawa, and it was too late to rearrange her arrival times at other destinations.

Why would he tell me his family was fine with me visiting? What kind of jerk is this guy?

She thought back to the many playful conversations she'd had with him in the past. Zak had always been friendly, even borderline flirtatious at times. He was one of the first from the online community she'd seen a picture of. She'd gotten the sense that the nineteen-year-old wasn't quite as mature as his appearance would suggest, but she'd never thought that he might leave her stranded. She had half a mind to chew him out when she did call him.

Frustrated, she swiveled around and stood, scanning the entertainment room behind her for any signs of Mark. At his insistence, she'd spent several hours watching one of his favorite TV series with him. Anything that warranted Mark's interest also seemed to require his exhaustive understanding of it. As a result, along with the watching came his frequent, although unsolicited, background commentary. He'd seemed content to continue watching for as long as consciousness would allow, but Angie had finally been forced to pardon herself.

It wasn't that the show was uninteresting. She simply didn't have his capacity for devoting so much time to a single activity. Now it seemed, in the absence of someone to share it with, Mark had given up and gone to bed.

She hoped she hadn't hurt his feelings, but at the same time, she couldn't imagine how it would help his social skills if she were to encourage his every excess. From what she understood, Mark had spent his entire educational life attending a private school for the gifted and talented. She was beginning to wonder if that sort of environment had been artificially tolerant toward certain areas of weakness. Not that she could imagine public school resulting in anything but total immersion in the opposite, soul-sucking extreme.

Quietly, she made her way across the lower level of the house. Godot laid curled up on the welcome mat at the front door. The contented animal only bothered to half-open his eyes when she passed.

As she rounded the corner to the base of the darkened stairs, she was suddenly able to make out the seated form of a person. Had she noticed any later, she would have tripped over them. The abruptness of that revelation caused her to jump back in reflexive alarm. She wasn't sure what had unsettled her more, the stillness of the form, or the oddness of the location given time of night.

Her body relaxed then, a moment before her brain caught her up to the recognition that the statuesque figure was Rob. The man had apparently fallen asleep there, his right shoulder inclined against the slatted wooden railing of the staircase. His elbow rested against his thigh, forming the support for his palm to hold up his chin. She remembered Sandra once mentioning that Rob had never been able to spend more than three or four hours in bed before having to roam the house. Perhaps he hadn't made it to the roaming part yet.

That's going to take some getting used to.

Angie managed to slip past without disturbing him, continuing up the stairs to the guest room.

June 13th,

I got into the city without any trouble, and I'm doing fine so far. Tired, but fine. I enjoy Mark's family very much. Although, Mark himself tends to leave me a little intellectually exhausted. I appreciate the stimulus, but it's a bit too much sometimes. I always feel like I'm fighting to remain on an equal level with him. I'm probably just trying too hard. I need to focus more on having fun.

I'm not sure how this will all pan out anymore. Zak sent an email that made it sound like there's a big problem with me coming to Ottawa. I keep thinking it's early in the trip...I could still go back home. But giving up so soon would feel like a huge failure. We'll see how I feel after a little longer in Detroit. Maybe I'm going about this all wrong. My attitude is pretty pathetic at the moment.

I haven't heard from Don at all. Part of me wonders if I should just leave him alone. All I can do is pray for the best. But for once, I'm going to try choosing hope over realism. Since my personal sense of realism tends to be nothing but thinly veiled pessimism, I figure I'm not losing anything in the venture. But for now, I sleep.

Mileage Log: 890 miles

~Ang

Chapter 5

Angeli heaved a sigh as she set the house phone back into its cradle on the nightstand. It was late in the morning, and Mark had been fidgeting in the doorway for the last five minutes of her conversation with Elsie. He was clearly more determined than she was to make it to the zoo before any animals had been fed.

"I don't know why I thought talking to her might make me feel better. She's all excited that she just got another letter from Anne Rice. I couldn't get a word in edgewise." Angie griped to herself as much as she was explaining the reason for the delay.

"Anne Rice? As in… 'Interview with the Vampire?' That Anne Rice?" Mark gaped at her, seeming to have forgotten the schedule he'd plotted out for the day.

"That'd be the one." Angie nodded, pushing off from the edge of the bed where she'd been sitting. "And I wouldn't have believed it either, if I hadn't seen the lockbox under her bed with each letter sealed in its own little plastic bag. Elsie claims that they're pen pals, but I figure the lady must just be really nice to some of her fans."

"That's impressive," Mark said, still marveling.

"Well, you know, Elsie is a pretty great writer. She wrote her first fan-fiction novel when she was fourteen. Maybe her talent is just being recognized and encouraged." Angie paused to consider before admitting, "Or, she's become so dedicated to a fantasy that she's forging letters to herself from a famous author. I can never be completely sure with her."

Mark emitted a low chuckle. "Well, if anyone could manage to get the attention of a respected author, I suppose it would be her. She seems like quite the character herself."

Understatement of the year.

Glancing to the oak dresser beside the door, Mark grabbed Angie's journal off the top of it and began inspecting the tome. "Speaking of writing—"

Before she'd fully processed the impulse, Angie lurched forward and snatched the slim book out of his hands. "That's…personal." She kept up a light tone in an effort to counter the defensiveness of her action. While she didn't believe she'd written anything negative about him, she didn't want to risk hurt feelings.

Mark looked all the more intrigued. "You keep a diary?"

Angie shook her head, removing the pen that marked her last page. "It's just a journal, for keeping track of things while I'm on this trip." Hoping to satiate his curiosity, she flipped it open to the back page where she'd maintained a record of identifiable road kill using categories and tally marks. "See? So far, the raccoons are winning. But the deer aren't far behind."

Mark peered over the list for a long moment. "Well, it's not exactly something out of Robinson Crusoe, is it?" he said, unabashed in candor. He groomed his fingers through his beard in an exaggerated gesture of contemplation. "So then, does your journal have a title?"

"I hadn't really thought about it." Angie shrugged. She snapped the book closed and tucked it under her pillow.

Mark snapped his fingers. "Oh, I know! You could call it: The Chronicles of Peril," he said, looking proud of himself. "…You see the double entendre?"

"Yes, that's very clever." She sighed, miming a courtesy applause before shooing him out of the room. "But I think that would be right up there with naming my car 'Oh no' —' just asking for trouble." She pulled the door closed behind them as an additional measure, having observed Mark to be somewhat oblivious when it came to personal space.

She was glad to be getting out and about. A good night's sleep hadn't done as much to improve her outlook as she had hoped.

~ ~ ~ ~ ~ ~ ~

On the whole, Angie was impressed with the Detroit Zoo. The grounds were lush and expansive, offering hours of self-paced sights and educational activities. Although, in Mark's company, she struggled to keep any sort of casual pace. The young man flitted from one exhibit to another, reading aloud from the plaques and offering an array of accompanying details he recalled from previous visits or books he'd read. She was reasonably sure that anyone overhearing would think that he was vying for a position as a tour guide.

At one point they passed through a tunnel-like construct overgrown with leafy vines and other foliage, supported by a grated iron frame that allowed sunlight to filter through. She called for Mark to stop for a moment while she took a picture. Angie hadn't noticed the hedges along either side were filled with white roses, until Mark spontaneously broke into a short musical number over them.

" . . .everything's coming up roses!" His rich voice carried as he did a tight spin and gestured to the flora. The outburst briefly drew the attention of a half dozen people nearby, who didn't seem to know what to make of it. If Mark noticed the stares, he didn't acknowledge them.

"What's that from?" Angie asked quickly, concerned he might progress to a full-fledged production if he wasn't redirected.

"Gypsy: A Musical Fable." He appeared momentarily aghast at her lack of recognition, clawing his upturned hands before himself. "It's only considered to be the -greatest- American musical of all time!"

Angie watched out of the corner of her eye as a passing woman steered her two small children by their shoulders, giving Mark an excessively wide birth. "Okay, sure. Gypsy," she said and then paused. "You know what? I like the sound of that." She gave Mark's shoulder a firm, congratulatory pat. "Thank you. You just found the perfect name for my car." She continued walking, taking the lead on their way to the Penguinarium.

Mark lifted a finger in a look of confusion before hurrying to catch up with her. "You're welcome?" He glanced at his watch, falling in line with her stride. "We ought to be right on time. This is my favorite habitat by far, even though they only have three of the seventeen existing species—"

Angie kept her camera in hand as they stepped into the cooled air of the rounded, concrete building. Her attention was immediately drawn to the cylindrical structure filling the center of the room. The rocky, three-sided habitat rose up surrounded by a glass-encased pool that stood well above waist level. As they moved closer, she could see the pool was continuous, flowing in a rapid counterclockwise motion around the central habitat. Penguins of varying sizes plunged into the water to swim against the current, taking on the characteristic underwater flying pose she'd often seen on television.

"Huh. It's like...a penguin treadmill," she mused aloud.

"Precisely." Mark shuffled to her right, watching as the largest of the penguin species were tossed small fish by their handlers. "It's one of the few zoos in North America to utilize this form of containment."

A sprightly young girl pointed toward the most sizable of the flightless birds. Too small to see over the top of the pool, her pigtails bobbed freely as she bounced up and down. "Look mommy! It's an Emperor Penguin, like from my book!"

"I wish it were." Mark bent slightly at the waist, coming closer to the child's level while giving her a singular pat on the head. "Actually, that's a King Penguin. It's an easy mistake to make, they're very closely related." His tone was pleasantly authoritative, as it tended to be regardless of who he was speaking to. He also appeared unaware of the irritation that soured the face of the little girl's mother.

"Oh," the child said, giving Mark a confused look before turning her attentions to a smaller penguin nearby. Her mother eased to her side, placing an arm around the girl while subtly positioning herself as a buffer between her offspring and Mark. Mark, however, showed no signs of recognizing this. He'd already moved on to another section of the habitat.

Angie followed after him. She was becoming convinced that her friend had no idea of when his behavior or choice of words could be considered off-putting. She knew he meant no harm whatsoever, but she also knew the general public wasn't privileged with the kind of background knowledge she'd accumulated about him. If today was any indicator of a "normal" outing for him, she had to wonder if his future would hold to a pattern of unwitting alienation. She also wondered if it would do any good for her to obey the urge to talk to him about it. After all, when it came to social graces, she was a far cry from savvy herself.

Several feet away, a boy she guessed to be around the age of six was staring intently at a section of information on the wall, struggling to sound out the scientific name for the Macaroni Penguin.

"E...you...youdip...youdipits cris...sol...pus..." The boy dragged his finger along underneath the word as he attempted the pronunciation.

Mark clasped his hands behind his back and leaned aside toward the boy. "Eudyptes chrysolophus," he amended, gesturing to a set of smaller penguins that were swimming past behind the glass. "They're closely related to the Eudyptes chrysocome, but you can see the difference in their crests."

Angie sighed at her friend, thinking he sounded a little too much like the character he most favored using for storylines in their online writing community—a mad scientist. She then noticed that a gruff-looking, middle-aged man standing a few paces behind the boy had frowned and shifted his stance.

Undeterred by the correction, or simply ignoring Mark, the young boy stepped aside to the next plaque and repeated his stumbling efforts with the King Penguin. "Ap...ten...odits... Pat...ago...nice..."

"Aptenodytes patagonicus." Mark piped up again, matter-of-factly.

"Excuse me...do you work here?" asked the man Angie had deduced was connected to the little boy. His tone was demanding and laced with agitation. He was tall and thickly built, wearing an old Harley Davidson t-shirt that must have started out black but had faded to gray. The scruffy start to a beard showed a salt and pepper mingling, which could have placed him as either an older father or a younger grandfather. Either way, he made for an intimidating figure.

Mark smiled as he looked back at the man. "Oh, no. But I have thought about applying for a seasonal position. I'm here nearly every week as it is." His expression brightened. "I highly recommend the membership program. It comes with a magazine subscription that I'm sure could improve his familiarity with Latin pronunciation," he said, gesturing to the boy.

The man folded his arms across his chest as he stared at Mark, his face darkening into what Angie interpreted as mounting hostility.

"Mark! Come on, I need to show you something," Angie blurted out, unable to come up with a better excuse for ushering him away. She gave the angry looking man an apologetic smile, grabbed a handful of Mark's shirt, and pulled him along toward the door.

Mark allowed himself to be led, but appeared thrown off over having his one-sided conversation interrupted. "What is it? This was supposed to be our last big exhibit."

Angie released him once the door of the building closed behind them. "Okay, so I don't actually need to show you something. I just didn't want you to get hit in the mouth."

Mark gave her a bemused look. "And why would you be concerned over something like that?"

She sighed, wracking her brain for the best way of illuminating the situation for him. "Because...you were starting to piss that guy off with critiquing that kid. I know you thought you were being helpful, but I'm pretty sure he wasn't seeing it that way."

"What other way was there to see it?" Mark gave her an incredulous look as he smoothed out the crinkled spot on his arm where she'd gripped his shirt.

"That you were being an arrogant know-it-all?" she said, bluntly.

"Nonsense! I was only—"

"Hey, you asked." Angie held up a hand to halt his brewing logistical argument. "I know you don't mean to sound that way, but you do sometimes." She held up her other hand to fend off the interruption. "People who know you know better, but in the rest of the world, people tend to make snap judgments about strangers. And when it comes to their kids, they're going to be protective and even less willing to try to understand where you're coming from. You need to be more careful. Establish a rapport with people first, you know?"

Mark considered this for a moment, his bright gaze bouncing over directional signs and passersby without any clear focus. "I thought I was being sociable." His insistence began to sound wounded.

"I know." She smiled in sympathy. "But being sociable includes showing that you're interested in other people, not just inviting yourself in on a topic you think you have in common. What you have to say doesn't tend to mean a lot to people, unless -you- mean something to them."

Mark frowned slightly. "That sounds...reasonable."

Though Angie wasn't certain that he'd understood what she was getting at, she decided not to press the issue. It didn't seem likely a single conversation would be enough to temper how he related to others. At least a potential conflict had been averted. "Come on, " she said. "I want to stop by the big cats again before we go. Maybe a few of them are done napping."

Mark's amiable expression returned. "I'd say the chances are good. Cats are most active at dawn and dusk, and the sun should be setting soon." He nodded to the west where the glowing orb was about to sink beyond the horizon. Taking long strides on short legs, he set the pace for them down the cement walkway in the direction of the feline exhibit.

Angie smirked to herself and shook her head, launching into a sprint to catch up to him.

~ ~ ~ ~ ~ ~ ~

Angie waited until after dinner to call Zak. She knew his high school classes wouldn't be over with for several more days, and she wanted the best chance of catching him at home. The phone rang several times before a woman picked up on the other end. Angie infused cheerfulness into her voice as she asked for Zak, hunching herself forward in the computer chair as she waited.

"Hello?" A mellow baritone voice came on the line.

She swallowed back her surprise. With the cost of long distance phone calls to Canada being twice that of calls in the US, she'd never actually spoken to him outside of a somewhat garbled computer chat function. "Zak? This is Angeli." She waited, allowing the information to sink in.

On the other end there came a sigh. "Look. Don't be mad. I didn't think you'd actually come. Lots of people make plans and talk big, you know? I just figured—"

"That I'd chicken out?" Angie said, blandly.

"Well, sorta." Zak confessed, tone filling with regret. "I'm really sorry. I'm going to break it to my mom tonight and see what I can do. I can't make any promises though. I mean, I can at least show you around when you get up here. I just don't know if I can convince her to let you stay at the house."

"I'd settle for a safe place to park my car, if you know of any parks or camping spots." She found herself sounding more dismayed than upset with him.

Zak seemed to hesitate. "I don't know that I'd feel great about that, but I'll look into it."

"If it helps at all, your mom can call and talk to my mom. And the family I'm staying with now can vouch for me not being psychotic. I'll send you an email tonight with the phone numbers."

"That couldn't hurt," he said. "Just give me a day or two and I'll get back to you, eh?"

"Okay. I'll be here a few more days. Let me know what's up as soon as you can," she said, trying not to sound pleading.

As Angie hung up the phone, she felt somewhat better. There was nothing to do now but wait for the verdict. She could at least try to enjoy herself in the meantime. Hearing Mark and his mother laughing in the dining room, she got up to join them. Cutting through the entertainment room, she was given only a slight start at finding Mark's father slumped over asleep on the nearest side of the sofa. She was beginning to regard him as a sort of randomly relocating effigy.

Sandra smiled after noticing her entrance. "There you are. Mark was just telling me about your little mishap with the car."

"Oh, that." Angie recalled with mild embarrassment as she sank into a chair beside Mark, across the table from Sandra. "I can't believe I left the door ajar while we were in the zoo. I'm just glad I had jumper cables with me."

"I can't believe I couldn't persuade anyone to pull their car around and give us a jump-start," Mark said in a bewildered tone. He gave Angie an inquisitive look. "And yet, somehow, you managed to coax the first person you asked into helping us."

"I shouldn't have asked you to flag someone down in the first place." Angie laughed. "We were in the middle of Detroit, at dusk, stuck at the back of a giant parking lot. You're a guy with a beard, who could pass for being ten years older than you are. And I'm...a generic eighteen-year-old girl. Guess who looks least like a serial killer between the two of us?"

"Well, that's...discrimination!" Mark forced a theatrical tone of outrage.

"You bet your Blarney Stone, it is." Angie chuckled. "But it's also survival instinct. I would have picked me, too." She reached over and gave his russet hair a good-natured ruffling.

"I'm not Irish!" Mark leaned away and immediately began grooming his hair back into place with his fingers.

His mother laughed. "I can just imagine it. At least you weren't stuck somewhere downtown. I'd think it would have been even more difficult to find a good Samaritan." Sandra stood and headed back toward the kitchen. "The tea should be about ready."

Angie looked to Mark. "Downtown... is that where we were when we passed the burning car?"

Mark bobbed his head in a nod. "Technically, yes. That was an unusual sight, in my experience. Even more unusual that there weren't any first responders on the scene yet." Mark's head twitched aside toward his right shoulder as he spoke.

Angie noticed the twitch, but being he didn't seem to acknowledge it, she decided not to ask. "Maybe somebody torched it for insurance money," she said. "All I know is, it scared the bajeebers out of me when one of the tires exploded."

Mark smirked. "It -did- sound reminiscent of a gunshot go—" He paused mid-sentence. His gaze had been wandering about as it usually did while he was speaking, but now seemed frozen on some point along the wall.

Angie's first instinct was to look across the room at whatever he'd fixated on. Unable to detect anything that seemed worthy of rendering him speechless, she looked back at Mark's face, unsettled by his silence more than she would have expected. "What is it?" She noticed a tic below his right eye, but nothing else by way of movement. It was as though everything about him had simply stopped. She snapped her fingers in front of his face, and then reached out to tapped his shoulder, increasingly alarmed by his lack of response. "Mark?"

Nothing happened.

She pushed her chair back and stood, pitching her voice toward the kitchen. "Sandy?" She decided her tone hadn't adequately conveyed the sense of urgency that flooded her mind. "Sandra?!"

Mark's mother came bustling into the room with the tea tray extended out at her waist, a wondering look sweeping from Angie to her motionless son. "Oh!" She hurriedly slid the tray onto the end of the table as she moved to the other side of Mark. Placing one hand on his elbow and the other on his shoulder, she bent down closer to him. "Mark. Sweetheart." She glanced down at her wristwatch.

"Do you need me to do something?" Angie asked, recovering her composure.

"No, no. Just give him a moment," Sandra said, looking more focused than anxious. "Mark?"

Mark blinked, his eyes resuming their darting course. He looked from his mother to Angie and back, straightening up in his chair. "I'm sorry, what were you saying?"

Sandra kept a hand on his shoulder as she eased back. "You're late on your medicine tonight, aren't you?" It was more of a statement than a question.

"Am I?" He glanced at his own watch and stood up. "Ah. I'll remedy that. Was I gone long?" He directed the question to his mother, who looked to Angie in uncertainty.

"Not...long." Angie answered. "Less than a minute?"

Having paused long enough to hear an answer, Mark made a low, contemplative noise and continued on into the kitchen.

Sandra went back to the tea tray and brought it to the middle of the table as she sat down. "And that would be why he doesn't have his driver's license yet," she said, looking suddenly worn.

Angie took her seat again and accepted the tea cup that was handed to her. "I take it that was a seizure." She'd never actually witnessed one before, but one of the advantages to having a nurse for a mother meant an awareness that not all forms of seizures involved overt convulsions.

Sandra nodded. "Nothing to worry about—they're fairly well controlled. But as you just saw, timing is everything. Especially lately, while they've been tinkering with his medication. I may need to have them adjust his doses again. They had such a hard time diagnosing him in the first place, I hate having to keep taking him back."

"That's got to be hard on you," Angie said, taking on a tentative tone as she settled back with her tea.

"It is, sometimes." Sandra took her time preparing her own cup. "Part of it is just being a mother. I know better than anyone how brilliant he is; how limitless his talents. It just hurts me to see things holding him back. He's already looking at all of these art colleges off in other states. In a year, it'll be so much harder for me to be there for him. And it's never been easy for him to make friends in new places, let alone ones that would look out for him."

Angie nodded, taking a long sip as she considered the opening she saw for bringing up a nagging concern she had about Mark's mannerisms. She was fond of Sandra, and she felt sure the sentiment was mutual. The last thing she wanted to do was distress her with an under-qualified impression — or worse, anger her. And yet, the woman had already dared to be straightforward with her out of genuine concern. The least she could do was return the courtesy. "Had I told you I worked for the school system for the last year as a classroom assistant?" she asked, attempting to broach the topic in a roundabout way.

Sandra shook her head and smiled, her soft features easing into a less worried state. "No, you didn't."

Angie smiled, looking up from her tea. "I ended up working with age ranges from preschool through high school, with all types of kids. Learning disorders, developmental delays, language barriers, behavioral problems—not all remedial classes, just kids who needed extra attention," she said, as a preamble. She cleared her throat then and met Sandra's gaze, hesitant. "I bring it up because…well…there are a few things about how Mark relates to people that I keep finding familiar." She waited for the woman to look insulted.

Sandra cupped both hands around her steaming teacup and leaned forward, showing nothing more than heightened interest. "How do you mean?"

Angie cast a look toward the kitchen to assure herself that Mark hadn't wandered back within earshot. "I was wondering…if you'd ever had him tested for Asperger's." There, she'd said the 'A' word. Not the worst 'A' word, but she'd know in a moment if she'd still need to use it to clarify.

Sandra sat back in her chair with a pensive expression. "High-functioning Autism…" she defined the syndrome out loud. Her voice came out detached, calm enough that Angie wasn't sure if she'd taken her seriously. "No, we've never had him tested for it, specifically. Although, I've considered it at one time or another. He's always done so well academically, I'm not sure we should risk him being labeled." Her brows drew together. "What makes you suspect it?"

Angie released a breath she'd been holding a little too long, relieved the woman had taken the inquiry without offense or disregard. Her respect for Sandra deepened. "It's…hard to explain. I just notice things from spending so much time around a big range of the spectrum. I can tell he thinks differently than most people, and not just because he's so logic-oriented. He doesn't seem to pick up on certain non-verbal communication signals. And I know he doesn't realize when he's dominating a conversation. I see how people who aren't used to him can…misunderstand his intentions," she said, as delicately as she could without being vague.

Sandra nodded after a moment of consideration. "Even when he was small, Mark always got along better with adults than he did with his peers. Other children could be so impatient with him. But, he's never seemed to have trouble making eye contact. I'd thought that was one of the indicators." She brought up the last point with an air of uncertainty.

"Like you said, he's brilliant. And he loves acting. I think that might be an expectation he adapted to, not something that comes naturally to him." Angie said, groping for the gentlest way of differentiating between book smarts and people smarts. "He knows to look at the people he's speaking to, but I don't think he knows how to read them while he's looking at them." She paused before giving in to the desire to backpedal. "But, I could be way off base. I'm sorry. I sure didn't want to give you something more to worry about."

Sandra gave the table top a light pat with her palm to go with her smile of reassurance. "Don't be sorry. It's good to have perspective from someone more…removed from the thick of things. Fresh eyes." She finished off her cup and poured herself seconds. "I think we'll probably wait and see how his first semester at college goes before we look into how much support he may need. I don't want to make him anxious if it turns out he can cope just fine on his own."

"I'll be praying he does," Angie said. She was sincere, but immediately wanted to kick herself for sounding trite.

Fortunately, Sandra seemed to take it precisely as it was intended, and even appeared touched. "Thank you, that means more to me than you can know." She inhaled deeply, as if to clear her head. "Now then, tell me about you. Did you get things straightened out with that boy in Ottawa?"

Angie stifled an exasperated sigh. "Not quite. I'll know more in a day or two, though."

Sandra gave her an empathetic smile. "You know, you're welcome to stay with us as long as you need to. It's so nice having another woman in the house."

"Thank you. I'm glad I haven't been a pain." Angie chuckled. "I may stay a little longer, depending on the weather. I know my stop in Toronto is flexible at least."

"We'll all be going into Windsor tomorrow night for dinner, so you can at least have a quick glimpse of Canada and be a little more familiar with the border-crossing. There's a Scottish festival going on over there we might even catch," Sandra said with pleasant anticipation. "But if you're going to enjoy a proper tour tomorrow, you may want to turn in early."

Angie nodded, wondering if she must look as weary as she was beginning to feel. She looked off to the kitchen as she stood, setting her empty cup on the tray. "I hope Mark is okay," she said, feeling a slight edge of guilt over not checking on him."

"He must have gotten caught up in one of his shows. I should see if I can convince him to get some sleep, too." Sandra gave one last warm smile before taking the tea tray off into the kitchen, leaving Angie to her evening routine.

June 14th,
Lions and Tigers and Penguins…Oh My!

It was a perfect, sunny day. Mark and I went to the Detroit zoo, which made for a good distraction from my personal little pity party. Being around Mark more is helping me to understand him better. He has a few peculiar tendencies that take some getting used to. Sometimes he reminds me a little of Elsie; extensive capacity for intelligence… attention span of a squirrel. I need to be more patient with him. His mother has been so kind to me, and I want to be good company for her.

Good news today to weaken my panic. My phone cards have been in my wallet all along. I'd just forgotten about the slot under the picture holder. This realization of course came to me while I was taking a shower. (I wonder if I'd have even more profound revelations if I spent more of my life in the shower.) Also, it seems that Zak hasn't abandoned me after all. But, I'll probably be extending my stay here in hopes that I won't outstay my welcome in Ottawa.

I can admit, I still wonder if I'm being incredibly stupid. It's not like I'm having second thoughts from being homesick or anything like that. But I'm way outside of my comfort zone. And once I cross into Canada, I'll be too far outside my 12-hour range for being able to drive straight back home. So maybe that will actually help me… to be so far along that I might as well keep going.

Status: Dead tired; mild sore throat.

~Ang

Chapter 6

In spite of the looming uncertainty overshadowing the Ottawa leg of her trip, the next several days flew by for Angie. Mark's parents were passionate about their favorite sights in the area, and their enthusiasm was infectious enough for her to find enjoyment in the historical aspects of Detroit.

Returning from a particularly full day, Angie took the time to check her email. She'd already resolved to call Zak again if he hadn't updated her by that evening. She was relieved to find a message from him in her inbox, though she was hesitant to read it. There was also a message from Don waiting for her, which lifted her hopes more than she would have liked. She decided to save it for last, in case Zak had bad news for her.

With a deep breath she opened Zak's email.

```
    Hey, I don't think it's going to work out.
It's not a problem with me, It's just... my mom is
extremely paranoid about things she doesn't
understand. It's also the timing. I just finished
my writer's craft exam (I think it went pretty
well), and have a history exam on Thursday... My
sister is due to have a baby any day now. My other
sister is graduating from the University. I'm
graduating high school... etc, etc. I also kinda
did spring it on her at the last minute, but she's
so uptight about anything related to the internet,
I doubt it would have mattered if I told her about
it three years ago. She did say that if you were
to come up another time you might be able to stay
here, but she's really hesitant about letting
```

someone neither of us have ever met face-to-face
stay over.
"What if she's some kind of freak murderer
and kills us in our sleep?"
lol
"She's doing what?! Is she crazy!?" etc, etc…
Basically, we'll just have to find you a
nice, relatively cheap place to stay. I'll start
looking. The day you'd be coming up is my last day
of classes, so try to hold off getting here until
after 4pm, and I'll at least be free to show you
around after that.
-Zak

Angie closed her eyes and held her breath until her lungs
burned. She wanted to hurl something across the room to vent her
frustration, however destructive and pointless that would be. Maybe
she -was- crazy. And maybe she deserved to run into trouble for
trusting Zak at his word when he'd told her that his family was fine
with her visit.
What was I supposed to do, demand to speak to his mommy?
She sighed, glancing around the office to be sure she was
alone before muttering a complaint to God. "I know we don't have
the exact same plans lined up, but could just a little more go -right-?
Are you trying to tell me I should go back home...?"
The recollection of her initial resolve seeped steadily into the
forefront of her mind. *Okay, so this doesn't have to stop me. I knew
I'd have to sleep in the car some, and it's not going to kill my bank
account to stay at a cheap motel for a night or two.*
She sighed, her emotional turmoil beginning to settle. Hoping
for a boost to her spirits, she opened Don's email.

I don't have a lot of time. They put me on
12-hour night shifts now. I just wanted to get
back to you before I grab a nap. It sounds like
your trip is falling apart. I'm sorry for that,
but it's probably for the best. You know I didn't
like the idea of you taking this on alone in the
first place. There's no shame in trying something
out and realizing it's not working for you. I'd
prefer you play it safe, but it's your call.

```
    Whatever you do, please take care of
yourself.
    -Don
```

Good grief.

It wasn't just what he'd said that she found so disheartening, it was what he didn't say. Consistent with his last few communications, Don had ceased to mention anything about "When I get out of the Air Force..." It also hadn't escaped her notice that she was now the one having to initiate all contact between them. The lack of personalization in his closure of the message also pointed to the same conclusion she kept coming back to — he'd given up on ever meeting her.

Either he'd found someone else to focus his attention on, or he was so down about having his service contract extended he was becoming despondent. The effect on her was essentially the same. She could either accept it, or be depressed over it.

As long as he's okay, it doesn't matter.

If she had to remind herself of that until her attitude lined up with it, then that's what she intended to do.

Without answering either message, Angie pushed herself away from the computer and headed through the kitchen. Sandra had already set everything out for them in the dining room. A cup of tea and a little girl-talk seemed like the most inviting way for Angie to work through her muddled despair. She was sure now that missing her Detroit hostess was going to be the hardest part about moving on.

June 15th-17th,

Be Flexible, or be Bent Out of Shape

I spent most of the day touring Detroit with Mark's family. Mark's dad gave a free history lesson along with the sightseeing. The old, rich neighborhoods were particularly impressive. All in all, it was a highly educational day.

I've been enjoying great in-depth conversations with Mark's mother every evening. For me, it's kind of like having an extra mom. She's fun to talk to, and she's been very understanding. I just hope that I'm not excluding Mark in the process.

Tonight I discovered that Don finally replied to my email. I suppose I made him worry with the last message I sent him. I've got to make sure I quit mailing things late at night when I'm feeling lousy. I'm relieved he seems to be alright, but I miss talking to him. I guess that must not be mutual though, or he would be putting more effort into keeping in touch.

Zak finally got back to me as well. It sounds like his attempt at explaining me to his mother didn't go well. Honestly, I can't blame the woman. Zak should have mentioned my visit a long time ago. I'm considering replacing his name with 'Jerkface' from here on out. If I'd known this would be such a problem, I never would have planned him into the trip in the first place. But at this point, I'm far from home and pretty much stuck in my forward momentum. I'm going to Ottawa. And I'll either have somebody to show me around, or I'll just have to wing it like a true American. Haphazardly.

Status: Sore throat again, but the fever has been better the last few nights.

~Ang

~ ~ ~ ~ ~ ~ ~

Standing on the front stoop, Angie returned Sandra's warm parting embrace. The morning was bright and calm, in stark contrast to the mood that had been hanging over her as of late. She was as ready to hit the road as she was ever going to be.

Sandra had insisted on making Angie breakfast before she left, and was currently sparing no measure of maternal fussing. "You're going to like Canada. It's got some beautiful countryside, and they keep things very clean. But aside from the metric system, it's not so different. In a lot of ways it reminds me of the U.S., twenty years ago. Just a bit more...French."

"Thank you so much, Sandy." Angie weighted her words with heartfelt sincerity. "I can't thank you enough. You've all been amazing to me."

"No thanks needed. Just come back through again if you can!" Sandra's soft face pinked with emotion. "Oh, I nearly forgot. Hold out your hands," she instructed, delving into her pockets.

Angie blinked in confusion but did as she was told, only to have Sandra deposit handfuls of Canadian coins into her cupped palms. "Oh, you don't have to do that!"

Sandra pushed her hands back toward her, adamant. "It's nothing, believe me, we have so much of it sitting around. You'll need it for the parking meters, if nothing else. Your credit card should convert anything else you need without any trouble," she said, cheerily. "Just promise me you'll let us know how things go?"

"Of course," Angie said, funneling the coins into her pockets. "I'll send you the same updates that my parents get."

"Good." Sandra beamed, clapping her hands together at her waist. "I'll have Mark help you load up. He should be bringing down your bag." The woman swayed aside through the open doorway and called up the stairs, "Mark?"

Mark came bounding down the staircase moments later, Angie's duffel bag slung over his shoulder and Godot at his heels. The dog charged past him out the front door, galloping in playful circles around everyone's legs. Angie bent to give the animal a farewell pat on the head before following Mark to her car. Flipping open the trunk, she gestured for him to toss the bag inside.

"Well I suppose that does it, my friend," Mark said, clearing his throat as though he were about to make a formal announcement. He raised his right hand and splayed it, deftly holding the middle and index fingers apart from the pinky and ring finger in a V formation, a la Mr. Spock. "I believe Shakespeare put it best: 'Love all. Trust few. Do harm to no one.'"

Angie chuckled. "You know, I think those are some pretty great words to live by. But, I think you've got your genres a little confused," she said, indicating his Vulcan salute.

Mark quirked a fiery brow and shook his head in rebuttal. "On the contrary; not only are Shakespeare and Star Trek compatible, but I find them to be complementary. Symbiotic, if you will. His works are directly referenced in four episodes of The Next

Generation. And Patrick Stewart was, after all, a veteran Shakespearean actor—"

Angie raised her own salute, cutting him short. "I'll take your word for it." She gave him a brief hug. "Your hospitality is greatly appreciated, but I'd better get going while I've still got a head start on the day." She walked around the driver's side of her car and dropped into the seat.

Mark locked his hands behind his back, peering through the open window at her. "You should have plenty of time to see Niagara. Assuming they don't decide to search your car at the border. We've never been searched before, but then, we've never stayed for more than a day."

"Okay, thanks." Angie stretched her hand out the window to wave to him and Sandra before pulling away from the curb. She'd gone a block before she allowed herself to grimace, recalling the signs posted outside of the border crossing. The parts about having proper identification wouldn't be an issue — it was the "no weapons" notice that concerned her. She wasn't willing to leave her Bowie knife behind, for both sentimental and self-protective reasons. She'd spent an hour the previous day looking for the best place to conceal it in the event her car was searched. It currently resided under her seat, secured by the strap of the sheath. But she had no confidence this would outsmart an experienced border agent. She would just have to hope she wasn't searched.

Being arrested was definitely not on her itinerary.

~ ~ ~ ~ ~ ~ ~

"Next!" croaked a middle-aged woman from behind the processing counter.

Angie stepped up and laid out her I.D., along with the written note she was given before being diverted to the tiny customs building. "The man at the guard house sent me here."

The older woman wouldn't have had a memorable face, if not for the puckered expression etched into a leathery tan. Her hair was short, ash-brown, and curled into meticulous rows. She wore a thick-framed pair of reading glasses, tethered to her neck by a colorfully beaded cord. Holding them pinched between two fingers, she whipped the glasses on and off as she scanned the note from the border guard. "Now, how old are you?" she demanded.

"Eighteen," Angie answered, wondering why the woman hadn't bothered to read the date on her driver's license. "—and a half," she added, immediately wishing she could take the words back. They rang of desperate immaturity.

Stay calm. They can't keep you out of their country on suspicion of being a moron. ...can they?

"And if I call your father to ask him about this, what do you suppose he's going to tell me?" The woman challenged in a patronizing tone.

"He'd tell you that I'm exactly where I said I'd be, and to say 'hi' for him," Angie said, maintaining her calm. Getting uppity would only make things worse. "You're welcome to call. My dad would still be at work, but my mom is probably home. She'll tell you the same thing. Do you have a pen and piece of paper?"

The woman scowled, crumpling her features enough to remind Angie of a wadded-up paper bag. She slapped a pen down on the counter between them and turned to peel off a sticky note. The phone beside her rang and she snatched it up. "Hello?" She paused. "Yes, I've got her right here and—" Her shoulders shifted downward. "Are you sure? ...alright. Alright," she huffed, setting the phone back down a little harder than necessary.

Angie held the pen poised and ready, watching the unfriendly clerk.

The woman snatched the pen from Angie and scribbled something down. "Take your things. You can go through."

"Thank you." Angie forced a small smile as she gathered up the papers and I.D.

"I'm not the one to thank. Running around meeting invisible internet friends—" The clerk raised her voice in disgust for all to hear. "And I won't be the one to blame either, when you get yourself killed."

Angie stiffened and turned away. *I doubt they pay you to give your opinion to complete strangers, you ornery she-bat!*

If the woman wasn't the only thing standing between her and the rest of her trip, Angie would have happily said it out loud. As it was, she was glad to get out of the building without looking anyone else in the eye.

Chapter 7

It was well past noon, and Angie had only seen hints of civilization in the last hour as she neared Niagara Falls. The road skirted around a few small towns, which remained largely hidden behind the dense tree line. It seemed sudden when the forest began to break up to her left — dark, jagged rocks signaling a change in the terrain. These openings became more frequent until she'd entered the town of Niagara, its buildings cropping up on the right side of the road while the left side narrowed to follow the sheer ledge carved out by the Niagara River.

Seeing the curve of Horseshoe Falls ahead she slowed, scanning for a parking spot. Groupings of tourists were scattered on both sides of the road, following the sidewalks to her right and the cliff-side walkway to the left. The low roar of endlessly crashing water already filled her ears.

She passed a multi-tiered parking deck, where a white sign with red letting declared: "Parking $10." Remembering her meager budget, Angie frowned to herself and drove on.

The road beside the falls ran out before she was ready, forcing her to turn right onto a side street. Parking garages became open lots. $8...$5... the fees were going down as she'd hoped, but she would have quite a walk in exchange. Nearing three-fourths of a mile from the turn, she decided she could safely manage the next lot's $3 fee from the pocketful of Canadian coins Sandra had foisted upon her. Fumbling with the unfamiliar currency, she bought a ticket from the lot attendant and started walking.

The sound of the falls registered in her mind, beginning as an ambient static and building to an unrelenting thunder as she neared its source. She picked up her pace. By the time she could see water, she felt the uncomfortable dampness of her exertion gathering along her forehead and at the nape of her neck. It made her look forward to the relief she expected to find near the water. With the sun at its highest point, the mist rising from the falls ahead hung against the translucent blue of the sky like a drifting, formless specter.

Angie wasn't aware of how mesmerized she'd become until she heard the blaring rebuke of a car horn to her left. She'd begun crossing the road to reach the overlook without minding where she was going. She winced at her carelessness and broke into a jog, offering an apologetic wave to the green Suburban.

Inattentive teenager coming through...

Once safely across, she headed for the railing of the semi-circular, cement observation platform. She thought there should be a protective fence around it, but beyond waist level there was only a set of taut metal cables. She lifted herself onto her toes and leaned into the top railing until one of the cables pressed just beneath her collarbone in restraint.

Her most immediate thought was that Horseshoe Falls was aptly named. The massive carving of darkened cliff face bowed to her right in a sweeping, concave formation. It was as though some ancient Titan had taken a bite out of the earth and the Niagara River now poured into the chasm left behind.

The surface of the river above appeared blue-gray and perfectly smooth, up to the moment it reached the precipice. As the water succumbed to gravity, the transition it made was abrupt, violent, and thoroughly captivating. Down in the lower river she caught sight of a ferry drifting in and out of the billowing mists. Its deck was covered in tiny blue dots she guessed to be people clad in rain coats, enjoying the closest experience that could still be considered safe.

The breeze shifted almost imperceptibly, sending a cool smattering of water spray against her cheeks. She closed her eyes and smiled as a tingling sense of awe dropped through her chest and shivered down her limbs. Even with her eyes closed she could still envision the vastness of the spillway and the raw power of its churning, as though the image was branded to the insides of her eyelids.

"Magnificent," she murmured in quiet admiration.

Angie opened her eyes and looked first to her left and then her right, realizing she wanted to see the reaction to this marvel on someone else's face. She needed some reassurance that her wonderment wasn't just a childish naiveté. To her unexpectedly deep disappointment, there was no one nearby. A feeling of abject loneliness struck her with an almost physical force.

Confused over the intensity of the sudden emotion, she scanned farther up the concrete sidewalk until she spotted an approaching group of tourists. They weren't close enough for her to read their expressions, and so the weight of her isolation lingered.

What's the matter with me?

She'd had years to grow accustomed to being on her own — why did it feel so wrong to be now?

Angie recalled reading somewhere that Niagara Falls saw at least twenty suicides a year. She wondered if they'd all been people who arrived with that intent, or if some of them had simply come to see the falls alone and been so entranced that their better judgment had abandoned them to their impulses. Looking at it now, she could understand why the falls had an appeal as both a dramatic and serene ending. She was also reasonably sure that "normal" people didn't entertain such morbid thoughts in the midst of such breathtaking beauty.

During a much darker time in her life, she would have been someone who shouldn't visit this place. When her depression had been at its worst a few years before, she had pondered a variety of horrible remedies. In truth, she'd never actually wanted her life to end. She'd only wanted release from the ever-gnawing pain that seemed to detach her from all things good and rational. She was ashamed to recall the perverse distortion of her former mindset, but at the same time, she knew it was somehow critical she never forget.

It would be an easy jump, she thought. The low barrier wasn't much of a deterrent.

She could imagine herself climbing up over the railing and perching there for a moment — gathering desperation and awaiting a pulse of fear to stop her, or compulsion to propel her. In her mind's eye she could feel the thrill and exhilaration of freefall – the cool moisture on her skin as the mists engulfed her form and obscured her vision. She wasn't sure if it would make it easier, not being able to see or gauge when her body would plunge into the water. Those precious few seconds would seem like a drawn-out eternity. And that would make the slap of impact and the frigid immersion all the more shocking to her body. Would she fight to the surface for air, or would her stunned senses hold her suspended in the tumultuous current?

Angie was somewhat certain she would end up fighting. If she survived the fall, that is. She was too much of a fighter to begin with, and she imagined the craving for air would override any other thought or intention. Base survival instincts aside, she felt sure her splash landing would wake her up to at least one glaring revelation: that the answer to penetrating loneliness couldn't possibly be found in dying alone, surrounded by darkness and cold. Even at her worst, she hoped she would have been able to reason that much.

Something nudged gently at the back of Angie's mind, reeling her in from her melancholy speculations. It wasn't healthy to entertain thoughts like that for long — she knew that much about herself full well.

"I know, I know… I'm not really alone," she whispered, forming a faint smile as her internal bearings settled. Realizing her pulse was rushing fast in her ears, she took a step back from the railing and concentrated on slowing it. There were distracting downsides to having a vivid imagination.

Behind her she heard the approaching crowd as they neared the overlook. Her thoughts shifted to the present, the practical. Remembering her disposable camera, she readied the advance switch and scanned over the nearest family as they arrived.

One couple stood out to her. Appearing to be in their mid-thirties, the man was tall, rail thin, and confident in stature, while the woman seemed tiny and demure by comparison. A boy who couldn't have been more than eight years old trailed close at the woman's heels, fiddling with an expensive-looking camera. She supposed them to be Japanese, based on the bits of conversation she overheard exchanged between them.

"Konichiwa!" She tested the theory in a friendly voice, waving with an open degree of uncertainty. All three stopped and looked at her with what she took to be immediate recognition. Before they had a chance to overestimate her linguistic skills, she held up her camera, pointing to it with her free hand and then motioning to herself. The man's expression brightened in understanding and he accepted the camera from her.

"Hai, onegai," she said in vague request, trusting he could figure out the device. She took several strides backward until she leaned shoulders into the cement portion of the railing. The man took care with the shot, shuffling to one side to include more of the cliffs with the falls behind her. When he'd finished, she gave him a dipping bow as she took the camera back.

"Domo arigatō," she thanked him. And unless they wanted her to count to ten, she'd just expended her entire arsenal of useful Japanese vocabulary. Fortunately, the man and woman just smiled politely and didn't seem to expect any further conversation. As they walked past her to the railing with the boy in tow, Angie stepped back to take in one last look.

She watched as the man hoisted the boy up to give him a better look at the falls and down into the massive gorge below. The woman spoke soft, rapid words to the child, in a tone that Angie thought held an air of reverence. The boy answered in a high, excited voice, pointing to something in the vicinity of the lower river. She felt herself warm at their shared amazement.

Almost without thinking, she advanced her film and snapped a quick picture of the awestruck family. None of their faces would be in the photo, but that didn't matter. It was the concept, not the specifics, she wanted to capture. Contented punctuation to her otherwise manic impression of the landmark.

~ ~ ~ ~ ~ ~ ~

Angie parked along the street in a quiet, middle-class suburb of Toronto, grateful to have daylight left to spare. She'd never met Daniel or his family before, but she was sure showing up in broad daylight would be more comfortable for everyone involved.

Though, she had no reason to expect a poor reception. Daniel had met his girlfriend on the same story writing community that Angie had met them on, and from what she understood, she'd flown in from Alberta for a visit just a few weeks prior. His family had to be somewhat used to the idea of long distance social networking.

With her bag in hand, Angie walked to the front door of the cedar-sided house and rang the bell. She'd called from a payphone to verify her directions, and so it wasn't a surprise when Daniel opened the door almost immediately.

He was a gangly young man, no taller than she was. Longish, mousy brown hair laid limp just past his ears. His facial features were fine, particularly for a male, and set against pale skin. His gray eyes would have appeared large behind the strong prescription of his eyeglasses, if not for their tendency to drift halfway closed.

"Hello Danny," she said, offering out a hand.

Daniel thinned his lips into a smile and clasped her hand in a firm shake. "Good, you didn't get too lost," he answered in a mild voice. He looked over his shoulder and swung the door open. "Come say hi, Mom. See? She's a real girl, just like I said."

Angie waved to the figure approaching from behind him. The petite woman appeared to be in her early fifties with straight, shoulder length hair the same hue as Danny's. Her expression brightened as she neared. "Oh, good. I just wanted to be absolutely sure. You understand, I hope—" she said in a high, rapid voice. She reached out and shook Angie's hand just as Danny released it. "I'm Mary. And I'm sorry we don't have a spare room, but you're welcome to the couch." The woman motioned behind herself and to the left toward the den. "You're a friend of Katie's?"

Angie nodded, smiling. "I wish I could have arranged my trip so I'd be passing through while she was visiting, but I wasn't done with my classes then. It sounded like she had a great time with your family." She stepped past Danny as the woman ushered her in.

"Oh, she was a delight to finally meet." Mary reached up to pat her son's shoulder. "I was more than a little worried when Danny flew out to see her over Christmas break. But, what could I do? He's twenty, after all. And he was so bound and determined." She leaned toward Angie to add, "He was a preemie, you know. I've worried about him his whole life."

Danny rolled his eyes and cast a light smirk between the women. "Thanks, Mom. I can take it from here."

Mary gave an apologetic smile. "You make yourself right at home," she directed to Angie. She pivoted then and trotted off across the hardwood floor toward what looked like the kitchen.

"She worries too much," Danny said. "I'll show you where the computers are, if you need to get in touch with anyone. And don't mind my little brother. He's skulking around here somewhere, but he shouldn't bother you for long if he does show himself."

Angie chuckled as she moved into the den to deposit her duffel bag onto the couch. She unzipped the bag and withdrew a square envelope, turning to offer it to him. "Here, before I forget. This is your -extremely- belated Christmas card from Elsie."

Danny raised his brows, though this didn't do much to alter his otherwise bland expression. "How...nice. Should I be terrified?" he asked, plucking it out of her hand and tearing it open on one side.

Angie laughed. "Maybe a little. This is Elsie we're talking about." She awaited his reaction as he opened the handmade card and read it to himself.

"Ah-ha. Thinly veiled threats and outright insults. I'm touched." He flipped the card over and pointed to an amorphous shape laminated to the inside with scotch tape. "And look, she made a sculpture of my soldier character out of belly button lint. I will treasure this forever." Danny's dry sarcasm conveyed the undertones of good-humor, though his voice and facial expression remained deadpan. She'd begun to suspect that this sort of emotionally-limited countenance was normal for him.

Angie rubbed a palm over her face and sighed. "Don't worry—it's just pocket lint. I saw her making it, I just didn't know what it was for at the time. But trust me, this is about as endearing as it gets with her."

Danny folded the card back on itself and slipped it into his pocket. "It's truly an honor."

Angie followed Danny up the hallway staircase to the second floor, where an open office loft overlooked the ground level. Three computers sat along one wall, each atop their own desk. Danny motioned to the farthest one. "Help yourself. I've got a few things to take care of, but we can go get something to eat later at the restaurant I bus at. I get a discount." He took a seat in front of the middle computer.

Angie settled in, going through her mental checklist. Once she'd finished with her mass email update, she spent another hour keeping entertained with online games, sitting in silence as her host went about his business. Bearing in mind the fact that she'd be leaving the next day, it didn't seem worth her dwindling energy to force conversation.

Her gaze occasionally drifted to a framed picture sitting on the desk beside the computer. She recognized Katie with her long, dark hair and narrow-framed glasses, standing in front of the railing overlook of Niagara Falls near the very spot where Angie had viewed it earlier in the day. The timid-looking girl was dressed in a red tank-top and jean shorts, standing beside a broadly smiling Danny, who had one arm draped across her shoulders.

Geeks in love.

In the den she'd seen a similar picture of the pair, affectionately huddled together in front of a vast, mountainous vista. The two had obviously seen the sights during Katie's visit.

While the most conscious part of her was happy these two had found each other, another part or her wrestled with an upwelling of gloom. Whether it was envy or the result of long nursed self-pity, she wasn't sure. Either way, she didn't like it.

Am I really that petty?

The last thing Angie wanted was to become the kind of person who felt entitled to resent those who'd found a counterpart. To her, that sort of angst was even more insufferable than the gushing declarations of the blissfully happy. She took one more intentional look at the picture, forcing herself to smile until she was sure it was sincere.

June 19th,

Oh Canada

It's been a memorable time so far. I ended up staying with Mark's family longer than I meant to, but I wouldn't trade my quality time with Sandra for anything. I was beginning to think I'd be heading straight back to stay with them again after I got stopped at the border. But, I guess when I didn't turn out to have a criminal background, they decided I wasn't trying to flee to Canada or something. They still gave me a hard time about my reasons for being in the country, but I don't really have a great defense on that one. I know how it sounds.

I got to Niagara Falls around 1pm. It was just as incredible as advertised. I didn't stay long, though. It was neat to be there and see it in person, but it made me sad for some reason. Looking back on it, I think it was because I didn't have anyone to share it with. I guess even -I- need people sometimes. It's not like I've ever thought I need someone to "complete me" or anything stupid like that. I'm fine with being alone. ...I just don't want it to always be this way.

I did get a little lost outside of Toronto. I don't think they give as much warning for upcoming exits here as I'm used to. I could see the CN tower from a distance as I was going through (it's hard to miss, what with it looking like a skewered UFO), but I didn't want to risk losing my daylight to get a closer look. I don't mind everything being in kilometers, but 100 kph sounds a lot more exciting than it actually is. Their speed limits here are pretty low, compared to U.S. highways. But everyone seems to make up for it by going 20 kph over the limit.

Danny is just as funny in person, but on the whole, a lot less talkative than he is online. And since he's working tomorrow, I'll have headed off to Ottawa before he gets back. Oh well. At least I got to meet him and put a face/mannerisms to the personality.

Tomorrow I'll find out if Zak has the guts to meet me.

~Ang

Chapter 8

"Hello?" Zak answered on the third ring, tiredness apparent in his voice.

Angie launched straight to the point. "Hey, it's me. I think I'm on your street, but I can't find your house."

"Oh, that's...weird," he said. "I'll come out and walk the street to see if I can find you. I just got home, so I'm still in my school uniform—white shirt. Should be hard to miss me."

"Thanks, that would help a lot." Angie sighed, relieved at the genial sincerity in his voice. "I'll keep an eye out. See you in a bit."

She hung up the payphone and sprinted back to the side street where she'd left her car. Here in the urban residential heart of Ottawa, the houses were old and tucked close together, shrouded in the greenery and shadows of lofty trees. Angie perched on the trunk of her car and observed the entire length of the dead-end street. She waited a minute; then two.

Nothing happened.

Something wasn't right, and she suspected that it was her fault and not Zak's. She grabbed up the map again and traced her finger along the short road, verifying the cross street and then expanding her search. Several blocks over, she realized her mistake. There was a half-mile gap between the road where she sat and the main street with the same name.

"Fan-freaking-tastic."

She pulled her car around and crossed several busy city blocks before turning onto the primary street. Sure enough, she spotted a lone figure walking away from her up the sidewalk. This individual was definitely male, judging by the build and gait, wearing an untucked white dress shirt with the sleeves rolled up past his elbows. She caught up to the figure and pulled alongside him, waiting to be noticed.

The young man halted, slouching low to see through her passenger side window. Then came the slow smile and a wave of recognition. Angie rolled down the window.

"Hop in! Sorry about that—I was on the wrong part of the street. There's another section of it a few blocks down from here." She suspended any further explanation as Zak immediately obliged her by getting into the car, folding his legs up to make the fit.

He turned to her with an easy half smile, extending his hand across himself in greeting. "Didn't know that, or I would have warned you. I was about to get worried."

Angie accepted the offered handshake as a welcome distraction.

She'd once seen a picture Zak had posted of himself standing with a gaggle of his high school friends, but it hadn't done him justice. Broad shouldered and lean in build, he had the sort of solid jaw-line that lined up in perfect balance with the rest of him. His face was bronzed, with high cheekbones and deep, dark brown eyes that suited the rest of his well defined features — all hinting strongly at a Native American heritage. His thick, glossy black hair was short on the sides and longer toward a central strip, which he kept spiked into a slight backward bent that reminded her of a cockatoo's crest.

The term "attractive" didn't begin to cover it. She couldn't recall ever seeing someone so remarkably good-looking in person. "Nice to finally meet you," she said, for a lack of a better conversation starter. "Mind pointing out your house?" She returned both hands to the steering wheel, fixing her gaze straight ahead.

"Just keep going, it's at the end on the left," Zak said, motioning down the street. "You can park in the drive for now. My car has a street sticker, and I don't want to risk you being towed."

Angie nodded once. "Okay, whatever you think." She found herself concentrating inordinately hard on coming to the end of the long street and turning onto the driveway. She parked alongside a two-story dwelling that would have reminded her of a quaint old farmhouse, if not for its neighbor sitting just a few strides away. She couldn't guess at its age, though the wood-sided house bore a design that had to put it beyond sixty years. A fresh coat of a gray-blue paint was accented by bright white trim around the open-air front porch.

Once parked, she got out and stretched. In need of a distraction to keep from gawking at Zak, she strolled back to examine the car parked along the curb. The ancient, two-door Dodge

Dart had once been tan in color, but was now half covered in rust and patches that had been painted a matte gray. "Is this your baby?" she asked, giving the vehicle a casual once-over.

"Baby? More like…disagreeable old man." Zak smirked, moving to stand beside her.

Acutely aware of his proximity, she looked aside and then up.

She knew he was tall, but only then did she grasp just how tall. She stood no higher than his shoulder, which she guessed would put him at well over six-and-a-half feet. She wasn't accustomed to being dwarfed. "Does he have a name?" Angie pressed on, perplexed with how off-balance she felt.

"I call him Chip…for obvious reasons." Zak stepped up to the car and scraped at a loose piece of roof paint in demonstration.

"Cute." Angie laughed, motioning back at her car in a sweeping gesture. "I guess I didn't introduce you to Gypsy."

"Ah, also fitting," Zak said, looking off toward the Geo with that same light smirk and then back to Angie. His hands sought out his pockets and he inclined his head toward the front porch. "Come on in. I guess you're used to this at your latitude, but it's a bit warm out for me."

"Oh, sure. As long as your mom isn't going to mind." She followed after him, noting he didn't respond to her concern. She hoped that didn't mean he was getting them both into trouble by having her in the house. Being she hadn't seen an "adult" yet, she slipped a hand into her pocket and felt for the small can of travel mace.

He did just put me through the wringer with his unreliability, she reminded herself. She didn't care how handsome the guy was, there was no reason for her to completely trust him.

The floorboards creaked as they entered. A small foyer funneled ahead into a hallway that ran between a staircase following the right wall and opened into a modest den to the left. The decor was minimal, with no particular theme that Angie could discern. Pinstriped blue and white wallpaper curled slightly where the seams met. The house was clean, but undeniably old.

"Mom bought this place two summers ago, so we'd finally have a house and she'd be close enough to walk to work," Zak said. "It needs some fixing up." He paused along the staircase, threading his arm through the slats of the wooden railing to pet the large, black cat sitting motionless on the fifth step.

Angie approached the staircase, taking a few slow steps up to sit beside the feline. The yellow-eyed creature turned its head to follow her movements, but didn't bother to move anything else. Satisfied the cat wasn't skittish, she stroked a hand along its back. "Hello there."

"That's Jinx," Zak said, with a fond note. "He mostly stays inside, but don't worry about it if he gets out, eh?"

Angie gave the cat one last scratch between the ears before standing up and following Zak on through the hallway, which opened into the back end of the house. There was a small dining area with a round breakfast table taking up a nook to the right, and a door set into the back side of the staircase she guessed to be either a closet or a cellar. Zak veered left into the kitchen. The small, square room had little counter space and the appliances seemed squeezed in wherever they happened to fit. Zak's presence in the room only made the space appear more cramped.

She stood by and watched as he stooped to grab a liter container out of the fridge, twisted off the top, and began drinking straight from the carton. He'd easily downed half of the contents before lowering it to take a breath. "Oh, sorry. You want something to drink? We've got...water, juice, and eggnog." He held up the carton in offering.

"I'm good with water." Angie peered at the container in his hand in mild bewilderment. Unable to help herself she asked, "Why are you drinking eggnog in the middle of June? And how is it still good?"

Zak closed the fridge and pulled open the freezer. He gestured to the rest of its contents, more than half comprised of tightly packed eggnog cartons. "The stuff freezes just fine. I stock up after Christmas every year. We've got an extra freezer in the basement just for this." He took another long swig as he went about finding a glass and dropping ice cubes into it. "I'm kind of addicted to the stuff, ever since I worked as a bag boy for a grocery store over the holidays when I was like...fourteen."

Angie accepted the glass of water he brought to her, looking away to conceal her amusement. "I guess there are worse things to be hooked on."

"No kidding." Zak leaned a shoulder against the entryway of the kitchen. "Some of the people I graduated with are already certifiable alcoholics. I hit legal drinking age this spring and figured out I don't have a taste for the stuff."

"Oh that's right, it's nineteen here," Angie recalled, surprised to find herself settled by the ease of their interaction. She had expected to be at least somewhat annoyed with him. Yet, so far he hadn't said or done anything to prompt another comfort-check on her can of mace.

"Right, and our grade levels go up to thirteen before college." The laid-back quality of his voice mirrored his unhurried mannerisms. "On that point, I think I like the American version better. I felt ready for college two years ago."

An abrupt combination of sound and movement called their attention down the hall to the front door, where a tall woman had shouldered her way inside carrying multiple grocery bags. "Zaky? Well, where is she?" the woman called.

"That'd be mom," Zak said, polishing off the remainder of his eggnog and giving the empty container a long toss across the kitchen into the garbage. "Let's get this over with." He sighed, rounding the corner and heading back down the hall.

Anxiety gripped Angie's stomach. Was she even supposed to be in the house? She deposited the glass of water on the table before following Zak, somewhat glad his towering form hid her from view. The effect was short-lived, as he reached the foyer and stepped to one side while taking the bags from his mother.

The woman stood a bit taller than Angie, with a solid but trim build. Her golden-brown hair was wavy, pulled back in a loose pony tail that fell past her shoulders. Her face was one that had seen regular outdoor exposure, but a notably lighter complexion compared to her son's. Vivid blue eyes stood out from otherwise even, unremarkable features.

"Mom, this is Angeli. Angeli—Mom." Zak nodded between the two women as he gave the introduction and then turned, heading back toward the kitchen with the groceries.

Feeling the irrational sting of abandonment, Angie stayed where she was and offered out her hand along with a smile she hoped would be taken as harmless. She hadn't read any anger from the woman's tone or posture, at least. "Hi there." Her voice came out small .

Please like me.

"Oh, good! You're not a forty-year-old escaped convict!" the woman said, with no small degree of jubilance. Her eyes brightened, and the light creases around her mouth and eyes became defined with sincere expression. Smiling brought out a beauty that Angie supposed must have been breathtaking in her youth.

Instead of shaking her hand, the woman embraced her in a quick articulation of relief. "I'm Cathy, by the way. I could swear I taught that boy better manners." She released Angie to have another inspecting look at her.

"Good to meet you, too." Angie laughed. "I'm so sorry for the confusion over my visit. I never meant to cause any problems."

"Well, that's not your fault. Zak really cooked it this time," Cathy said, in blatant agitation. "But now that you're here, I don't think there's any need for you to get a hotel. The couch folds out into a bed." She gestured to the sofa as she walked past the living area and headed for the kitchen.

Angie trailed after the woman, on the verge of shock over her change of heart. "That's...very kind of you. I can always stay in my car if you'd prefer. I don't want to make anyone uncomfortable."

"No, no. I won't have you sleeping outside." Cathy said over her shoulder before leaning into the kitchen. "Zak, how does seafood sound? I thought we'd all down to that little place along the canal. We could show your friend around a little afterwards, if there's still daylight."

"Uh, sure." Zak's low voice answered from somewhere in the kitchen, carrying a trace of surprise. "Have you heard anything from Evie?"

Cathy leaned back and nodded. "I just talked to her before I left work. She's still having contractions, but they aren't any closer together than they have been all week. She'll call if there's any change."

"Alright," Zak said. He reappeared in the hallway and moved past Angie, flashing a relieved smile. "I'm starved. Just let me grab my keys."

The day had cooled by the time they arrived at the restaurant. Cathy requested a table out on the broad patio deck, with a view overlooking the Rideau Canal. They found a place near the lacquered wood railing and settled in.

"Is that any good?" Angie laid the menu down, looking to Zak at her right as she set her finger beneath the "Shark Burger." The item had stood out to her as something she'd never tried, but always been curious about.

Zak made a face. "I'm not really a fan of shark meat. Kinda dry and not a lot of flavor. But, I mean, they might do it well here."

"Oh, he's just a picky eater." Cathy piped up from across the table. "Give it a try if you've never had it. You may never get a better opportunity."

Angie nodded. Noting that it was one of the less expensive things on the menu, she settled on it — in case her hosts insisted on paying for her food.

Once they'd all ordered, Zak kept to himself while his mother began a subtle cross-examination of Angie. Cathy asked about her siblings, her parents professions, her schooling and extra-curricular activities. Angie answered readily, feeling she owed her hostess that much. Their food had arrived by the time she got around to the harder questions.

"Well if you're already in college, what is it you're going for?"

Angie paused, peeking under the bun in front of her at the slice of off-white meat while racking her brain for some way of not sounding fickle. "I'm just getting an associate degree in liberal arts for right now. I'll probably take a break after that. I know people change their major a few times on average, and I didn't want to risk wasting money until I was sure what area I want to go into." She took a testing bite of the burger, tasting mayo along with a fishy flavor, combined with a chewy texture she'd never encountered before.

Cathy leaned forward over her salad. "Well, what interests have you narrowed down to?"

"I'd like to be a writer, but from what I can tell it doesn't really pay the bills." Angie said. "I've considered becoming a nurse, since I'm already familiar with the lingo. I'm just not sure I'm ready to give in and officially become my mother." She chuckled, working on another bite as she considered further. "I've thought about becoming a Minister too, since it's kind of in the same vein with helping people."

Cathy grimaced. "A woman Minister?" A thought seemed to dawn on her. "I suppose they do have those. Still, if you want to be of some real use to people, you'd be better off going into nursing. Can't be much good to the soul if the body's falling apart."

Angie nodded in appreciation of the woman's opinion, however quickly it had been given. She wondered at the disapproval Cathy seemed to have tempered, but decided it wasn't the best time to ask about it. "I also haven't ruled out going into the military. I know a lot of people who thought long and hard about it after the 9/11 attack."

Cathy's scrutinizing gaze seemed to soften. She speared a few small shrimp with her fork and paused to speak before eating them. "That was a terrible thing to watch. I'm glad we didn't have something like that happen here." Her voice carried a detached sort of empathy. She was quiet for a few long moments before asking, "Which branch of the military are you considering?"

"The Air Force," Angie said. "I have a friend there now, and from what he's told me, I think I'd do pretty well there." Thoughts of Don surfaced, but she willfully suppressed them.

"Ah." Cathy intoned with a measure of approval, if not respect. "My oldest daughter's husband served in the Canadian Air Force. It was a good experience for him. Instilled a solid sense of discipline, I'd say."

Angie smiled to herself, considering it an victory that the woman had at least found something relatable about her. Their chatting became lighter as they neared the end of the meal, with Cathy shifting to focus on Zak with graduation-related inquiries. Just as Angie had guessed, Cathy picked up the check while brushing off any argument about it.

"We've still got a good hour of light," Cathy said as she got up and headed across the deck. "I'm going to run to the biffy, and then we can show you a little more of the city."

Angie waited until the woman was out of earshot before turning to Zak. "Biffy?"

"Bathroom." Zak smirked, pushing his chair back to stand.

Following suit, Angie tucked in her chair and walked down along the deck railing to the overlook point closest to the waterway. The canal mimicked the blue of the sky, save for where the surface was broken by the path of a small watercraft. Along both banks she noted a smattering of color, reds and yellows dominating. She bent forward, straining to identify the flora causing this picturesque affect.

The colors reached as far as she could see in both directions. Zak came alongside her and leaned into the railing.

"What kind of flowers are those?" she asked.

"Tulips." Zak glanced her way, dark brows lofting. "It's kind of what Ottawa is known for. We've got millions of them all over the place. The Netherlands gives us like ten thousand more every year." He made an open gesture down one length of the channel. "You should have seen it last month during the tulip festival. Toward the end of May, the shores are almost solid color."

"Must be beautiful," Angie said. She stared out at the shorelines for a long moment, envisioning the sight. "But why would another country give you a boatload of flowers every year?"

"We took in a Dutch Princess for a few years while World War 2 was going on, during the Nazi occupation," he said. "Ever since then, the royal family keeps sending us more bulbs annually in thanks. This year was the fiftieth anniversary." His expression grew slightly embarrassed as he went on. "I heard the Princess's daughter came over for it and everything. But...I wasn't really paying a lot of attention. Most years I'd go to the festival concerts with my friends, but this time everybody was more worried about exams and graduation."

"I'm sure it's a lot easier to take for granted when it's basically going on in your back yard every year." Angie felt a wistful smile settling and turned to look back out over the canal. "That's a great story. Much less depressing than the main thing my hometown is known for."

"And what's that?"

Angie grimaced. "Site of the largest mass execution in U.S. history."

Zak flinched. "Yikes."

Angie nodded, keeping her eyes fixed on a bridge spanning the channel in the distance.

Zak paused for a time before uneasily picking up a different topic. "Hey, uh, don't mind my mom. She's got strong opinions. And she's still kinda mad. I guess she used to go to some kind of church when we were little, but when my dad left us and they got divorced, the people there acted like it was her fault. So, she's not real keen on religious people."

Angie wasn't sure if he was simply navigating away from the previous subject out of discomfort, or if he'd been planning the explanation all along. "Well that makes two of us." She gave a sympathetic smile and shook her head. "That's exactly the kind of thing I'd try to fix, if I did end up going that route. Churches are supposed to take care of people." She noted the look of confusion that came over him, but decided that if he wanted her to clarify, he'd ask.

Any further discussion was cut short by Cathy's return. She called them away from the railing as she emerged from the restaurant. "Let's get going, you two. We're wasting daylight."

And with that, the driving tour of the canals began.

Cathy took over driving, and Zak compacted himself into the back seat so Angie could take the passenger's side. Tulips were a prevailing part of the scenery everywhere they went. Beds of them decorated street corners, lined bike trails, and accented the immaculate open parks. Bursts of yellows and reds were joined by vivid oranges, pinks, whites, and even shades of violet. She'd never had much interest in flowers, but she couldn't deny the charm of their application throughout the capital city.

Crossing over a bridge that spanned the Ottawa River, Cathy mentioned to Angie that they were entering the province of Quebec. The city of Hull sprawled along the northern bank directly across from Ottawa, offering a striking view of Parliament Hill and the neo-gothic buildings that comprised it. While Ottawa was surrounded by farmland and largely flat, the fringes of Hull were thickly forested and took on steeper inclines. They stayed in Quebec just long enough for Cathy to park at a favorite overlook along the river.

Everyone exited the vehicle — the women to take pictures, and Zak to stretch his legs. Cathy produced a camera with a sizable lens and began walking along the bluff snapping photos. Angie frowned at her disposable camera, knowing it couldn't adequately capture the splendor of the fiery red and orange sunset reflected off of the water.

Angie looked over her shoulder at Zak while pointing across the river toward the tallest spire on Parliament Hill. "So, we're going there tomorrow?"

Zak looked up from his slumped position on the hood of the Dodge. "Yup. I think they do the changing of the guard at 10AM every morning. It's supposed to be worth seeing." He smirked to himself. "I'll try to wake up in time for it. I'm not much good to anybody without my twelve hours of beauty sleep."

Angie gaped at him for a moment until she decided he was being serious. "And I thought -I- was sleeping a lot with having Mono. How were you getting by with school if you're hard pressed to get up before ten?"

"Not very well," Zak admitted with a slow shrug. "That'd be one of the reasons why school wasn't agreeing with me. I don't know how I'm going to do it when I get a job over the summer. I grew three inches in the last year, and I'm probably not done. Takes a lot out of me."

"Oh, he's always slept like the dead," Cathy inserted as she came trudging back toward the car. "The best thing I could do was send him to bed early and hope I wouldn't have to pour water on him in the morning." Her tone held equal parts complaint and fondness.

"Well in that case, I guess once we get back you should turn in." Angie kept her voice light with amusement.

"Yeah, probably." Zak chuckled, smoothing a hand over the carefully shaped crest of his hair before sliding off the car.

It occurred to Angie that, despite how much she was beginning to like Cathy, her presence was making it harder to figure Zak out. He seemed more prone to conversation when his mother wasn't close by. Had Cathy not been there, she imagined she might have worked up the nerve to sit beside him on the hood of the Dodge to watch the sunset.

Why am I thinking about this?

Angie shook her head and looked to Cathy, awaiting her signal for their departure.

June 20th,

Ottawa has turned out to be an incredibly beautiful place. I should have looked up more about it before I got here. There's so much well-kept greenery and a huge variety of architecture...most of which, I know nothing about. The canals and lakes are so much a part of the landscape and lifestyle, I think this place would be a photographer's dream. I doubt I'd even mind it here in the winter. Zak told me the Rideau Canal turns into the longest skating rink in the world. I think I'd like to see that.

I was afraid Zak's mom wouldn't like me at all, but she warmed up to me the moment she saw I wasn't older or more criminal-looking than advertised. I even get to sleep on the couch, now! Zak and I seem to be getting along pretty well. I guess he's not completely asinine, after all. Tomorrow I'm supposed to get a foot tour of Parliament Hill from Mr. Tall, Dark, and Handsome. I'm not sure what to expect, but it sounds nice and historic. If Zak wakes up in time, I should get to see the changing of the guard. It sounds about as British as it gets without actually going to England.

All in all, I'm just very thankful that things are turning out so well. It's clearly been a stressful week for Zak's family, what with Zak's oldest sister being one week overdue with her first child. I'm going to do my best not to place any additional stress on them while I'm here.

Mileage Log: 1,548 mi

~Ang

Chapter 9

Angie awoke the next morning as Cathy was getting ready for work. Concerned she might interrupt her hostess's routine, she pretended to be asleep until the woman left the house. Pretending turned into reality, and she startled herself awake some time later. The wall clock revealed it was nearly nine-thirty. She hadn't heard any movement from upstairs, so she doubted Zak was up yet.

She ascended the groaning wooden staircase and surveyed the tight hallway. To her immediate right was an open doorway into a bedroom that was too floral and unoccupied to belong to Zak. Making a guess, she eased further to the right and peeked into a small space with a harshly sloped ceiling — the laundry room. By process of elimination, that left just one place he could be.

Angie approached the door at the opposite end of the hall, paying no mind to the random squeal of loose floorboards underfoot. Stealth wasn't the goal, after all. Her primary hesitation was invading Zak's personal space. Seeing the door standing open a few inches emboldened her, and she stepped up to peer inside.

The room was small and untidy, strewn with crumpled articles of clothing. A humble desk sat beside the door with an aging computer poised atop it. A hockey poster tacked to the far wall offered little by way of decor. Beneath the window at the back of the room she spotted a twin bed — which seemed absurdly small for Zak. And yet, there he was, laying face down with his feet hanging off the end of the bed and his arms folded over his head in defiance of the glaring daylight. The curled, inky form of Jinx lay across his lower back, amber eyes half open as the feline lazily took note of her.

"Zak?" Angie cleared her throat, nudging the door open a few more inches. She pinpointed the background sound of talk radio to the alarm on Zak's nightstand. There was no telling how long it had been trying to wake him. *Cathy wasn't exaggerating.*

"Zak!" she hissed with more urgency, looking around for something to throw at his sleeping form. The cat's eyes opened wide, but Zak didn't stir. She considered walking in, but then decided against it. *Too invasive.* Instead, she went bounding back down the stairs, encouraging each step to protest her weight. She snatched a pillow off of the couch and went charging back up.

She'd hoped the ruckus she made might have sufficed, but when she stuck her head back into Zak's room it was clear she'd had no such luck. She wound her arm back and hurled the pillow across the room, landing a direct hit to the side of her friend's head.

"ZAK!"

Startled by the sudden motion, Jinx leaped straight up and landed between Zak's shoulder blades, tail bushed. One, or perhaps all of these combined elements resulted in Zak's head jerking up from his pillow.

"Wha—?"

Angie didn't give him any time to recover his faculties. "Morning, Rip Van Winkle. It's nine-thirty. How fast can you get ready?"

Zak turned his head, giving her a glazed look. "Guess we'll find out," he mumbled. "Give me a couple minutes." He waved her off and turned over. The cat gave a feeble cry of complaint as he was dislodged from his perch.

Angie headed back downstairs. She wasn't ready herself, and it was dawning on her that sweat pants wouldn't be appropriate for the day's activities. Though she doubted they would make it into downtown by ten, she was determined it wouldn't be for a lack of trying on her part.

~ ~ ~ ~ ~ ~ ~

Half an hour later they were in her car, scouring side streets in search of a parking space. Zak had skipped showering, but insisted on taming his hair. Much to Angie's exasperation, he'd continued to groom using the visor mirror while giving her driving instructions.

She finally spotted a car pulling out and claimed the open spot. She jumped out and fed the parking meter, bringing the count up to two hours by the time Zak had eased his way onto the sidewalk.

He matched her jogging pace up the sloped sidewalk toward
Parliament Hill without having to exert anything beyond long-legged
strides. A bell began to toll somewhere nearby.

"Is there any time left? Do you think we should be running?"
She looked to Zak in blatant urgency. By this time, she'd concluded
him to be the kind of person who consistently needed a fire lit under
him — if not a full blown inferno.

"Ease up...its ten now," Zak said, unconcerned. "I'm pretty
sure it's over with quick. We probably won't catch anything."

"Probably?" Angie repeated, skeptical. Zak was silent as he
kept up with her, either lacking the breath or the motivation to argue.

Three structures rose to fill the hazy sky as they approached,
all unified in neo-gothic design with their many steep sandstone
arches. The angular, peaked sections of roofing stood out with the
distinctive matte-green of oxidized copper. The Peace Tower stood at
the center, the highest point on any of the buildings, fixed with an
enormous clock face that overlooked the area. The center block was
symmetrical, set back from the east and west buildings behind a level
expanse of lawn.

Zak tapped Angie's shoulder and pointed out over the grassy
field. "It'd be happening out here. Looks like we missed it."

Angie refused to pause until she'd reached the middle
walkway leading to the Peace Tower. Several dozen people were
coming and going, most at a pace suggesting sightseeing rather than
going about government duties. There was no one in uniform
anywhere in sight.

She released a defeated sigh.

"Sorry about that," Zak said, rubbing a broad palm over the
back of his head. "It's really not that big of a deal, though. Don't
worry about it."

Angie cast him a frown and pulled out her camera, taking
several distance shots of the Parliament buildings before she noticed
the raised, circular fountain in the middle of the walkway. The stone
monument consisted of a narrow moat, collecting the water
cascading down from its sloping central platform. The inner piece
was fixed with evenly spaced plaques bearing the coat of arms from
each Canadian province and territory. The water originated from a
domed apex, atop which the centennial flame burned on despite its
incompatible surroundings.

*I'm sure there's a metaphor behind that, s*he mused, snapping a picture of the fountain.

"Here, sit and I'll take a picture of you in front of it," Zak said, holding a hand out for the camera.

Angie wasn't sure if he was trying to make up for her missed opportunity, but she accepted the offer. She wasn't all that annoyed with him, anyway. He wasn't the only one who'd overslept.

Several pictures later, Zak led her off along the left side of the Parliament building toward a tour group. The guide was explaining to those gathered that they would be entering the Peace Tower in fifteen minutes, and he recommended everyone first pay a visit to the Parliamentary Cats.

"The what?" Angie asked aside to Zak, unsure if she'd heard correctly.

Zak chuckled at her, motioning with a tilt of his head in the direction the others were drifting. "You'll understand when you see it. This is the best part, in my opinion."

Deciding to take his word for it, Angie moved along with him to the untamed back portion of the lot, where people had gathered along a cast iron fence. The trees grew thick beyond the fence amid an array of underbrush. The sight drawing everyone's attention turned out to be a chest-high, wooden replica of the Parliament building sitting among the trees. More than a dozen cats of all sizes and markings lounged along the deck that served as the foundation for their apparent commune. Bowls of food and water were placed here and there, and none of the feline colony appeared undernourished.

"They're strays," Zak said, leaning forward over the railing. "It's not a bad exchange. They control the rodent populations around the government buildings, and the Humane Society makes sure they're taken care of."

"They just…come and go as they please?" Angie wondered, noting the bars of the fence would easily allow the animals passage. It struck her as a novel idea that someone had created a safe haven that allowed them the freedom to roam.

"Yep. And they always look pretty happy about it." Zak smiled faintly as an orange tabby came sauntering along in front of them. If the animal had any actual interest in them, it didn't bother showing it.

"Well, it seems a lot nicer than keeping them in little cages hoping someone will eventually adopt them," Angie said, looking over at Zak and then down at the tabby. It occurred to her that the blithe, effortless movements of the cat reminded her of Zak's demeanor. Cat-like ease — that seemed like an accurate description. On the other hand, it made her wonder what it would take to get his fur to bristle, so to speak. He had such a perpetually steady way about him, she doubted she'd get the chance to find out.

As the tour group began to reassemble and migrate toward the front entrance, Angie and Zak tagged along behind. Since the group wasn't in any hurry, Angie took the opportunity to bring up a question she'd be saving for just such a lull.

She gave his arm a nudge with her elbow. "So, what's Zak short for, anyway? Zachary? Zachariah?" She tried to ignore the inordinate amount of courage it had taken her to achieve such a trivial degree of physical contact.

Zak formed a smirk. "Actually it's not short for anything. It's just Zak." He shook his head, looking somewhat amused. "My dad named all of us, and he didn't like names with more than one syllable. So my middle sister, the one who just graduated from the University, is named Leigh. And my oldest sister, the one about to have a baby, her name is Eve. You'll probably meet her later."

"Eve. That's pretty," Angie said, contemplating what little inflection she could glean from his voice. She thought he seemed distant when referring to his father, but she didn't detect any anger. Though, for all she knew, this was as much anger as Zak ever displayed.

"My mom likes to say he proved his god complex when he named her. He wanted to call her Eve because she was the first woman he created."

"Wow. Healthy ego, huh?" Angie watched his face intently.

"He's…kinda hard to be around," Zak admitted, giving a slow shrug. "I didn't really have much to do with him until last summer, when he started paying me to help him on the weekends."

Angie nodded, processing this information for a long moment before asking, "When did your parents split up?" She didn't want to get too personal, but was spurred on by his tolerance toward her curiosity.

"When I was like a year old. Dad left, and my mom had to take care of us by herself. She'd been trying to finish college, but she never got the chance with having to work so much." Zak answered in a factual in tone. "It's not like I remember things being any different. Not like my sisters. They still don't want to have anything to do with him. Not that he's really tried to connect with them at all... Just me."

Angie absently shuffled forward as the line of visitors began funneling through the entrance. "It doesn't bother you that he's not trying with your sisters like he is with you?"

"Sometimes it does." Zak pocketed his hands and looked away toward the eastern government building, as though it had suddenly become interesting. "It's not fair, I know that. I don't pretend to know why he's the way he is. But I mean... he's the only dad I've got. My grandparents are dead, so he's the only one that can tell me anything about that side of the family." He paused at length before looking to Angie again. "My dad is full-blooded Blackfoot. That makes me at least half. I didn't even know that until last year when he showed me some of the genealogy."

Angie nodded quickly in understanding. "I get it. It's harder to figure out where you're going without an idea of where you came from," she said. "I'm glad you're getting a chance to get to know him. Even if the most you get out of it is figuring out what kind of person you -don't- want to be. That's still worth something."

Zak gave her an easy half-smile, his shoulders sinking as they seemed to join the rest of him in relaxing. "Yeah. It's kinda like that."

As they headed up the steps, the entryway opened into a cavernous chamber the guide referred to as Confederation Hall. Angie was immediately impressed by the cathedral-like detailing. The smooth, inlaid marble floor was primarily white, with accenting patterns of deep green radiating out from the central column. The ceiling was steeply vaulted, and the limestone walls were covered with sculpted imagery, giving the building's interior a more elegant feel.

A line formed to the right with visitors emptying their pockets into small bins before stepping through a set of metal detectors. When it was her turn, Angie dumped her keys, wallet, and all of her remaining Canadian coins into the gray container and walked through without setting anything off. On the other side she turned to wait for Zak.

Suddenly, she became aware of a large, looming presence approaching from her right just before hearing a low voice of inquiry.

"Ma'am, are those your keys?"

She glanced over to see who the voice was being directed at. A hefty, dark-skinned security guard was looking down at her with a furrowed brow while pointing to her keys, which a nearby female guard was holding up. He didn't seem angry — maybe just concerned. She couldn't imagine why.

"Yes, those are mine." Angie said, nodding. There was no mistaking them, given the can of mace and numerous plastic keychain plaques hanging from of the central ring.

"I'm going to need you to come with me," the male guard said, taking on a reluctant but firm tone as he motioned to a narrow hallway leading away from the main chamber.

"O...kay?" Angie said, after a moment of bewildered staring. *Obviously, I'm not about to get a private tour. What the heck did I do?*

She began to follow the guard, having all but forgotten about Zak until she heard him call out behind her.

"What's going on?" Zak caught up in a few quick steps, his inquiry directed more to the security guard. "She's here with me. Is there a problem?" He'd become straight-faced and almost professional in tone. A sort of situational maturity, Angie decided. *At least he isn't pretending he doesn't know me.*

"Yeah, there's a problem." The broadly-built man swiveled his torso partway toward Zak. As he did so, Angie caught a glimpse of his name badge. John. Knowing his first name was a little more reassuring to her for some reason. "We found mace with her belongings. It's illegal for civilians to carry weapons," he said in a brooding tone.

"Mace?" Zak gaped at the guard in disbelief. "The spray stuff—that's illegal?"

"You live here and you didn't know that?" Angie spoke aside to him.

John heaved a sigh. "It's not as commonly known as it should be. The same applies with Tasers. There were cases a few years ago of people committing robbery using them, and they passed the law to keep it from happening again."

"Somebody robbed someplace...using a can of mace?" Angie had to admit, it sounded ridiculous enough to be true.

"It's okay. We'll get this cleared up," Zak said, mild agitation detectable in his voice.

The guard led them to a door at the end of the hallway and held it open to let them pass into a bleak, square room containing a round table surrounded by chairs. The addition of two uninteresting watercolor paintings only succeeded in making the space look like a waiting room.

"Just have a seat," John said. He stepped out and closed the door, though his back remained visible through a small, square window.

Angie pulled out a chair and numbly sank into it, staring at the door for a short while before glancing to Zak. "Are they going to arrest me?"

Zak leaned back in his chair and folded his arms across his chest. "No, they're not that stupid. We'll call your embassy if we have to."

"Embassy?" she repeated at a murmur, folding her hands in her lap. "I keep forgetting I'm not in the States anymore."

"I'm sorry. If I would have known it was illegal—or that you had it—I would have warned you." Zak's dark brows pulled together in a look of pensive aggravation.

"I wouldn't have told you I had it," Angie said. It was the truth, after all — and she didn't see any reason he should blame himself for their predicament.

Zak cut his eyes toward her and his lips curled into a smirk. "See, I don't think you have the kind of crazy death wish my mom was assuming."

Angie managed a small smile. "Just crazy—no death wish."

They chatted idly over the next hour, waiting for whatever was supposed to happen next. The room wasn't as intimidating as the interrogation rooms Angie had seen depicted in movies, but she was still glad Zak was with her. If he wasn't, she probably would have been asleep in her chair by the time a stern-faced man came striding in with a clipboard and sat down across the table from them.

He appeared to be yet another security guard, although she wasn't sure she would have been able to distinguish security from actual police. This man was short in stature, slim, with neatly-combed ginger-blond hair and a thin mustache to match. He carried himself like someone attempting to appear larger and more important than they actually were. She didn't take this as a good sign.

It made her feel somewhat better when John came in from the hallway and pulled a chair out so he could sit along the wall facing them. Now that she had a better look at him, Angie surmised that John was older than the man with the clipboard by at least a decade. His hair had gone gray at the temples and along the light stubble of his jaw. Despite being built like a bear, his dark eyes held underlying warmth that granted him a paternal air. Angie decided she would much prefer talking to him over the upstart with the clipboard.

If John reminded her of a bear, the younger man reminded her of a ferret — and a mean ferret, at that. His eyes were an icy blue and deep-set, giving them a cunning edge. Opening with a long string of identity verification questions, the man never looked away from Angie's face for more than a split second as he jotted down her answers. After a while, his curt inquiries became specific to the problem at hand.

"And what, exactly, were you planning on doing with that mace?" The man sounded as though he'd taken personal offense to her error. Angie knew he had a name badge on, but the way he was seated kept it hidden from view under the table. The complaint she'd begun writing in her head would have to make do with a physical description instead of a name...for now.

"I was planning on defending myself, in the event I was attacked," Angie answered, hoping to convey respectful candor.

"You hadn't thought about, say, spraying a tour group while they were trapped in a confined space?" Ferret Man pressed, leaning forward.

She stared back at him, allowing her mystification to trump her annoyance. "I can honestly say that never crossed my mind until you suggested it."

Don't get snarky, it'll just make things worse...

"Come on, you can't be serious," Zak interjected. "She's just a first-time visitor from the U.S. She didn't know any better. And this isn't giving a great impression of how we treat tourists." His defensive tone seemed out of character. Angie wasn't sure if he was embarrassed or angry, but she was grateful he was standing up for her.

"Ignorance is no excuse for breaking the law," Ferret Man snapped. His gaze lanced back to Angie. "So you mean to tell me that when you crossed the border, you didn't notice the signs posted about prohibited items?"

Angie's shoulders stiffened from some combination of tension and struggling to keep herself from fidgeting. "I read the signs. No drugs, exotic plants, weapons—"

"So you admit you knew about the weapon's policy?"

Angie worked her jaw and glanced toward John. The man had shifted position, his focus primarily set on Ferret Man. At the last question he'd given a sigh that suggested he wasn't any more pleased with the smaller man than she was.

"I didn't know that mace was considered a weapon here—I didn't see that specifically listed," she said, struggling to hold a patient tone with the belligerent interviewer. "My dad gave it to me because I was going to be traveling for a long time by myself, and I'm not familiar with most of the areas I'm visiting. It's a pretty standard personal defense measure where I'm from, especially for women."

"Yeah," Zak piped up again. "Most of those American TV shows and movies, you always see ladies carrying mace in their purses. It's dangerous down there."

"Well, it may be a different world south of the border, but nobody needs things like that here in Canada. We don't just go around attacking each other," Ferret Man said, looking between them both with an expression Angie took as sneering. Part of her objected to this Canadian impression of America as one big cesspool of violence and depravity. Another part of her wondered if playing it up might work in her favor.

Just keep quiet. This can't be worth turning into a patriotic martyr.

John spoke up abruptly, drawing everyone's attention. "Come on, now. Don't act like we've got a crime-free society." He nodded to Angie in obvious sympathy. "You know, I've got a daughter about her age. And the way her college campus is after dark...I'd have bought her mace to carry if it were legal. I guarantee you that." His deep voice was even, but his broad nostrils flared with conviction.

Ferret Man tapped his pen against the table, looking angry over being undermined. "This isn't about personal views. This is about the law, and the fact that it's been violated."

Someone rapped their knuckles against the window of the door before opening it partway. A young man, also dressed in a security uniform, leaned in and handed John a small stack of papers. They murmured back and forth for several seconds before John nodded and waved him off. The large man stood slowly, scanning over the papers before announcing, "Clean record." John exchanged a significant look with Ferret Man before motioning to Zak and Angie. "You two, come with me."

Angie shot to her feet, reasoning she'd rather be almost anywhere else as long as it was away from her pitiless interrogator. Though Zak was closer, she beat him to the door and trailed close behind John down the length of the hallway. John waited to speak until well after the door closed behind them.

"We're going to let you go with a warning. You should know though, we could have had you arrested. I just don't see how that would accomplish anything. You be sure to read over everything more carefully before you visit us again," the hulking man advised, directing a consoling smile to Angie. He reached into his pocket and pulled out her wallet, change, and keys — minus the mace — offering them out to her.

"What happens to the mace?" Zak asked, keeping a step behind them both.

"Taken to be destroyed. I'm sorry, I don't have any control over that. Consider it a small price to pay to keep your freedom." John glanced back over his shoulder, pausing as the hallway opened up into the ornate entry. "It's too bad it was a chemical and not a knife or something multifunctional on that order. A knife we could have just held and given back once you'd exited the building."

Angie accepted her belongings. She was having trouble sorting the logic of the man's claims, but she wasn't about to question him. "Can we still see the Peace Tower?" she asked, a sense of irony occurring to her after a delay.

John adjusted his belt and nodded. "Go right on up with this group. They won't even notice you joined them." He urged them onward with a wide motion. "You two have a good day now, and stay out of trouble."

"Thank you...we'll try." Angie gave the man a grateful smile, and then made haste across the marble floor as she caught up to the other tourists.

"It would have been better if you'd brought a knife into the building? What a bunch of hosers." Zak griped aside to her once they were clear of security, following the tour group as they filed into a small elevator. "I'm really sorry about all that."

Angie gave him a weak smile. "It's okay. I can replace it as soon as I get back into the States. That's not a long time to go without it."

June 21st,

It's been an interesting day. Zak and I ended up missing the changing of the guard, but we did get to visit the cats that live on Parliament Hill. I suppose that's almost as good. But while attempting to get to the top of the Peace Tower, we were spirited away by security and detained for close to two hours. Evidently, it's illegal to carry mace in Canada. So there you go, I learned something today. I'm so glad they only detained me for a little while. Getting arrested in a different country is definitely NOT on my to-do list for this trip.

Anyway, so we saw the Peace Tower and moved on to the Ottawa Mall. We had a nice lunch in the market, and went to see the free sections of the National Gallery of Canada. After that, we crossed over the bridge into Quebec to visit the Canadian Museum of Civilization. It was a muggy day and the long walk kind of knocked us out, but it was worth it.

Zak's been a total gentleman so far, I just wish he'd stop trying to pay for everything. His personality is really close to what I figured he'd be like: very easy-going. And we seem to have a similar level of tolerance before becoming bored with something. Hopefully I haven't annoyed him too badly by turning him into my tour guide.

Zak's sister is still in labor, but nothing hospital-wise yet. We'll see what tomorrow brings.

~Ang

Chapter 10

On Saturday morning, Angie awoke to the sound of the front door closing. She had the impression that Cathy didn't work on the weekends, and so she guessed the woman wouldn't be gone long. She changed out of her sweats before heading to her car and hunting through her box of food. Settling on a cinnamon streusel muffin mix, she went to see what she had to work with in the kitchen. It was 10AM, and she figured she had plenty of time before Zak returned to the land of the conscious.

The muffins had nearly finished baking and Angie was in the midst of plating a cheese omelet when Zak appeared in the doorway. Not only was he up and dressed for the day, but he'd already finished his complicated grooming routine. His slack expression didn't reveal him to be particularly refreshed, but he was awake.

"And here I was afraid you'd been up forever, bored silly," he said, leaning his shoulder into the door frame.

"You're up before noon...and without having anything thrown at you." Angie gave a teasing smirk and handed him the omelet. "Does this constitute a miracle?"

"If you ask my mom, it does." Zak grinned, staring down at the plate as he accepted it. "I think my nose woke me up. We don't usually do breakfast. Nothing cooked, anyway. Mom never has time." He picked up the fork with his other hand and poked at the folded envelope of egg. "Don't take this the wrong way, but...what is it?"

Angie blinked at him. "It's an omelet. It -should- be edible," she said, donning a mismatched pair of hot-mitts and cracking open the oven. "You don't have to eat it."

"No, I mean, it smells really good. I just can't remember ever eating an omelet before." Zak said, clutching the plate closer while backing up a couple of paces toward the table.

Angie chuckled to herself, setting the muffin tin on top of the range to cool. "Then you're seriously breakfast-deprived." She grabbed a carton of eggnog out of the fridge and took it to the table to set in front of him. She didn't bother bringing a glass for it, relying on her previous observation of his habits.

Zak gave a nod of appreciation. "Eggnog goes with everything."

There was something different about him that made Angie take pause. It took her a moment to realize that, for the first time since she'd met him, he'd smiled broadly enough to show his teeth. Being that they were white and perfectly straight, she doubted that he'd been hiding them intentionally. No, it seemed more likely he either didn't invest much effort into his expressions, or this was some sign that he was becoming more comfortable with her. Regardless of the reason, she was glad for the effect it had on his already appealing features.

Some part of her worried she might be a little -too- glad.

Footsteps on the porch snapped her attention to the front door just as it opened, revealing Cathy and her very pregnant eldest daughter.

"Something smells amazing," Eve said, sniffing the air. Though she was every bit as tall and well-built as her mother, she had a softer, more melodious voice. She wore her hair down, falling perfectly straight to her hips in a sleek, mocha-brown curtain. Her complexion and features were dark, more similar to Zak's than to Cathy's. She moved down the hall toward Angie with a distinctive swayback and waddle. "You must be what all the fuss was about." The young woman's tone was pleasant, her expression curious.

Angie produced a smile and a small wave. "Hi. I'm Angie."

Eve had nearly reached her when she paused, placed a supporting hand against her distended belly, and held up her index finger with the other hand. At the same time, she took in a series of puffing breaths.

Cathy, meanwhile, closed the door and came up behind Eve to lay a hand on her shoulder. "Steady now."

Angie stood by uncertain as she watched the woman work through the contraction. "Are you okay? Do you need some water or something?" she asked, after the intensity of the moment seemed to ease.

Eve nodded. "I wouldn't mind a cup of something. And one of...whatever it is I smell."

"You just sit down a while." Cathy urged her daughter onward until she'd taken a chair across from Zak, who had resumed inhaling the remainder of his omelet. He raised his fork in brief salute to his laboring sister.

Angie stepped aside into the kitchen to stay out of the way, and while she was there she went about stacking the muffins high onto a plate. She brought them out to set in the middle of the table, along with a glass of water for Eve.

As everyone procured one of the baked goods, Cathy glanced to Angie in vague confusion. "Did you whip these up from scratch?"

"No, no." Angie held up her hands to shun the credit. "I brought a mix. But I did need to use a few of your ingredients. Sorry about that. I left some money on the counter to cover the eggs, milk, vanilla—"

"Don't be ridiculous." Cathy chortled. "Who makes food for someone and then tries to pay them for the ingredients?"

Apparently, I do. Angie forced a small smile, picking up a muffin for herself.

Cathy gave Eve a five-second shoulder rub before walking off down the hallway with a muffin in hand. "You two keep Eve company for me. I've got some laundry to attend to." She turned the corner and her footsteps receded up the stairs.

"I don't need pregnant lady-sitters!" Eve protested. Her voice dropped then as she addressed Angie and Zak. "I just didn't want to be at home alone while Peter is working. No sense in going to the hospital, either. They've already sent me home twice saying I'm not progressing," she said, helping herself to another muffin. "The things we go through. This is why I've been telling Zak-Zak, whenever he gets someone pregnant, I'm going to personally see to it that he waits on her hand and foot."

Zak groaned and sank lower in his chair.

Eve laughed. "Oh, look. I've embarrassed him." She winked at Angie and patted the chair beside her.

Angie laughed and took the offered seat, quickly warming up to the twenty-something woman. "I think that's the prerogative of an older sister. My little brother likes to pretend he doesn't know me when we're in public. And I'm pretty sure my little sister wishes I wasn't related to her at all."

"Leigh and I fought all of the time until we both finally moved out." Eve leaned to one side as she spoke and grabbed a picture frame from the bookshelf along the wall. "It gets better, I promise. Now we even like each other sometimes." She set the frame on the table and slid it toward Angie. "That's Leigh. Well, and her boyfriend, Evan. You almost got to meet her, but they took off straight after her graduation for two months of backpacking across Europe."

Angie picked up the picture for a closer inspection. Posing on a slanted rock face wearing hiking boots and backpacks, the couple looked like an advertisement out of an outdoors magazine. Leigh was a petite version of her sister, though her facial features were finer and more exquisite. The strapping young man with her projected a poise and confidence that was backed by a strong jaw and flawless smile. "Sounds like the trip of a lifetime," she said, handing back the picture.

"It does, doesn't it?" Eve sighed. "I just hope Evan doesn't plan on dropping Leigh once it's over. They've been seeing each other since her first semester of college, and he's been real dodgy on commitment. I kept telling her, 'Leigh, don't make it easy for him now or he'll just expect he can be lazy later. Make him prove he's worthy of you.' Not that she listens to a word I say. But, what do I know? I've only been happily married to a great guy for the last five years." Her sarcasm came across as cheerful rather than bitter.

"Some would probably call that luck," Angie said with a faint smile. Internally, she was impressed. Not only was she finding Eve likeable, but there was a level-headed astuteness about her that Angie already admired.

Eve shrugged, seeming to downplay the obvious passion she had for the subject. "Luck is for rabbits and the unprepared." She paused after the declaration to take a bite of her muffin before adding, "I had a good screening process. Saved me from a world of heartache."

Zak sedately monitored the exchange between the women. "Evan had better come through, or he and I are going to have an unfortunate...chat." He eyed the picture long after Eve had replaced it.

Angie glanced to Zak, wondering if his assertion was some sort of vague threat. At the very least he seemed protective of his sister. She liked that.

"When you say 'talk,' do you mean something on the order of the warning you gave to Peter before our wedding?" Eve raised her brows slightly at her brother before turning her attention to Angie. "Oh, yes. My then fourteen-year-old baby brother took my fiancé aside to let him know he planned to 'break his face if he ever broke my heart.' That sound about right?" She looked to Zak, playful in tone.

Zak slunk lower into his chair.

"That's just about word for word." Eve continued, directed at Angie exclusively. "I think he'd been watching too many action movies. It was absolutely adorable." Her last syllable came out strained and she looked down, taking in a deep breath as she smoothed her hands over the cream colored maternity tunic that hugged her belly. She seemed to momentarily block out the rest of the world as she focused on a breathing exercise. "Hee hee hoooo…hee hee hoooo—"

Less disquieted this time, Angie watched Eve for a moment before glancing to Zak to gauge his reaction. His brows pinched together in a look of concern. Without a word, he got up from the table and wandered into the kitchen, taking his empty plate and one of the remaining muffins with him.

"I can't wait for this to be over." Eve's pleasant smile returned as the moment passed. "I didn't think a baby could be so stubborn. Peter insists he's getting that from me." She sighed, giving her belly an affectionate pat. "Let's hope not."

Angie smiled. "What's his name?"

"Obie." Eve beamed, in spite of an underlying weariness. "It's different, I know. It's Peter's Grandfather's name. They were close when he was growing up. I didn't really like the idea at first, but it grew on me. Now I can't imagine calling him anything else."

"I like it," Angie said. "I prefer unique names. There were two other Angies in my classes in elementary school, and we never knew which one of us the teachers were calling on. I finally had to start using my full name." She glanced over her shoulder, noting Zak was pacing the kitchen. He hadn't taken long to do the dishes, and now seemed lost without a distraction.

"He gets like that when there's too much estrogen in the house," Eve said, lowering her tone as she leaned toward Angie. Her warm brown eyes held a humored gleam. "You should get him outside for a while. Did you have any plans for the day?"

"None that I'm aware of, yet. We did the museum and historic thing all day yesterday."

Eve brightened. "Oh, then you didn't make it to see the Canadian Shield." When Angie didn't show recognition, she elaborated. "It's part of a mountain range. It extends into the United States as the Adirondack and Appalachian Mountains, if I remember correctly. Lots of great hiking trails, and there's a cozy little French village we like to picnic at. You have -got- to go into Quebec and see it while you're here," she said, tone brimming with enthusiasm.

Angie was already sold on the idea. "Are they going to be annoyed that I don't speak any French?"

"Pfffffft. Of course!" Eve laughed. "But that's Quebec for you." She gestured toward the kitchen where Zak had continued to seclude himself. "Zak isn't quite fluent in French, but he's got enough down to get by with the locals. Just remember that if you go to eat somewhere, don't bother asking for a nonsmoking section. They get all huffy about that. The last time we ate out in Quebec and asked for smoke-free seating, they turned up their noses and pointed to Ontario."

"What, now?" Zak reappeared in the doorway.

"You're going to give me a tour of the Canadian Shield. Just as soon as I get dressed for hiking," Angie informed him. When she was met with Zak's puzzled stare, she got up and headed down the hall.

"Wear something light! It's sweltering out there." Eve called after her.

Donning a pair of shorts and a pale green halter top, Angie made her way back down the staircase several minutes later. To her surprise, Zak was at the bottom of the steps waiting for her. He'd changed into a blue polo shirt and khaki pants, looking ready to leave.

"Whoa," he murmured in surprise, looking her over. "I think I'm overdressed."

Angie froze on the second to last step and glanced down self-consciously. "Was this a bad choice? I don't normally go hiking."

She gave herself a half turn in preparation to dart back up the stairs. "I never wear shorts. This is like my only pair," she added, attempting to sound less defensive than she felt.

"Why not?" Zak gave her a look of confusion. "You'd be doing the world a favor."

"Ha ha." She rolled her eyes, shrugging off his remark. "I was in a car accident when I was twelve—I got knocked off my bike and my legs were run over by a pickup truck. I had tread mark-shaped bruising for weeks. They've been a little messed up ever since." Bending, she patted her left knee to indicate the nickel-sized scar she bore as lasting evidence. "I still can't feel anything to the left of this kneecap." She expected Zak to join with the majority of people she'd ever mentioned this to and declare disbelief. Instead, he gave a slight wince and ventured an assessing sweep of her legs.

"Well, they look fine to me. You should let them out more." His brow furrowed then as he seemed to reconsider his choice of words. Angie thought she caught a flash of embarrassment before he cleared his throat, turned, and strode toward the front door. "Let's get going before it gets any warmer out, eh?"

Angie stared after him for a bewildered moment. *Was he just flirting with me?* She'd never been much good at picking up on that sort of thing. Even if he had been, did it mean anything—? Probably not, she decided. She stepped down and around the banister.

"Just a sec. I want to say goodbye to your sister in case she's gone by the time we get back," she called over her shoulder, following the sounds of conversation between Cathy and Eve back into the dining area. Considering how engaged they were in talking, Angie was sure they hadn't overheard the awkward moment between her and Zak.

That was a relief, at least.

~ ~ ~ ~ ~ ~ ~

Half an hour into Quebec, tall buildings gave way to forested hills and minimal civilization. Save for offering basic directions as they approached turns, Zak kept to himself.

He eventually directed Angie down a road that sent them winding around a deep mountain lake. Much of the terrain surrounding the clear, glittering water was made up of steeply angled shale and granite, with the occasional bit of vegetation clinging to the near-vertical surfaces. Several minutes beyond this, they arrived at a small gravel lot that proclaimed itself — in both French and English — to be the start of a nature trail.

With the sun at its highest point, the shade of the rugged walking trail was a welcome reprieve. Zak set a leisurely pace along one of the least demanding routes. Less than a mile in, they reached the flat clearing of a precipice overlooking a vast swath of the Quebecian countryside. The view was like nothing Angie had ever seen.

Well below them at the base of the mountain range, the forests and grasslands stretched out for miles with only gently sloping terrain. The vista made it appear as if they were situated on a hilly plateau overlooking the rest of the visible world. To their right, one long, continuous cliff face had been carved out of the landscape into a gently curving backward C shape.

"That's…the Shield?" Angie asked, once she found her voice.

Zak stood off to her left with his arms folded, surveying the landscape with a pensive smirk suggesting he was proud to be showing off the sight. He looked to her and nodded. "Nice view, eh?"

"It's incredible," Angie agreed, still genuinely in awe.

Their trek back to the parking area was over a mile long as they completed the trail circuit, but it was well worth the effort in Angie's mind. The scenic overlook had given her the same sensation as being up close to Niagara Falls, but without the bitter aftertaste of solitude. She'd had an pleasant companion to share the experience with, and there was something profoundly validating about that.

It doesn't hurt that I could really like having this guy around. She had to admit that much to herself.

Zak directed her onto a rural road, where she noticed the occasional weathered cabin cropping up behind the tree line. A handful of aged but well-kept buildings clustered around an intersection ahead, and Zak motioned to a dirt lot in front of a small storefront. Angie glanced around at the little shops as she parked — all constructed out of raw logs and planks to give the impression of a French village with rustic influences. The overhead signs were in French, which didn't help to orient her.

Stepping out of the car, she caught the smell of fresh bread and sweet pastries pouring out of the open door directly in front of them. The sign overhead was fashioned from wood with elegant lettering. The background was darkened by charring, which caused the name to stand out: La Boulangerie.

"Bakery?" Angie guessed, looking across her car's roof to Zak as he got out.

"Yep." He gave an easy smile. "I'm not real hungry yet, but I thought we could grab a few things and go walk around."

"I like this plan."

As divine as she found the enveloping smells, the sound of water slapping against stone drew her attention to the village square behind them. "Photo op!" she announced, noting a trio of other visitors standing around a fountain exchanging cameras. "Come on. I don't have any pictures of both of us yet." She motioned for Zak to follow her and she jogged over to the fountain before the tourists moved on.

Handing off her camera to an affable old man, Angie backed up to stand in front of the three-tiered, circular construct of gray stone and flowing water. Zak caught up and moved to her right, standing so close their shoulders brushed. While the older man sized them up with the camera, Zak casually wrapped an arm around her. She caught her breath in surprise. Unsure what to make of his proximity, she forced herself not to move until the picture was over with.

Still nonchalant, Zak withdrew his arm and stood by while she retrieved the camera and thanked the man.

Angie stole a quick glance at Zak, but he was already heading back toward the bakery. *Don't read into it.* She had to guess the gesture was nothing more than friendly. To assume otherwise would be unwise — if not wishful thinking — on her part. She wasn't about to do that to herself.

Zak tilted his head to one side as they approached the back of her car. "Normal people worry me?" He glanced her way, a single dark brow arched.

Angie let out a short laugh as she realized he was reading her bumper stickers. "'Normal' is such a socially skewed term."

"I love dorks," Zak went on, nodding in approval. "All that is gold does not glitter; not all who wander are lost." He smirked at the J.R.R. Tolkien quote and shifted his gaze her way. "That one fits you."

"I hope so." Angie smiled in cautious satisfaction. She wanted to ask him which part he considered most befitting, but quickly thought better of it. "I tried to express my personality in a thought-provoking, but minimally offensive way. That happens to be a real challenge when you have an abrasive personality."

"I don't think you're abrasive," Zak said, flashing an amused smile.

Angie's stomach skipped a beat. "Only because I've been on my best behavior." She managed a factual tone, looking to the back of her car to keep herself from staring at him.

Okay, get a grip.

The inside of the bakery was stifling. Cramped and unadorned, there was barely enough standing room for six people between the door and the cash register. Display cases on either side of the central counter showed off rows of pastries to the right, and crowded shelves filled with rolls and loaves to the left. A young blonde girl manned the cash register while a squat, older woman went bustling back and forth between the front cases and the ovens behind her. Angie counted three oscillating fans, one making sweeps of the standing area, and the other two presumably making conditions in the back more bearable.

"So what's good here?" she asked Zak, who seemed to be engrossed with the piles of fresh bread.

"Everything." He motioned toward the more dessert-oriented display. "Pick yourself a few of anything you'd like to try. Go nuts."

While Zak struggled through his French vocabulary in giving instruction to the older woman, Angie shifted herself over to survey the delicacies. The younger girl behind the counter smiled and patiently ran a pair of tongs over each row as Angie pointed out three different sweets that caught her eye. She had no idea what they were, but if they tasted half as good as they looked, she wouldn't be disappointed.

The cashier placed the goodies in a white paper bag and set them on the central counter, where they joined the three wrapped loaves Zak had picked out.

"I got it," Zak said, stepping to the cash register with an open wallet. "I had to get extra for my mom and my sister, anyway. They love this bread."

Angie wasn't sure if he was using courtesy to his family to cover for his continued habit of paying for her, but she decided not to protest his generosity.

What she -was- fairly certain about was that their doe-eyed cashier, who she guessed to be around the age of fifteen, was taking every opportunity to stare at Zak while she rang up his purchases. Zak didn't seem to notice.

Angie couldn't blame the girl. It was almost as though he possessed his own gravitational pull. The fact that he seemed completely unaware of this only compounded the effect — so much so that she'd already caught herself unconsciously leaning toward him on more than one occasion. To her it was an unfamiliar phenomenon, this unnervingly literal take on the term "physical attraction." She'd been hesitant to acknowledge it, but the effect was becoming impossible to ignore.

"Merci," Zak thanked with a nod. He grabbed up the bread loaves and headed for the door while the cashier followed him with her eyes.

Angie thought the girl looked ready to swoon over the fact that he'd spoken to her. Suppressing a chuckle, she grabbed up her small bag of sweets and followed Zak out.

Leaving two of the bags of bread in the car, they made their way across the tiny village to a dirt path that wove its way into the forest. They walked side by side, with Zak passively leading the way. Soon the trees became widely spaced, permitting countless shafts of sunlight to breach the canopy and illuminate the mossy ground.

Angie thought of the woods behind her house, where she'd often wandered as a child. As calming as their shady depths had been at the time, the image of steeply knifing ravines with their thick carpeting of dead leaves paled in comparison to this. She looked to Zak, though he was ever intent on monitoring the trail ahead of them. The silence between them was a natural one, and she was surprised when he was the one to break it.

"Here," Zak said as the forest around them gave way to a clearing. "This place is really old. Eighteen hundreds, I think." He pointed ahead several meters to a framing line of decaying iron fence before wading into the tall grass.

Angie followed after him, curiously surveying the meadow. Toward the middle of the clearing the greenery was studded with rounded stones of varying sizes — none more than a foot and a half in diameter. As they drew closer she noticed their spacing was oddly regular. By the time she'd become certain of the intelligent arrangement, the purpose of the place dawned on her. She stopped in her tracks several feet away from the first row of overgrown markers.

"It's...a cemetery?"

Several paces ahead, Zak came to a halt and turned back to her with a vague look of concern. "Yeah. I mean...you're okay with that, right? Not too creepy in the middle of the day?" He formed a dubious smile. "I'm pretty sure it's been a good century since they added any new residents."

"No, not creepy." Angie laughed, deciding she wouldn't have to conceal the fascination she already had with the place. She made her way down one of the rows, searching for discernible markings that might still remain etched into the headstones. "I've just never seen a cemetery that was so...I don't know. Pretty?"

"Peaceful?" Zak volunteered, slipping his free hand into the front pocket of his khakis. He stood by, casting a sweeping gaze out across the meadow.

"Peaceful." She nodded in agreement. The small graveyard was unlike any she'd ever visited. In spite of its purpose, there was no sense of foreboding or rigid order. The forgotten quietness was more charming than disconcerting.

Angie stooped to brush away caked dirt and other debris from the worn face of one of the basketball-sized stones. The shape of a dove was still visible carved into the upper portion, and half of the name below the year. She moved on to the next stone. "1828 to 1834... 1826 to 1833... 1830 to 1834." She spoke the dates aloud to herself at first. In a tentative tone, she finally shared her suspicion. "Zak...I think it's a children's cemetery."

"Take off. ...Really?" He breathed out, a look of intrigue lighting his features. He walked several dozen yards off to the farthest row of stones and began his own investigation. After several minutes he seemed convinced. "I don't see any that made it to twelve." He frowned. "I remember hearing something about a cholera outbreak in my Canadian history class. That would probably explain why most of them were put here within the same year or two."

"That makes sense. How sad..." Angie murmured, though the words were more obligatory than heartfelt. The idea of so many children being buried here was certainly dismal, but cemetery itself didn't evoke any sadness in her. For whatever reason, she felt just as tranquil as she had before the revelation.

"I keep thinking I should feel worse about it, you know?" Zak said, looking conflicted. "I mean, it's horrible all of these kids died before they had a chance—even if it was a really long time ago. Is it weird that I always liked it here?"

Angie gave Zak a reassuring smile. "I don't think it's weird. Like you said…it was a long time ago."

If anything, we're both weird. And that's just fine with me.

Zak gave an absent nod and turned, motioning for her to follow him. Across the cemetery the path resumed, taking them deeper into the forest. Angie gave him some time to his thoughts before making an attempt at lightening the mood.

"Are we going to eat that, or are you using it to leave a trail once we find the gingerbread house?" she joked, pointing to the bread loaf he'd been carrying in the crook of his elbow.

"We're almost there." Zak glanced her way, smirking.

Ahead, the gurgling sound of moving water grew to fill the air just before the forest floor yielded to the broad banks of a creek bed. Clear and fast-moving, the water surged over rounded chunks of sandstone and slapped at the ferns that encroached along its borders. An old wooden bridge arched over the creek, connecting the paths on either side. When Angie started toward it, Zak held out his arm in a staying motion.

"Hang on, I'll go first." He stepped forward as he spoke, cautiously testing his weight over small sections of the weathered planking.

Angie held back, idly considering methods of rescue in the event he fell through into the water. Not that she thought he'd actually need rescuing. From studying his movements more intently, she had the distinct impression he was prepared to spring out of his relaxed demeanor at a moment's notice. Something about the broadness of his shoulders and the taut movement of the muscles along his back made her want to shiver, in spite of the heat of the day.

Oh, good grief. Down girl.

She shook her head slightly to clear it.

By then, Zak had reached the middle of the bridge and turned toward the railing. He eased into a crouch and then sat down, allowing his legs to dangle over the water. "It's fine. Come on," he called, waving to her.

Angie made her way out to join him, careful to follow close to the route he'd taken. The boards complained at her weight, but none threatened to give way. Dropping down to sit, she settled herself as close to him as she dared while keeping her gaze on the creek below.

Zak slid the bread out of its bag and broke the loaf in half, handing one portion to her. He pinched off a crusty piece of his own half and ate it, brushing the crumbs off his knee. The moment the sprinkle of bread bits touched the water, a swarm of minnows darted to the surface to claim them.

"Do you think those kids are in a good place? Like, heaven, I mean..." Zak voiced what had apparently been weighing on his mind. He turned his head aside and his dark eyes assessed her. His expression was enigmatic, but his tone carried a distant air of concern.

"Yeah. I do." Angie answered with certain ease, giving him a reassuring smile. "No reason to think anything else."

"Maybe that's why it feels okay to be there." Zak went on, making short work of his remaining bread. He brushed his lap clean and used his arms to prop himself up as he lounged back, staring up at the sky where the canopy parted. "I don't know much about all of that afterlife stuff... easier not to think about it. But I figure somebody like you must know how it works."

Somebody like me. What does he mean by that?

Angie made slower progress on her bread. She savored each bite, finding comfort in the familiar smell and taste. "Well, I know life is short. For some, incredibly so." She looked off down the path for a moment. "And I know no one's guaranteed to have a tomorrow. So, to me, it's worth doing a lot of thinking on it." She stopped herself from any further rambling, afraid of sounding preachy. She wasn't sure if Zak was genuinely curious, or just thinking out loud.

"So is that what getting run over by a truck did for you—?" He gave her an amused half-smile. "Made you all deep?"

Angie mustered a small smile. "It did have a pretty significant affect on the way I see the world." Finishing her bread, she dusted off her palms and eased back onto her elbows, mimicking him in reclining.

"Eve keeps talking about looking for a church once Obie finally gets here. I might go with them, if they find one." Zak said, after an extended pause in which he seemed preoccupied with a passing cloud. "You know...maybe becoming a mom is having the same affect on my sister as being in a car accident had on you."

Angie gave a light chuckle. "That's an interesting theory. You might have something there." Perhaps his astuteness rivaled that of his sister.

As cloud watching brought a return to silence, Angie found herself weighing an impulsive idea.

If he actually wanted to, this would be a great time to hold my hand.

She glanced down at their hands — there was less than an inch between them where they rested. She debated working up the courage to brush her fingers against his, if only to see his reaction.

I could make it seem like an accident...

After several failed minutes of willing their hands to touch, she made an inquiry in her mind. *What do you think, God? Should I just suck it up and grab his hand? That ought to make it perfectly obvious I like him.*

As if to answer her question, she abruptly recalled a conversation she'd had with Zak several months prior. He'd complained to the online community that he was skipping his prom because no one had asked him to it. Still sore over her own disastrous prom experience, Angie had questioned why he wasn't the one doing the asking. He'd teased her about being old fashioned, and then asserted his preference for not being the one to 'make the first move.'

That made sense. If he did like her then, in all probability, he was waiting on her to do something about it. All she had to do was work up enough nerve—

She cut the thought short when another consideration surfaced. Her mother had always assured her that she should never have to chase after a guy. Rather than citing it as a matter of tradition, it was explained as an adage that now latched onto her mind like the jaws of a indomitable pitbull: "Don't expect a man will try any harder to keep you than he did to get you."

If the mom-ism held true, then she had to consider if she wanted to set a precedent for being the one in pursuit. It was enough to dampen whatever power her fluttering stomach held over her logical mind.

And then, of course, there was the possibility of being outright rejected. *What would he want with a plain-looking, impossibly weird American girl, anyway?* her cynicism demanded.

Finally settling on inaction, she rocked forward and sat up, pulling her hands into her lap.

Zak broke off his fixation with the sky and gave her a lazy smile. "Ready to head back?"

"Sure."

Angie returned the smile, silently hoping she wouldn't end up regretting the opportunity she'd just let slip away.

June 22nd,

Another enjoyable, fascinating day. I was introduced to Zak's oldest sister, Eve. Not wanting to be stuck home alone, she stayed here today. I liked her right away. Despite being in the early stages of labor, she was remarkably pleasant. And if she thought I was crazy, she at least did a masterful job of keeping it to herself.

Zak and I did some hiking along the Canadian Shield, followed by lunch at a historic little village. When we got back, we made nachos and just hung around watching late night comedy shows. Eve went home in the evening. I doubt now that the baby will be coming while I'm still around. I guess I'll have to find out over the phone how Zak handles becoming an uncle.

Zak has been great company. Even though I think we're both still a little unsure about each other, he's been nothing but sweet. It's probably for the best that I'm leaving tomorrow. I think it would be easy for me to get too fond of him. I know, I know…there's something cliché about that. The heroine initially wanting to clobber a protagonist male, but later realizing that he's grown on her and she actually really likes him. Technically, I'm not supposed to find that appealing. But maybe real life is a lot more cliché than anyone wants to admit. Or maybe there's just a fine, subjective line between the cliché and the poetic.

I really wish I didn't have to leave tomorrow. I never expected Ottawa to become one of my favorite places. I'm honestly going to miss it here, but I know I have to keep going. New York awaits.

Status: Still sleeping more than usual, but I haven't noticed a fever since I crossed into Canada. Maybe the worst is behind me.

~Ang

Part 2

"An adventure is only an inconvenience rightly considered. An inconvenience is an adventure wrongly considered."
– G. K. Chesterton

Chapter 11

June 23rd,

A Fond Farewell

I'm sitting still in line for the border crossing right now, and the wait looks pretty bad. So, I might as well write.

I attempted to leave Ottawa after dropping Zak off near his friend's house. After he left, I realized that I couldn't find my keys. I had myself a little freak-out moment (like the pansy that I am) and went looking for Zak. Since I didn't know for sure where he'd gone, I ended up disturbing his still very pregnant sister, who happened to live close by. She called him back along with his friend, and we looked all over the place for those keys. Finally, Eve figured out I'd dropped them in the engine while I was checking the oil. I don't think I had any pride left by then.

Zak and his friend took off right away, but Eve was kind enough to invite me into her home for drinks and a nice chat. She even showed me Zak's baby pictures. (He was adorable, of course.) When she wasn't putting up with contractions, she was witty, perceptive, and all around fun to talk to. I think I'd be doing all right if I ended up more like her one day. She's happy, and she has a functional life. No minor accomplishment there.

Before I left, Eve told me that Zak had gotten into a big argument with his family a few days before I came into town. They were all understandably upset that he was planning on meeting some strange American who he only knew from the internet. But evidently, he was convinced that I was trustworthy and wouldn't back down, despite the concerns of his sister and mother. Eve sounded like she was proud of him for it, since he isn't usually assertive about much of anything. It warmed my heart to find out he'd thought well enough about me to defend me to his family... and before we'd even met in person.

I left Eve, promising to pray she not need a C-section. I can't blame her for not wanting them to take the baby out through the emergency exit. But with how exhausted she's been, I'm pretty sure she'll just be glad to be holding Obie... regardless of how he gets here.

~Ang

~ ~ ~ ~ ~ ~ ~

Gripping the steering wheel until her knuckles ached, Angie slowed to make out another street sign. She'd pulled into the small town of Oldwick, New Jersey, well after dark, and her written directions had ceased to be of any use.

Four hours prior, she'd called her next host from a gas station to warn him she would be late. Since then, she'd gotten lost twice while trying to navigate a poorly-lit construction detour. She was stressed to her limit and desperately tired. Her shoulders felt like they were strung together by overstretched rubber bands.

The road to her right looked promising, but she couldn't be sure. The second half of the street name was covered by a tall bush.

Don't people around here know how to use hedge clippers?

She turned down the dark lane, straining to read the house numbers as she crept past each dwelling. She was looking for a "weekend home" — whatever that looked like. When Scott told her about it, she had pictured a cabin in some rural setting. But this was clearly a suburban street with average-sized houses. All very nice houses, from what she could tell.

Okay, so they could afford to -hire- someone who knows how to use hedge clippers...

Further along, Angie came across a lone figure walking on the right side of the road. She wouldn't normally have paid much attention, but it was late for a stroll and the person's attire wasn't well suited for the activity. A pair of baggy beige pants stood out as the most headlight-friendly part of the ensemble, while the dark T-shirt blended into the darkness. The vigilant part of her brain suggested she hit the door locks. Catching a glimpse of the young man's face as she passed, recognition tingled at the edges of her mind. She'd gone on several yards before a muffled sound from outside of the car provided the last clue.

"AAANNNGGGEEELLLEEEEEE!"

The bellowing cry caused Angie to stomp on her brakes. She put the car into reverse and backed up to pull alongside the lone figure. Her passenger side door opened and Scott's strapping frame slid into the seat beside her.

"I was about ready to call Elsie and see if you'd checked in. You seriously need to get a regular cell phone," he said, though he wore an easy grin that softened the scolding. "You couldn't have found another pay phone and thrown me an update?"

"I'm really sorry," Angie said, awash in relief over having been found. "The highway disappeared on me and I kept getting off on the wrong road—" Her excuse sounded weak. The truth was, she'd been so frazzled over getting lost it hadn't occurred to her to call him again.

"Hey, I'm just glad you're okay. You are okay...right?" Scott asked, a vague look of concern lighting his swarthy features.

"Yeah. Just tired is all," Angie said. Scanning his face, she understood what had thrown her off in identifying him on the road. In all the pictures she'd seen, Scott had been wearing his shoulder-length hair down. Presently, his dark, unruly mane was tamed back into a blunted ponytail — it suited him better, she thought. His hair had called attention away from his face, which was smooth, save for the soul patch that wrapped under his strong, angular jaw. He bore almost no resemblance to his cousin, Elsie.

"Well, let's get moving." He gestured ahead. "The house is down here on the right. My dad and stepmom left a couple hours ago to head back into the city, but my friends are still hanging around. We can catch a ride with them." Scott's voice came out low and decisive, just as it had in countless phone conversations they'd shared in the last year since Elsie introduced them.

Angie nodded, following his instructions until they'd pulled into a broad driveway. They got out, and Scott transferred her duffel bag into the back of a black Lexus SUV that shared the drive.

"Lock up," he said. "Your car should be safe here for the week."

Angie secured a wallet-chain she'd brought along for this part of the trip, then double checked the locks and patted the trunk affectionately. "Thanks for not making me drive into the city. I'm not sure I could handle that."

"No problem." One corner of Scott's mouth tugged upward as he looked from her to the vehicle. "It's easier this way. Don't have to worry about you getting stuck in traffic or finding a place to keep your car."

"Exactly." Angie nodded.

Scott gave her a curious look and pointed to the link on her belt. "You know, I didn't picture you as the wallet-chain type."

"I remember you talking about how tourists get targeted by pickpockets," she said. "I just thought I should come prepared. I don't really carry anything valuable—I just can't afford to lose my driver's license."

"Huh." Scott mused. "It's kinda punk. I like it." He flashed a grin, projecting the confident bearing she'd come to expect. "Let's get the guys and get out of here." He led the way and Angie followed, the cool evening air reviving her.

The back door deposited them in a warmly lit kitchen, where polished oak cabinets overlooked black granite countertops. A pristine set of copper-bottomed pots and pans hung on display along the wall, and in combination with the studio lighting, made Angie think the place belonged on a gourmet cooking show. The space was open, with only a half-wall separating it from the living room. A sizable island bar sat in the middle of the stone-tiled floor with a trio of tall brass chairs pulled up along one side.

The middle chair was occupied by a bored looking young man, whose attention was fixated on the television mounted over the refrigerator. Like Scott, he was somewhat above-average in height and well built. His complexion was fair, however, and further washed out by the white designer T-shirt and matching baseball cap he wore with the bill cocked to the right.

"Hey James, I found her. We can head out," Scott announced as he trudged across the kitchen, his nylon track pants making a swishing sound as he moved.

A game controller in hand, James's focus barely deviated from the first-person shooter he seemed enthralled with. "Kay. Lemme finish this round," he answered vapidly.

Not waiting for an introduction, Angie followed Scott to the living room. She caught a blur of movement as a figure went sprinting in front of them, hurdled the brown leather sofa and disappeared behind it. A moment later the agile young man popped back into view, craned his arm, and pitched something brightly-colored across the room. The object, which turned out to be a miniature football, was captured just short of its impending collision with a bay window by the bulky form of another young man.

"Guys! What'd I say about throwing stuff in here?" Scott barked.

"Try not to hit the breakables?" The big one offered in a deep voice, tinged with a faint accent Angie couldn't identify. A mocking grin spread across his rounded face as he feigned a snap throw, which would have been aimed at Scott's head. His expression ebbed then when he caught sight of Angie. "That the girl?"

Scott, seeming to know the hefty fellow well enough to predict his behavior, didn't flinch. "Yeah, this is Angie," he said, looking back at her with a lingering smile. "Angie…Tonga."

"Your name is Tonga?" Angie asked, uncertain if she'd understood correctly.

"No. Tonga is the country I come from." The young man beaming smile stood out against his rich, dark skin. He was dressed more formally in a blue button-down shirt with gray pinstripes, paired with black pants. His hairline came to a pronounced widow's peak above his brow, and his tight, black curls were trimmed to a clean half-inch in length. "My name is long and hard to pronounce. It's easier to call me Tonga, trust me."

"Tonga's a diplomat brat—just like Yosh over here." Scott motioned to the considerably smaller young man who was crossing the room toward them. "We all went to the same school."

"Hideyoshi." The diminutive young man amended the introduction, tapping his fingertips to the center of his chest as he sauntered closer. His face was ovular, with almond-toned skin laid taut over stoic features. Around his head he wore a white bandanna with a red disk imprinted front and center, which Angie recognized as the Japanese flag. His baggy jeans hung low enough to make her wonder what mysterious force was preventing them from falling down around his ankles. His chin jutted upward as he gave her a scrutinizing once-over. "But, I'll let you call me Yosh-sama." His dark brows arched and fell as he made the offer, a smirk curling his lips.

"And why would I do that?" Angie asked. "I thought 'sama' was a suffix used for addressing someone of higher rank or age." She was reasonably sure she recalled the cultural morsel correctly, but glanced to Scott in hopes of verification.

Scott broke into a snicker at Yosh's expense. "I told you, man. She's smart."

"It would be either 'san' or 'kun', wouldn't it?" Angie went on, quietly pleased that something from her collection of random knowledge had proven useful.

"San's too formal." Yosh looked disappointed but nodded once, begrudgingly. "Nice find, Scottie. Tits with wits." He looked Angie over again before turning back to Scott. "Get her a little makeup and some decent clothes, and she could be a seven."

It took Angie a moment to grasp that Yosh had not only insulted her, but in the same breath managed to rate her as though he were the judge at a dog show. Even in giving him the cultural benefit of a doubt, she was no less astonished. She had known several Japanese students in her Aikido classes, and had always found them to be significantly more respectful than American students at large. That left her to conclude Yosh was some sort of vulgar anomaly.

"And that's why he can't keep a girlfriend." Tonga rumbled out a laugh, shaking his head as he moved into the kitchen.

"Yeah, don't mind Yosh." Scott chimed in after clearing his throat. "He talks first and thinks later."

Having accepted that she was an outsider, and therefore unlikely to be defended, Angie folded her arms before herself as she sized up Yosh. "Well, since it sounds like you're actually younger than me, maybe I should be calling you Yosh-chan." She injected an artificial sweetness into her tone for the suffix, which she knew to be most appropriate when directed toward small children or cute animals.

Scott laughed, and Yosh shot him a sneering look.

"Call me that again, and we'll see how long you last riding back on the luggage rack." Yosh cocked his head to one side as his gaze snapped back to Angie.

"Touchy." Angie clicked her tongue. But when it occurred to her that the Lexus parked in the driveway might belong to Yosh, she decided it wasn't in her best interest to perturb him any further.

"Okay, play nice," Scott said, stepping between them. "Let's just get out of here. It's getting late."

"This ain't late—The Yosh can go all night long." The shorter of the young men bounded his fingertips off of either side of his chest before turning and stalking off into the kitchen.

The Yosh? Angie mouthed to Scott.

Scott rolled his eyes.

"Right." Angie sighed. "Well if it's alright with you, I'm going to hit the bathroom before we leave."

"Third door on the left." Scott motioned to the hallway to the right of the kitchen. He turned then, surveying the damage to the living room. "I gotta clean this place up quick, anyway."

Angie made her way down the hall, pausing to straighten an ornate wooden mask that had likely been bumped off-center by one of the cavalier houseguests. She remembered Scott mentioning that he had some interesting friends. Now, she was beginning to see now why he hadn't gone into detail.

~ ~ ~ ~ ~ ~ ~

Angie drifted in and out of an exhausted, dreamless sleep on the ride into New York City. A map put the distance at around an hour's drive, but that wasn't taking the city's traffic into account. Wedged between the back left window of the SUV and Scott's shoulder, she dozed, catching only pieces of their entry.

They had a long wait at a toll booth while Yosh hunted through the front seats for his EZ-Pass, cussing angrily in both English and Japanese. Sometime later, she had the vague impression of an illuminated suspension bridge in the distance and an endless line of glowing tail lights. She'd glanced up at the clock on the dashboard. Was traffic really this bad at midnight? She heard the muffled refrain of car horns at one point, but found her eyelids too heavy to open.

The sound of someone shouting jolted her awake, and confusion greeted her as she struggled to make sense of her surroundings. The low throb of rap music vibrated through every inch of the vehicle's interior. Lifting her head, Angie realized it had been pillowed against Scott's shoulder. Solid, but more forgiving than the window, she wasn't surprised at where she'd migrated. But she was now alert enough to be embarrassed.

"I'm sorry." She sat up straight and checked Scott's shirt for signs of drool. Finding none, she felt only marginally better.

"I'm not." Scott gave her a glib smile when she looked up. He lifted a hand to pat his shoulder and added, "It's there whenever you need it."

On the other side of him, Tonga groaned. "Don't you two get all cuddly. Yosh's driving is making me sick enough as it is." He leaned forward, making it obvious just how much of the back seat his frame filled out. "Why can't I be up front?"

"Cuz' you can't appreciate the sunroof, King Kong," Yosh shot back.

Angie's attention shifted to the open sunroof and James — who stood on the front passenger seat, projecting his upper body through the opening. He let out a howling cry into the night air, and it suddenly became clear what had startled her. She looked out her window at the streets of New York, where the night life was in full swing. A blonde woman navigated the sidewalk across the street, clad entirely in black leather while propped up on impossibly tall stilettos. Angie guessed James's vocal display had been directed at her.

The cat-calling continued, as did their journey through the grid-like maze of streets. Yosh maintained an unhurried cruising speed. Though the city was lively in the small hours of the morning, traffic wasn't as dense as it had been on their way in.

Deciding to make the most of her confined situation, Angie tried to strike up a conversation with Tonga. "So what's it like in your country? And…where is it, exactly?" she asked, leaning forward to look past Scott.

"It's a little island in the South Pacific, sort of near Fiji." Tonga perked up at the inquiry. "It's always warm. And there's -lots- of coconuts," he added, seeming happy about the subject but struggling with what to say.

"Do you miss it?"

"Not usually. Most people leave the country to finish their educations, so there's just a lot of old people and nothing to do." He seemed to reconsider. "When it's winter here, I miss it. Too cold for me."

Angie cut the interview short as the SUV jerked off the road and parked in front of a tiny liquor store. James slunk back down into his seat, and the neon "spirits" sign overhead filled the vehicle with an ethereal blue glow.

"Why'd we stop?" Scott eased forward to place the question directly into Yosh's ear.

"So Tonga can run in and score me a fifth of vodka," Yosh said, turning down the booming music.

"I thought you bought a new I.D. card off Sanders," Tonga objected. His hairline fell dramatically as he furrowed his brow.

"Yeah, but my dad caught me with it." Yosh looked back over his shoulder and set his jaw. "Says he's shipping me back to Tokyo if I %&*# up again. James got his pulled by that bouncer last week, and Scott ain't legal til' next May. So it's on you."

"Come on, man. Can't you drop us off first?" Scott interjected.

"My ride, my rules." Yosh shot back.

Tonga grunted as he left the SUV, closing the door harder than necessary. He disappeared into the store, and Yosh turned the music back up to half the original cruising volume. James rolled down his window and stretched his legs out until he'd propped them on the side mirror. While the two in the front seats bickered back and forth about who owed who a cigarette, Angie turned her attention to Scott.

"You don't have a fake I.D.?" she asked, trying to sound casual. Angie had yet to decide if Scott's look of apprehension was due to his friends, or his concern for how well she was tolerating their behavior. She was determined to act indifferent. At best, she reasoned that voicing her disapproval would earn her a self-righteous label. At worst, she wouldn't put it past Yosh to kick her and Scott out in a bad part of the city.

"Not anymore." Scott shook his head. "I can't play the diplomatic immunity card like they can. I got in trouble enough when I first started staying at my dad's for the school year. I was starting to make him look bad." Scott's tone held a twinge of resentment. "He told my mom, and she said I'd have to go back to school in Virginia if I didn't shape up. So, I shaped up."

"And Virginia is...bad?"

"Not bad. Just boring," he said. "And the school system is crappy. I'd never have gotten into the college I'm going to this fall if I hadn't been in private school."

"So then, Tonga's older than you?" she presumed after a contemplative pause.

"No." Scott hesitated, casting the front of the store an uneasy glance. "Tonga's fifteen. But he looks a lot older and he's the least likely to get asked to show I.D. Maybe it's his size, I don't know."

"He's only fifteen?!" Angie gaped at him. "So, this is all kinds of illegal. That's just great," Angie breathed out in a sigh, sparing no sarcasm. Still travel-weary, her facade of indifference crumbled. Trying to imagine how she was going to afford to post her own bail was making her downright cranky.

Scott frowned, dark brows pulling together. "Look, I'm sorry about this. I didn't think we'd be coming back with—"

The rear right door opened and Tonga lurched in next to Scott. He entered with enough haste to make his side of the vehicle dip low before the shocks could absorb his substantial weight. "I got carded—GO!"

"What'd you tell em?" James peered back over his shoulder.

"I made like I couldn't speak English. What else was I gonna do?" Tonga folded his arms across his broad chest as he leaned back and settled in.

Yosh pulled away from the curb and back onto the street, only to be rebuked by the horn of a taxi he'd nearly sideswiped. He growled out a series of expletives, offered up the one-finger salute, and cranked the stereo volume into the range of blaring.

After roughly ten more minutes of Yosh's erratic driving, the SUV pulled up in front of a towering non-commercial building. Everyone exited the vehicle — Tonga to stretch his legs, and Yosh to hop onto the hood where he began puffing away at a cigarette. James pulled himself out through the sunroof and made a show of leaping off of the luggage rack at Tonga. Tonga sidestepped him, and James landed in a crouch on the sidewalk with a heavy *smack*.

Scott walked around to the back to unload bags. Angie followed to assist him, but he waved her off.

"Look at you, all helpful." James smirked at Scott before turning his attention to Angie. "How many points does he gotta earn before he gets lucky?"

Angie was caught off guard by the question. It was all she could do not to snap back with something emasculating.

I don't know what your problem is, but I'm sure they make a medication for it.

She stood seething for a moment, wondering how to set the boy straight without embarrassing Scott in front of his friends.

"Virgin-Scottie ain't gettin' lucky." Yosh called out. "The ladies respect skill. No experience, no skill." He took a long drag off of his cigarette before jumping off the front of the SUV and strutting toward them. "Now The Yosh," He curled his fingers in toward himself, indicatively. "The Yosh got skills."

"Oh, here we go—" Tonga rolled his gaze skyward and started off down the sidewalk, as though he'd spontaneously decided to take a walk. His departure was largely ignored.

Angie had reached her limit. Fists clenched at her sides, she didn't spare Scott a glance. She wasn't looking for permission. "First of all, nobody's getting 'lucky,'" she told James, eyes narrowing as she gave Yosh a more pointed look. "Secondly, plenty of women happen to find it endearing when they don't have to worry about contracting something itchy or potentially life-threatening from a guy."

"Just shut up, Yosh." Scott spoke at last. His tone came out as flat and hard as the street underfoot. Angie looked aside at his face and gathered what his voice had already told her; he'd had enough.

Yosh looked from Scott to Angie, throwing up his hands as if in concession. "That's alright. This honey couldn't handle The Yosh." He attempted a sneer in her direction, but his pomp had suddenly deflated.

"Actually this…'honey'…tries not to handle anything if she doesn't know where it's been," she said.

Great, now he's got me talking in third person.

She planted her hands on her hips before she could stop herself. "And you can cut the over-privileged gangster wanna-be crap. No one's impressed."

Yosh eased a step back, hands raised as if intent on diffusing tensions. As it turned out, he was merely acting as a distraction for James, who had skulked around behind Scott. In an abrupt flurry of activity and shouting, James de-pantsed Scott and darted for the safety of the SUV. Yosh backed up farther and let out a whooping endorsement.

Scott's reaction was quick, suggesting this wasn't an unusual hazing maneuver. In one extended motion he dropped Angie's duffel bag, hurled his backpack at James, and yanked his pants back up.

Out of the corner of her eye Angie caught a glimpse of blue boxer shorts covered in some form of cartoon character, but decided to pretend she hadn't noticed. The backpack caught the back of James's head and sent him stumbling to the right, where he rebounded off of the tail light and clamored around the side of the Lexus.

Yosh had already dashed around the front of the SUV and started the engine. James dove halfway into the passenger seat through the open window and they took off, tires squealing. They got less than a block before Tonga came barreling at them from the sidewalk, waving his arms. They stopped just long enough to pick him up before resuming their overly dramatic getaway.

Angie watched the *diplomat* license plate recede into the distance. Aside from walking a few unhurried paces to retrieve his bag, Scott made no attempt at pursuit.

"Well that was charming," she said, sardonic. "Now, why is it you hang around these guys?"

"They're not so bad," Scott said. He let the backpack slide off his shoulder and deposited it on the ground beside her bag.

"They remind me of some of the guys from my high school. Well, mainly the ones that threw things at my head between classes," she went on. Angie's temper was cooling, but she was still annoyed with the juvenile antics. She turned aside to survey the building, tipping her head back as she lost count of the number of stories that made up the high-rise. "You live here?" she asked Scott aloud, though she hadn't meant to. It was an inane question, which she was sure highlighted the fact that she'd never seen a building this tall in person.

"Yeah, most of the year." In one exuberant motion he caught her wrist, spun her around, and pulled her into an embrace. "It's so weird…you're a real person!" He laughed in her ear.

Feeling her feet leave the ground, Angie was momentarily stunned by the display of affection. While he was just a few inches taller than her, his upper body strength caught her by surprise.

"Scott, I think we established the reality of my existence a couple of hours ago." Angie chuckled. "Put me down!" She found it difficult to scold him for the manhandling when he seemed so sincere.

"Sorry." He eased her back to the ground and held her at arm's length, as if to get a better look. His playful grin ignited a warmth in his honey-hazel eyes. "That's for all the times you put up with my philosophical ramblings."

Angie smiled, giving a casual shrug. "Hey, I'm pretty sure everybody starts wondering about the meaning of life from time to time. It helps to bounce things off of somebody else." As she spoke, she was aware he was still clasped her by the elbows, which hadn't allowed much space to return between them.

"Yeah, it did help me—a lot," Scott said. His balance seemed to sway and he leaned in closer to her. A shock of a thought lanced through Angie's mind.

He was going to kiss her.

She reacted unconsciously, twisting at her waist and bending to grab up her duffel bag. It was a defensive deflection of attention, which she bolstered with words. "So, where am I staying? My brain is about useless, and I still have Mono. I should really get some sleep."

That's it, mention the Mono. Everyone knows it's contagious.

Scott caught the strap of his backpack and hefted it onto one shoulder, a genial smile still affixed to his dark features. He didn't show any signs of disappointment or expectation. Angie decided that she'd probably imagined it. Her mind wasn't at its sharpest, after all.

"Come on." He motioned for her to follow as he went striding into the building. "My dad thought you should have the spare apartment so you'll have more privacy." A doorman emerged to hold open one of the double glass doors while they passed into the elevator lobby.

As she trailed after him, it occurred to Angie that she had no idea who Scott's father was or what he did for a living. Whatever it was, it apparently supplied him with the means for two Manhattan apartments and a swanky weekend home in New Jersey. She could only hope everything might feel a little less surreal after she'd had a good night's sleep.

This is going to be interesting.

June 23rd,

I Heart NY?

I arrived almost 2 hours late in New Jersey, and eventually found the right house in Oldwick. Scott was literally out roaming the streets looking for me. His father and stepmom had already gone back to the city by then, so we rode back with his rowdy friends. The traffic was insane.

Scott's friends reminded me of a bad stereotype from a sitcom. Oh sure, they're amusing in their own way. But I can see how they've gotten Scott into trouble in the past. (Or at least, he makes it sound like that was past-tense.) They're the kind of guys that prove testosterone and immaturity are a combustible combination... like gasoline and Styrofoam. Add a little spark of boredom, and bad things are bound to happen.

It looks like I get my own place for the week! It's like a studio apartment; all one big L-shaped room with a separate bathroom and kitchenette. Evidently, Scott's dad rents it for him just so he has a place to hang out with his friends. There's a pool table, a big entertainment center, and a couple of couches. I'm sleeping on the couch that converts into a bed. So far, it's amazingly comfortable. I'm sitting on it now, clearing my head before I pass out. The main apartment is five floors down. I'll get to see it tomorrow, when I meet Scott's dad and stepmom.

Scott is pretty much what I'd expected. Just like with the other people I've met, it's not like meeting someone new. It's more like... placing the final pieces of a puzzle you've been staring at for a long time. Within a couple of minutes it all feels normal and familiar.

~Ang

Chapter 12

Scott showed up at Angie's door in the late morning and invited her on a grocery run. She'd been awake just long enough to change out of her pajamas and pull her hair up into a pony tail, but for that much she was grateful.

As they emerged from the building, it was obvious it had rained recently. Puddles lingered along the gutters, while a gray haze overhead was steadily yielding to the noontime sun. The streets smelled like a strange blend of things chemical and organic. To Angie, this translated to the unpleasant scent of road tar and wet dog.

Scott set a marching pace. Angie strode alongside him on the broad sidewalk, not about to be outdone by his athletic gait. There seemed to be an excess of sound and movement everywhere with people coming and going, half of them carrying on phone conversations. The unfamiliar atmosphere scattered her attention, compelling her to focus on her host as they walked.

"So, are New Yorkers as surly as television makes them out to be?" she asked.

"Surly?" Scott's brow furrowed.

It took Angie a moment to realize he didn't recognize the word. "Rude." She tried again, wondering if her vocabulary was going to stand out in this part of the country as much as the slight, unconscious emphasis she placed on her vowels.

"Oh." Scott looked off ahead of them again, growing somber. "Well, yeah. A lot of them were before the terrorist attack. But ever since then, it's been different—people are nicer. It got a lot of people thinking."

"Trauma seems to have that effect," she said, monitoring his face with sidelong glances.

"I mean, it'll probably wear off." Scott rolled his shoulders in a cynical shrug. "People are good at forgetting stuff and going back to taking everything for granted. But while it lasts, it's a good time to be visiting."

Angie nodded, pausing at length before asking, "What was it like, being there when the planes hit the towers? I know Elsie was on instant messenger with you that morning—she called me after school freaking out that you were describing things and then suddenly went offline." She hoped enough time had passed that she wasn't hitting a raw nerve. As much as she wanted to, she'd never asked him about it before. It seemed like something better done face to face.

"I was on the front steps of my school. I didn't have to go to first period," Scott began. His walking pace slowed. "I had my laptop open, and I was just playing around when the first plane hit. I didn't really know what was going on at first...I just saw the smoke off in the distance." He stopped at the street corner and backed himself against the side of a small bakery, as though he could no longer think and move at the same time. "About the time the second one hit, people started coming out of the school to look. Nobody was talking. And all you could hear were more and more sirens."

Angie mimicked Scott's stance against the wall, studying his burdened expression. "How close was your school to the financial district?"

"I dunno...just a few miles. Close enough." He lowered his head, as though something near his shoes had caught his interest. "When the first one fell, that big cloud of dust swallowed up everything. All we saw was this gray wave coming at us. It looked like a bad storm cloud." His gaze flickered up to meet hers, then darted away. "People started screaming and running back inside. I think that's when it started to feel real." Scott paused. "They just kept playing the close-ups over and over on the news. It was like...the world was ending or something."

Angie nodded, finding it hard to swallow. "I sort of thought that too, at first. I couldn't get my head around it." She kept her voice low. "What did you do? Just...watched the news until somebody came to pick you up?"

"They wouldn't let us leave at first." Scott shook his head. "They didn't know if the attacks were over, and I guess they weren't sure how dangerous the dust was. I think that was the first time I ever prayed and really meant it." He held her gaze at last, his hazel eyes deep wells of thought. "I tried to call my mom in D.C. when I found out the Pentagon got hit too, but the cell towers were jammed. I couldn't let her know I was okay until the next day."

Angie absorbed his account, picturing it in her mind and filing it alongside her own vivid recollection of that infamous day. "Wow," she murmured. It was an inadequate word, but it was the only one that found its way from her thoughts to her mouth. She reached out and laid a hand on his shoulder, hoping the action would convey more than words could. They shared a significant look. "At least your family was okay. Elsie and I were worried for days before you checked back in."

"I got luckier than a lot of people," Scott said. "I didn't know anybody who died. Not directly. My dad did, though." His expression eased to something more apologetic. "Didn't mean to worry anybody. It was just crazy for a while there."

"Have you been to Ground Zero yet?" Angie asked, withdrawing her hand and clasping it to her other wrist behind her back.

"No." Scott looked down.

"I'd like to go there. I need to see it." Angie said, more insistent than she'd intended. When his face contorted with skepticism she elaborated, "I want to pay my respects. I need to make sure it's real to me...so I never forget." Hesitating, she added, "I can go on my own. I just need a map, and for you to tell me how the subway works."

"Yeah, like I'd send you wandering through Manhattan alone." Scott gave a sharp exhalation through his nose. "I'll take you there sometime this week. I probably should have gone sooner." He pushed off from the building and resumed walking. Though he moved with purpose, he was careful to make sure she kept up beside him.

Angie fell into step. She considered arguing that she was perfectly capable of taking care of herself, but in truth, she was finding the city more intimidating than she'd expected. The idea of navigating it alone made her uneasy.

"What else do you want to see while you're here?" Scott's tone lightened with the change of subject.

Angie shrugged. "The usual touristy things—Times Square, Central Park, The Statue of Liberty, The Empire State Building..." She searched her mind for other hallmarks of the city. It occurred to her then that, as with Ottawa, she should have done more research ahead of time. She'd planned out the travel portion of her trip carefully, but not the sight-seeing. "I'd like to try to see a Broadway musical," she heard herself blurt out. She didn't really, but she'd always heard it was something not to be missed while in New York.

"I think I can arrange all that." Scott cast a beguiling smile her way.

He has beautiful eyes, Angie caught herself thinking.

She couldn't help but make the observation. In spite of his unkempt appearance, she'd begun to find him handsome. It caught her by surprise, given the self-satisfied air he projected.

"Well don't go out of your way. I don't want to be an inconvenience..." Angie trailed off as she caught sight of a homeless man sitting in the middle of the sidewalk ahead of them.

The scruffy, older man had a full gray beard — stringy tendrils of matching locks protruded from under a brown stocking cap. Though it was the beginning of summer, he was dressed entirely too warm in what looked like faded military fatigues. As people passed, he held up a plastic cup to collect the charity of those who made a point to notice. Angie slowed as she considered him.

It isn't compassionate to enable him if he's an addict, the commonly recited argument surfaced in her mind. *You can only love Jesus as much as the person you love the least*, countered an assertion she'd once read on a dorm room inspirational poster.

Scott realized she'd fallen behind and stopped to let her catch up. As Angie was busy wracking her brain for a balanced answer to the moral conundrum, he followed her gaze in a bemused effort to determine what had distracted her. He looked at the homeless man, and back to her, brows lofting as it dawned on him. He started to shake his head, but Angie had already made up her mind.

Stepping out of the flow of sidewalk traffic to stand beside the panhandler, she bent down and asked, "Are you hungry?"

"What?" The old man looked up at her blankly.

She wasn't sure if he was hard of hearing or just surprised someone was talking to him. Feeling odd about standing over him, she crouched down to his level. "I don't carry cash on me, but if you're hungry I can take you to get something to eat," she said, gesturing across the street and down a block to the deli she'd spotted.

"I ain't givin' up my spot!" the panhandler all but growled. His weathered face pinched into a suspicious expression. He looked over her shoulder and eyeballed Scott, as though he were a likely competitor.

Angie hid her amusement. Deciding there was a spark of validity to the man's paranoia, she amended her approach. "I could bring you back some breakfast then, if you tell me what you'd like."

"I'd like a little cash," the man clarified in a slower, more forceful tone, as though he found her dimwitted. As an afterthought he added, "I'll take a cigarette, if ya got one."

"Sorry, I don't smoke," Angie said, perplexed over how poorly the conversation was going. "And like I said, I don't keep cash on me."

"You got a credit card, don't ya?" The old man narrowed his eyes, addressing her with an edge of impatience while jerking a thumb to his right. "There's an ATM right around the corner." When he turned his head she noticed his nose was crooked. Given his apparent attitude issues, she had a guess as to why.

"Here, man." Scott's voice came out low as he produced a cigarette and offered it to the panhandler, who snatched it up with grumbled thanks. While the man was busy pawing at his jacket search of a lighter, Scott hooked his hand around Angie's elbow and urged her to stand. Once she complied, he secured his arm around hers and guided them onward.

Angie was too preoccupied with her internal review of the exchange to protest being towed away. "I didn't see it going that way in my head," she said, throwing a backward glance. She suddenly felt like a naive country girl.

"If you're gonna try to feed every bum we pass, we'll have to leave a lot earlier for sightseeing," Scott joked once they were well out of earshot. He shook his head in some combination of amusement and disbelief. "Don't they have homeless people where you're from?"

"We have them. Well, one that I know of," she said, defensive. "Just ask your cousin. She actually knows Punk Rock Freddie personally."

"Punk Rock Freddie?" Scott repeated, looking at her expectantly. She didn't realized how long he'd kept a comfortable hold on her until he finally released her elbow.

"He's this crazy old homeless guy who wanders our town," she said. "He's covered in tattoos and piercings, and his hair is always dyed some neon color. All of his earthly possessions are in this little rolling suitcase he keeps with him. He's a nice guy—really friendly."

"Okay, that's a different kind of homeless guy than the ones I'm used to." Scott laughed.

Angie smirked. "Elsie's heard his whole life story. According to her, he was a completely normal guy until he was in a car accident. He thinks he died and was brought back to life by the spirit of Punk Rock." She smiled to herself in recollection. "Before Elsie could drive, she used to ride her bike around town on the weekends looking for him. She'd follow him around and get him to tell her stories, like he was her adopted grandfather or something."

"Oh my god, that sounds just like her!" Scott smacked his palm to the middle of his face. "Er, sorry. Does that offend you?" He peered at her through splayed fingers.

Angie gave him a blank stare. "Does what offend me?"

"'Oh my god?'" he repeated, his voice taking a dip in its usual confidence.

"No," she said, considering carefully. "I mean…I don't personally use the expression unless I really mean it. It just seems too much like crying wolf, you know? When I -do- say it, I want it to be so rare that it puts God on full alert."

"I guess that makes sense." Scott looked off ahead of them again, smirking. "I just know you're kinda religious, and you can't swear and all that. I mean, I've never heard you when we talk on the phone, anyways, so I just figured—"

"I can swear. I'm pretty good at it, actually," Angie interjected, unsure at first of where she was going with the argument. "What I mean is, it's not that I can't… it's just a habit that doesn't bring out the best in me, so I try not to." She shrugged. "And I'm not religious." The word had been afflicting her like a mental splinter from the moment he'd used it.

"You're not?"

"No, I don't think so." She smiled when his puzzled expression deepened. "It's too much of a blanket term. Lots of negative connotations attached to it." Pausing, she struggled to compress her thoughts into a proverbial nutshell. "I think people can be religious about a lot of things. Sports, politics, education, cooking… Anything with a rule system you can attach rituals to. To me, it's just not the right description. I love Jesus. We're close. I talk to God a lot, and I try to pay attention and catch what He's trying to tell me." She gauged Scott with frequent sideways glances. "It's not about rules or rituals, it's about a personal connection. If that makes any sense."

"I guess it sorta does." Scott said, meeting her gaze curiously. "So you aren't 'religious,' you're spiritual," he inferred, looking halfway pleased with himself.

Angie weighed his wording for a few moments, turning it over in her mind as though it were a tangible object. It wasn't a perfect fit, but it didn't have the jagged, unforgiving barbs she associated with the first label he'd used. "That makes me think of a hippie commune for some reason. But if you have to call me something, I think I like that better."

Scott's mouth shifted into a partial grin. "So, if you don't say 'Oh my god', what -do- you say?"

"Oh…Mylanta?"

"Yeah, I figured it would be something lame like that." Scott laughed, tensing when she shot him an exaggerated look of annoyance.

Noting that he seemed ready for it, Angie gave his shoulder a solid punch. He rocked with the force of it, still looking smug. When he stopped walking she thought he was playing up the punch, but then noticed they were standing in front of a grocery store. She tailed him into the building.

Inside, Angie was taken aback by the elaborate ambiance. A wall separating the entrance from the checkout counters was comprised of latticed mahogany, stacked with an array of fine wines and draped with faux grape vines. The displays at the head of each aisle were ornate, if not elegant. The color scheme was earthy and warm, complimented by the mingled scent of fresh produce and baked goods. One word came to her mind as she strained to identify the classical music piece drifting about the store's interior: Expensive.

She imagined this was the sort of grocery store that threw away food within a week of its expiration date, rather than risk looking tacky by offering it at a discounted price. She found herself both loving and loathing the place at the same time. Love for the serene atmosphere, and loathe for the snobby undertones.

Scott paused to pat down the numerous pockets of his pants before locating his wallet. He pulled out a credit card and held it up.

"Ooo. Ahhh." Angie kept her tone lukewarm, wondering if she was supposed to be impressed. "I have one too."

"It's my dad's," Scott clarified. "He told me to pick up some stuff for dinner tonight, and to make sure you got some snacks for the week." Expecting the protest that was already forming on her face, he held up a hand. "I've gotta answer to him, so don't be difficult, okay? Just pick out a few things you want and meet me back up here in five minutes." He ended on a pleading note, giving Angie a look that reminded her of a sad puppy.

She released a disgruntled sigh and nodded once. "Fine."

As they split up to undertake their separate food expeditions, she wondered at what the rest of her host family would think of her. She was sure she'd already made a bad impression by being late with her arrival and failing to call. And while Yosh's observation about her clothing had been exceedingly rude, it wasn't inaccurate. She didn't own anything new or particularly nice. Would it matter to them? Some part of her mind pointed out the chosen attire of Scott and his friends, and she decided she was over-analyzing.

High school is over. These are adults, she reminded herself. Or at least, it seemed reasonable to hold out hope.

~ ~ ~ ~ ~ ~ ~

After returning to the guest apartment for the afternoon, they broke into the cookies and Vanilla Coke that Angie had brought back. It wasn't the healthiest lunch she'd ever had. In fact, she was sure the sugary pairing had no actual nutritional value. But it was far more enjoyable than the gas station hotdogs that had sustained her the day before.

To kill time they discussed comic books, their respective martial art of choice, and played many brutal rounds of various video games from Scott's collection. It became clear to Angie early on that Scott wasn't above bragging, and his competitive nature proved too pervasive for him to go easy on her. Her own competitiveness reared its head in response, and along the way their friendly antagonism deteriorated into rivalry. The banter between them became comfortable, and by the end of the afternoon, Angie was grateful for the mindless downtime.

With the approach of evening they headed down to the apartment serving as the main residence. While the front door was unassuming, Angie found it difficult to conceal her amazement once they'd entered the condo. Polished wood floors stretched out from the entryway into a spacious dining area. To her right, a cast iron railing was the only separation between the upper living area and the sprawling den located on a recessed level — which was accessible via a wide staircase.

From the railing overlook she took in the black leather sectional-sofa, which was positioned in a U shape and angled toward the largest flat-panel television she'd ever seen. The back wall of the den wasn't a wall at all, but a section of floor-to-ceiling windows that ran two stories high, offering an acrophobic view into the chasm between them and the high rise across the street. The wall décor was made up of large abstract paintings and fabric swaths, rich in color and expertly arranged. The spotless condition of the apartment topped off a sense of class with the impression the place was barely lived in.

"You coming?" Scott's voice pulled her focus to where he stood in the doorway to the left of the dining table. She closed her mouth and took quick strides to make up the distance between them.

"Yeah, sorry." Angie looked side to side when they ended up in a kitchen space at least the size of the one at the weekend home. Here the countertops were all composed of beige stone, given contrast by the stainless-steel appliances. To the right was a preparation area, and to the left, a walk-in pantry. "What did you say your dad does for a living?" she asked, curiosity finally getting the better of her.

"I didn't," Scott replied evenly. He veered right, first placing groceries in the refrigerator and then filling a tea kettle with water. He looked intent on his tasks, and Angie guessed he was either delaying or stringing her along in an effort to seem mysterious. She was about to drop the subject when he finally looked at her with an air of reluctance. "He works in insurance."

Angie eyed him warily. "So, is that code for 'he's in the mafia?'"

"No, worse." Scott's expression slackened with amusement. "He's the regional president of an insurance firm. My dad is 'The Man.'" He threw up two fingers of each hand into mimed quotations, disdain evident in his voice.

"And you never mentioned this before because...what, you're embarrassed by him?" she asked, puzzled.

"Not exactly." Scott thinned his lips, considering for a long moment before he began a search through the upper cabinets. "It's hard enough to know who your friends are. It's just about impossible when people think you have money."

Angie watched him set out a pair of sapphire-blue cups, along with a bag of loose-leaf green tea. Before saying anything more she turned, hopping up to perch on the end of the countertop. "So what you're saying is, you wanted to make sure I liked you for who you are and not because your dad is some kind of big-shot?"

"Something like that." Scott glanced up at her and then away.

"That's...kind of dignified, actually." She broke into a congratulatory smile, admiring his discretion.

"It wasn't like I didn't trust you...I just didn't think it should be important." Scott relaxed visibly. "I don't even think Elsie knows about my dad. Her mom and my mom aren't close. I haven't seen her in person since we were little kids. I just found her email in a Christmas card one year and we started talking."

When the kettle began to steam he removed it from the heat and dropped the tea into the upper part of the vessel.

Angie slid off the counter and accepted the two earthenware cups as Scott offered them out to her. "I haven't known Elsie to ask for much personal information," she said, following as he carried the kettle out of the kitchen. "And she's not keen on sharing anything profound about herself, either. I think she's afraid of getting too close to anybody."

How sad is it that we're best friends and we hardly know each other?

"Now that you mention it, I guess we mainly just talk about games and TV shows." Scott mused aloud, stepping out into the dining room and veering left down the main hallway of the condo. He passed several doors and nudged the last one open with his foot.

"These are pretty," Angie remarked, admiring the ornate cups as she trailed after him. "Where did you get them?"

"Japan," Scott answered, matter-of-fact. "My mom and I went for two weeks over spring break. It was her trip of a lifetime, and I got to tag along." He used his feet to push low piles of clothing out of the way as he entered the room, which Angie presumed to be his. Notebooks and papers covered a twin bed in the left corner. Hanging scrolls covered in hand-painted Japanese Kanji lined the walls, and an unimposing computer desk sat against the right wall. It was the computer he seemed to be clearing a path toward. "Here, I figured you'd want to check in with people."

"Oh, thanks. That'd be great." Angie sank into the computer chair, setting the two cups down on the left side of the desk. She marveled that she'd gotten so caught up with everything, she hadn't even thought about sending her routine newsletter to let everyone know she was still alive. "So, how was Japan?" she asked, glancing back to her host to show she didn't plan to completely disengage from conversation.

Scott poured tea into each cup, claiming the one closest to him before setting the kettle on a sparsely populated bookshelf in the corner. "It was great. Beautiful. If I got to go back, I'd want to stay at least a month or two," he said, thoughtful. "I just wish my sister could have gone with us. She got married last year, and something about her husband's religion says they have to live in a mud hut in Guatemala for a year. He's a decent guy and all—I just don't see why they can't have some vacation time. Or at least a computer. She has to write me regular letters." Frowning, he picked up a leather-bound book off of the shelf and pulled out an envelope he'd been using to mark his place.

"I'm sorry," Angie said in sympathy. "You'd mentioned a few times that you two were close. Is she much older than you?" She lifted up her cup and sniffed at the tea before tasting it. The liquid smelled like grass clippings and jasmine. Fortunately, its taste was mild and dominated by the floral aspect.

"No, we're just two years apart. She took care of me when we were kids—after my parents got divorced." Scott turned the book over in his hands. "I got this journal while we were in Japan, so I could record all of the stuff she missed and everything I wanted to talk to her about. I'm going to send it to her when it's full."

Angie smiled, endeared. "I'd love it if my little brother thought that well of me."

"Glad you think so." Scott smirked at her roguishly. "You help yourself to the computer, and I'm going to catch my sister up on you." He made his way back to the bed and flopped down without bothering to clear himself a spot.

Angie scowled over her shoulder at him. "Do I get to screen it for accuracy?"

"Not a chance," Scott shot back, turning his full attention to the journal.

She grumbled back at him in forced exasperation — her way of shrugging off what she was tempted to perceive as a veiled compliment. Opening her email, Angie caught some part of herself hoping to find a letter from Don sitting in her inbox. Having no such luck, she internally scolded herself for failing to accept reality.

Quit being a silly little girl and just let him go.

She realized then that the only new mail she had was from Zak, and her disappointment was partially replaced with intrigue.

```
     Way to freak me out. My mom calls me up at my
friend's place at like 12 am and says you haven't
called yet. I didn't sleep too well last night...
Did you underestimate the drive? I told you it was
more like 8 hours...
     Anyway, I hope you liked your stay. Sorry if
things didn't turn out the way you might have
expected. Uhh, and sorry I sorta left you with my
sister after you lost your keys, but she's not so
hard to get along with is she? I know that was all
really awkward at the end. I have no idea why my
friend came along with me when my sister called me
back. I guess I didn't know what to do after that,
so I just left. Whatever... Hope you're ok.
     Found the keychain you left me. Cute. At
least now I've got something to remember you by.
     -Zak
```

Angie smiled to herself. *Aww. He was actually worried about me.*

She had debated slipping the keychain under his door before she'd left. It was a favorite from her collection, featuring a sleeping housecat with a witticism about relaxation that seemed to fit him. Now she was glad she'd summoned the courage to leave it behind. Though her visit to Ottawa had ended on a clumsy note, she would always remember it with fondness.

At least he must have cared about me a little, in his own way.

She typed up a quick report and included Zak in the send list, tacking on a personal note promising to call him within the next day or two. She hoped by then he would have some good news about his sister and nephew.

"Alright, I'm done." She swiveled around in the chair to square off with Scott. "Now, what sort of libel are you fabricating about me?"

Scott finished the sentence he was on before snapping the journal closed and setting it aside. A grin played across his face. "Just telling her how I can't believe you tried to buy a homeless guy breakfast. It was so…tourist. Right up there with running into things while staring up at the buildings." He laughed, polished off his tea, and walked over to collect her empty cup. While his room was an organizational disaster, he at least appeared to be conscious about keeping things sanitary. "And doesn't that kinda go against the whole Bible code? You know, 'God helps those who help themselves?'"

Angie gave him the flattest expression she could manage before realizing he was serious. "Scott… that's not in the Bible. That's just a saying people like to use when they're too lazy to help people."

Scott's brows knit together. "Oh." He processed the revelation a moment longer and then shrugged. "Sorry. You know, I actually tried to read it to figure out what all is in there and what isn't. But it got pretty boring after that second chapter…er…book. You know what I mean." He turned and strode back to his bed, rummaging through the clutter until he produced a nearly ancient King James edition. Balancing it in one upturned palm, he brought it to her. The leather binding was cream in color, with dry cracking and fracture lines along the edges. "This is the one my Grandmother gave me a couple of years ago. It was hers when she was a kid." He spoke with obvious affection, offering it out to her.

Angie stood up and accepted the book. Scott's fingers grazed hers in the process, unnerving her. She glanced up, but when he didn't look at her she decided to shake the sense it had been deliberate. "Wow." She gently turned over the inside cover and scanned until she found the print date: 1927. "So let me guess. You made it to about…Numbers?" She glanced up at Scott again, his surprised look confirming her assessment.

"Yeah. How'd you know that?"

"Because that's mostly what that book is—numbers. It's not exactly what you'd call easy reading." She chuckled. "You're probably better off starting in the middle instead of trying to read it front to back like a normal book. Both testaments are important, but it might be easier to understand if you start with the New

Testament." She opened the book and leafed through until she found Matthew. She turned it around and handed it back to him. "And a study version would be really helpful. Something with footnotes to explain the customs, traditions, units of measurement—the stuff that's hard to relate to because of that whole two-thousand-year generation and culture gap. Not to mention the language barrier—"

"Yeah…the Old English thing made it pretty slow going," Scott said, cradling the book in the crook of his arm. "Same reason I sucked at Shakespeare."

Angie smiled. "It's a great heirloom, but I'm sure we can find you a version that'll make it fairly painless. Are there any bookstores nearby?"

"I think I've seen one. I'll look it up," he said, nodding. "So, does that mean you'll keep teaching me more about this faith stuff?"

Angie laughed, appreciating his sincere lack of piety. "I don't really think I'm qualified to teach anybody anything. But I'm happy to talk about it anytime you want."

"I'm pretty sure my grandma would love you for it." He smirked. "She's great. I'm thinking about driving out to Wisconsin to see her at the end of the summer." He paused, probing gaze locked onto hers. "If I can get that far on my own, I could go a couple hours more to see Elsie and her family. Then maybe me and you could hang out again, if you're back by—"

"Scott? Are you home?" An older female voice carried in from the front room of the condo.

"That'd be my stepmom," Scott said, looking vaguely annoyed at having his train of thought interrupted. He gathered the cups and kettle, then cut through his room and headed back down the hall. Angie followed him out as far as the dining table, where her attention arrested on a smiling, middle-aged woman.

Clad in a short-sleeved gray blouse and fitted jeans, she appeared unremarkable on a physical level. The woman stood several inches shorter than Angie, built slender enough that her form was nearly devoid of curves. Her shoulder length, ash-brown hair was pulled back into a loose pony tail, and her bangs curled under just above thin eyebrows of the same hue. If she was wearing any makeup, it was too scant for Angie to detect. Her features were fine and regular, set with eyes an unmemorable shade of gray and lips encircled by the patent wrinkle lines of a long-time smoker. Her only jewelry was a gold wedding band.

If not for the possessive manner in which the woman clutched a small Siamese cat to her chest, Angie would have been tempted to think she was the housekeeper.

"Angeli...so glad to finally meet you." The woman's flowing alto voice came out with a husky finish. "I'm Martha."

"The food's in the fridge," Scott said, detouring into the kitchen.

Martha waited until the door closed behind him before edging closer to Angie and dropping her volume to a secretive level. "Scott's talked about you coming to visit for months. He's been so excited to show you the city." Her eyes glimmered with a pleasant zeal Angie was immediately drawn to. "You're good friends with his cousin Elsie, aren't you? I haven't met her yet, but she sounds fascinating."

"Oh, she's definitely one-of-a-kind." Angie smiled, reminded that here she was "a friend of Scott's cousin," and not "that potentially psycho girl from the internet." The change of expectation was refreshing. "You have a beautiful home," she added, glancing around in admiration before turning her focus to the feline lounging in Martha's arms. "Who's this?"

"This is Iris...my only child. Well, unless Scott lets me count him one of these days." Martha laughed as she raked her fingernails between the cat's ears. "I never really considered having children— or getting married, for that matter. Scott's father was a surprise."

Angie reached out to graze her fingers down Iris' sleek coat. "She's beautiful."

"Here, you're welcome to hold her," Martha extended her arms to offer the cat to Angie, who readily accepted the warm bundle of fur. Iris, for her part, remained indifferent despite changing hands. "There now, she likes you." Martha said. "Would you mind keeping her company for me while I cook dinner? She won't give me a moment's peace otherwise."

"You mean, while you warm up dinner?" Scott was back, and taking the opportunity to point out the prepackaged state of the food.

"Well, I've never made myself out to be a master chef." Martha countered Scott in a light tone, placing her hands on her narrow hips. Angie halfway expected the woman to stick out her tongue at him to complete the picture, but she didn't.

"I'll keep her out of your way." Angie said.

"Thank you. It shouldn't take me long." Martha smiled and headed into the kitchen.

"We normally go eat out," Scott said, sounding irritated. "I don't know why they wanted to do the pretend homemade-meal-around-the-dinner-table thing."

"So, do you have a problem with refilling your own drink, or with doing dishes afterward?" Angie allowed a snide undertone to her query, hoping to distract Scott from his familial angst.

"It's not like that. I hate being waited on." Scott sounded defensive. His impassioned look told her he was gearing up for a lengthy explanation.

The cat, which had seemed ready to fall asleep in Angie's arms, suddenly opened her blue eyes wide and twisted her head toward the front door. Angie followed the animal's gaze just as the door opened and a well-dressed man entered. There was no question in her mind as to who he was — the resemblance to his son was too striking.

He was older, of course. His full, thick hair had dulled to a distinguished gray, which he wore neatly cropped. He was an inch or two taller and rounded heavily in his midsection, darker skin tone owing to a full-blooded Portuguese background. Yet, there was no mistaking the balanced cut of his brow and cheekbones, or the deliberate way he set his mouth. Their eyes were almost identical — turbulent and hazel. He shrugged off his suit coat and draped it over his left forearm.

"Well young lady, you made it! So sorry we couldn't bring you back ourselves—I had a meeting early this morning." The man's tone was expressive and warm — the voice of a businessman. "What do you think of The Big Apple so far?" he asked, with what seemed like a more subdued version of Scott's smile.

"It's definitely big." Angie said, for a lack of better commentary. "I haven't gotten farther than the grocery store yet. I think we're going to try to see some of the major landmarks tomorrow." She glanced to Scott for confirmation, and he nodded.

"The weather is perfect. It might be a good night for you to see Times Square, if you're up for it after dinner," Scott's father suggested.

"That sounds great." She smiled. "It must be amazing at night."

"It's okay." Scott twisted his mouth off to one side, looking unenthused. "It's kind of a long walk from here."

"Take a taxi, then." His father gave a low chuckle. "I'll give you some cash for it." He retrieved his wallet from his back pocket and pulled out two bills.

Scott held up a hand, protest written all over his face. "I wasn't asking for money—"

"I never said you were." The older man held out the bills, insistent. "But in the event that our guest gets tired of walking, you shouldn't have a problem getting a ride." There was a calm firmness to his voice as he gave Angie a genial smile and then turned his expectant gaze to Scott.

Feeling caught in the middle of a father-son battle of wills, Angie buried her fingers deeper into Iris's fur and glanced between the men. It seemed like a long while, but she knew in reality it was only a few uncomfortable seconds before Scott relented. He took the bills, folded them twice, and jammed them into his pocket.

"Well then, what's for dinner?" The older man asked, tone pitching cheerfully. He rubbed his palms together in anticipation.

"Stuffed pasta shells, I think." Angie piped up, more than happy to encourage a new topic of conversation. "And some kind of chocolate torte for dessert."

"Sounds good to me," Scott's father said, starting for the kitchen door. "I might poke my head in and see if I can help speed up the process."

Scott stepped up to the table and pulled out a chair, motioning Angie toward it in an exaggeratedly chivalrous gesture. "Have a seat," he said, voice thick with sarcasm. "The show's about to start."

Angie weighed Scott with a skeptical look, but decided not to ask what he meant. Instead she sank down into the plush, high-backed chair and settled the cat into her lap, resolved to pay close attention to the family dynamics of the evening.

~ ~ ~ ~ ~ ~ ~

In spite of Scott's ongoing tension with his father, Angie warmed up to the older man throughout their unhurried dinner conversation. She found him to be cordial, even charming. Once Martha joined them, it set her mind at ease to learn that his first name was Shaun. She didn't have any intention of calling him that to his face, but simply knowing it made him seem less imposing.

And it didn't hurt that she thought "Shaun" would make a terrible name for an evil villain.

After dinner, a forty-five minute walk landed Angie and Scott in the middle of Manhattan's vibrant theater district. Angie intended on asking Scott about his strained relationship with his father on their way, but the pace he set wasn't conducive to any real conversation. She decided to delay bringing it up, guessing physical activity was Scott's preferred method for blowing off steam. Once they were within sight of the brilliantly lit intersection that made up Times Square, Scott had returned to a more indulgent mood.

After Scott's standoff with his father at the beginning of the evening, Angie decided they wouldn't use the taxi money. Her resolve buckled, however, when it began to rain. After fifteen minutes of huddling under an awning, they both agreed that they could either hail a taxi, or be wet and miserable. Scott brooded all the way back to the apartment, his pride seeming to have taken a hit over dipping into his father's money.

Though she was tired, Angie challenged him to several more rounds of a video game tournament back at the apartment in hopes of cheering him up. Her effort paid off, as it didn't take long before his usual gall returned. The next thing she knew, he'd goaded her into arm wrestling.

Scott had at least twenty pounds on Angie — all of it muscle. She wasn't surprised when he was able to beat her matching their right arms. She put up a stubborn fight, but it was little more than stalling on her part. When they matched their left arms, they wound up in a straining deadlock. The advantage shifted between them until her endurance slowly won out over his brute strength. Scott growled something under his breath and took a walk around the pool table, shaking out his arms at his sides.

"What's the matter? Don't like losing to a girl?" Angie teased, too proud of herself to feign humility.

"Don't like losing, period." He laughed, eyes narrowed in challenge.

At Scott's insistence, the arm wrestling continued until they were both exhausted. Angie called for a pause, and they both flopped down onto the couch, still bickering amiably about whether or not the need for a break meant she was conceding defeat. Scott nudged her shoulder with his in lethargic provocation, and she nudged back.

They went back and forth like this until they were both reduced to inane snickering. It was late, and they were officially punchy.

"You're pretty tough, you know. For a girl." Scott smirked as he spoke, closing his eyes and resting his head back.

"Thanks. I think." Angie chuckled, allowing her eyes to drift closed for a long moment as silence stretched between them. She listened to his steady breathing, along with the gradual slowing of her own heart rate. It helped her tune out the muffled sound of traffic coming from far below the apartment windows. Her mind drifted in a gathering haze, and she knew she was close to dozing off. She also knew she ought to shoo Scott out so they could both get some sleep.

She turned her face toward him to address the issue and her lips brushed along some soft, warm part of his face. Until that moment, she hadn't realized how close they were.

And then, somehow, they were kissing.

Angie felt a dull sense of astonishment, mingled with confusion over which of them had started it. Had it been her? She didn't know. She was acutely aware of him, yet she couldn't focus to form a coherent thought. They shifted toward each other, lips moving together with an almost involuntary ease. Languid and dreamlike, the expression between them seemed to have a will of its own. Having lost her perception of time, along with her base sense of caution, there was no telling how long the kiss went on before it concluded just as inexplicably as it began.

The moment their eyes opened, they were fixed on each other. Angie saw the storm of uncertainty in Scott's face, dispelling any thought she might have had about him planning this. Her wits came flooding back to the forefront of her mind, accompanied by a large jolt of anxiety. She felt intensely vulnerable — not to mention stupid.

"So…what was that?" Scott murmured.

Oh, like he doesn't know. Get some distance!

Even the sarcastic part of her mind was edging toward panic. She stood up abruptly and headed for the front door. "You should go," she said, attempting a quiet command.

"Sure." Scott got his feet.

He didn't sound sure, but Angie didn't want to look at him. She needed to think, and he had become distracting in more ways than she'd thought possible. After pulling open the door, she stood holding it as he walked out of the apartment. Only when he was in the hallway did she venture to look at his face again. He appeared more dazed than dejected, and some small part of her was grateful for that. "Good night," she said, in as steady a voice as she could manage.

"I'll call up in the morning." Scott squared his shoulders, reestablishing his composure. "Night."

Once he'd left, Angie eased the door closed, locked it, and then rested her forehead against it. She lifted her head and let it drop forward with a light *thud* several times, thinking she might deserve to be smacked in the face quite a bit harder.

Still thrumming with bewilderment, she pulled out the couch bed and dropped onto it. Picking up her journal out of nightly habit, she opened it and stared at a blank page. She waited for words to come to her. After several minutes of futility, it dawned on her that she didn't have enough brain power left to brush her hair, let alone express whatever it was she was feeling.

Sleep on it, something in her advised.

Finally allowing herself to lay her head down, she was immediately swallowed by merciful unconsciousness.

Chapter 13

"So, about what happened last night—" Scott got straight to the point. It was a clear, sunny mid-morning, and they were heading for the nearest subway station. He had obviously been impatient to address the incident from the moment he met Angie at the elevator and they'd ridden down to street level. His fidgety state seemed to have overwhelmed him after less than five minutes of neutral conversation regarding their plans for the day. "Who kissed who first?"

"I don't know." Angie shook her head, less eager to talk about it. She was still dismayed to have woken up with no better idea of what had come over her. From the way Scott spoke, she began to wonder if it was something that had happened to them, rather than something either of them truly intended.

"It was a mistake." She finally met his gaze. "You could end up getting mono because of me."

"It was worth it," Scott said, without missing a beat.

Caught off guard, she looked away.

"You're embarrassed?" he asked, incredulous.

"You're perceptive," Angie said, unable to withhold the dry bite to her tone. She watched his perplexed expression shift to one of blatant amusement.

"Why?" Scott sidestepped to give her shoulder a playful nudge as they walked. "I mean, that couldn't be your first kiss. You're too good at it," he said, sincere in his praise.

Angie tucked her chin, thankful that she wasn't prone to blushing. "No, it wasn't." She locked her gaze on the sidewalk ahead of her, absently counting the cracks in the cement. "That was the second time."

"So, who was the first guy?" Scott asked, his tone guarded.

"Just some guy I went to school with."

"And—?"

"And, what?" she snapped, with more agitation than she'd intended.

"You still got a thing for him?" Scott pressed.

Angie wondered then if it was envy she was detecting in his voice. She might have been flattered, if she hadn't been so flustered over the entire situation. Exasperated, she turned her head to look him straight in the eyes for a drawn out moment. "Scott, I was twelve years old. A guy I thought I liked asked me over to his house after school. He told me he liked me, and then he asked if he could kiss me. I let him."

"Twelve, huh? That's kinda cute." Scott chuckled, his voice regaining a lax quality.

"It was cute—" she agreed, turning her attention back to the sidewalk. "—until he told me to take my shirt off."

"What'd you do?" She could hear the unsettled surprise in his voice.

"I may have been a kid, but I still had -some- sense of self-respect. My mom had enough talks with me by then to make sure of that." Angie's tone evened out and she glanced aside to him. "I told him no, and I left. I never spoke a word to him again. Pretty awkward, considering I had classes with him every year for all of middle school and high school," she said, using a safely vacant tone. "But he managed it without so much as looking at me ever again. Like it never happened...and I didn't exist."

"Wow—that sucks. What a douchebag." Scott scowled. His dark brows knit in earnest. "You know, I'd -never- do something like that."

Angie felt his hand brush and then envelop hers in a loose, reassuring hold. A warm sensation hummed up her arm and settled in her already knotted stomach. "Good. Because I'm a lot more capable of violence now than when I was twelve." She smirked, defaulting to sarcasm in her attempt to conceal nervousness.

"That reminds me—I've got a Kendo class this evening." Scott broke into an easy grin that reached his eyes. "I was just going to skip it while you're here, but then I thought maybe you'd want to sit in on it and see what we do." He released her hand with some reluctance, grasping instead for a hand rail. They had reached a concrete stairwell that broke from the sidewalk and descended into the ground.

Angie followed close at Scott's heels as they moved below street level, relieved by the change in subject. "I'd love to watch, if your Sensei is okay with that. You shouldn't have to miss out on something just because I'm here."

Cool air swallowed them as they approached the base of the steps. The concrete walls of the station were a flat gray, given random color by a medley of signs, posters, and professional advertisements. The mellow, resounding tones of steel drum music echoed through the crowded transit space. Scott used a card to get them through the turnstile gates and onto the platform, where they waited for the next train to arrive. The tiled floor of the station was dingy, but Angie noted it was relatively free from garbage. For whatever reason, she'd expected more trash lying around and even some sign of rodent activity.

I guess I've been watching too much TV, she mused.

Spotting the source of the warbling Caribbean melody, she made her way toward the performer who stood with his back against a squared cement pylon. The tall man's skin was the color of dark roast coffee, which made his broad smile seem all the more luminous in contrast. He tapped away at the set of metal cylinders in front of him, looking immensely pleased with anyone who paused to watch. A tip jar sat on the floor in front of him, and Angie noted the meager handful of coins and small bills occupying the bottom of it. She was beginning to regret her 'no cash' policy.

"These guys are everywhere, just so you know," Scott said, seeming less impressed with the performance.

"Well, it's the first time I've ever seen someone play them in person." Angie shrugged, watching the musician to keep from looking at Scott. He'd come to stand at her left side, hovering close enough for their shoulders to touch. As much as she didn't want to admit it, she liked the nearness. Something about her perception of him had changed in the last eight hours. Was it simple physical attraction? She wasn't sure how to define it. It seemed similar to the nervous pull she'd felt when she was around Zak, yet different somehow. She found this new awareness intriguing, but at the same time, alarming.

What am I feeling, God? Why is this so confusing?

She waited for a thought to hit her; some spark of insight that might help to clear her head. Instead, a squealing roar invaded her mind, drowning out the buoyant trill of the steel drums. A train slowed and pulled up to the platform.

They found a set of open seats in a half-empty car and settled in for the ride. Scott was relatively quiet while he focused on determining their destination. Though Angie was initially relieved to have his attention elsewhere, an inequality between them began to nag at her. She waited for the rumbling of the train to even out before taking a deep breath.

"Fair is fair. Who was your first kiss?" she asked, trying for a casual tone.

Scott pulled his gaze from the map overhead and looked at her. "My ex-girlfriend, Ashley. Three years ago." He answered more quickly than she expected. Bracing his forearms against his knees, he leaned forward in his seat and hung his head. "Just so you know… you're only the second girl I've ever kissed."

Angie considered him for a few moments. "How long were you and your ex together?" she asked. As often as they'd talked, it had never occurred to her to pry into a subject this personal. Now that she was considering him in a different light, she felt somehow entitled.

"Over a year," Scott answered in a bland voice. "But most of that it wasn't serious. Not til' the last few months. Mostly, I think she just liked it that her dad hated me. He couldn't stand it that my hair was longer than hers." Scott smirked to himself and smoothed a hand back over his well-subdued locks.

"Is that why you broke up?"

"No. She broke it off because I…turned her down." His gaze shifted side to side, as though he were concerned someone might overhear.

"Turned her down, how?"

"You know what I mean." Scott sighed in aggravation. "She just kinda threw herself at me one day. I don't know if she was trying to get back at her dad for something, or what. It just didn't seem…right." He looked down again, almost guiltily. "I told her that. She got real mean all of a sudden, and then it -really- didn't seem right." Scott grimaced in recollection before venturing an uncertain glance at Angie. "And that was pretty much it. We were done."

"That's impressive." Angie commended him with a smile. "I don't think most guys would have had enough willpower to do that."

Scott cast a dubious look her way. "Yeah? Try telling that to Yosh and them. They never let me live it down."

Angie shook her head. "Why do you care what they think? Those guys didn't strike me as poster children for good judgment." When he didn't answer, she prodded him in the side with her elbow. "What, now -you're- embarrassed?"

"Ya think?"

She stared at him expectantly.

He made a guttural sound of frustration and eased back in his seat, folding his arms tight to his chest. "Look, it's different for guys. We're not supposed to say 'no.'"

"Right. Men are supposed to be easy." Angie rolled her eyes. "So, then what made you buck the social norm?" When Scott responded with a glazed expression, she rephrased. "Something must have given you a reason to say no. What was going through your head?"

Scott mulled her question over, absently toeing at an abandoned newspaper on the vibrating floor of the train. "A couple of things, I guess. I'd just started taking Kendo classes, and my Sensei kept going on about having discipline and honor, and not just while we were in the Dojo—" he began, seeming lost in thought. "And then, my mom had always told me when I met the right girl, I'd know. She said I should wait until I was sure it was forever. When I looked at Ashley, I wasn't sure."

"Well, I'm proud of you." Angie had expected him to credit his choice to simple fear, but his answer turned out to be far more complex and interesting. "Whoever the 'right girl' is, you did her a favor. Trust me." *If it were me, I'd be grateful*, she thought, though she kept herself from vocalizing that part.

Another thought sprang up in her mind, demanding to be analyzed.

What if I'm the right girl?

She glanced over at Scott and caught his enigmatic stare.

"Thanks," he said. In that moment he regarded her with such intensity, it caused her stomach to seize. Had the same thought occurred to him?

Angie forced herself to shrug and bounced her gaze to an empty seat across from them, pretending to be interested in a wad of chewing gum that had been left on the back of the seat. The logical part of her mind tallied Scott's positive attributes. His scorecard was compelling, but that didn't silence any of the practical arguments against him. All of this swirled together in her head until one aggravating question remained: *What the heck is wrong with me?*

The train lurched as the brakes ground somewhere under the floor, yanking her back into the reality of her surroundings. Scott flashed a quick smile her way and stood, then grabbed a metal support pole and slung his backpack over one shoulder.

Relieved that the strange tension between them had evaporated, Angie latched onto a hand-strap above her and waited for the doors to open.

~ ~ ~ ~ ~ ~ ~

Their first stop was the architecturally elaborate Grand Central Terminal, where they grabbed an early lunch. From there, they moved on to the Empire State Building.

After a long ride in a stuffy elevator, they were deposited onto the observation deck on the 86th floor. Angie took advantage of the 360-degree vista and snapped pictures from each corner of the building. After she'd captured a shot of the arching crown and spire of the Chrysler Building, Scott extended a hand through the bars to point out a skyscraper to the right of it. Up until this point, he'd seemed patiently disinterested in the landmark, which he'd no doubt visited many times before.

"That's where my dad works," he said, tone tinged with reservation.

Angie acknowledged with a polite nod, deciding she didn't want to seem too interested.

It still seems so surreal.

Just as Scott promised, they came across a half dozen more steel drum players as they traveled. Self-employed entertainers were plentiful. By the time they boarded a ferry for Liberty and Ellis Island, Angie had also seen two guitar players and a one-armed man who played the fiddle while holding it with his feet.

When they left the ferry station an hour later, they made their way north on foot. In this part of the city, it was the sidewalk artists that commanded Angie's attention. Their mediums and styles varied widely, but there was a consistent and haunting theme appearing in the majority of their pieces. She found it vaguely unsettling that this theme was also their next destination — Ground Zero.

There was no blatant indication that they were close to the former site of the Twin Towers, and so it came as a surprise when the tranquil blue of the sky seemed to gain sudden domination ahead of them. Of course, the sky had always been there. It's appearance was striking simply because of what -wasn't- there. In this area so crowded with immense buildings, the yawning gap they approached was equally imposing.

They paused at a street corner on the eastern side. Angie was immediately unsettled by the sense that she was standing at the bottom of a man-made canyon. The surrounding buildings varied in height; their dull, windowless faces fitted with expansive lengths of what looked like orange mesh. Recalling that several of these buildings had been damaged beyond repair and would eventually be torn down, she supposed the netting was meant to catch any debris that might break off from the structure and threaten the streets below.

At a distance, she noted a chain-link fence stretched to encompass the rectangular length of the massive rift. A chorus of low rumbles and metallic groans filled the air — the off-key song of heavy construction equipment.

When Scott crossed the street and came alongside the fence, Angie tagged along close behind him. As distracted as she was with her surroundings, she was careful not to lose track of him. Passersby walked more slowly on this side of the street, many of them pausing to stare. She stopped when Scott did and they both pressed close to the barrier, straining for an unobstructed view of the enormous cavity plunging five stories below the level of the sidewalk.

The heaping mounds of jagged debris she'd seen on television had been cleared away, leaving an excavation site laden with tan dirt and segmented along the edges by strips of concrete. Bulldozers, backhoes, and cranes of all sizes went about their business below them, directed by a small army of workers wearing white hard hats.

In her mind's eye she tried to picture the Twin Towers in that place; how looming and majestic they must have been up close. The image she conjured was marred by the mental replay she'd seen again and again from different camera angles; visions of fire, smoke, and panic.

She remembered everything about the day the towers fell. Halfway across the country, she'd been sitting in her morning art class at the University when she first heard of the attack. The radio had been left on in the back of the room, as it always was for the sake of ambient background music. That day there was no music. She recalled being bemused by the tone of the newscaster's voice as the live report was given. At first, Angie had dared to hope what she was hearing was some sort of a radio play — perhaps someone's slightly more feasible version of *War of the Worlds*. She remembered the bewildered faces of her mute classmates, and not wanting to be the one to voice the obvious question.

To answer it for herself she sprinted down two flights of stairs to the lobby, where she knew she would find the nearest wall-mounted television. What she also found were dozens of other students, all standing eerily still as they stared up at history unfolding. She had known then that it was real.

In a daze of uncertainty, Angie had returned to her class and distracted herself by working on a black and white abstract piece. A dark amalgamation of ink, pastels, and charcoal took shape while the radio repeated the same basic information — the Towers were burning; people were trapped. It became an ominous droning in the back of her mind.

She wasn't sure how much time passed before the report suddenly changed, announcing the south tower had collapsed. If not for the fact that all of her remaining classmates had looked up in disbelieving unison, she would have assumed she'd misheard. Until that moment, it had never occurred to her that such mighty buildings could fall.

The echo of the emotions from that day came rolling back over her in slow waves. Angie clenched her stomach to regain control, drawing her camera out of her pocket to provide herself with both diversion and documentation. Holding the lens up to the center of one of the diamond-shaped openings in the chain-link, she snapped a picture. Scott motioned to her when she finally glanced to her left again. He seemed to have a destination in mind, and she was in no mental state to argue.

They moved south along the fence. As they rounded the corner to the right, Scott paused, gesturing to something with his chin. Set on a tapered cement pedestal, overlooking the remnants of Ground Zero, stood a rusted metal cross.

From what Angie could see, the slightly warped T-beam had writing scrawled on it in various places, though it was too far away for her to make out the lettering. She wasn't sure if the artifact was something the excavation workers had fashioned, or if it had been discovered in that precise shape. Regardless, the sight of it was soothing to her amid the semi-apocalyptic surroundings. She exchanged a significant look with Scott before he nodded and they continued on into the shadowed south side.

Concrete barriers directed them away from the fence to the other side of the street, creating an opening for construction workers to come and go. It didn't take long before they reached the southwest corner, where a large white banner was tacked to the slatted wood side of a staging building. Signed by The Port Authority, New York and New Jersey Police, it read:

Thank You America
For Your Prayers and Support For
All Those Lost And Their Families

The banner also signaled the end of what the public could view. Angie turned to retrace their steps, but Scott tapped her shoulder to redirect her attention. A handful of somber onlookers walked past into what looked like an outdoor hallway, formed against the base of the building behind them. Angie followed him behind the plywood wall, supposing the poorly-lit space was a crowd control measure meant to funnel them back to the nearest open street. As it turned out, it was much more than that.

She sucked in a deep breath as they entered.

The red painted wall of the building was barely visible under a tight layering of mementos. She recognized the uniform patches of every form of rescue worker, interspersed with department T-shirts that had been folded to display their message without consuming precious space: Houston Police; San Francisco Fire Department; Denver Police Department — every major city seemed to be represented. Crowded in among all of this were small American flags, photographs, hand written notes, and colorful drawings left by children. Sawhorses ran the length of the hall, draped with signature-covered T-shirts. Fresh bouquets of flowers lined the base of the wall.

This place was a memorial — a beautiful and heartbreaking American mosaic. Angie wanted to inspect every inch of it, but reasoned it could take her days to do it justice. She swallowed to ease the tightening sensation in her throat and then stepped back to take several pictures. If they turned out, she would study them later.

Stepping closer to the wall again, she suddenly wished she had something of herself to leave behind. She had come to pay her respects, but now understood she would be leaving with more than she could possibly give. Angie stared down at a loose bunch of white daisies someone had leaned against the leg of a sawhorse.

I'm sorry.

Something about the sawhorse itself drew her attention. She reached out and touched the uncovered end of the suspended two-by-four, grazing her fingertip along the smooth surface of the wood. Her finger cut a line through a thick blanketing of dust.

For dust you are and to dust you will return.

For the first time in her life, the concept took on a very real meaning. Hundreds of the casualties from the attack had been almost instantly cremated in the ensuing moments after each plane collided. In this place, the powder of crushed cement was indistinguishable from the remnants of human beings. Innocent victims and terrorists alike; their corporeal essence had been scattered by the wind. For a fleeting moment, she thought she could fully grasp the magnitude of the loss.

Startled by a harsh choking sound, Angie took a step backward. She began to look around, though she was dimly aware that she couldn't command her eyes to focus. The sensation of tears flowing down her face didn't register until they were dropping onto her collarbone. It was then she caught up to the fact that the sound had come from her own throat. Somewhere inside of her, a dam broke.

Overwhelmed, she turned around to heed the instinctive desire to flee from her own emotions. Instead, she collided with someone's chest. Strong arms locked around her, and she heard Scott's voice low in her ear.

"It's okay... it's okay."

Angie didn't know if he was telling her that it was okay to cry, or pleading with her to stop. In truth, it didn't matter. She was sobbing uncontrollably, and there was nothing to do but allow it to run its course. Distantly, she wondered how strange it was to grieve for people she'd never met. People died every day — many people. Intellectually she knew this, but the thought had always seemed mercifully illusive, hovering only at the fringe of her mind. She had wanted 9/11 to be real to her, and now it was. More real than her heart could bear.

However embarrassed she was over the gut-wrenching intensity of her reaction, she was glad Scott was with her. She didn't know how long he stood there letting the wet spot on his shirt grow before he finally led her away. Despite her condition, she did note that Scott never commented on the display, or seemed put-off by it. He even allowed reflective quietness between them for the remainder of their return trip. For all of those things, she was grateful.

June 25th,

Today was a long day of sightseeing. The Empire State Building was an interesting experience. When nobody was looking, I fulfilled my dream of spitting over the edge of it. (I know, I know, I'm as uncivilized as I am unsanitary.) I didn't really think about the people on the sidewalk below until we came back down to ground level and joined them. Maybe spittle evaporates before it ever reaches the bottom? I have no proof of this, but I can hope.

Lady Liberty was actually a lot smaller than I was expecting. She was also closed to the public, so I didn't get to climb up into the torch. That part was a little disappointing.

After that, we visited Ground Zero. It was so weird to see that gaping hole. It struck a hollow note in my soul to see it in person at last, even nine months after the fact. I was fine until we passed a memorial to all of the fallen police and firemen. I just couldn't handle that. I guess there's some part of me that's always going to believe that heroes shouldn't die.

I'm sitting on the sidelines now, watching Scott's Kendo practice. I've been here for an hour already. Their routines are pretty brutal, and since there's no air-conditioning, they have to circulate the air with floor fans. On top of that, they all have to wear helmets and padding. It's starting to smell pretty rank in here. At least I'm getting a chance to get my head together.

Yesterday was a rest day for me. We stayed inside mostly, playing video games and talking. Somehow though...and I'm not sure why...but, Scott and I ended up kissing. I suppose with the close proximity he's been keeping, I should have seen this coming. I'm really confused with myself right now. At least Scott seems almost as confused as I am. Obviously, there's some sort of attraction between us. I really like him, but I have a lot of doubts.

I don't really know what to do yet, but I'm going to discourage this...if only because I don't want to screw up our friendship. It's even more confusing now that I realize I also found Zak attractive on different levels. But then, what about Don? Am I really this much of a fickle idiot? I'm badly in need of some wisdom and direction here. There must be something seriously messed up in my head.

~Ang

~ ~ ~ ~ ~ ~ ~

After a much needed shower, Scott showed up at the guest apartment and the two of them wound down from the day by watching a movie. Angie picked out a comedy, which served its purpose in lightening the mood without demanding any real depth of thought. Once the credits began to scroll, she felt far enough removed from the events of the day to express herself.

"Thanks for giving me the tour." She looked aside to Scott and smiled. "And...sorry I got so emotional."

"Hey, it was a good reason to get emotional." Scott returned her smile with a lazier version of his own. "It's not like I thought you were invincible or something." He peeled himself up out of his sprawling recline against the couch, sitting up straight beside her. "People handle big stuff like that differently, right? I know when it first happened, I wanted to quit school and go back to D.C. to be with my mom—in case something worse happened."

Angie nodded in understanding.

"When I got over that, I was just pissed off. I wanted to hunt down Osama bin Laden myself." He snorted, his way of acknowledging just how irrational the idea sounded.

"I felt like I should have been here to help," Angie said. "I seriously thought about joining the National Guard, but my dad wanted me to wait until after I finished college. I'm still thinking about signing on for some branch of the military, if I can't figure out what I want to do after I get my Associate's degree this fall."

Scott's face shifted into an ardent frown. "Come on, you don't wanna do that. People who can't make it in college join the military — not somebody like you."

Angie flashed him a sharp glare. "Who told you that? My dad was in the military." She saw the immediate regret on his face, but drove her point in further. "I've got friends back home that are joining up, and I promise, all of them could handle college. They just wanted to -do- something instead of sitting around talking about it."

Scott backpedaled, throwing up his hands in surrender. "I didn't mean it like it sounded! I just don't like the idea of you doing something that dangerous, okay?" He gave a heavy sigh. "I'd worry about you."

Angie folded her arms, trying to maintain a look of irritation she no longer felt. His voice, strained with sincerity, had defused her temper. After all, this wasn't the first time she'd known him to open his mouth and insert his foot. "I can take care of myself," she said, quieting her tone. "Besides, I'd probably end up in one of the less hazardous branches, like the Air Force. My interview with the Army recruiter was kind of a letdown."

"You already talked to a recruiter?"

"A few months back." Angie nodded, a faint smirk forming on her face. "He told me tanks are considered front-line, so they don't let women drive them."

A slow grin spread across Scott's face. "Too bad. You would've made a kick-ass tank girl."

"Yeah, I know." She laughed.

Scott's expression sobered. "Seriously, if I get a vote at all—" He reached out to brush her hair back from her cheek, leaving his palm to linger against it. "Stay. Find something else you want."

Doubting he referred solely to her career path, Angie averted her gaze. An unnerving heat crept up through her neck to fill her face. "We'll see. I haven't decided anything yet." She fought for what remained of her composure as she spoke. It seemed strange now that she had been mad at him just a moment ago. Even stranger that she had no desire to pull away from his touch.

Angie sensed his weight shift and knew what was about to happen. Though she remembered her determination to dissuade him, she felt sure an immediate rejection would cause him needless pain. *Just keep it short*, she told herself.

But then their lips met, and all cohesive thought ceased.

His mouth was warm, moving over hers with a persuasive sureness. Angie responded without effort, engulfed in a pleasant sense of drifting that bordered on dizziness. Her instincts seemed to fill the void her brain left behind. She was only distantly aware it felt different this time — that there was something to this contact more powerful than affection. The potency of it was elating, and at the same time, terrifying. It went on much longer than she'd intended before she managed to pull herself back. Even then, he tried to follow, and she had to lift a hand between them to enforce the pause.

Once again, her wits came rushing back to their abandoned post. Reminded there was prudence in putting more distance between them, she turned off the brewing internal debate over whether that was what she actually wanted. She barely recognized her own muted voice when it came out, "I think you should—"

"—go?" Scott asked. His tone was questioning, but his eyes were resigned.

"Yeah." She gave him a small smile and looked down, embarrassed.

"Right."

Angie didn't follow when he got up and made his way to the door. She wasn't at all confident in how stable she would be on her feet. Besides that, she didn't want to risk an encore good-night kiss in the doorway. "Hey, Scott?" she called out when she heard his hand on the doorknob. She twisted in place and looked over her shoulder at him.

He stopped and turned, a half-smile forming on his face. "Hey, what?"

"Don't like me too much," she said, earnestly. "I don't know what I want, but I know I don't want to hurt you."

Scott worked his jaw in thought. He looked like he wanted to say something, but then decided against it. "See you tomorrow." He pulled the door open, stepped out, and was gone.

Angie released a pent-up sigh and wilted forward, draping her upper body over the arm of the couch. Her arms dangled to the floor, and all she could see was the repetitive texture of the soft, beige fabric.

This -can't- be a good idea. ...can it?

She was in over her head — that much she wasn't confused about. Her mother had once told her that women tended to shoulder the bulk of the responsibility in controlling the boundaries of a physical relationship.

If that was true, then she could be in serious trouble.

Chapter 14

"I can't believe you read that entire book." Scott grumbled as they departed Barnes & Noble, plunging headlong into the broiling heat of the day.

"It was just a graphic novel." Angie cut her eyes his way, struggling to keep up with him. "And it only took me an hour. Usually when I loiter at a book store, I'll stay four or five hours and polish off an actual novel."

"Great, so you're a bookworm. That's adorable." His tone started off sardonic, but it eased by the end. "Don't you know how to have any real fun?"

"To me, that -is- real fun," Angie said, her annoyance with him mounting.

Scott hadn't been exceptionally patient with their day thus far. Adding to her frustration, there was a strange tension between them that seemed exacerbated by the unforgiving weather. They'd left early in the morning to stand in line for half-price Broadway tickets, only to learn after an hour's wait that *The Lion King* was sold out. He'd made a point to take her by the book store on their way back, but was antsy the entire time they perused the enormous building. While she'd sat in a window and read, he'd paced the store, various magazines holding his interest for only minutes at a time. It was the most significant disparity between them she'd noticed thus far — her idea of paradise seemed to be his idea of purgatory.

That doesn't bode well.

"See, you're tame," he said. "You've even got this road trip thing all planned out like a class schedule, right?"

Angie looked straight ahead without answering. *Well it's not like much has been going according to plan. You included.*

Likely taking her silence for anger, Scott's tone reverted to something more concerned. "I'm just saying, if you're gonna go out and find yourself or whatever, you should try being a little impulsive." His pace slowed, his restlessness sapped by the weighty humidity.

"I get it, I'm boring." She sighed. "I'm working on that." Remembering the study Bible she'd bought, she slid the straps of the plastic bag into her palm and thrust it out toward him in offering. "This is for you."

He accepted the bag from her with obvious skepticism."You got me a book?"

"Okay, so I'll work on being less boring tomorrow."

Scott's dark brows knit as he peered inside the bag. "Oh." His demeanor seemed to soften as he cast her a more sedate look. "Thanks."

He remained silent for several minutes, seeming lost in his own contemplations as he deftly navigated them through bustling crowds and harrowing crosswalks. Angie stuck close beside him, glad for his improved mood. She didn't promote any further conversation, afraid they might revert to the inane bickering they seemed to keep falling into.

Before she could catch herself, she'd begun reading aloud from a sign she saw up ahead. "Free Personality Testing! No Obligation." The white A-frame sign stood in front of a nondescript storefront.

Scott overheard and glanced her way. "What, they test to see if you have a personality?"

"I don't think it's pass or fail." She cracked a smile. "Have you ever taken one?"

"Nope." Scott shook his head. "I don't take any more tests than I have to."

"You should sometime—they're fun." She scanned the darkened windows of the storefront. "It helps to get to know yourself and why you react to things the way you do."

"There's gotta be a catch to this, though." Scott slowed as they reached the sign, giving it further scrutiny.

"Yeah, there usually is—" Angie said, only to be interrupted by a petite woman in a pale blue business suit.

"Oh no, no catch!" Her voice was high and breezy as she stepped from beside the sign to address them, offering a pamphlet from the small stack she carried. "This is a free service for the betterment of the community." Angie guessed the woman to be in her mid-twenties, graced with thin, flawless features and crowned by a halo of rich brown curls. A bar nametag on her suit jacket read 'Debbie.'

Scott accepted the pamphlet and scanned over it.

Angie took one as well, curiosity trumping her wariness. "So, what form of personality test is this based on...Myers-Briggs? Hippocrates' four temperaments—?" When she glanced up, the woman had a bemused look on her face.

Scott smirked. "Don't worry about it. She just reads a lot." He tipped his head toward Angie.

"I'm not really sure, actually," Debbie confessed. "I'm not familiar with other tests. But, I know it's very accurate—there are over a hundred questions," she added with renewed enthusiasm. "They're just about to start another session, if you'd like to come in. I'm sure one of our analysts can answer any questions you might have." She pulled open the door and a rush of refrigerated air enveloped them.

Angie felt herself sway toward the promise of relief. She looked to Scott, catching his uncertain gaze. "So, how about being impulsive?" With a mischievous smile, she motioned toward the open door.

Scott's confident smirk returned to meet her challenge. He moved inside the building, catching Angie's hand as he passed to pull her along with him.

Inside, the front room offered little to look at. Sterile white walls rose up from blue, low pile carpeting. No company name was visible.

A set of long tables took up most of the room, surrounded by folding chairs. A balding, older man sat in one of the chairs, one elbow propped on the table in a listless pose. To the left the room was sectioned into several small offices and a hallway.

It was from the hallway that a tall, square-jawed man in his early thirties appeared, and introduced himself as Gerald. Like the woman out front, he had a professional air about him that coincided with his crisp slacks, tie, and dress shirt ensemble. While his pale eyes sparkled with charisma and his demeanor was welcoming, Angie felt uneasy with him. It had something to do with his smile, she decided. Combined with his rigid good looks, his smile seemed phony and plastic. He reminded her of a life-size Ken doll.

Gerald explained that they would be shown a short video, and then led them down a narrow hall to a viewing room with a projector screen and seating for roughly two dozen people. As they sat in the back and awaited the video, Angie felt the seed of unease grow into anxiety.

"Do you see any other way out of this room?" she whispered aside to Scott .

Scott's eyes narrowed as he gave the room a slow sweep. "Nope. Just the way we came in." His brow furrowed. "What's that mean?"

"Aside from this being a death trap if there happened to be a fire? I'm not sure." Angie pondered the prickling sense of caution that refused to resolve. "Just remember, we're not buying anything. And if anybody offers you Kool-Aid, don't drink it." She expected him to tease her about being paranoid. Instead he remained quiet, arms folded across his chest as he began to regularly glance back at the door.

The video began abruptly, and both of them jumped in their seats. They looked at each other then and chuckled nervously. Scott amused himself by mocking the old man who began the narration, and later the dated hair styles and clothing of the people featured. The only other person in the room with them was the bald man, who sat at the front and dozed off early on.

Angie strained to pay attention over Scott's covert heckling, but she wasn't able to discern the point of the video. They were definitely selling something — that much was clear. She didn't recognize anything regarding personality traits or types, only nebulous concepts about negative thoughts and insecurities. The assertions seemed as broadly applicable as the message in a fortune cookie. By the end of the showing, she was regretting their little detour.

Gerald returned and herded them back to the front room, where they sat down at the tables for testing. There were a lot of questions. Initially, Angie thought that might be a good thing. But as she went through it she found many of them to be vague. Scott finished before she did, which seemed to please him. Gerald took their tests to an office, then returned to show them graphs representing their results.

"Very interesting," Gerald said, laying out papers before them. "As you can see, you two scored similarly in most areas."

Angie's gaze flickered to Scott, though her surprise dissipated quickly. *That probably explains why we get on each other's nerves.*

Gerald leaned in between them as he gestured to the spiking lines on each of their graphs. "Abnormally high scores in aggression and drive—unusually low in self-esteem. You've got a few things within normal boundaries, at least. Don't worry too much about the negative scores—our training program can help with that."

Ah, Angie thought. *The catch.*

They listened as Gerald dissected their results in an authoritative tone. He stressed all of the scores that were 'abnormal,' taking on an air of deep concern. The impression she received was clear: 'You are fatally flawed.' That much Angie could believe. It was his continual emphasis on their 'program' being the answer that made her suspicious. When she finally cut to the quick and asked about the cost involved, Gerald mentioned something about a preliminary two hundred dollars and promised to be right back with a schedule and payment plan. She waited until he'd gone into one of the tiny offices before snapping her attention to Scott.

She looked from him to the door and back, voice lowered with urgency. "Run for it."

Scott's brows quirked in surprise, but the instruction was all it took to get him on his feet. They split up, darting around opposite ends of the table before breaking into a sprint. Angie hit the door first, putting her weight behind her shoulder to throw it open. Together they bolted down the broad sidewalk, spurred on when they heard Debbie calling after them. Scott grabbed Angie's hand and took the lead, running for three blocks before their overly dramatic escape ended in heaving, breathless laughter.

"That was crazy." Scott grinned rakishly, leaning back against the stone face of the nearest building. "According to them, we're pretty messed up, huh?"

"According to them, we're a plague upon humanity." Angie struggled to straighten up, more from mirth than from exertion. "If we're so defective, you'd think they could have at least offered to 'fix' us for free." She was very aware that he was still holding her hand, but she didn't want to withdraw it and risk hurting his feelings.

That's not the only reason. She had to admit, it felt good.

"Anything else you want to try out on our way home?" Scott asked, pushing off from the wall to resume their progress.

Angie found her thought process slowed with preoccupation over having his fingers laced with hers. In spite of this, she managed to keep her tone casual. "I want to try some authentic New York Cheesecake, if you know someplace that sells it. "

"They sell that everywhere," Scott chuckled. "But, we should save it for tomorrow. My dad and stepmom wanted us to go to dinner with them tonight."

"Is it a fancy place?" she asked, concealing her concern.

"It's French." He shrugged. "We go there a lot. I don't think there's a dress code or anything."

"Well if they let you in, then I know they'll let me in," she teased.

Scott just grinned.

~ ~ ~ ~ ~ ~ ~

After changing into the nicest clothes she had with her, which amounted to a knee-length denim skirt with a violet wrap blouse, Angie met her host family in the lobby and together they took a taxi to *Jubilee*. The modern French restaurant embodied refinement, from the fastidious décor and stiffly-postured waiters to the menu prices that made her cringe. She felt a keen sense of guilt over realizing the cost of one meal should have easily been enough to feed her for a week. But Scott's father was insistent that she order something she'd never had before, and she wanted to be a gracious guest.

"I've never had escargot," she said finally, setting her finger over its description on the menu.

Scott groomed his wild, unbound hair behind his shoulders with one hand, revealing the blatant disgust on his face. "Snail? That's an -insect-, you know."

Angie barely refrained from rolling her eyes and volunteering her biology scores. She'd gathered that he was wearing his hair down in an effort to annoy his father in public, and she didn't want to encourage his contrary mood.

Martha spoke up in a concerned voice, "That's brave of you, but are you sure? The duck and pheasant are both very good."

"I've actually had both of those before. We have a few hunters in my family," Angie said. "Although, I'm sure the experience is more enjoyable when you don't have to mind every bite to keep from breaking a tooth on a BB—"

Scott's father broke into a rumbling belly laugh that drew the attention of a few nearby tables. Once he'd collected himself, it became apparent that he'd found her candor endearing as well as amusing. He asked what type of game Angie thought was the most exotic, and she thought for a moment before explaining her mother's recipe for barbecued squirrel. That was enough to elicit murmurs of fascination out of both Martha and Shaun. Scott feigned a look of nausea, which she decidedly ignored.

Once their orders had been taken, Scott's father beckoned a waiter to him and requested white wine for everyone at the table. Angie shifted in discomfort when the man came by to fill her glass, waiting until he came to Shaun and began a light conversation about the quality of the wine before she leaned aside to Scott.

"Does your dad know how old I am?" she whispered.

"Relax. They always have wine with dinner," Scott muttered, sounding irked. "Seriously, take a break from the goody-goody thing."

Angie resisted glowering at him as she straightened up in her chair. *He probably thinks I've never even smelled alcohol.*

While drinking wasn't a pastime her immediate family had ever taken an interest in, it wasn't something she was oblivious to. Alcohol had often been blamed for her grandfather's meanness and her uncle's ailing liver. She knew full well that too much of it made sensible people stupid and stupid people dangerous.

No big deal. Just don't overdo it.

Picking up the glass of pale-gold liquid, she brought it to her lips. She expected it to be bitter, like the Chardonnay her mother occasionally sipped to soothe back spasms after a long day, but this wine was smooth and sweet. She was glad — that would make it easier to avoid being rude.

Shaun turned his full attention to Angie once the waiter had moved on. "What destinations do you have coming up next on your trip?" he asked, admiration for her venture carrying thick in his voice.

"One day in Lancaster, Pennsylvania; then all the way down to Georgia for two weeks near Atlanta; five days near Miami; and then maybe a few days somewhere near Birmingham, Alabama." She paused, reviewing the map in her mind. "I'm not really sure after that. I had to cut out a stop in Arkansas, so I don't know what way I'll head home yet."

"You know, Scott will be staying with his mother in D.C. for the rest of the summer," Shaun said, glancing to his son with a questioning look. "If you have any interest in seeing the Capitol, you might want to think about coming back that way."

Seeming caught unawares, Scott sat up at attention. "Yeah, I mean, that could work. I can check with mom."

It had to be the first time Angie had seen him agree with his father with any degree of enthusiasm. "That might be a good option. I'd love to see Washington D.C. in person," she said, smiling in appreciation.

The food arrived, diverting the discussion while everyone tended to their meal. Angie's dish was served on a circular plate with a dozen half-sphere hollows, which had been filled with a steaming mixture of butter, garlic, and herbs. The escargot wallowed within each depression, requiring her to use a pronged utensil to spear the morsels. Once she was sure everyone else had started eating, she popped one of the shapeless bits into her mouth and chewed before she could deliberate on its origins. The piece was rubbery, but void of the sliminess she'd braced for. The flavor itself was unremarkable, as the meat had taken on the essence of the butter and garlic.

Martha went into fond detail about each of the proposal attempts Shaun had made before convincing her to become his fifth wife.

"I made him propose once for every previous wife," she joked, giving Scott's father a good-humored smile. Scott sat by impassive, appearing bored with the story he'd no doubt heard many times.

In spite of her initial concern over the evening, Angie felt confident it had been a success by the end. But as they all got up to leave, she felt the floor of the restaurant suddenly tilt. She grabbed the back of her chair to steady herself, glancing around to see if anyone else had noticed the phenomenon. Scott's father and stepmother were busy chatting, unaware of her misstep.

Scott did notice, however. Eyeing her, he sidestepped closer and touched her arm. "You okay?"

"I think I ate too much," Angie lied, rummaging through her memory for the number of times her wine glass had been refilled. Twice? She hadn't paid it much attention, presuming the food would absorb the alcohol. She had felt perfectly normal while she was seated. But now that she was standing, her head swam and her balance was questionable.

You idiot, she chided herself.

Arm in arm, Shaun and Martha headed out the front door. Angie poured all of her concentration into her footing as she turned to follow the couple out, aware that Scott was still watching her. *You're fine. Just make it to the taxi.* She wobbled slightly at the threshold but covered it by placing a hand on the door frame. Stepping out onto the sidewalk, she was just in time to be struck with dread as Scott's stepmother made a suggestion.

"It's such a gorgeous evening, why don't we walk back?" Martha gave Shaun's doughy midsection a playful poke. "Some of us could use a little exercise."

Angie stifled a whimper, seeing no clear way to keep from humiliating herself. When they set off at a strolling pace she kept far to the right, praying she wouldn't trip. The cement felt wrong under her feet, more like sifting sand than a solid surface. Scott noticed her irregular gait and slipped his arm around hers. She was as grateful not to have to ask for the assistance as she was to have a stable anchor.

"Are you...tipsy?" Scott leaned aside, whispering in disbelief.

"No!" she hissed. Revising her assessment, she frowned. "Maybe."

"Just take it easy," he said, crooking his elbow in a genteel motion.

Angie secured herself to his arm and allowed him to escort her along. Part of her expected Scott to deride her lack of discretion, but to her relief, he seemed more concerned than amused. They fell in line behind Shaun and Martha, pausing at storefronts as the older couple window-shopped. The night air was thick with humidity, though the temperature had eased and a light breeze carried through the streets. By the time they arrived back at the high-rise Angie had regained her poise, along with some of her dignity.

"Can I come in for a while?" Scott asked, leaning his shoulder into the wall as he watched Angie unlock the door to the guest apartment.

"I don't think that's a good idea," she answered, palming the knob and pushing the door open a crack. In her mind, she'd made enough questionable decisions for one day.

Scott folded his arms, looking offended. "Look, I know I'm not the greatest influence—"

"I'm not blaming you for anything," she said, sifting through her thoughts. She'd been trying to weigh her feelings ever since things between them became complicated. "I just think we need to be more careful and not spend so much time...alone."

"Don't trust me?" His expression transitioned into something more wounded.

"Right now, I don't trust -me-," Angie stressed. She averted her gaze for a long moment. "When we get too close, it's like my brain switches off."

"Is that such a bad thing? You do kinda think too much." Scott's tone came out genial, though his smile bordered on smug. She hated how handsome it made him look.

"It could be—" Angie began.

Her breath caught when he stepped up to her, his face inclined mere inches from hers. Though he had completely invaded her personal space, it didn't occur to her to take a step back.

Seeming to interpret her lack of retreat as an invitation, Scott closed the remaining gap between them. His lips captured hers in a swift, sure movement. At once, she understood the friction that had grated between them throughout the day. Her palms lifted to his chest to push him away, but before she knew it, she'd forgotten why she placed them there.

Independent of her intentions, her lips followed his lead. Some remote part of her mind registered the faint, acrimonious taste of cigarette smoke. Just as she'd gathered herself enough to create a pause, the kiss deepened. He pulled her tighter against him. Though there were no hands where they shouldn't be, the demand she sensed was more dizzying than the wine.

Somewhere down the hallway a door opened and closed as a tenant left their apartment. The sound was enough of a distraction for Angie to recover control and pull away. They stood in unsettled silence for a moment while an elderly woman scuttled past, her footsteps receding to the elevator. Angie groped for some way to transform the lingering tension.

"I thought you were going to quit smoking," she said, deliberately dredging up an old point of contention between them.

Scott shrugged. "I've been trying. Stress makes the cravings worse, ya know." He leveled his gaze on her.

"Sorry," she muttered, looking down toward the elevator to avoid his gaze. "Don't worry, I'll be out of your hair in a few days."

"Yeah, about that—I've been thinking." He raked his fingers back through his espresso mane, clearing a few stray locks from his eyes. "You know, you could just stay here for an extra week or two if you wanted. My dad wouldn't care, I already asked him—"

"No, I need to keep going." She cut him off, gently. "I live over a thousand miles away from you, Scott. It just wouldn't work out. We shouldn't be pretending like we can be more than friends."

"But what if we could be?" Scott spoke with enough earnest emotion to stun her into silence. "If we both wanted it bad enough, we could make it work. I know it'd be hard, but I mean—" His voice lowered and then faltered as he locked eyes with her. "I think...I might be in love with you. And I know you at least feel -something- for me, or you wouldn't kiss me back like that."

Angie shook her head, feeling a deep sense of panic clawing up from her stomach. "No, no you're not. You shouldn't throw that word around." She found herself arguing, voice strained. "I know there's this crazy...pull...between us, and I don't understand it. But I care about you too much to jump into something."

Scott opened his mouth and then closed it, looking confounded by her reaction. "So, you think we should slow down?" he said at last.

"I think we should stop and back up," she clarified. "I don't think we've been thinking straight."

Scott lowered his head, leaning his shoulder into the wall beside her door. "I guess you're right," he agreed, working his jaw side to side.

Angie sighed inwardly as she watched him. *Better to hurt him a little now than a lot later on.* "I need you to do me a favor."

"Anything you want." Scott answered without hesitation, though his voice was glum.

"Could you give me the day to myself tomorrow? I need some time to think."

Scott nodded. "No problem. I guess it wouldn't be a bad idea if I took some time, too."

"Thanks for understanding." She wanted to touch his arm — offer some light and reassuring gesture. But instead, she stepped into the apartment and began to ease the door closed between them. More than anything she wanted clarity. And she knew the more distance there was between them, the clearer her thoughts would be.

"At least now I know it wasn't all one-sided," Scott said, unmoving as he watched her.

She paused, leaving the door cracked several inches. "What wasn't?"

The left corner of his mouth quirked upward. "You—making me crazy." He rocked away from the wall and started down the hall.

"Good night, Scott," Angie murmured after him.

Angeli drifted across the apartment, kicking off her shoes as she went. She pushed her way into the bathroom and surveyed the white marble-topped vanity. Deciding it was sturdy enough, she hopped up to sit with her feet in the sink, curling her arms around her knees as she stared into the mirror at her own serious eyes. Her way of peering into her soul.

She could remember doing this often when she was a small child, finding solace in focusing on her reflection as it appeared against the sheen of her muddled brown irises. The habit had led to the discovery that her eyes would become hazel when she was in a brooding mood. She'd even known them to turn bright green on the occasions she'd been upset enough to have a good cry. Eventually looking up this phenomenon, she'd found it had something to do with stress and blood pressure. She couldn't recall the exact explanation, only that it had eased her concerns at the time.

For the moment, her eyes shown hazel as they stared back at her — and with good reason. This thing with Scott was causing her strain, and she still didn't know how she should feel about him.

Alright, soul. What's your problem?

The logical part of her mind wanted to give a relationship with Scott a chance. After all, he was available, open to faith, chaste, undeniably good-looking, and definitely interested in her. She'd never before come across such a promising combination of attributes. And she never would again, for all she knew. Yet, she couldn't shake the sense that it wasn't enough.

Greedy greedy makes a lonely girl, she mused.

Rubbing at her eyes in weary resignation, Angie cut her introspection short by pivoting and sliding off the vanity. She decided she would catch up on some much needed sleep and make a few phone calls in the morning. One thing she was sure of, at least — tonight wasn't the time to make any important decisions.

Chapter 15

"Here, Martha wanted to make sure you got something to eat," Scott said, thrusting a deli box at Angie as he stepped into the apartment. His gaze shifted restlessly as he edged around her and moved to the pool table, busying himself with chalking the end of a stick.

"That was sweet of her." Angie passed the pool table and moved to sit in the back window sill, while there was still ample sunlight. "I went out and found my own food just fine yesterday, though. I could have managed again." She noted when she neared, Scott stepped back to give her clearance. The distance he was keeping was a stark contrast to the first few days of her visit. So much so that she felt compelled to ask, "Are you mad at me, now?"

Scott's head snapped up as he pulled his attention away from the ball return. "Mad? No. Why would I be?"

Angie shrugged a shoulder, using her lap for a table as she unwrapped a generous club sandwich. "You're acting weird."

"I'm just…tryin' to back off, like you wanted. Tessa should be over in a few minutes to hang out, so we won't be alone. I've told you about her before—"

"Right, the girl from Vermont. Parents divorced last year, and she's living with her lawyer dad who completely ignores her?" She recalled the most immediate information she tied to the name. Scott had often described Tessa as his closest female friend, and a point of concern to him when it came to her partying habits.

He smirked. "That's the one."

"Good. I'd like to meet her."

"Just remember she's a little…different." He hesitated. "Don't say anything about it."

Angie shot him a vexed glare. "Scott, remember Elise has been my best friend for years? I'm good with different." *Takes one to know one.*

"Yeah, okay. I guess you've got a point." Scott tipped his head down in a low chuckle. He had a more stoic expression when he looked her way again. "So, did you get in all the thinking you needed?"

Angie swallowed a bite of sandwich. "Some," she answered tenuously. "I still need to talk to my mom. She wasn't home when I called."

Scott set out the triangular rack and occupied himself with placing six billiard balls into one corner of it. "I called my mom this morning and told her about you," he said. "She's usually pretty good with advice."

Angie looked up in surprise. "What did she say?"

Scott set out the cue ball and eased around the table, delaying his answer as he sized up angles with the pool stick. "She said…I should quit touching you. She thinks that would make it easier on both of us." His voice rang with conflict.

Angie released a burst of relieved laughter before she could catch herself. When Scott looked up at her in confusion, she quickly offered, "I think that's -great- advice. Your mother is obviously a smart woman." Watching him nod in reluctant agreement, she opted to steer the topic. "I'm glad you're close enough to her that you can talk about things like this. I didn't think most guys talk to their moms."

"Well, who else am I gonna talk to?" He finally committed to a forceful break. The balls ricocheted around the table, none finding a pocket.

"I don't know—your stepmom is pretty nice," Angie said, knowing better than to suggest his father. "I can tell she cares about you."

"She's alright," he said, begrudgingly.

"She's not quite what I was expecting," Angie admitted. "After the way you talk about your dad sometimes, I mean."

"What were you expecting?"

She considered for a brief moment. "I don't know... some young, gorgeous, high-maintenance trophy wife?"

"That was his second wife...the one he left my mom for."
Scott's tone darkened. "I'm pretty sure the third and fourth wives
were on the rebound. They only lasted a few months each."

Angie sensed she was treading into an emotional minefield,
but it only slowed her approach. "Is that why you're so angry at your
dad all the time?"

Scott straightened up. His eyes were fixed on the cue ball,
but she could still read contempt behind them. "You know, when my
parents first split custody and my dad made it big, he used to try to
buy us off. He'd take us along on his overseas trips—like that made
up for what he did or something." Scott sneered. "He took me to
England with him once, just after he met Martha. One night there, he
told me he was sorry for everything. First time in ten years I ever
heard him say sorry to anybody." He shook his head, as if still in
disbelief.

Angie crumpled up the sandwich wrapper and pivoted to face
him, maintaining her position on the sunny ledge. He'd earned her
undivided attention. "And what did you say?"

"I told him he was a selfish prick, and sorry didn't change
that." Scott all but snarled. "I told him how I had to listen every night
while Mom cried herself to sleep. How much she changed after he
left, and what the depression did to her..." His grip on the pool stick
tightened until his knuckles blanched. Then he lifted his chin,
projecting some combination of pride and anger. "I told him I'd
never forgive him for what he did."

"How can you say that? Like, you think it's noble of you to
hate your own father—" Angie exclaimed, before tempering her
reaction. "If you won't forgive someone in your own family, are you
going to go around holding a grudge against everybody that hurts
you somehow?"

Like against me, for instance?

A raw look of bewilderment flash across Scott's face. "It
wasn't just me he hurt—that bastard tore our family apart!" Scott
recovered from his shock with a fit of righteous indignation. "He just
about killed my mom from the inside out. He deserves to be more
than sorry! You think I'm supposed to just let him off the hook?"

"Yeah, I do." Angie answered, finding her tone had calmed
as incrementally as his had become hostile. "And not for your dad's
sake, for yours." She paused. "Besides that, I know for a fact that
God doesn't want us hating -anybody-."

"If you're gonna preach, save some for him—cuz I know it's gotta be a sin to cheat on your wife and abandon your kids," Scott growled back, dropping the pool stick onto the table in a clatter of disregard.

"That isn't the point, Scott." Angie wavered, unsure if his temper would allow him to process anything she was saying. He was worked up enough that, were their places reversed, she couldn't see herself being receptive. She waited, watching as he half-circled the table back and forth several times, pacing. "You know the saying about how bitterness is like drinking poison and expecting the other person to die?"

Scott paused to look at her. "No."

"Oh." Angie's line of thought faltered. "Well, it's true, anyway. You're causing yourself a lot more harm than you're causing your dad. You need to forgive him."

"At least it's doing him -some- damage. Karma sure hasn't kicked in otherwise." Scott looked away, defiant. "If God doesn't like it, then he shoulda brought down some justice a long time ago."

Angie lowered her head in exasperation. She felt repulsed by Scott's demeanor, which now stood in brutal disparity to some of her recent feelings for him. "You need to rethink this vindictive thing, Scott. It's not healthy—and it's really ugly on you."

A rapping sound came from the front of the apartment and Angie rose to answer the door. She passed Scott on her way and he moved aside, rubbing the dark scruff along his jaw in sulking silence. She pretended not to notice his mood, turning her focus to the new arrival.

Standing no more than five feet in height, the lithe girl on the other side struck up a radiant smile. "You must be Angeli?" she said, offering out a dainty hand — the arm it was attached to clinked with countless plastic bangles. "Tessa." She brought her free hand up to splay against her own shoulder, indicatively. Her left arm was equally stacked with multicolored bracelets.

Angie shook the offered hand and motioned for her to enter. "That's me. Good to finally meet you," she said, concealing her surprise. After Scott's vague cautioning, she hadn't been sure what to expect.

Tessa was somewhat pale in complexion, with small features that Angie saw as fragile and lovely. Her large, pale-blue eyes adopted a lavender hue thanks to expertly placed eye makeup and the vivid amethyst hair she wore in a face-framing bob. Six silver rings lined the cartilage of her right ear, with the same number of silver studs filling out the left. She wore a close-fitted pair of glossy black pants, while her slender form failed to fill out the tattered band T-shirt that draped her shoulders. Tessa's uniqueness was stunning, and Angie was fascinated.

"Hey," Scott greeted. The fire in him seemed to die down. He sat cross-legged atop the pool table, sifting through a deck of cards.

"I hope we're not playing for cash." Tessa's voice came out light and brisk. She looked over her shoulder to Angie with a mischievous smile. "The guys are no good with odds—or at reading women. I always clean them out on poker night."

"That won't be happening." Scott held up the back of the deck to display the name, and then continued his complicated shuffling routine. "We're playing Uno. And I'm the grand master of Uno."

Tessa cast Angie a sly smile. "Aww, he's showing off." She bent to remove a pair of studded leather boots and hopped up onto the pool table opposite Scott. "You're from Minnesota, right?" she directed to Angie. "Isn't that the state with the governor who used to be a wrestler?"

"Yep, that's us." Angie chuckled, placing herself at the end of the table facing both of them. Scott seemed to be putting a great deal of effort into not looking at her, and so she gladly continued to give Tessa her full attention.

"I liked that guy. He finally made politics interesting." Tessa nodded in approval. "I read that interview where he said that 'religion is a crutch for the weak-minded...' Good stuff."

Scott paused and cut a glance toward Angie.

Under the sudden impression she was being tested, Angie smiled to herself. If either of them expected her to become uppity and offended, she was determined to disappoint. "Well if nothing else, I think our state should get credit for trying something new." The reply earned her a beaming smile of amusement from Tessa.

"You have to tell me about Minnesota. I always figured it must be a lot like Vermont; all forests, fields, and cows—god, it's boring up there." Tessa swatted at Scott's knee, coercing him into dealing the cards.

~ ~ ~ ~ ~ ~ ~

"So, you and Scott—" Tessa opened the conversation as she sat down at a small table in the least-crowded corner of Starbucks. Angie trailed close behind carrying both of their drinks — a mocha for her, and a vegan-friendly chai latte for Tessa. "—are you two official yet?"

Angie had already come to appreciate the girl's pithy-yet-pleasant disposition during their many rounds of cards. She'd been charmed enough to ask her to coffee afterward, with the intent of relishing a female-exclusive outing and any insight it might bring. "Ah, no. We're not," she answered, setting the drinks down as she sank into the opposite chair.

"Well what's the holdup, chick-a-dee?" Tessa brought her drink to her lips for a sip. "It's obvious the chemistry is there. You already have a guy back home or something?"

Angie cupped her mocha with both hands, allowing its heat to build against her palms. "No. Nothing like that."

"I didn't think so, or Scott would have mentioned it—seeing as he's been talking about you for months now." Tessa laughed. "He even asked me what he should get you for your birthday. Me. Like being a girl made me an expert."

Angie squirmed in her seat. "You mean, that mix of music he sent me—"

"My suggestion," Tessa said, proudly. "I could already tell he had it bad then. Not that he'd admit it."

Angie's shoulders slumped with the onset of guilt. "I didn't realize that."

"So, you like him, right?" Tessa said. "I mean, guys don't come much better looking than Scott. He's a little obtuse sometimes...but most of them are."

"I like him." Angie nodded, nursing her mocha. "But I don't know if we should be more than friends. I hear long distance relationships don't usually work out, and I don't think it's worth either of us getting hurt."

"Well nobody said you had to marry him or anything." Tessa laughed. "Or are you really all old-fashioned like he says?" Feigning a dramatic gasp, she leaned in closer across the table. "Wait, are you one of those girls that still believe in white knights and happily-ever-afters?"

Old-fashioned. Out of date. Pathetic. The taunts of Angie's former classmates echoed through her mind. She bit back annoyance at the girl's condescension.

"I just don't want to start a relationship with somebody if I'm not serious about them. And I don't know if I could be serious enough about Scott." It was the best way she'd been able to explain it to herself thus far, though she knew it left something to be desired.

"I think you should go for it," Tessa said. "Experiment a little—live it up while you can." She clicked her barbell tongue piercing against her teeth in contemplation, then shook her head in wonder. "Sorry, maybe that archaic conformist mentality is still big where you come from, but I don't see how you can stand being so…repressed."

Huh. The girl with the purple hair thinks I'm weird.

Angie couldn't decide if she was reading pity or concern from Tessa's expression. "I don't think I'm repressed, I just don't want to play around with someone's emotions while I'm trying to figure out my own." She struggled to keep from sounding defensive. "I knew a few people in high school who lost it over bad breakups. Two attempted suicide. I may not have a lot of personal experience with this sort of thing, but it's not a game to me." Angie settled an earnest gaze on the girl's face, silently willing her to understand the respect she had for something she knew held the power to shatter emotions. "I don't want to hurt Scott. I don't want to hurt -anybody-."

Tessa leaned back in her chair, her expression shifting as she considered. "See, those people you're talking about? They wouldn't have overreacted if they'd realized that love is just a word. Nothing more than a chemical reaction in the brain tied to physiological needs." She spoke with finality. "It's not like humans are naturally monogamous. If they could just accept that, they wouldn't have taken it so personally."

Angie balked internally at the odd philosophical turn the conversation was taking. Instead of finding common ground, they were teetering on the edge of an argument she hadn't seen coming. *Okay, so how to I pull out this little conversational nosedive?*

Frustrated and confused, she collected her thoughts — watching silently as Tessa abandoned her drink in favor of fiddling with her bracelets. The girl's demeanor cooled to remoteness, which made Angie suspect there was more to her opinion than callousness or even researched conviction. "I don't see it that way. I think love is a choice, not just something you feel. Devotion is supposed to hold things together when emotion falls short," she began, maintaining a peaceable tone. "I know half of marriages don't make it, but then again, half of them do. Statistically, it's not the worst bet you could make. Especially if people take the time to find out what makes them succeed or fail—"

"Yeah, and most of those only stay together because people are too complacent or scared to go find something to make them happier." Tessa's retort came laced with cynicism.

Angie allowed a pause before cautiously venturing, "Your parent's divorce must have hurt you pretty bad."

Tessa shook her head, turning a hand over to examine her fingernails. "No I was glad, actually. I was sick of them walking around like zombies, pretending they didn't want something better for themselves. Narcissism is a natural mechanism of human survival. Why fight it?" The girl's tone grew clipped and adamant.

Angie rallied a soft smile. "I think...because that's another part of human nature—the fact that we fight it." From their conversations back at the apartment, she had already determined that Tessa was exceptionally bright. Thanks to their current discourse, she'd also gathered that the girl was as convinced of her perspective as Angie was in disagreement with it. Doubting an intellectual debate would accomplish anything aside from hard feelings, she opted to redirect the discussion. "So, do you have a boyfriend?"

"Sure." Tessa shrugged. "He and I have an understanding. I see other guys while I'm in the city, and he does his thing. Whenever I go back home to visit, he gets what he wants." She raised her brows, as if daring Angie to be shocked.

"Do you love him?"

Tessa pursed her lips, then screwed them off to one side. "The chemical effects of enamorment haven't worn off yet, so I guess you can say that." She returned to her chai, sounding more distant. "Think what you want, but it's a lot better than what I had with my last boyfriend. At least I don't come back with bruises."

Heaviness coiled around Angie's chest. Though they had come to very different conclusions about the world, she detected something agonizingly familiar in Tessa's guarded countenance. This was further supported in her mind when she caught glimpses of the thin white scars that the distracting bangles otherwise concealed. The girl projected herself as strong-willed, but she was also fragile. "I'm sorry."

We're not really so different.

Tessa shrugged. "Don't be. It's my life." The vapidness in her tone suggested she was withdrawing from the conversation.

In an effort to avoid any more points of contention, Angie spent the next several minutes asking about Tessa's college plans and an assortment of other aspirations. She was relieved to find that, unlike her, the girl seemed under no immediate threat of becoming aimless. Tessa had been accepted into an Ivy League college on a partial scholarship and was favoring law school. Though the rest of their discussion remained safely superficial, Angie was satisfied that Tessa's thoughts weren't void of hope for the future.

"Anyway...Scott's a good guy. But I don't want you to think I'm trying to tell you what you should do," Tessa mentioned aside as they got up and headed for the door. "I'm sure whatever you decide will be the right choice for you."

"Thanks," Angie said. *Diplomatic but -so- not helpful*, she thought, managing to keep the observation from falling out of her mouth.

Tessa shouldered the door open and paused on the sidewalk, smirking as she motioned to their left. "Looks like he didn't want you too far out of sight."

Angie followed her gaze and spotted Scott leaning beside the front window of the coffee house. He snubbed out his cigarette and gave a casual wave of acknowledgment as they approached.

"I've got stuff to do." Tessa half-smiled, quickening her pace. "Thanks for the drink. Maybe I'll catch you later."

Angie guessed the parting words were obligatory friendliness. "Sure. Thanks for the chat!" she called after the other girl as she halted at Scott's side.

Scott pushed off from the wall and waved to Tessa in passing. "She's in a hurry," he said, glancing back to Angie. "Took you two longer to duke it out than I was expecting."

"We didn't fight." Angie frowned at him. "We didn't exactly see eye to eye on much, but it stayed nice and civil." She sighed, watching the slight girl disappear as she rounded the block.

"I didn't figure you two would get along," he said, motioning with his chin for her to accompany him. "Girls with strong personalities usually butt heads, you know?"

"She's not as strong as you think." Angie said and then reconsidered. "But in a way, I suppose she's probably stronger. I know, that doesn't make a lot of sense. What I'm trying to say is…keep looking out for her, okay?" She glanced to Scott. He was staring back at her in confusion. "She's not just tough, she's hurting. She needs somebody to care about her. And not because they have to, or because they want something from her."

"Hey, no problem. I'll watch her back." Scott's slumping posture straightened as he pulled his hands from his pockets. "I've called her taxis after the last few parties, just to make sure nothing bad happens to her. Not that she probably remembers…"

"Don't expect applause for doing the right thing. Just do it." The mom-ism was out of Angie's mouth before she thought to stop herself. Hoping to soften the directive, she gave him a smile, and motioned down the sidewalk. "The apartment's back this way, right?"

Scott nodded, seeming distracted as he set off in the direction she'd indicated. He remained silent for a short while before brushing the back of Angie's hand with his. "Hey, uh…I was thinking about what you said earlier. About my dad—" he began, hangdog expression matching his reluctant tone. "Sorry about that. I thought you were just being a know-it-all."

Angie frowned, scanning his contrite profile before focusing on the sidewalk ahead. "If I didn't care, I wouldn't have brought it up. It would have been easier to just agree and not risk pissing you off," she said, pointedly. "But I'd rather you being mad at me than not say what I really think."

"Yeah. That's something else I kinda like about you." Scott cast a sidelong smirk her way. "I've decided I'm going to work on the forgiveness thing. If it'd make you happy, I can at least try." He caught her hand as they walked.

Subdued by the warmth of the gesture, Angie looked at his face and then away. She smiled, relieved at the change in his countenance from earlier in the day. "Do it for yourself. And while you're purging the metaphorical toxins, you might want to consider a literal angle and quit the cigarettes."

"Alright, alright—" Scott grumbled, though he didn't appear resentful. Instead he wove his fingers with hers and changed the subject. "Some of the guys are on their way over. I don't know how late they'll hang around, but it's not an official party or anything." He seemed hesitant about her reaction.

Angie gave a quick nod. "That's fine. I'll catch up on sleep tomorrow if I need to." Silently, she hoped the gathering would prove more pleasant than her first meeting with his friends.

June 28th,
The City That Never Sleeps

I got a hold of Zak again and discovered that Eve finally had her baby via C-section. Obie ended up being eleven pounds. No wonder he was having trouble making his entrance! At least they're both fine now.

As for me and Scott, things are finally clearing up a little. After several days of confusing feelings on both our parts, I took some time to myself. I'd intended on talking to Mom, but it turns out she's out of town for something with her job. Elsie wasn't around either...not that she probably would have been much help. So when I called Zak to check on his sister, we had a long talk. I hadn't meant to tell him about everything...it just worked out that way. He was really calming and kind, and he kept telling me I should just be honest and not so guilty over hurt feelings. That helped a lot.

By the time I saw Scott again, his mother had apparently advised him not to touch me. That's probably the best idea. Though he isn't following that so very well, I think it's at least changed his attitude. I feel a little more comfortable now. I think everything will be alright between us.

Scott's pack of guy friends came over this evening. They're still here...being guys. The quieter ones seem okay, at least. The rest are about to drive me insane with all of the macho/gangster crap. After they started comparing nicknames for their genitalia, I decided it was a good time for me to go sit out on the fire escape for a while and catch up on my journaling.

I kind of like it out here, being so high up. There's a building blocking most of my view, but I can see the East River off to my left. I assume the sun will be rising from that direction, and I hope to catch it one of these mornings. That might make up for not being able to see the sky at night. I miss the stars. New York is a fascinating place to visit, but I don't think I could live here.

~Ang

Chapter 16

"Ow! Holy crap, woman—" Scott bellowed, holding his head with his free hand.

Angie winced, lowering the unfamiliar bamboo sword she wielded. Her arms still vibrated from the percussive force of the practice weapon. "I'm sorry! You told me to give it everything I had—"

"I slipped on the blocking, okay? You didn't give me enough time," Scott said, letting his sword drop onto the grassy knoll and pressing the other palm to his head. "Seriously, I can feel my brain. Were you getting me back over your leg? I told you that wasn't on purpose."

Angie's sympathy for him was short-lived, having already been strained by the day's activities. The plan of visiting Central Park and teaching each other the basics of their respective martial art forms had rapidly gone downhill. Scott cooperated with her demonstration for less than five minutes before his competitive nature resulted in a grappling brawl, complete with gawking spectators. Things went just as badly with him assuming the role of teacher. Now, she wished they had joined the tranquil Tai Chi class meeting at the front of the sprawling park.

"That wasn't revenge. I was just doing what you told me to do," she said, pivoting away from him to resume practicing her stance. "This thing feels so different from the bokken I'm used to." Gripping the hilt, she arched the false sword high over her head, then snapped it down as she took a lunging step forward. She forced herself to ignore her throbbing knee, a casualty of her companion's passionate resistance to instruction.

"I shoulda brought my helmet." Scott's griping continued. Angie repeated her movement numerous times before he addressed her again. "Don't take such a long step," he said, settling cross-legged into the shade of an aging oak tree several yards away.

Angie went on with the repetitions until her arms began to ache. Scott prolonged his self-soothing, rubbing at his temples and the back of his neck. It had gone on long enough by then that Angie suspected she may have caused him some legitimate injury. Not wanting to end her last day in the city on a bad note, she walked over and offered him a hand up. "Let's go get you some aspirin. I could probably use some, too."

"I think there's a drug store on the way to the Café," Scott said, hefting himself up without letting her bear much of his weight. "We've got an hour before we're supposed to meet Martha for dinner."

Angie retracted her hand as soon as he had his footing. The previous day had been low key and enjoyable, but it had brought with it the need for her to reassert her belief that they shouldn't entertain a relationship beyond friendship. However hesitant she still felt over rebuffing him, she considered it far worse to lead him on. "Well, thanks for giving this a try. It was…interesting." She gathered up the two practice swords to hand to him.

Scott's cell phone chirped out an Asian melody, and he answered it with one hand while rolling the swords into his side with the other. He led the way onto the paved walking path, immediately engrossed in conversation. Angie followed after him. She remained a few paces behind for a time, until she found herself too preoccupied with the way his dampened t-shirt clung to the solid span of his back. Shaking her head to clear it, she strode to walk alongside him.

Scott held the phone away from his ear as the person on the other end emitted a loud exclamation. "She's here now—you talk some sense into her," he directed into the phone, punching a button with his thumb. "You're on speaker."

"She can hear me?!" Elsie's voice projected from the device.

"Yeah, I'm here." Angie chuckled.

"I'm told you're still planning on hitting the deep south," said the disembodied voice. "I'm with Scott, I say skip it. You don't know what it's like down there."

Angie glanced from Scott to the phone he held outstretched, skeptical. "And you do?"

"I watch the news! That's enough to keep me from being caught dead below the Mason/Dixon line."

Angie cut her eyes from Scott to the phone. "Your prejudice is duly noted, but I think I'd rather see it for myself."

"I've been to North Carolina, does that count?" Scott offered. Angie shook her head, quelling her exasperation.

"Fine, be that way," Elsie's voice groused. "But if you hear one of those inbreeders play dueling banjos, you'd better get out in a hurry." She gave the barest pause before shifting in tone and topic. "Hey, my mom said you called looking for me the other day. What'd you want?"

Angie flashed a glance to Scott and then took the phone from him, holding it out so he could still hear his cousin. "It was nothing. I just wanted to catch up."

"Well if we're all caught up, I need you to do me a favor—" Elsie said. "Get Scott to take you by a cross-dresser boutique. I need you to pick me out a decent pair of red pumps."

"Do what, now?" Scott yelped.

"You heard me!" Elsie's voice picked up fervor. "Do you have any idea how hard it is to find decent women's dress shoes in size thirteen!? I know they'll at least have them wide enough—"

"Forget it." Scott shook his head, adamant.

"Angie, would you kindly explain to my cousin that I have snowshoes for feet?" Elsie pressed on through the speaker. "You've seen them!"

"I'll work on him," Angie promised, chuckling in spite of herself. She turned off the speaker phone and handed the device back to Scott.

Scott slowed their pace as they emerged from the greenery back onto the Manhattan streets, spending several more minutes in good-humored argument with Elsie before the call ended. Muttering to himself, he tucked the phone into one of his pockets.

"So, aspirin and pretty clown shoes." Angie prodded him, playfully. "Think we can round those up and still make it to dinner on time?"

Scott heaved a sigh of resignation and motioned ahead to a drug store they were approaching. "Let's start with the pain killers."

~ ~ ~ ~ ~ ~ ~

While dinner with Martha was a pleasant experience, Scott's complaints of his physical condition increased as the evening wore on. By the time they'd returned to the apartment he was guarding his neck, carrying himself with his shoulders hunched. It was clear to Angie that he wasn't just being dramatic. Feeling somewhat guilty, she offered him a shoulder massage.

"If you're sure you know what you're doing," Scott said, with some reluctance. "I mean, you can't make it any worse—right?" Crossing the guest apartment, he eased himself onto the couch. He attempted a slow roll of his head and grimaced.

Angie trailed after him at a distance. Regardless of his condition, she was suddenly assailed with apprehension over the idea of being too close to him. "I never made my dad worse. He used to get sports injuries all the time when I was growing up, and I could always make him feel better," she said. "I've taken a few massage workshops. I even thought about becoming a masseuse for a while, but the school I toured was too expensive."

"Alright, you can give it a shot," he agreed. "Where do you want me?"

Angie gnawed at the inside of her cheek in contemplation, rounding the pool table to survey the line of windows. "Can you make it onto the fire escape?"

Scott cocked a skeptical eyebrow. "Yeah, I guess so." He got to his feet and joined her at the window. The warm night engulfed them with suffocating density as they eased out onto the metal grating of the small balcony. "What am I supposed to—"

"Sit with your legs through the railing." Angie motioned toward the side that faced the river. When he complied, she sat behind him and splayed her fingertips along his taut shoulders. As she began to apply pressure, he leaned forward until his head rested against the rails. "You're all knotted up."

"You have that affect on me," Scott said, humor seeping into his voice.

Angie frowned to herself, kneading the pads of her fingers deeper into his muscle bands. When he flinched she eased off, noting where she would have to use more care. After several minutes, the muscles warmed and yielded to her manipulation. "Thanks for everything," she murmured as she worked, deciding it would be easier to say goodbye if she started early.

"I can't do anything to convince you to stay a little longer?" Scott spoke up in a meditative tone. "Or…to let me go with you?"

Angie smirked faintly. "It's tempting. I can't think of a better way to prove I'd make a lousy girlfriend than for us to be trapped together in a car for hours."

Scott made a throaty sound, but didn't directly argue her theory. "So, who are all these other people you're staying with?"

"People I've known for a few years," she said, deliberately cryptic.

"You mean, people you know from online?"

"I've talked to them on the phone too. Just like you." She shifted her focus to her thumbs as she worked at the back of his neck.

"Yeah, but that's different. I started talking to you because of Elsie. What are you supposed to have in common with the rest of these people?"

"Writing."

"What, like chatting?"

"No. Like… story writing." Angie elaborated, though she wasn't confident he would understand. "Short stories...text-based role play games. Stuff like that."

"Nerd stuff."

"Watch it." She paused in her efforts to flick his ear. "I prefer the term 'geek.'"

Scott ducked his head, snickering. "What's the difference?"

"A few handy social skills and the lack of a pocket protector," she answered. "And that first part is debatable."

"Nah, you're better with people than you think." Scott gave a slow shake of his head, which he transitioned into a cautious stretching motion as he tested his flexibility. "You're like me. Good, but stubborn."

"Stubborn is an understatement." Angie smirked to herself, smoothing her thumbs along his neck and across his shoulders. "'Surly' is probably the right term."

"If you say so." Scott was quiet at length before speaking up again on a more sober note. "I've been thinking about that personality test. Just because those people giving it were freakish doesn't mean the test was wrong, does it? "

Angie paused to consider. "No, I actually think the tests were fairly accurate—we do have a lot of similarities." She patted his shoulder to indicate completion. "Feel better?"

"Yeah, way better. Thanks." He rolled one shoulder and then the other, straightening up as he looked back at her. His pensive expression indicated his mind was still hard at work over something. "I thought the tests were pretty dead-on. I've never met anybody like you before. I guess that's because I've never met anybody like me before." He met her gaze and hesitated. "So…do you think that might make us soulmates or something?"

Angie cringed at the expression. The concept had always struck her as a vague and fanciful term, immune to verification. "I don't think so," she said, gentling her tone. "I think a soulmate is supposed to be someone who complements your personality. Their strengths would compensate for your weaknesses, and vice versa. We're -too- much alike for that."

That's it, isn't it? That's why I don't feel right about it?

Angie felt as though she'd had a revelation. A relationship with Scott wouldn't work out because they weren't different enough. They were both temperamental, obstinate, and brooding. Being together only seemed to amplify these traits to the point of dysfunction.

The corners of Scott's mouth twitched downward at her response. "You're saying we don't complement each other?"

"Something like that."

"Well, I can fix that. You have amazing—" He paused to scan over her from head to toe and back up again, a roguish grin forming. "—eyes."

Angie rolled her allegedly 'amazing' eyes at him, though she was relieved to see him in good humor. "Ha ha. You know what I mean." She hoped he knew, at least.

In a sudden motion, Scott caught her arm and pulled her around to his side in a tight embrace. Awash in the disorienting sense of nearness, she had just enough presence of mind to turn her face away. The strength of his arms was inviting — she couldn't deny that. The spiced scent of aftershave almost canceled out the trace of secondhand smoke that clung to his clothes.

"I still think I love you," he murmured into her hair.

Angie sighed, swallowing anger with herself over failing to deter his attachment. "That's just the backrub talking."

"I don't think so." Scott nudged her temple with the side of his jaw, his soul patch scrubbing coarsely against her skin. "Since you've been here I've been…happier. Even my dad noticed. Thanks to you, we had our first decent talk in years."

When Angie drew her head back to see his face, he looked away, staring down through the rails to the busy street far below. "Did you forgive him?"

Scott smirked and shook his head. "We didn't really talk about that. He just wanted to know about you…and how I felt, I guess."

"What did you tell him?"

"That I've never felt like this before." He shrugged, casting her a sidelong glance. "I asked if I could apply to a college in Minnesota, and he said it'd be alright with him. He could make sure I get set up nice—"

"Wait…you're so opposed to taking money from him, but you'd accept his help to move to Minnesota?" Angie sensed a knot of agitation forming in her belly.

Scott's dark brows lifted in surprise. "Well…yeah. Then at least we could be together."

"You don't want to do that." She shook her head. "I can't ask you to leave your friends and family. There's nothing to do there, and you'd just end up resenting me."

Looking stung by her avid disapproval, Scott's shoulders hunched forward. "But isn't that what you have to decide when you love somebody—if you'd be willing to leave everything for them?"

"It's a nice thought, but you don't know me well enough to make a decision like that." Angie twisted aside to grip one of the painted metal bars of the fire escape railing. Her mind sifted through a range of arguments. "Where do you see yourself five years from now? Do you even know what you want to major in?" As much as she hated sounding like a guidance counselor, she felt a need to weigh Scott's response to the pressure she was so familiar with. She couldn't recall him mentioning any dreams or aspirations he might have for his life. That bothered her.

Scott's jaw slackened. "I guess…graduated and traveling the world? I dunno, I just figured I'd take a few classes first and see what I liked." His certainty seemed to crumble into bewilderment. "I just take stuff one day at a time, you know?"

"Yeah, I know," Angie said. Somehow, she'd known all along that he was just as lost over the future as she was. Satisfied that she'd gotten him thinking in broader terms, she leaned forward out of his grasp to peer between the railing bars.

"Would you wait for me?" Scott asked, on the heels of a long pause. "Give me a chance to grow up...or whatever it is you want?"

"Please don't hold out hope on me," Angie pleaded. "That's not fair to you." She turned her face toward him at last. "I've been thinking about it—praying about it. And this just doesn't feel quite...right." Seeing his expression dim, she knew she'd won the battle of wills.

Scott released a gruff sigh. "But, you've never given a guy a chance before. How do you know what it's supposed to feel like?"

"I know it's an important enough decision to me that I should feel at peace about it," Angie said. "And I don't."

I just wish I could explain -why- I don't.

"Not now? Or...not ever?"

"I don't know." She took in a deep breath, sensing her resolve begin to waver. "But right now, I need you to respect my decision."

Scott worked his jaw for a long while before finally nodding once. "Alright. I can do that." He formed a morose half-smile, raising his voice to a positive note. "Still friends, at least?"

Angie managed a smile of certainty. "Still friends."

June 30th,

Scott and I spent yesterday just hanging out. He took me to "John's", a great pizza place that still uses the old brick ovens that are totally against modern fire codes. I've never tasted a better pizza. After a quick tour of the Sony building (and yes, I played with all of the displays), we went to see Lilo and Stitch. This was possibly the best Disney movie I've ever seen. And so, it was actually a nice day. I had to rearrange the last portion of my trip, so right now I'm planning to come back up the East coast and stay in D.C. for a few days before heading back home. I think I'm kind of winging it now.

We went to Central Park today. It was nice to see that there can be real green in New York. I tried to teach Scott some Aikido, and then he tried to teach me a little Kendo. In the end though, we were basically reduced to beating the ever-loving crap out of each other. I'd call it a draw, as I was left with a welt on my wrist and bruised knee, and Scott ended up with what might be a mild concussion. Oops.

This evening Scott's stepmother took us out to "Café Paris. " It was such a beautiful night, we decided to eat on the patio and do some stargazing, (which, in this city, means keeping an eye out for passing celebrities.) I could have sworn I saw Jackie Chan crossing the street, but I didn't get to my camera in time. Oh well.

While we were out yesterday, I noticed Scott was still treating me like a girlfriend. We had a talk about it, and he backed off. But then tonight we ended up talking things over again until almost dawn. He thinks...he's in love with me. And he doesn't understand why I can't reciprocate. Maybe I don't understand, either. I just can't ignore my instincts. I asked him to respect my judgment, and he says he will. I think he's still hopeful I might change my mind, but I'm praying my absence will drain those feelings from him. I hate seeing him hurt.

Tomorrow, I move on.

~Ang

Chapter 17

Two hours of driving brought Angie through the rolling green hills of Lancaster, Pennsylvania. The relatively short drive seemed agonizing, as she couldn't help but use the time to review her visit with Scott. Before she left he had kissed her beside her car, seeing her off with an air of gloom. In addition to a nagging sense of guilt over causing him pain, she'd begun to doubt that she was capable of being in love at all.

Better off alone than with the wrong person.

Angie couldn't remember where she'd heard the adage. She often wondered if other people took in select words of wisdom and wove them into their consciousness as completely as she sometimes did — embracing them like old friends — allowing them to shape the way she perceived life. To her, these were the truest kind of friends. They could be counted on to tell her what she needed to hear, and not just what she wanted to hear. Still, she desperately wanted to get in touch with her mother and have a live person verify that she'd made the best decision. But that would have to wait a few more days.

In dire need of distraction from her thoughts, she found it first in the peaceful Amish countryside. Watching a horse-drawn buggy rambling between the fields set her mind to imagining a simpler, unhurried life. Further distraction came in the form of her next host.

Brant met her in a bookstore parking lot, where he pulled up in a hulking old Buick. Angie had to hold her amusement in check when the gangly, diminutive seventeen-year-old emerged. She'd seen his sophomore year photo when he'd posted it to the story-writing community, but up close he appeared even younger — no more than thirteen. Puberty had yet to be kind to him. His straight, white-blond hair was feathered to frame large, intelligent blue eyes, while a sprinkling of acne and a none-too-subtle set of braces vied for attention. He couldn't have been more than three inches over five feet, which struck her as particularly comical when he stood beside his cumbersome vehicle.

It was little wonder why he preferred to write about burly, heroic characters.

"Well if it isn't Peril, The Road Warrior Princess." Brant's voice was amiable, and more fitting to his age than the rest of him. He offered out his hand, projecting a whimsical confidence.

"That's a lot more extravagant than I deserve, but I'll take it." Angie grasped his hand in a quick shake.

"Are you kidding? You're my hero. Er...heroine." He flashed a metallic grin. "I wish I could pull off what you're doing. I can't even stomach the idea of driving to the next state." He turned to lead the way as they started for the front door of the bookstore. "Sorry about not being able to put you up for the night. If my parents figure out where you came from, they'll ground me until I sprout roots."

"It's no big deal, I don't want to get you in trouble." Angie assured him. "Just show me where I can park for the night and I'll be fine."

"Well, we can hang out for a few hours at least." He sprinted to catch the door and held it open. "We've got a pool at my house, if you want to cool off."

Entertained by the young man's exuberant courtesy, she chuckled to herself. "Are you sure it's a good idea if I go to your house? Won't your parents ask questions?"

"Considering I've never had a girl over before...yeah, they're going to ask questions." Brant rubbed his palms together in anticipation, as though he were looking forward to the interrogation. "I doubt they'll ask you anything. They'll wait until after you leave and then grill me. If they do try to talk to you, just remember your backstory: You're my friend Steven's second cousin, visiting from Kalamazoo, Michigan. You're studying to be a herpetologist, and you have a cat named Atonic." He rattled off the information with rapid ease.

"I—what now?" Angie caught up to his sense of humor after a brief delay.

"You're right...we should just hope they don't ask you anything." He grinned as he steered them toward the store's cafe. "You drink coffee, right?"

"Oh, definitely." She nodded. "I wouldn't have made it this far without Jesus and gas station cappuccinos."

"Good. I was online until three A.M. this morning, and I'm still barely conscious." He motioned for her to file into line ahead of him. "Everybody's talking about your trip. Kalvin is still expecting you in Georgia by tomorrow night, and I think Vincent wants you to call and let him know if you're still swinging by Alabama."

"Alabama is still up in the air." She frowned with uncertainty, stepping up to the counter as the line advanced. "It was going to be on my way to Arkansas, but now that Don is out of the picture..." In light of the persistent heat of the day, she ordered a frappe'. When she attempted to tack on Brant's drink, he pulled out his wallet and shooed her back.

"I got this."

"I can at least pay for mine—" she protested.

"After you drive all this way and bother working me in for a face-to-face?" Brant laughed and dismissed her with a wave. "The least I can do is buy you a coffee."

July 1st,

Just before I left New York, Scott gave me a going-away present. I now have a traveling buddy; a huggable-sized stuffed version of Stitch. Scott must have really logged it away when I mentioned that I'd love to have something like Stitch for a pet. It's nice he was paying attention.

It sounds like I'll be visiting D.C. next month, and then letting Scott follow me back as far as Wisconsin on my way home. He's got his own little road trip planned for seeing relatives before he starts college this fall. I just hope by then it won't be weird for us to spend more time together.

I still don't know what's wrong inside my head. Lately, it's like the whole idea of love is a lost cause to me. I still don't understand it. People talk about falling in love like it's just as easy and pointless as falling down a flight of stairs. So many things about Scott fits what I'm looking for in a guy, but I couldn't seem to let myself be in love with him. I just don't think we were much good at bringing out the best in each other. But now, I'm beginning to wonder if I've set myself up to always be alone. I don't know, maybe I'm over-thinking this.

I arrived in Lancaster today around 5pm, and spent the next four and a half hours with Brant. The kid was even more of a cut-up than I'd expected. I didn't really get to talk with him about anything profound, but then, I guess there wasn't really time for it. We paddled around in his family's swimming pool until it got dark, and then he showed me a safe place to spend the night in my car.

This might be one of the stupider things I've ever done. At the moment I'm parked near a field behind his neighborhood, getting by on peanut butter crackers and jerky. The sun is down, but it's still over 90 degrees. I'm afraid I'm in for a rough night.

~Ang

Though the temperature and humidity were both miserable, Angie had locked herself into her car with the windows cracked only an inch. While it came as a relief whenever a breeze happened to stir the air, she didn't dare allow any opening to the outside large enough for an arm to enter. On the off chance that someone did try to break in, she wanted ample warning.

With the back seats laid flat she settled, fully clothed, on top of her sleeping bag with the lower half of her body extending into the trunk. It was far from comfortable, but it was the most secure setup she could arrange. She waded restlessly into the night, lying on her belly with her arms grappling her pillow. It was certain to make her look pitiful from the outside, which was one of the reasons she'd chosen the position. The other reason being it allowed her immediate access to the bowie knife she'd hidden under her pillow. She had bought a new can of mace to hide between the seats, but it was useless while she was in such a confined space.

Brant assured her his neighborhood was safe, but she wasn't taking any chances. Well...any *additional* chances. The darkness of the field flanked her car on one side, while the dull glow of suburbia illuminated the other. The longer the night wore on, the more the residential lighting dimmed. Enveloped by a droning chorus of crickets, she eventually drifted into a shallow slumber.

A sound startled her awake. Keenly aware of her pounding heart and the raw burn of adrenaline pumping through her limbs, Angie strained to identify the cause of her alarm. She lifted her head from her pillow and peered into the darkness. The silhouette of a vehicle had come to a stop along the nearby road, its headlights shown toward the dead end where they were diffused by tall grass. A car door closed and footsteps started toward her.

Angie's first thought was to calculate how fast she could extract herself from her sleeping pallet, throw open the side door, and go tearing off through the adjacent field.

Not fast enough, she decided.

That left her with plan B: Play Possum. She lowered her head to the pillow and squeezed her eyes shut, forcing her ragged breathing to slow so she could monitor the figure's approach. At the same time she gripped the leather sheath of her knife with one hand, curling her fingers around the handle with the other. In her mind's eye she could picture the blade, curved at the tip and facing away from her.

The footsteps stopped, and she waited for something to happen. There was a pause and then a rustling sound. She opened her eyes to thin slits and saw the ominous frame of someone staring in at her through the left rear window. Angie drew in a slow breath and pulled the bowie knife halfway out of its sheath. Why hadn't she just found a cheap hotel? The question floated out in the middle of all of this, but she didn't have time to answer it.

A blinding white light invaded the interior of the car. She winced at the sudden constriction of her pupils, and her brain told her the offending object was a flashlight. Before she could guess at why a serial killer would be wielding such an attention-drawing device, it switched off. The figure turned and began a sauntering walk back toward the idling car.

Angie lifted her head. The figure was a man, of that much she was certain — broad shouldered and sure in gait. She caught the short hiss of static along with a garbled radio voice, and realization offered her a full serving of relief. Her visitor was a police officer. A closer study of his vehicle's outline confirmed this.

I almost pulled a knife on a cop. Fan-freaking-tastic.

She planted her face into her pillow, held her breath, and waited. Hearing the squad car turn around and head back down the road, she released a sigh. Perhaps he'd been on patrol and was just making sure that her car hadn't been stolen or abandoned. At least he'd done his job without knocking on the window to give her a sound scolding.

Angie spent several more minutes breathing out her tension into the sticky night air before she gave sleep another chance.

~ ~ ~ ~ ~ ~ ~

July 2nd,

I survived my first night sleeping in my car...barely. I have to say, I hope I don't ever need to do that again. What little sleep I did get was lacking in quality. I gave myself a wet-wipe sponge bath this morning and managed to leave by 6 am. It was a particularly long and lonely drive this time. I still had a lot on my mind.

Oh, and I received my very first speeding ticket around noon. I got careless and forgot to set my cruise control coming out of Richmond, Virginia. Being an out-of-state driver this close to a holiday, I guess I shouldn't have bothered hoping for mercy. I know I technically got what I deserved, but I'm pretty miserable over it. That fine is really going to stress my trip budget.

I arrived in Toccoa, Georgia right around 6 pm, and met up with Kalvin in the Wal-mart parking lot. I thought I recognized him right away, but for some reason I kept losing my nerve to get his attention... maybe because he's so tall in person. It's not like he's scary or anything, though. He speaks and moves slowly, and he always seems sad. The way he talks reminds me of Eeyore from Winnie the Pooh (I'm not even exaggerating.) I don't know if it's just the way his personality is, or if it's because of his issues with depression. I know I'm not exactly happy-go-lucky, but it's almost as though negativity is an embedded part of his mindset.

Kalvin lives with his mom in a little townhouse nearby. They've both insisted I make myself at home, so I've taken up residence on the couch. They're still living out of boxes from having moved in a few months back. Kal hasn't bothered to unpack at all, since he'll be moving to Atlanta at the end of the week to start at a technical college. Having type 1 Diabetes seems to have made him a bit of a shut-in, so I'm happy he's about to try living on his own. I hope I can at least make myself useful and help them with the move.

Mileage Log: 3,023 mi

~Ang

Chapter 18

"Kal, are you awake?" Angie called down the narrow hallway of the single-level townhouse. It was well after noon when she'd finally awoken, the only sound she'd heard was the muffled clicking of a keyboard coming from his room.

"Yeah. Unfortunately." The young man's reply was heavy-laden, which she recognized as his usual inflection. "I'm decent—you can come on in. If you can make it past the door."

Taking his offer as a warning, Angie pushed at the door. It yielded several inches, forcing her to put her shoulder into it when she met resistance. As the gap widened, it became obvious what had hindered her. Mounds of clothing spilled over from where they'd been stacked atop a constricting maze of boxes. Among the discernible clutter were scores of toys; most of them cars or action figures. There had to be hundreds of them. Kalvin himself was wedged in the back corner at a tiny computer desk, his pasty features awash in the glow of the screen. He continued typing, in spite of her arduous entrance.

"Good afternoon," she offered, wading in several feet.

"Is it?" Kalvin's voice droned as he cast a sluggish glance over his shoulder.

Angie opted to overlook his prevailing cynicism, diverting her gaze in a sweep of the room. "Well, this is…quite the collection you've got." She attempted a tone of admiration but didn't quite make it beyond astonishment.

"It should be—been collecting since I was five." Kalvin pivoted and stood, up to his knees in the mire of his living conditions. "My so-called father tried to make me sell it when they divorced, but mom wouldn't let him. It's the only part of my childhood he didn't take." He looked as though he was trying to work up the gumption to sound angry, but defaulted to weariness instead.

Yeesh. Trying to cheer this guy up could be a full time job.

Surveying her friend, she formed a sympathetic smile. Though Kalvin was well over six feet in height, there was nothing imposing about his slim frame or the slumped manner in which he carried himself. At twenty years old, his dark hair was already thinning at the crown. His features were even, long in the nose, and graced with mournful cobalt eyes.

"Oh, here, Elsie sent a present for you," Angie said as she recalled the trinket, delving into her pocket until her fingers closed around the thin metal chain. She held out her hand and waited for him to close the distance. She wasn't about to venture in further and risk setting off a domestic avalanche.

Kalvin took his time, a skeptical look dislodging the melancholy. "Why would she do that?" He tentatively accepted the dog-tag chain and examined the small, squared charm that hung from it.

"It reminded her of you." Angie shrugged. "It's a pet I.D. tag. She had it made with your real name, and the names of your characters underneath."

The barest hint of a smile lit Kalvin's features as he looped the chain around his neck, holding the tag up. "She spelled my name with a 'C' instead of a 'K'." He sighed.

Angie winced at the error. "I'm sorry. I guess she hadn't seen your real name, she's just heard me say it—"

"No, it's fine." Kalvin formed a fleeting smile as he tucked the chain under the collar of his video game-themed T-shirt. "That's the way my name was supposed to be spelled. My dad just didn't care enough to get it right on my birth certificate."

Finding it probable that her friend's struggle with depression was rooted in paternal neglect and abandonment, Angie stored the deduction away for later. For the time being, redirection seemed like the best way she could help him. "So, what are we doing today?"

Kalvin frowned. "We've got two options, I suppose. I could show you around the interesting places in town. That won't take long." Though his voice was mild, the sardonic edge was hard to miss. "Or we can get me ready for the big move. But that'd be boring, too. I just need to pick up supplies and get a haircut."

"I don't bore easily," she assured. "Hey, I could save you a little money and cut your hair for you. I've given a few of my friends haircuts before. I'm not fantastic at it, but it doesn't look like you do anything too complicated with it."

"Sure." Kalvin shrugged, shuffling around her as he exited his room and headed for the kitchen. "It's not like you could make me look any worse."

"That's it, never mind." Angie uttered an exasperated sound as she followed him. "The haircut can wait—we've got all week. I think it'd do you some good to get out."

"Okay." Kalvin paused amid dropping a slice of bread into the toaster, though his expression never shifted from a default glumness. "We could check out the new coffee shop," he said. "Or we could go see Toccoa Falls. But I'll warn you, it's not as impressive as it sounds."

"What's not impressive about a waterfall?"

Kalvin snorted to himself, the closest thing to a laugh she'd heard from him. "It's more of a glorified trickle. The thing is supposed to be taller than Niagara Falls, but it's no bigger around than I am wide."

"Well, I'd like to see it anyway. I need to stretch my legs, and it wouldn't kill you to get some fresh air and sunlight."

"It might," he countered with a grimace. "I guess we'll find out."

Angie shook her head, reclaiming a degree of mirth. "That's the spirit, Kal."

~ ~ ~ ~ ~ ~ ~

Just as Kalvin had claimed, there was nothing particularly entertaining about his small hometown. The week wore on in a largely uneventful fashion, while Angie filled her time with watching movies, running errands, and urging Kalvin to see life from a slightly less dismal perspective. They settled into a comfortable sibling-like way of relating to each other, with Kalvin eventually confiding in her the struggles that he and his mother had faced at the hands of his abusive father.

As the last full day of her visit waned, she had noted a modest lightening in his demeanor. It relieved her to hear him speculating on the move and his future.

"Well, I've had a lot worse," Kalvin said, sipping away at the sugar-free frappe Angie had ordered for him. She'd insisted on celebrating his exodus into a new stage of life by treating them to whatever the town's only cafe had to offer. Despite the fact that they were indoors, he continued to wear a broad pair of sunglasses. Angie had learned early on that he guarded his eyesight well, as the degenerative effects of diabetes threatened blindness for anyone as brittle as he was considered to be.

She sat down across from him at one of the round tables, beside a line of windows that had once been part of a retractable garage door. The full interior of the one-time auto repair shop had been painted an uninteresting shade of beige, accented by fake plants and paintings that appeared to have been procured from a local elementary school. Between them, Angie deposited a plate piled with triangular slices of chicken salad sandwiches. "Sorry, it looks like just the drinks are diabetic friendly."

"Doesn't surprise me." Kalvin eyed the sandwiches and reached for the clip on his belt, lifting the rectangular black box that housed his insulin pump. He adjusted the settings on the device, as she had seen him do whenever he was about to eat.

Angie decided to act on the opportunity to bring up a nagging concern. "You know, you should educate your new roommates on what to watch out for. In case your glucose levels get too high or too low and you can't help yourself."

"You sound like my mother." Kalvin huffed. He took a bite out of a sandwich and frowned as he chewed. "I get to start over, someplace where nobody knows or has any preconceived ideas about me. I don't want to screw it up by telling them I'm medically defective." He sighed. "I'm not even bringing most of my toys with me, just so I have a chance at seeming...normal."

"Normal is overrated." Angie blew across the top of her steaming latte. "You can always hang out with Jeff if you don't happen to get along with your new roomies," she said, reminding him of their mutual online friend who would be acting as her next host in Atlanta. "But at least give them a chance. Out of three other guys, odds are at least one of them is going to like video games and action figures."

Kalvin attempted a dubious smile, but it refused to stay on his face for more than a moment. There was a short lull between them while they ate, which he broke without any preamble. "So, you're some kind of Christian?"

Caught off guard by her friend's sudden directness, Angie nearly choked on her coffee.

"What...gives you that impression?" she asked, stalling as she sorted her thoughts. Faith wasn't a subject they'd ever broached before, and she wasn't sure what had sparked his inquiry. Worse yet, with his eyes concealed behind the sunglasses she had little idea where he planned on going with it.

"You bowed your head before dinner the last few nights," he said, analytical in tone.

Angie strained her recollection over his claim. "I guess I did. I've been pretty grateful for your mom's cooking." She shook her head. "But that could mean anything—"

"It doesn't though," Kalvin deduced. He leaned back in his chair, studying her. "I'm right, aren't I?"

She smiled faintly at his certainty. "Yeah, you are."

"So, I have a question for you—" He eased his sunglasses off to set on the table before him. His poignant blue eyes bore into her with unwavering scrutiny. "Why bother?"

She considered him for a long moment, deciding she didn't detect any signs of hostility or entrapment. "Do you want the long or the short version?" she asked. *Not that either one would be adequate.* When Kalvin gave a shrug, she took a slow sip of her drink to clear her throat as well as her mind. "Cliff notes? I've seen and been through a lot of things that got me to this perspective. Some stuff, you probably wouldn't believe. There's a lot I still don't understand, but I've gotten enough answers to keep me going." She spoke quietly, monitoring his reaction. "I guess the main thing is, I know God saved me—in more ways than one. I know He cares enough to have some sort of plan for me, and I want to know what it is." She smirked then. "It's not like things tend to go the way I plan them, anyway."

Kalvin made a contemplative sound, his thick brows drawing together. "Your ears aren't pierced." He used a wary tone in making the observation.

Perplexed by the seeming randomness of his statement, Angie reached up and touched one of her bare earlobes. "No. Not yet, anyway. I have metal sensitivities, and I'm a wuss about putting intentional holes in myself," she said, hoping his rabbit trail was going somewhere.

"No tattoos?"

"No, but I've had two in mind for a while. I figure if I still want them a couple of years from now, then I won't regret it when I do get them." As she spoke, a thought occurred to her. "Are you trying to figure out if I belong to a fanatical cult or something?"

The hint of a smile graced Kalvin's face. "Yeah, pretty much."

Angie snickered to herself. "No, I'm just really boring. Sorry to disappoint."

"At least you earned your belief in something," Kalvin said. "Most people around here just say they believe whatever their family believes. They don't bother thinking for themselves," he grumbled on. "And the less they know, the louder they believe it."

"I don't think that's just the people around here." She smiled in genuine sympathy.

Kalvin's expression grew confiding and he leaned forward. "I always thought God existed—I just don't understand Him. The first time my blood sugar got too high and landed me in the emergency room, I was hoping I'd go into a coma and not wake up. I was so sick of everything...I kept asking God to get me out of here." He shook his head, a weightiness in his voice. "But that didn't happen—"

"I'm glad it didn't," Angie interjected, frowning. "You've got a lot of living left to do, Kal." While she'd grown accustom to challenging his more fatalistic perspective, his latest admission troubled her. If he weren't about to start a whole new life, well removed from the stifling confines of his hometown, she would have been downright worried.

"Yeah, I guess nobody would have been left to take care of my mom." He conceded at last, leaning back in his chair.

The stubbornness she detected in him was enough to ease her immediate concern. Still, she decided to check in on him more regularly once she'd moved on. "You're a lot more valuable than you let yourself think."

"If you say so," Kalvin said, poking at another half-sandwich.

She gave him a stern glowering. "Kal."

"Alright, alright—"

Angie let a pause drag out between them as she considered her words. "Are you angry at God about being diabetic?"

"Maybe sometimes." He shrugged. "But then I feel bad, because I know there's always somebody that's got it worse than me. I'm not asking life to be fair—I know it's too screwed up for that. I just want to know why He lets people hurt each other."

"You mean...like your dad?"

Kalvin nodded. "Everybody, I guess. Why let all this crap go on when he could just -make- us all love each other instead of telling us to?"

"You know how they say freedom isn't free?"

"Freedom is overrated." He made a dismissive motion.

Angie considered arguing, but after some thought, decided to pose another question. "Do you think you'd love somebody more if you -had- to, or if you were free to choose them?"

He met her gaze for a long moment before shaking his head. "I don't know."

"I don't either." She gave a faint smile. "But I think it might mean more when love is a decision—not just some reaction you get no say in."

And maybe one day I'll know for sure.

"I suppose." Kalvin's tone remaining pensive-yet-skeptical. He drained the last of his frappe, then paused as a thought seemed to occur to him. "Thanks—for not beating me over the head with the God stuff."

"Thanks for asking about it." Angie bobbed her head. Whatever his reasons, she was grateful he'd put his curiosity into words. It wasn't often she was given the opportunity to explain herself. "It would have been easier for you to just assume whatever you wanted about me."

"Well, you know me. I never manage to do things the easy way," Kalvin said, dryness returning to his voice. "I hope you're right though—about God caring. Maybe He'll pay attention to something I ask for once and keep you out of trouble."

"If you're trying to say that you'll be praying for me, thanks. I appreciate it." Angie chuckled. "I'm pretty sure I need it."

July 7th,

I've been on the road for almost a month now. It seems so much longer than that. I don't know if it's because I've seen and experienced so much in that time, or because I'm starting to miss home. Maybe it's a little of both.

Kalvin and his mother have been incredibly kind to me. I've never once felt like a stranger. I knew before coming here that Kal was carrying a lot of pain from his past, but in the last week I've realized that he and his mother are both very wounded people. They have a good, strong relationship at least. Which makes sense. They're all each other has. I wish I could have done more to help them. I see now why Kal has such a toy obsession...that's how he copes. Despite that though, I really think he needs to have a garage sale. There's so much he could stand to get rid of...literally and figuratively.

Scott hasn't called or emailed me since I left. Part of me is relieved that he's done what I asked and let me go. But then, there's the stupid part of me that thinks it shouldn't have been so easy for him. By now, he must have come to his senses and realized the difference between love and infatuation. I know I should just be grateful instead of letting it gnaw on my self-esteem.

I finally got a hold of mom on the phone tonight and we had a good, long talk. It eased a lot of my anxiety just to explain things out loud. I told her about everything... giving up on Don, the crush I had on Zak, and all of the confusing feelings I've had for Scott. By the end of it, I must have sounded neurotic. But hey, I guess I probably am sometimes. Of course, she told me I'm not crazy. (She's my mom, what else is she going to say?) More importantly, she reassured me I shouldn't settle for something that doesn't feel right. She thinks I've been putting too much pressure on myself to decide what I want in a relationship, on top of trying to pick a career. I know I don't have to have everything figured out with my life and my future. It would just be a lot more helpful if I did, that's all.

After I got off the phone with Mom, I went for a walk and had a little monologue with God. I let Him know that

He'll have to make it glaringly obvious when I do come across the right guy one day, because I'm done agonizing over it. I don't want to worry about confusion, hurt feelings, or making a bad choice. I want to find something real, or not at all.

Status: I think I'm finally over the Mono now. I just have to be careful not to overdo it so I don't relapse.

Tomorrow I'll help Kal with his move to Atlanta. I'll be killing a few days there before moving on to Florida.

~Ang

Chapter 19

It was late on a Sunday afternoon when Angie set out on her ten hour drive south through Georgia and into Florida. Along the way she was treated to the eerie beauty of the Spanish moss that hung from many of the trees, stirred into gentle motions by the humid breeze. The Florida Turnpike proved to be a long and lonely stretch of road, taking her through a more level landscape interspersed with orange groves and wooded marshland.

Her next host, Antonio, lived in the coastal town of Boynton Beach — an hour north of Miami. It was 1am by the time her directions led her into a quiet little neighborhood, and she was invited into a weathered, single-level home.

"Sorry it's so late," Angie whispered, clasping the young man's hand in greeting.

"Don't worry about it. My grandparents have been asleep since like eight o'clock." Antonio smirked, giving his dark eyes a lackadaisical roll. Standing a half a head shorter than her, the sixteen-year-old was chunky in build, with a preference for oversized t-shirts that failed to conceal his roundness. His dark hair was buzzed short and even, calling attention to his plain features and café-au-lait skin. "Abuelo set that up for you." He pointed to an air mattress taking up a good portion of the nearby living room.

"Thanks." Angie shuffled over to the pallet and sloughed her duffel bag off her shoulder, relieved by the promise of sleep. "Sorry to keep you up waiting on me."

"You didn't." Antonio shrugged. "I'm usually online until three. That way I catch less flak from my grandma. She thinks I should get a job or something."

Angie glanced around the sparsely decorated innards of the dwelling. The furniture appeared many decades old and well worn. The carpet was a dull shade of green, and likely surpassed the furniture in age. Even the smell of the place told her it was old; the lingering hints of musty peppermint reminding her of a foot lotion used by her own grandfather. "Got anything planned while I'm here?" She turned her waning attentions back to her friend.

"I figured you could drive me and my sister up to Orlando one of these days and we could hit a theme park." Antonio shifted his weight side to side as he spoke. "Other than that, you can hang out and do whatever you want. The beach is just a quarter mile down the road."

"You go there a lot?" she asked, sinking down to test the firmness of her sleeping accommodations.

"Naw." He shook his head. "Me and the sun don't get along so great. All I need is my computer and I'm happy."

It wouldn't take Angie long to realize just how much he meant this.

~ ~ ~ ~ ~ ~ ~

Angie spent most of the next two days to herself either on the beach or in the back yard of her host's home, sitting in the shade of a mango tree. Antonio's grandfather was a hardworking man of few words, who spent all of his daylight hours manning a carpentry shop. He seemed indifferent to Angie's presence.

Antonio's grandmother, on the other hand, was a shriveled, moody woman who hobbled about the house seeming paranoid that her grandson's guest was eating all of their food. Angie avoided the old woman as much as possible. She ate all of her meals from what she had stored in her car, unless invited to do otherwise.

Antonio rarely left his computer, and when he did, he carried along a hand-held gaming device to keep himself occupied at all times. Though Angie knew she had no business complaining, the degree of his addiction struck her as absurd.

His fifteen-year-old sister, Josephine, showed little interest in conversation on the rare occasions she wasn't out with her friends. Angie hoped her sense of isolation would be lifted by the time their trek to Orlando arrived, but acting as their driver and theme park chaperone didn't seem to forge any further connection to the disinterested siblings. By Thursday, Angie had given up on engaging them at all. She had even called Elsie to vent her frustration, but her best friend's usual avoidance of depth only left her feeling that much more alone by the time she'd hung up.

Angie stood barefooted along the damp sands of Boynton Beach, staring out over the ever-shifting expanse of the Atlantic Ocean. It was late in the day, and only a few scattered souls remained to enjoy the coastline. That suited her just fine. She preferred the honest seclusion to the illusion of companionship. A sense of morose descended over her. It accumulated with unnoticed subtlety, like falling ash.

She absently pulled out her wallet and withdrew the picture of Don from the window pocket, sparing it one last glance. This seemed as good a place as any to lay something to rest. She edged up to the lapping reach of the water and bent, setting the picture down just as a cool surge reached her toes.

"Goodbye," Angie murmured. The water ebbed back, carrying the small picture along until it was unceremoniously sucked beneath the next wave. She took a few steps back and watched the last of the color drain from the sky, turning the surf to liquid smoke and sapphire.

As dusk fell, so did her spirits.

"I want to go home," she whispered, gaze flickering upward. A thin blanketing of clouds hid the stars from her. It was six weeks into her two-month journey, and she was finally homesick. On top of that, she felt like a failure. "I made it to the other side of the country, and I still don't think I have any better idea of who I am, what I want to do with my life, or who I'd want to share this mess with," she said, unsure if she was talking to God or just complaining.

A gentle breeze sifted through her hair, carrying the briny scent of sea water. She closed her eyes and inhaled deeply. Florida was beautiful, she had to admit. But just as it had at Niagara Falls, the wild natural beauty only seemed to underscore her solitude.

Irritated with her own nagging insecurity, Angie came to a decision. She would cut her trip short and start out for home in the morning. This meant skipping her stop in Alabama, but she couldn't think of any major landmarks she would be missing out on there. And though she was curious about her final host, tiredness had begun to outweigh all other considerations. Her eyes snapped open and she turned, starting back for Antonio's house before she lost her nerve. *Not that it actually takes nerve to go running back home...*

"Hello?" Vincent answered his phone in a friendly, quizzical voice.

Angie was surprised he'd picked up to a strange area code. She had been prepared to leave him a message, but found the promise of a live conversation to be oddly preferable. "Hey Vince, it's Angeli," she said, apologetic. "Am I interrupting your night?"

"Hey! No, I just stepped out of class." Vince's tone warmed with recognition. Just as with all of their previous phone conversations, Angie was struck by how amiable he sounded. If she didn't know better, she would never guess he had a flair for coming up with most of the villainous mastermind characters that kept their story-writing community on their toes.

"Oh, sorry. I forgot you have night classes."

"Don't worry about it. What's up?" he urged. "Still think you'll make it here by five tomorrow?"

"That's what I wanted to talk to you about," she began. A sense of guilt caused her to falter. "I'm sorry to do this on such short notice, but I'm thinking I might pass on Alabama altogether and just start heading back to Minnesota."

"Are you okay? What happened?" Vince asked, voice shifting to wary concern. "Is Antonio treating you alright?"

"He's not treating me...badly."

"But—?"

She frowned to herself. "I think I'm an inconvenience to him, that's all. He's pretty much ignored me the whole time."

"Ignored you?" Vince sounded incredulous.

"I think he likes his friends better when they're not face-to-face," she explained, attempting to verbally shrug off the topic. "I'm tired. I think it's probably best if I just call off the rest of the trip."

"Hey, I'm sorry Antonio doesn't have as much sense as I thought he did," Vince interjected. "I don't think you should give up on your trip, though. Weren't you going to get a tour of D.C.?"

"Yeah, that was the new plan. But I'm changing it...again."

"So, I'm the only one who doesn't get to meet you." He didn't disguise the disappointment in his voice.

"It's nothing personal, Vince—"

He seemed to seize on her growing hesitation. "Look, I promise I won't ignore you." An edge of humor crept into his tone. "Or smother you with too much attention. I can totally walk that line and not weird you out."

Angie found herself laughing for the first time in days. Vince had always possessed a certain humorous charm over the phone, and it was swaying her. "I'm really not that needy."

"Come on, you've only got a week or two left, right?" he persisted. "I already made sure it was okay for you to shadow me at my job and everything."

Angie felt her most recent determination evaporate. He was right, she only needed to keep herself together for a little longer. And aside from that, she hated the idea of inconveniencing him when he'd already gone to some trouble on her behalf. "Okay. I'll still be there tomorrow," she said, giving herself some leeway by adding, "I just might leave a day or two sooner."

"Hey, whatever you need." Vince sounded pleased. "Just be careful. I'm a long haul from where you're at."

"I'll be fine." Angie smiled to herself, realizing she was glad to have been talked out of a rash decision. "I can let you get back to your class."

"If you're sure." His tone gave no indication that he was in a hurry. "Call me anytime—even if you just need to talk. I'll keep my phone on me."

"Thanks, Vince. I'll see you tomorrow."

July 18th,

There's No Place Like Home?

Yesterday I drove six hours total to and from Orlando, bringing with me Antonio, Josephine, and one of her friends. It was about the only thing I've done worth noting while I've been in Florida. Even though we were all stuck together for the whole day, none of them really talked to me. I don't know if it's because I'm an outsider, or if it has something to do with them being younger than me.

Today I slept in to recover. Since I couldn't convince Antonio to leave the house, I ended up spending another day browning on the beach. I'm actually eager to leave for Alabama tomorrow. I think its best that I do, since I seem to be getting in the way of Antonio's computer time. I've decided he reminds me a lot of my little brother. I guess it's the enthrallment with video games and the overall apathy toward real life.

I've had a few more phone conversations with Vince now. I had a weak moment today when I thought I should just cancel the last of my trip and head straight back home, but he talked me out of it. I'm grateful he did. I'm sure I would have regretted quitting early. I'll get to thank him in person tomorrow, if all goes well. I've got a twelve-and-a-half hour drive ahead of me this time.

Mileage Log: 4,083 mi

~Ang

Part 3

"Sometimes you find yourself in the middle of nowhere; and sometimes, in the middle of nowhere, you find yourself." –Unknown

Chapter 20

It began to rain as Angie crossed into Alabama and took the first exit for Cropwell. After a mile of nothing but dense forest on either side of the road, she decided she'd made an error. She didn't see the gas station Vince had mentioned, and felt sure there should be more signs of civilization.

A service station with a barn-like roof grabbed her attention, but it wasn't the one she was looking for. She turned in anyway and, to her relief, spotted a payphone tacked to the far side of the building. Once she'd gotten a hold of Vince, they quickly figured out that she'd turned off two exits too soon. Fortunately, Vince seemed familiar with the area and claimed he could be there within minutes.

Angie eased back into the front seat of her car to take shelter from the warm sprinkling as she waited. She used a baby wipe to wash her face, then leaned into the passenger seat to adjust her Stitch plush toy so it peeked up over the door with its hands and face pressed into the window. Her little navigator had already earned her the approving honks of many bored truckers.

"Well, this should be interesting," she murmured, resting her head back as the weariness of the drive set in. It occurred to her then that she'd never seen a clear picture of Vince. The only thing she had to go on was a poorly angled high school graduation photo he'd once posted for their story-writing community. In it, he'd taken on a grandiose pose wearing black robes while one of his cousins bowed down at his feet. She wasn't sure if that was a good indicator of his ego, sense of humor, or a little of both.

A large, white sedan pulled alongside her car, and she turned her head to have a better look. The driver was a lean, clean-shaven young man who barely looked old enough to be driving. As he got out and stood she noted his attire was well put-together — a gray button-up over a white undershirt and black cargo pants. His close-cropped hair was bright copper in color, meticulously groomed and gelled into a spiky state. He was staring at her.

That has to be him.

Angie pushed her door open and stood, offering a smile and a tentative wave. "Vince?"

The young man broke into a cool smile. "I'm glad you didn't get yourself too lost." He stepped around the front of his car, speaking in the same easy tone he'd used over the phone.

Up close Vince could almost pass for a college student, thanks to the saving grace of intent green eyes and a confident bearing. Standing even with her in height, his thin features were distinguished but not quite sharp. Though he was somewhat pale, he'd seen enough sun to bring out a smattering of freckles across high-set cheekbones.

Before Angie had time to determine whether their first meeting warranted a hug or a handshake, Vince turned and motioned to the building. "I'll be back in a minute."

She followed him into the service station, pretending to be interested in the candy bar aisle while her new host weaved back through the store and disappeared. Seeing food made her realize how long it had been since she'd eaten. By the time he returned, she'd grabbed up a bag of chips and stood perusing the refrigerated section for a bottle of juice.

"You hungry?" Vince asked as he neared. "We can stop and get something at Sonic."

"Oh...okay," Angie said, though she wasn't sure what a "Sonic" was. She returned her impulsive dinner plan to its shelf and followed her new host as he went striding back outside.

The rain had dissipated, leaving the warm air heavy and the roads wet.

"Stick close—I won't let you lose me," Vince called over his shoulder before getting into his car. Angie hopped back into Gypsy and fell in behind the white sedan as it pulled onto the main road. They continued on through a few long stretches and curves before a pocket of urban expansion began to unfold around them.

What she saw of the city made it seem small. The roads were well kept, but the buildings were showing their age. They passed a handful of gas stations, a grocery store, and an abundance of hardware and auto shops before she spotted a sign for the Sonic — a drive-in burger place with outdoor seating.

Angie parked beside Vince and rolled down her window to let in the scent of the fresh rain. As she did, she heard a car horn play Dixie. Craning her neck back to locate its source, she spotted a mud-spattered pickup truck. The shirtless young driver leaned out his window and shouted something unintelligible to a car passing in the opposite lane. Deciding that gawking wouldn't be the best idea, she reached over then and patted the head of her Stitch toy.

"I don't think we're in Kansas anymore, Toto," she muttered to her inanimate companion before taking a deep breath and hauling herself out of the car.

Vince was wearing a set of reflective blue sunshades as he stood with his arms folded, studying one of the menu boards. "Order whatever you want." His genial tone contrasted with what she'd begun to perceive as an aloof demeanor.

It didn't take her long to decide on a BLT and a strawberry shake. Vince repeated her request and his own to the disembodied voice that came through the speaker.

The two sat down at one of the tables and made small talk during the short wait for the food to be brought out. Vince asked about a few of the others from the online community she'd spent time with, and she obliged him with brief summaries of a few misadventures.

"So, what about Danny?" Vince asked, referencing her host in Toronto, who she knew he considered a creative sparring partner of sorts. "What's he like in person?"

Angie allowed herself a little more time to consider as a bleach-blonde girl carried a tray out to them. Vince handed the waitress a bill and waved off Angie's insistent attempts to pay for herself. She finally accepted his gesture with thanks. Having downed the first bite of her sandwich, she said, "Danny was probably the most different in person. You know how he's really clever and quick-witted in written form? He was actually pretty quiet in real life. Still on the sarcastic side, but I mean, he didn't talk much at all while I was visiting. Introverted, I guess."

"Huh," Vince mused, collecting a spoonful of his frito chili pie. "That must make it hard to get laid."

The crass remark caught Angie off guard. She paused midway through her second bite, glancing up with a flash of irritation. "I wouldn't know." Being unable to see his eyes behind the sunglasses only added to her annoyance. They finished eating in awkward silence.

At this rate, it could end up feeling like a long visit in a big hurry.

Vince didn't press for any more conversation, and afterward he led her on a fifteen minute drive south between miles of open sod farms. Patches of water appeared to her left as a lengthy lake came and went from view. Rundown trailers and sheet-metal sheds cropped up with some frequency, spaced by small stretches of pine forest. They passed someone selling wares in a dirt lot alongside the road, and Angie gaped when she spotted a large Confederate flag draped in front of one of the tables.

She was steadily beginning to feel like she'd entered a different country.

Half a mile after passing a volunteer fire station, Vince's car hung a left into a wooded area lined with mobile homes, many parked alongside pontoon boats. Just as it began to occur to her that any of these trailers could belong to Vince's family, his Pontiac turned into the driveway of the first and only foundation-seated house they'd encountered. The two-level home was plain and rectangular — white vinyl siding and a broad cement slab for parking.

Vince stepped out of his car and walked back toward Angie's window.

"Mom isn't here. She should have beat us home. Hang on a sec, I bet she's down at the bar." He held up a finger and walked to a chain-link dog kennel, which sat just a few feet from the basement entrance. Inside the kennel, a rotund miniature pincher bounced up and down, eagerly awaiting its release. Vince swung the door open and the animal bolted for the house. After letting the dog inside, Vince locked the door and eased back into his car.

Angie broke her vague interest in the interaction and backed her car out to resume following him.

Did he just say his mother is at a bar...in the middle of the day?

~ ~ ~ ~ ~ ~ ~

The bar they arrived at was located a half-mile from Vince's house, at the end of a small island mass that jutted out from the lakeside community. On their way in, Angie marveled at the tiny, weathered trailers — all packed tightly along the muddy banks on either side of the road. Minnesota was known for its lakes, but homes along the water were coveted and always seemed to go to someone who could afford an upscale cabin. These humble dwellings seemed out of place in her mind.

The Islander Marina was aptly named, Angie decided as she found a parking spot on the gravel lot beside the tin-roofed building. "Restaurant and Lounge" was the claim painted in blue cursive below the swinging wooden sign. Logan Martin Lake's vast and murky waters stretched out a few yards from the wide front deck of the establishment. A boat-launching ramp led into the waters at the front of the parking lot, flanked on both sides by creaky wooden piers where dozens of houseboats sat bobbing in place like giant, mechanical ducks.

Vince rummaged through his glove box before emerging from the vehicle with a black case several inches in length. As she approached, he opened and turned it around to display rows of throwing darts, all with the number eight pool ball featured on the feathered end. "Not as much fun as pool, but I do pretty well when they have tournaments." He motioned with his chin for her to accompany him. Angie wasn't sure if she was supposed to be impressed by his alleged dart-throwing prowess, so she simply nodded and followed him across the front deck.

Inside, the atmosphere was a blend of rustic and nautical. Broad wooden beams spanned the bare ceiling, and the bracers between them were strung with fishing nets, colorful Christmas lights, and various women's undergarments. Tall, round tables dotted the right side of the room, with half a dozen electronic dart boards lining the wall.

The bar itself extended along the left side, and the far back wall featured a raised karaoke stage. Country music filled the dim space — piped in from wall-mounted speakers. The scent of stale cigarette smoke was lingering but faint. A bald man behind the bar looked up from running a towel over a freshly washed glass and gave Vince a nod. He was a tall fellow in his early fifties, who seemed to be trying to make up for the lack of hair atop his head by sporting a dark, bushy mustache.

"Hey, Joe." Vince nodded as he passed.

"Well, there you are!" The high, warbling exclamation came from a buxom, middle-aged woman who'd swiveled to face them from her seat along the bar. "And you brought yer lil' travelin' lady friend?" She was high-cheeked and fair skinned, her fox-red hair framing deep brown eyes before falling in waves past her shoulders. She sat tall, wearing a lime-green halter matched up to blue jean shorts and a pair of worn flip-flops. Casting a long-neck bottle of Bud Light onto the bar to free up her hand, the woman caught Vince in a hug and planted a kiss on his cheek.

Squirming free of the woman's affections, Vince motioned to introduce them. "So…this is my mom. Mom, this is Angeli."

The woman cast Vince a scolding glance and took hold of Angie's hand, giving it a squeeze and a shake. "I'm Marie. Pleased ta meet you." She patted the stool next to her. "Have a sit with me, girl. You want anything ta eat? Joe here makes a great burger," Marie proclaimed. Her drawl was thick enough to slice. It was then Angie realized Vince had somehow bypassed the standard southern accent.

"Oh, no thank you. We just ate." Angie smiled at the woman's warmth and perched on the offered barstool, looking to Vince then in hopes of some direction. To her dismay, he'd already walked off to speak with an older, bearded man sitting at a nearby table. After a brief discussion, Vince and the older man moved to one of the dart boards and began a game. Angie was on her own, and completely out of her element. Fortunately, Marie seemed the chatty type.

"So, Minnesota. I hear it's plenty cold up there."

Angie chuckled, "It can be. The winters are longer than I'd like."

"Vinny was sayin' you've been drivin' for a while already," Marie said, maintaining a lively tone.

"About six weeks now."

Marie leaned into the bar and sipped her beer. "Yer underage, aren't ya? You like sweet tea?"

Angie hesitated, wondering if she should conceal her ignorance. Curiosity ultimately won out over pride. "Sweet tea? Is that like iced tea?"

Marie's brows raised and the laugh lines at the corners of her eyes deepened. "Well that tears it. Joe? Could ya bring my girl here a sweet tea?" she called over her shoulder, patting the bar top with her free hand.

A few moments later, Angie accepted a red tumbler and found herself as glad to have the refreshment as she was to have something to do with her hands. The drink wasn't iced tea, per say — at least not as she knew it. To her, iced tea was made from a powder mix and matched to a citrus flavor. This tasted like the brewed black tea she normally drank hot, except it was on ice and sweetened with either honey or brown sugar. Not exactly an exotic new experience, but pleasantly different in its own way.

At Marie's expectant look, Angie raised her glass in appreciation. "It's good! Thank you."

Marie toasted Angie's glass with her empty beer bottle and grabbed another out of the sweating metal bucket Joe had left on the bar behind her.

The bubbly woman was forthcoming with personal information. She informed Angie that she was a "Yankee" herself, having grown up on the East Coast — something that wasn't discernible, considering how thoroughly the woman embraced the southern vernacular.

Marie had discovered that college wasn't for her and joined the Army just a few years out of high school. There she'd met Vince's father, and moved with him to his home state of Mississippi after they eloped. They'd lived and worked on the state penitentiary grounds until Vince was 14, before moving to Alabama. Marie had found work at the state government in Birmingham. It sounded as though she'd also been responsible for getting her son a clerical position in the same department.

While they bantered, Angie attempted to track the progress of Vince's dart game. She couldn't see the score from where she sat, but judging by Vince's nonchalant expression and his opponent's agitated mutterings, he was winning. Several more patrons trickled into the building in the meantime, most looking worn from whatever the day had brought.

Vince shook hands with the bearded man as their match ended. He came walking back toward the bar just as his mother was explaining to Angie where in the living room she could find an album with his baby pictures.

"Mom!"

The overhead music changed, and the atmosphere of the place shifted enough to catch Angie's attention. The dull constant of background conversations yielded to a murmur of approval. Several patrons got to their feet and took a dance partners in the narrow clearings between tables. She couldn't recall ever seeing such an automatic reaction to a song, aside from the National Anthem. It took several more bars of the upbeat guitar hook before she was able to identify it as none other than Lynyrd Skynyrd's *Sweet Home Alabama*. She couldn't help but smile to herself at the quaintness of it all.

"Son, why don't you get out on the floor with Miss Angie?" Marie said, making urging motions at both of them.

Angie's stomach knotted. Thanks to high school, she had nothing positive to associate with the concept of dancing. And aside from that, she wasn't sure she was getting along with Vince yet. Dancing seemed like an uncomfortable stretch. To her relief, a gauging glance at the young man told her he wasn't about to yield to the coercion.

"Mom, I don't dance. " Vince gave a groan of annoyance. "And if I did, it wouldn't be to the redneck theme song."

Marie gestured with her beer as she looked aside to Angie. "Don't you listen ta him, he can too dance. And he sings. I oughta find you that video of him singin' the Mississippi Squirrel song." Delight glimmered in her eyes she gave Angie's arm a conspiring nudge.

"I was ten—I didn't know any better!" Vince threw up his hands in a dramatic combination of exasperation and mock horror. He caught Angie's gaze and inclined his head toward the door with urgency. "I think that's enough quality time. You ready to get out of here?"

Angie nodded, chuckling to herself as she slid off the swiveling chair. "It was nice to meet you. Thanks for the tea," she said, leaning closer to Marie to be heard over the music. She then found herself buried in the woman's ample bosom, caught in an enthusiastic parting embrace.

Marie released Angie and leaned back into her chair, calling out after them, "Any time, girl. Ya'll have fun!"

Vince paused at the door to look back, forcing Angie to stop short. "Hey Mom? Don't stay out too late," he called, a sincere edge to his voice.

Angie heard Marie laugh, but didn't catch her reply.

It was nearly dusk as they made their way back to their cars. Angie caught a pensive expression on Vince's face as she passed him. "Something wrong?" she asked.

Vince pulled a set of narrow-framed eyeglasses out of his shirt pocket and slipped them into place as he got into his car. "Nah," he answered, reaching to pull the door closed. "I just get worried when she stays out on nights when my Dad isn't in town. His job sends him out-of-state for training a few times a year." He draped his arm along his open window and shrugged, changing the subject. "Follow me back? I rented some movies the other day." He half-smiled and backed his car out.

How strange, Angie thought, sliding into her driver's seat . Was there some level of child/parent role reversal going on, or was Vince just overplaying his concern? Worrying about her own mother staying out too late at a bar wasn't something she'd ever had to consider.

Maybe just a case of one person's "normal" being another person's Twilight Zone.

The short drive back to the house didn't leave her with much time to mull it over.

~ ~ ~ ~ ~ ~ ~

Halfway up the stairs to the main level of Vince's house, Angie was startled to come nose-to-nose with the black and brown dog she'd seen earlier in the day. She wasn't sure what was more unnerving, the dog's sudden appearance at the top of the stairwell, or the statuesque silence that accompanied its stare. She'd never seen a Doberman of any size up close before. In spite of it being a miniature, its sharp ears, along with the angle at which she was forced to approach, combined to make the animal seem menacing. She didn't realize she'd stopped in her tracks until she heard the creak of the step behind her and felt a tap on her elbow.

"You okay?" Vince asked, hefting the duffel bag he'd insisted on carrying for her.

"Yeah, it's just…your dog surprised me," she said, recollecting her resolve and continuing on.

"Back up, Bud," Vince called from behind her, unconcerned.

Nails clicking on the pale linoleum, the dog gave Angie space as she reached the landing. The top floor opened into a lighthouse-themed kitchen, with a porch on the right that faced a tree line along the back side of the house. To the left was the living room, featuring cinnamon carpeting and a ragged blue sofa. To her immediate left and right were short hallways leading to bedrooms.

She turned around in the kitchen and glanced down at the dog again as she waited for Vince to indicate where he was taking her things. The dwarf canine afforded her the briefest sniff before centering all of its attention on its owner. His black nub of a tail squirmed back and forth with recognizable enthusiasm. When Vince rounded the corner and veered into the hall to the right, the dog went prancing after him.

"His name is Bud?"

"Budweiser Jack-Daniel's. Bud for short," Vince said, grimacing over his shoulder as he nudged the door open. "I was eight when we got him. I didn't get any say in the naming," he added.

"Oh, so your parents—"

"—named him after their favorite beer and whiskey."

"Gotchya." Angie kept her tone carefully nonchalant, in case he expected her to be appalled by the information.

Vince lowered her bag to the floor as she scanned around the wood-paneled walls. The room was spacious and tidy, arranged with a computer desk on the far left and a steel framed bunk bed in the far right corner. The bunk bed was painted a vivid red, with a full size futon for the lower portion and a twin bed on the upper level. Budweiser had already jumped onto the futon and curled up at one end. Each wall held at least one poster featuring dragons as the central theme. On the wall adjacent to the door sat an old oak dresser, topped with a collection of framed pictures. Beside it was a small television on a low stand, its shelving packed with video games.

"This is your room?" Angie guessed.

"Yep."

She hesitated a moment, chewing at the inside of her lower lip. "Where…should I be sleeping?"

Vince gave her a blank look, cupping his hand to the back of his neck before using it to make a sweeping gesture toward the bunk bed. "Well, I thought you could stay here." He looked uncertain, as though no other possibility had crossed his mind. "I mean, I'm not planning on watching you sleep or anything creepy."

"I just...don't think I should stay in your room," she said, groping for a way to keep from offending him. "I don't think that's going to look good to your mom."

"Mom won't care, trust me." Vince's tone came out bland. "Neither of my parents would mind. They're kind of...more like friends than parents sometimes."

Angie was bewildered by the concept he presented so factually, while part of her wondered if she'd caught a note of sadness in his voice. "Well, I'd be more comfortable with the couch, if that's alright."

"Probably not." Vince frowned. "It sags in the middle and it's got a bunch of broken springs. Oh, and Mom gets up around four-thirty every morning, even on weekends. Being quiet isn't exactly her forte." He paused to consider. "There's the basement though, we've got a spare bed down there if you want to check it out." Abandoning her bag, he moved to his computer, switched it on, and sank into the chair in front of it.

"Okay, thanks." While her host appeared otherwise occupied, Angie retrieved her bag and made her way back to the stairs.

Every one of the painted wooden steps creaked on her way down into the unfinished basement. She hadn't paid much attention when they'd first passed through, and now she regretted it. At the base of the stairs was an open workshop, strewn with benches, shelving, and countless power tools positioned along the walk-in cinderblock foundation. No sign of a guest room. She veered to the left, passing the wall that supported the staircase on one side and a wall lined with posters of bikini-clad women on the other.

She found a light switch, noting the only window seemed to be located near the entry door. Not that there was much daylight left for it to offer.

In the back corner sat a well worn trap set, and she resisted the urge to inspect the instrument. There was only one portion of the basement left to search: a partial room on the back left side that looked as though it had been erected as an afterthought.

Angie rounded the corner and found a full-sized bed. The room itself was bare bones at best, with blank drywall surrounding and the same poured concrete floor as the rest of the basement. The room had no door. Bare rafters and pipes hung overhead, and the only light source for this semi-secluded corner was a small lamp perched on a nightstand. She turned it on, but found herself disappointed with the dull glow meant to illuminate the lonely space. The bed was neatly made at least, layered with a hodgepodge of colorful blankets.

Forcing herself to ignore the general eeriness of the room, she sat on the edge of the bed. The mattress offered little give.

Still, it has to be better than sleeping in my car again.

From where she sat, she detected the mingling scent of motor oil and sawdust drifting in from the workshop. She stared out from the open section of wall where a door should have been, wishing the window wasn't so far off.

Out of the corner of her eye, a sudden movement drew her attention to a clear Mason jar that sat in front of the lamp on the nightstand. A tightening sensation gripped her chest. Startled, she turned only her head to peer at the vessel.

The glass was more distorted than it was clear, but she caught the shifting of something dark toward the bottom of it. Whatever was in the jar, it was alive — and it was much larger than she would have liked an unidentified living thing to be. Every muscle in her body pulled taut in unison as her curiosity barely outweighed her impulse to flee.

Vince looked up from his computer as Angie shuffled back into his room and let her bag slide off her shoulder. "Change your mind?" His lips quirked slightly at the corners in what she guessed to be either a pleased or smug affect.

Angie stared at him for a moment before she approached his desk, holding out the Mason jar in front of her. She set it down and slid it toward him, monitoring his reaction.

Vince looked genuinely perplexed with her, though he turned his attention to the drinking mug she'd set before him. He leaned forward to look over the rim at its contents.

"What are you... HOLY mother of... it's alive?!" The exclamation was accompanied by him launching to his feet and backing away from his desk with enough force to knock his chair into the wall behind him.

This immediately abated Angie's suspicions of any malicious intent. "I found that by the bed downstairs. So, I take it this isn't part of some punk-the-Yankee thing?" she asked, glancing down at the brown scorpion as it skittered uselessly against the slick walls of its confines.

Vince recovered from his initial alarm and returned to the cool, composed expression he seemed to default to. He cleared his throat and stepped back up to the jar, going so far as to pick it up to inspect the trapped arachnid. "I guess it must have fallen in from the ceiling—" he said, glancing back up at her again. "I didn't put it there, I swear."

"From the ceiling?" Angie gaped at him and then glanced upward, as though she might find more of the creature's kin lurking overhead.

"They come in sometimes in the summer looking for water. My dad told me once that they like the condensation on the pipes." His brows gathered in what she guessed to be an apologetic expression as he set the jar back down. "Usually we only see the dead ones. They're not deadly—they just have a mean sting, kind of like a wasp."

"Oh, that's comforting," she said, openly sarcastic.

"Sorry. I'll go down and do a sweep...make sure there aren't any more," Vince offered, pulling open one of his desk drawers and rummaging around until he located a utility flashlight. "Just make sure you check your shoes before you put them on in the morning. Sometimes they like to crawl in there."

"That's okay." Angie held up a hand. "You know what? It's kind of scary down there -without- the threat of scorpion bombardment. If the offer is still open, I'll take the top bunk." She sighed, just to make sure he knew she wasn't thrilled with the compromise.

"Sure, whatever you want," Vince said, and then hesitated. "Will you mind if I keep the radio on all night? I need background noise to drown out my brain, or I can't sleep."

"Not a problem—I can get used to noise." Angie retrieved her duffel bag and hefted it onto the top bunk. "So if the scorpions aren't poisonous, what do you have around here that is?" she asked. "You know, so I can keep an eye out."

"Brown Recluse spiders, Black Widows, Copperheads, and Water Moccasins," he answered, as though he was reading a grocery list.

"Great." She frowned. "You don't really have to worry much about the great outdoors in Minnesota. The cold must keep away the poisonous critters."

"The Water Moccasins are just around the lake," Vince added with a dismissive air as he picked up the Mason jar and headed toward the door with it. "I've only seen one since we moved here."

"Where are you going?" Angie called after him.

"I'm evicting your former roommate. By way of the garbage disposal."

"Wait! Don't kill him," she said. "I named him Harvey. I'll let him go in the woods tomorrow or something."

Vince stopped in his tracks and turned back to her, a dumbfounded look on his face. "You -named- it?"

"Yeah." She shrugged, quietly pleased by his astonishment. "Just leave him on the dresser. It's not like he can get out or anything." She'd decided that if she was going to spend several days in close quarters with this guy, she ought to go out of her way to make sure he didn't get too attached to her. What better way to prevent that than by being herself?

"O...kay." He relented after a pause, carefully setting the jar atop the dresser. Vince shifted to the television then, grabbing several rental movie cases. He held them up and fanned them for her to see. "Take your pick."

Angie selected a comedy to start out the marathon, exchanging it for a sci-fi action movie halfway through when it proved to be more stupid to her than funny. As far as she could discern, Vince was indifferent to the swap. Though, he seemed more entertained by the first movie than she was. This observation underscored their differences in her mind, and his relative silence through one movie after another made her suspect he found them to be a convenient excuse to avoid talking to her.

Angie wasn't sure at what point during the fourth movie she fell asleep on the futon, but when she opened her eyes, the gray glow of predawn seeped in from the window behind her. The little television across the room droned out the low hiss of static, mingling with the muted pulse of rock music from the radio on the wall. Her neck was stiff from being slumped to one side. Blinking away the fog of confusion over her whereabouts, she peered down at what she now realized had roused her.

Budweiser had wedged his sausage-like body into the gap between her and Vince. His back conformed to his master's side, which left his legs free to stretch and swipe at Angie. The dog was clearly dreaming about chasing something.

Vince was asleep as well, propped up at an ungainly angle with his head tilted back. She couldn't imagine the position to be healthy, let alone comfortable. She gave brief consideration to letting him know she was clearing out of the way, but decided against disturbing him. This turned out to be a pointless effort, as the bunk frame squealed when she hoisted herself onto the top bed.

Vince leaned forward as she settled overhead. "Where're you going?"

Angie peered down at him over the side, wondering at the amused smile he wore. "To sleep. You should too."

"You don't have to leave. I was sleeping just fine," he said through a stifled yawn.

"Good night," she called down, tone mild but firm.

"Good morning," Vince corrected at a mumble.

Budweiser grunted in protest over being repositioned, but that was all the more Angie heard from below before sleep reclaimed her.

Chapter 21

Dead pine needles crackled underfoot as Angie stepped into the thick tree line. Continuing on for several yards toward a crumbling tree stump, her eyes scanned the ground for any signs of movement. If not for her scorpion encounter the night before, she wouldn't have given her steps a second thought. Today she was committed to respecting the fact that she was in unfamiliar territory — particularly if it saved her a trip to the emergency room.

Holding the Mason jar at arm's length, she overturned it, forcing the vessel's occupant to drop out. No worse for wear, the scorpion landed upright and wasted no time darting across the top of the stump. Angie didn't wait to see which direction the creature went. Pivoting in place, she retraced her steps at twice her original speed.

As she cut back into the relative safety of Vince's backyard, she noticed her host leaning against the fender of his car, watching her. At least, she was fairly sure he was watching her. Much to her chagrin, his eyes were again concealed behind the mirror lenses of his sunshades. There was a better excuse for it today, as the skies were an unbroken blue and the sun hung high overhead. Arms folded loosely across his chest, he wore a faint smirk, shaking his head as she approached.

"So, where are we going?" she asked, initiating conversation in hopes of avoiding any commentary on her arachnid altruism.

"We're going to meet up with my friend Grady and his cousin," Vince said, shifting to pull open the passenger side door for her. "I figured we'd all go see a movie. Not much else to do around here."

"Sounds good to me." Angie slid into the car, making a point not to balk at his gesture. She couldn't recall ever having a car door opened for her. It didn't occur to her to thank him for the courtesy until after he'd shut it behind her. But by then, the timing for it seemed to have passed.

While he walked around to his side, she took in the all-gray interior of the car. It was a spacious vehicle, clean and free of clutter. A number of ornaments dangled from their place of honor beneath the rear view mirror. Among them, an intricate wooden pirate ship — complete with a tiny skull and crossbones flag — twisted side to side as Vince got into the driver's seat.

"Welcome to the Corsair." Vince gave the steering wheel an affectionate pat. "Or, that's what I call him anyway. If you hear anybody call me Captain Vince, now you'll know why. This thing is kind of a land yacht." He tapped the pirate ship with his finger to persuade it into a pendulum swing.

Angie recognized a Catholic pendant suspended from a silver chain behind the ship, and she reached out to examine it more closely. She identified the small St. Francis of Assisi engraving on the back after running her thumb over the raised image on its front.

"From Meme'—my grandmother, " he said, one side of his mouth pulling in a faint smirk. "For when they come to visit and I have to pretend I'm Catholic."

"Keeping the peace, huh?" Angie smiled as she released the charm. "So then what do you consider yourself, if not Catholic?"

"Open to suggestion. If it's the kind that makes sense."

"Fair enough." She glanced around the rest of the vehicle's interior while she waited to see if he would take the opportunity to make any inquiries of his own. But his attention transitioned into backing the car out and taking them to the main road. Angie glanced behind her into the back seat, spotting a pair of leather work gloves lying atop a folded uniform, weighed down by a yellow, brick-sized radio. "What's all that?" She motioned over her shoulder with her thumb.

Vince adjusted his rear view mirror, giving him a momentary glimpse into the back seat. "Oh, you mean the fire department stuff? That's my call radio and a few things I'd need to work a scene. Everything else is at the station just up the road."

"Oh. Are you supposed to be on call this week?" Angie peered out her window at the brick-walled volunteer fire station as they approached, remembering it from the day before.

"Not while you're here," he said. "I haven't taken call much since I started college, but I did just about every night back in high school. I'm trying to stay in shape for it though, in case my class schedule eases up next semester."

Angie's conscience took her back to earlier in the day, and she reluctantly second-guessed the irritation she'd awoken with toward her host. They'd slept until close to noon that morning, and Vince had gotten up ahead of her only to launch into an extensive routine of push-ups and sit-ups. Though he wasn't noisy about it, he'd executed the workout on the floor just in front of the bunk bed. Presuming this display to be some attempt at showing off, Angie had feigned sleep to avoid acknowledging it at all. Now, she suspected she'd been too quick to dismiss its merit.

"Have you seen a lot of fires?" she asked with growing interest.

"If you mean structure fires, I've only been on a handful of those calls." He spoke in an absent tone, his focus on the road. "Most of the time we just end up being the first on scene for car wrecks— usually drunk drivers or people who don't know how to drive in the rain. We got to use the Jaws of Life once, but it doesn't normally come to that."

"So what got you into it? Hero complex, or thirst for adrenaline?"

"Wanting to be more like my dad, I guess." Vince's thoughtful candor gave her pause. "He was a fire chief when I was growing up, and we didn't share a lot of interests. I think it disappointed him that I wanted to stay at home and be on the computer instead of fixing cars or going out hunting and fishing with him." And then, as though he wasn't at ease with remaining serious for long, another smirk played across his face. "That, and I've always had a thing for fire. Most of the guys I volunteer with are borderline pyromaniacs."

"Well, that's good to know." Angie laughed. "At least it's a positive way to direct the fascination."

"Sometimes to stop a fire, we'd get to start one." His voice gained a measure of liveliness. "The National Forest near here had problems with wildfires a couple of years ago, and we got to go out there and control-burn a perimeter to keep it from spreading."

"Firefighters who stop fires by starting fires. Ironic," she said, amused. While they'd only managed a few minutes of genuine conversation, Angie was pleasantly surprised at how much more comfortable she'd become with Vince. For whatever reason, he seemed less contrived and more like the affable friend she'd enjoyed talking to over the phone and online. With any luck, her first impression of him as a standoffish jerk was nothing but a fluke.

Something about the abundant vegetation rushing past them began to strike Angie as unusual, and she tapped a finger against her window to call Vince's attention. "What are all of those vines covering everything?"

She wasn't exaggerating. The plants she referred to carpeted the ditches and crept upward to envelop tree trunks and telephone poles alike in a sheath of dense, rounded leaves. They adhered to rock formations and arched over abandoned farm equipment, reminding her of enormous hedge sculptures.

Vince glanced out her window and back several times before the confused expression on his face was lifted. "Oh, that's just Kudzu. It grows everywhere. I think it's some kind of weed."

"So that's what it looks like," Angie said, sounding more enthralled than she'd intended. "I guess it depends on your definition of "weed." It's actually native to Japan. It was brought over here to help control soil erosion, but it got out of hand. I think it's in the legume family."

"That's...interesting," Vince said in a less than convincing tone. "I didn't know you had a thing for plants. We can swing by the botanical gardens later if you want," he offered, though he didn't expend any enthusiasm on the idea.

She laughed, somewhat embarrassed at her spontaneous fact regurgitation. "I just read about it somewhere. Sorry. I'm not actually all about botany, I just tend to store useless trivia." She had also read somewhere that Alabama alone produced half of the peanut crop for the United States. Though, she wasn't about to earn herself any more geek points by throwing that in.

They lapsed into an uneasy silence for a time, which Angie accepted as deserved on her part.

So much for being more comfortable with each other.

Vince soon turned onto highway 20 west toward Birmingham, leaving the sprawling countryside behind. At some point, he began to fiddle with the radio. Angie didn't pay the background music much mind until a song came on that she knew. Even then, she was only half aware of it as she stared out her window. The rolling greenery of the Appalachian foothills held her fascination. Thick, shaded forest flanked the interstate, remaining unbroken for miles and giving the impression of massive gaps in civilization. She wasn't at all cognizant that she'd been reciting song lyrics aloud until Vince's voice drew her out of her haze.

"You know this song?"

Angie blinked, collecting her thoughts. She turned toward him, noting the astonishment in his face. "Um…yeah?"

"A girl like you—you listen to rap?"

Angie's bewilderment was overcome by a resurgence of irritation. "What, do I not fit the goodie-goodie mold if I happen to know a few songs?"

At that, he was silent. She took it as confirmation.

Angie forced herself to finish out the song at a more brazen and audible level, though she had to stare out her window all the while to maintain her nerve. It wasn't the first time her self-consciousness had been trumped by her determination to prove a point.

"For the record, that was the only song of his that I like." she said, evenly. "And that's mostly because I found the music video hilarious."

"You're full of surprises." Vince chuckled, casting her a sidelong glance.

"Only because you seem to be full of assumptions." Angie immediately regretted her bluntness. She reviewed her choice of words in her head, and then reasoned that it was for the best. *Keeping him at arm's length was the goal*, she reminded herself. She must have guaranteed her success by this point.

Vince drummed the pads of his thumbs against the steering wheel for several seconds, as if keeping beat to some tune in his head. "Touché," he said finally, with an air of respect. "Alright. No more assumptions."

~ ~ ~ ~ ~ ~ ~ ~

After meeting up with Grady and his cousin Steven in an expansive theater lobby, the group stood off from the ticket counter attempting to reach an agreement. Angie earned herself some measure of approval by expressing no interest in any of the romantic comedies. The others seemed to be leaning toward an action movie involving dragons.

"You'd probably like that one—the computer graphics were great." She singled out Vince with a nod. "But, I just saw it last week."

Grady held up a hand, offering Angie an amicable smile. "Hey, I'll go with anything you feel like." A former classmate of Vince's, Grady displayed a laid-back demeanor that contrasted somewhat with his professional choice of attire. Like Vince he was average in height, but his build was broad-shouldered and solid. His dark hair was frosted at the tips and sculpted into pristine peaks. A rich complexion and warm brown eyes suggested a Mediterranean heritage.

"Way to be decisive, G," Vince jabbed.

Steven spoke up for the first time, shoveling his hands into the pockets of his jeans. "I'm cool with whatever." Though he stood almost a head taller than Grady, he carried himself with a slight slouch that seemed to reflect a more timid personality. Pallid, lanky, and crowned with shaggy, golden-blonde hair, the only features he shared with his cousin were his eyes.

"There's one I'd be more than happy to see again," Angie said, pointing to the poster on the far wall advertising for Lilo & Stitch.

"A cartoon?" Vince groaned. "Seriously?"

"Trust me—it was funny," she said, insistent. "Give it a chance."

"Yeah, that one looked alright." Grady agreed more quickly than Angie had expected. He looked to Steven, who concurred with a quick nod. "And there you have it. We made a decision." Grady spoke with a hint of satisfaction.

At that, Vince's protests were cut short. Motioning for the others to follow, he stepped up to the ticket counter. When Angie filed in to buy her own, he waved her off. "You're still my guest," he said, as though she were trying to usurp a sacred local custom.

"Well where I come from, when the guy pays it makes it a date," she said, allowing annoyance to her tone.

"Here, it's called good manners." Vince countered. "Besides, what kind of crappy date would I be taking someone on if I brought Grady along for it?"

"Hey!" Grady complained from behind them, overplaying a wounded expression. "I happen to think I'd make a first class…third wheel."

Angie stepped out of the line, waiting as the rest of the group bought their tickets and then migrated over to the arcade to kill time until their theater opened. Grady and Vince gravitated to a cooperative game involving a large screen and a set of plastic handguns. A handful of quarters later, the duo were engrossed in shooting at an endless parade of virtual assailants. Angie watched for a time before shuffling to one side where Steven stood by, monitoring the scores.

"Have you ever played this before?"

Steven shook his head.

"Me neither," she confided. "If there's time left after they're done, I'll play you."

"Sure." Steven looked slightly amazed at the suggestion. "You a gamer?"

Angie shrugged. "Nintendo mostly. I'm not a huge fan of first-person shooters, but I've played a few. I prefer games with a storyline."

"This game has a story!" Grady made the declaration without taking his eyes off the screen. His replica gun emitted a clicking sound every time he pulled the trigger.

Angie laughed. "I mean an actual plot—beyond shooting every bad guy that pops up from behind a shipping crate."

"Picky, picky." Grady cracked a grin and then grunted as his avatar took too much damage and his side of the screen began a countdown. He fed the device quarters until it allowed him back into the action.

Vince, in the mean time, had never seemed to break or even divide his concentration from the game. He'd gained a substantial point lead, which continued to grow as they completed the level objectives. By the time they'd reached a stopping point, it was clear he'd won.

"You really get into it, don't you?" Angie said, as Vince turned the plastic weapon over to her.

Vince smirked but Grady chimed in before he could answer.

"He's a machine. Back in high school, he used to play through a new game in two days." Grady's tone was one of reverence, giving the impression he found this feat to be somehow legendary. "He could go the whole weekend without eating or sleeping."

Angie was vaguely horrified. "That -can't- be healthy."

Vince appeared more embarrassed than proud of himself. "It's an ADHD thing. Once I get fixated on something I'm doing, I don't really notice time passing."

"Your Mom didn't check on you or remind you to take a break?"

Vince rolled a shoulder in a shrug. "If she did, I didn't notice."

Angie decided not to probe any further, as Steven had already begun adding quarters to start a new game. She focused on her side of the screen and hoped she'd be able to keep up.

The game lasted five minutes before she conceded defeat. She was satisfied to have held her own for a while, at least. By then their theater had opened, and the group filed in. Angie found a seat between Grady and Vince.

"Hey, do you want some popcorn or something?" Grady asked her as Steven arrived, arms loaded down with drinks he then handed to each of them.

"Oh yeah, I brought food," Vince said. "Thanks for reminding me."

He had stopped at a gas station on their way in and picked up snacks, which he'd smuggled into the theater via the many pockets of his cargo pants. As he retrieved the items, Angie collected the inventory into her lap, beginning to wonder at her host's nutritional status. Two packages of gummy worms, a pouch of Doritos, three bags of miniature cookies, and a chocolate bar for each of them. The candy bars, however, had been forgotten in his pocket long enough to have liquefied within their sealed wrapping.

Angie held up one of the chocolate bars and demonstrated its condition by squeezing the packaging.

"Okay, so that wasn't the best idea I've ever had," Vince said.

Grady gave the candy bar a pained expression as he selected one of the bags of cookies. "What a waste."

"It's not wasted. It's just...more challenging," Angie said. To support her argument, she gingerly pulled open one end of the candy bar and borrowed the straw from her soda to spear into the middle of the gooey mess.

"That would be awesome if it actually worked," Grady said with a low chuckle.

Angie put the straw to her lips to test her theory. The dark liquid was thick, but not to the point of collapsing the straw. To her surprise, it climbed up the tube with relative ease until she tasted chocolate.

"Wow." Steven's voice came from the other side of Grady, where he'd leaned forward to watch.

"That is probably the single coolest thing I've seen in like a month." Grady sounded genuinely impressed.

"And what does that say about your life, G?" Vince heckled from the other side of her. Despite the satire, he seemed just as entertained as the other two.

As silly as it was, Angie couldn't help but smile in triumph.

The movie was a complete success as far as Angie was concerned. She ceased monitoring the reactions of her three companions halfway through, satisfied they were all enjoying it as much as she was. As they left the theater, the boys encouraged her to choose their next location. A bookstore nearby caught her attention, and she was relieved when her suggestion was met without skepticism.

In a short period of time the group had settled into a natural cohesiveness, the likes of which she'd rarely experienced even among friends she'd known for years. Grady had a dynamic, sociable way about him that kept a light banter going between them all, while seeming to act as a catalyst for Vince's sharp wit. Steven contributed a pleasant, calming presence, flavored by infrequent but thoughtful commentary. Despite being the only source of estrogen among them, Angie found herself at ease.

Inside the bookstore, she browsed the bestseller rack before combing through the magazine aisles. It took her several minutes to realize her three cohorts were following behind her like lost ducklings. Amused, she shooed them off, suggesting they meet up again once they'd all found something to read.

It was dark by this time and the store wasn't busy. Still, Angie decided they ought to stay out of the way of the more legitimate customers. They regrouped near the back of the store, where Angie claimed a set of cushy chairs. Grady dropped into the chair beside her, toting a computer hardware guide. Vince followed close behind with a game design manual and perched himself on the chair arms between them.

"Not exactly light reading, guys," Angie teased, cracking open a local Birmingham magazine that boasted of the city's renowned restaurants, fine arts, and vibrant night life. Considering most of the Alabama-related images in her mental Rolodex were in black and white and revolved around the civil rights movement, she hoped to update her outlook on the city.

"Hey, I have certifications to study for if I'm ever going to get decent pay," Grady said.

"I'm pretty sure there's some kind of law against reading for fun while you're in college," Vince added, plaintively.

Steven headed their way with a thick graphic novel in hand. Angie recognized the book at a distance. "I just read that one when I was in New York," she said as he neared. "It was good, especially if you like that character. It answers a lot of background questions." Steven's pale brows lofted, and he turned the book over to scan it before settling cross-legged onto the floor near his cousin.

Grady marveled aside to Vince in a dramatic stage whisper, "Dude, where did you find this girl? She's smart, she games, she reads comics, and she gets our sense of humor. I don't think she's real."

"I ordered her off the internet," Vince whispered back, deadpan.

Angie felt herself shrink at their approval. Unsure how to take the public compliment, she lifted the magazine to hide her face. With her concerns over her awkward first day fading into obscurity, she was actually beginning to enjoy herself.

Chapter 22

After giving his cousin a ride home, Grady had made his way
back to Vince's house to meet up with the other two. It was nearing
midnight by the time they all arrived, and the lengthy night drive had
made Angie drowsy. Her host and his friend seemed to think the
night was still young, and so she rallied a second wind.

Grady went through Vince's media shelves and pulled out
several amateur films they'd both participated in. The first was a
James Bond spoof. The second short movie was a modern
reenactment of the assassination of Julius Caesar. In it, Grady played
Caesar and Vince assumed the role of Brutus. The film ended with
Grady delivering a long-winded speech as Caesar while standing at
the end of a dock. After which, he was hurled into the lake by a mob
led by Vince.

Angie glanced over her shoulder at Vince, recalling several
villainous characters he'd created for the story-writing community.
"Why am I not surprised you played the bad guy?"

Vince grinned. "I like to stick with what I'm good at."

"It was supposed to be for a history project," Grady said."But
somehow, we didn't get points deducted for being historically
inaccurate on pretty much everything."

Vince smirked. "I don't think we cared about accuracy. We
just wanted an excuse to throw G in the lake."

Grady shot Vince a wary look. He craned his neck side to
side, eliciting a few low popping sounds before muttering something
about his back bothering him.

"It's probably from cramming yourself into that girly little
coup for two and a half hours every day," Vince goaded. "You know,
you could trade it in for a -real- car."

"Hey, it's a perfectly manly vehicle." Grady bickered back at a near-whine. "And I've almost got the thing half paid off."

"Not at the rate you've been getting tickets in that cop-magnet." Vince laughed. He edged around Angie, gathering up the movies. Angie absently noted how quick he was to put them away. Vince had been entertainingly dramatic in the films — possibly even talented, she thought. Yet he didn't appear to relish the attention.

"I might be able to fix your back." Angie looked to Grady, gauging his receptiveness to the idea. "I'm pretty good at massage."

"Seriously?" Grady's bark brows raised in surprise. "Are you going to school for it or something?"

"I might after I finish my Associate's degree," she answered, hesitating. *I -might- do a lot of things, if I could just make up my mind.* "I've taken a few classes on it. It's pretty expensive to get certified, and I don't know if it would be a good idea to end up with a job where I'd be so dependent on my hands."

"Yeah, but it pays really well." Grady looked around the room, seeming uncertain. "What do I need to do?"

Angie waved a hand toward an open area of the carpet in front of the dresser. "Just lay flat on your stomach." After he'd complied, she knelt beside him and placed her hands against his shoulder blades. She could tell she would have some difficulty, given how muscled he was.

"I'm next," Vince said as he stood and meandered back to the futon. He'd put in one of the rental movies, seeming content to entertain himself as he lounged.

"We'll see how much trouble he gives me first," Angie said before rising. "Okay, so I could wear myself out trying to tenderize you the old-fashioned way…or I can try this." She placed the pads of her bare right foot between Grady's shoulder blades and slowly added more of her body weight behind it.

Relenting to the pressure, the air was forced from Grady's lungs in one long, whimpering groan. The end of his deflation was punctuated by a simultaneous round of popping sounds. Angie felt the abrupt chorus resonate up through her leg, and she smiled to herself in satisfaction.

Vince shuddered. "You know what? Never mind. I'm good."

Grady shrugged his shoulders as Angie lifted her foot. "No, actually…that feels a lot better." He sounded surprised. "What is that, the Japanese back walking thing? Shiatsu?"

"Close." Angie chuckled. "'Shiatsu' means 'finger pressure,' I believe. 'Ashiatsu' is 'foot pressure.'" She reached out and placed a steadying hand on edge of the dresser, mindful not to jostle the pictures and knickknacks. "Hold still," she warned, placing her lead foot flat along one side of his spine before using the dresser top to reduce her weight as she pulled up the other foot.

Grady sucked in a breath and grunted. He continued to hold that breath while she steadied herself and began rocking forward and back. She shuffled her feet by tiny increments upward as he finally exhaled, rolling onto the balls of her feet to concentrate her weight between his shoulders. Several more cracking sounds resulted, and she hopped back onto the floor to give him a chance to recover.

"Wow. I'm pretty messed up, huh?" Grady muttered, muffled in part by the carpet.

"Did you break him?" Vince called from his side of the room.

Angie nudged at Grady's side with her foot. "Can you still wiggle your toes?"

Grady bent his toes and then rolled his ankles, though he seemed sluggish about any other movements. He eventually rolled himself onto his side and then up into a sitting position. "That feels a -lot- better."

Angie smiled. "Good. But I'm not done—turn around." She folded herself down to sit behind him. Picturing the location of his trapezius muscles in her mind, she began kneading her fingers along his neck and shoulders. As brawny as he was, she had to switch to using the flats of her knuckles with a twisting motion to address the deeper points of tension.

Grady became even chattier as his posture melted into a forward slump. They talked at length about their shared interest in a particular punk rock band, which led them into other commonalities in their backgrounds, and even personal beliefs. Angie was pleasantly surprised by the ease of their conversation. Like her, Grady came from what he considered to be a somewhat functional family and had grown up in a church where his parents were active members. As a result, he'd taken any sort of personal faith for granted until his mid-teens. In the retelling, he spoke with an openness that Angie appreciated.

Once she'd finished her work, he turned around to continue their conversation face to face. By that point, Vince had long since fallen asleep sprawled across the futon, and they made an effort to keep their volume low.

"My sister must be about the same age as yours," Grady said, after they'd touched on the topic of siblings. He pulled out his wallet and offered her a picture of the sixteen-year-old in question.

Angie took it from him to examine. The slender young girl shared her brother's dark, expressive eyes and tanned complexion. Her heart-shaped face was one of pleasant features, enhanced by an expert layering of makeup. Shoulder-length hair had been lightened, highlighted, and ironed to fall in a silky curtain around her head.

"She's gorgeous," Angie said with a smile as she handed the picture back. "I bet she's popular at her school."

"Yeah, she does pretty well for herself." Grady formed a fond smile, tucking the photo back into his wallet. "She's always entering some sort of pageant. My mom must have dropped a couple grand on dresses for her already," he grumbled, and then seemed to think better of his tone. "Not that I think it's -bad-, it just all seems a little…shallow. And she's not a great judge of character yet, so she's got all of these loser guys chasing after her who only want one thing. I end up being the one to run off the worst of them."

"Not easy being the oldest, is it?" Angie gave a commiserating chuckle. She patted at her pockets to locate her own wallet and drew out a picture. "This is my little sis."

Grady plucked the photo from her hands and flipped it around. His eyebrows shot upward. "Wow."

Angie expected that reaction. Her sister was just as stunning as Grady's, by her estimation. Her hair was a warm, golden brown and waist-length, framing her petite face in loose waves. Her eyes were large and shown a brilliant blue. To top it off, she touted a flawless smile from behind full, pouty lips. "Yeah. She gets people's attention, too."

"She's really pretty," he remarked, seeming enthralled. "And…you know…dainty. She looks like a pixie."

Angie nodded. "I know. Most people find it hard to believe we're sisters."

"I can see why." Grady stared at the picture a moment longer before handing it back, looking suddenly abashed. "I mean, you're pretty too! Just…in a different way."

Angie formed a dismissive smirk, shaking her head as she replaced the picture. "We're different on just about every level—

which is probably why we've never gotten along. But, hopefully once we both move out we can figure out how to be friends."

"So, you've really never dated at all?" Grady diverted back to a point from earlier in their conversation, which she guessed was an attempt to recover from his verbal blunder.

"Nope." She shrugged, replacing her wallet. "I couldn't even get a date to senior prom. And I asked four guys to go with me just as friends, so it's not like I didn't try."

"The guys up there must be morons," he groused.

"It's okay—it's starting to feel more like an accomplishment." Angie mustered a half smile, glad she'd gotten to the point where she honestly meant it. If the road trip had done nothing else for her, it had at least given her that much growth. She was done with feeling sorry for herself. "I think it was an expected part of high school for people to play relationship musical chairs. But I didn't want to risk hurting somebody unless I was serious about them." She paused for a few seconds to consider, drawing her knees up to her chest in reflection. "So I guess I'm kind of...intense. I'd probably be too much for most guys to handle, anyway."

Grady shook his head, holding up a hand in assurance. "Hey, at least you're up-front about it and not all into mind games. The girls around here are crazy."

"I don't think that's a regional thing. Most of the girls -I-know are crazy." Angie laughed. "I mean...I'm not claiming sanity here. I have been driving around the country by myself for weeks."

"Yeah, but that's an awesome kind of crazy." He grinned in admiration.

Uncomfortable with the praise, Angie looked back across the room at Vince's sleeping form. His face was turned away from them, but from what she could tell, he hadn't moved at all in the last hour. "Tell me about Vince," she heard herself say before realizing she'd put the thought into words. She looked back to Grady with a tight smile. Trying not to come across as too interested, she added, "I haven't had much luck getting to know him since I got here."

Grady raised a single brow in surprise. "Really? Vince is pretty easy going, usually." He hesitated, casting a glance toward his sleeping friend before returning his attention to her. "Well, he's a great guy. We've been like brothers since we met in high school." He diverted his eyes upward , seeming to collect his thoughts. "He started out at some private school in Mississippi, and I guess public

school here was kind of a joke in comparison. He was always ahead
of everybody and bored to tears."

Grady chuckled in reflection and then seemed to sober. "He
hasn't had it easy, though. I think his parents get along fine when
they're not drinking, but…they drink too much sometimes. I used to
stay over all the time, and it seemed like his parents were always
coming home from the bar screaming and cussing at each other.
Weekends, weekdays, it didn't seem to matter. He'd have to go break
them up and make them go to bed. I don't think he'll ever drink—he
knows how ugly it can get."

Angie felt her brows pinch in sympathy. "Oh. That must have
been hard on him." She secured her arms around her calves, allowing
her chin to rest atop her right knee.

Grady shrugged a shoulder. "I know it sounds a little messed
up, but he's been doing that since he was a kid. To him, it's normal. I
think he's just glad they stayed together this long." He shifted
uneasily. "His parents are really nice people—they just…do their
own thing. You know, free spirits. As long as Vince got good grades,
they didn't bother him. Sometimes I wished my parents were that
lax."

Angie frowned. "I don't think you would have liked feeling
responsible for your parents."

"Yeah, maybe not," Grady said, brow creased with concern.
"It's just hard to imagine swapping places with him, you know?"

She nodded, knowing precisely what he meant. She'd been
trying to picture herself in Vince's position from the moment Grady
began sharing his observations, but the idea impressed her as
altogether foreign and devastatingly lonely.

Grady wasn't one to let silence linger. "Anyway, so Vince
started going to church with my family. He'd never really been
before, and he had a lot of questions. He picks stuff up fast, so when
it got to where I couldn't answer something, I brought him to the
youth pastor. They got along pretty well, so Vince started coming to
the youth group with me and a few other guys. We all ended up
getting baptized together. Formed a band in Vince's basement... We
were really fired up for a while there." He recounted with a wistful
smile and a liberal use of hand gestures. "Things were pretty good.
And they stayed that way until around the middle of our senior year."

Angie sat up a little straighter, curiosity piqued.
"Did…something happen?"

"Alaina happened." Grady made a face, rubbing at the back of his neck as though some of the tension had returned. "One of the girls we hung out with a lot. She was kind of like you—tough, smart, different. She was just like one of the guys, up until she and Vince ended up in a play together. They had this scene where they kissed. It wasn't a big deal, but after the play was over, a couple of her friends kept telling Vince that Alaina was in love with him. They begged him to ask her out."

"And…he did?"

Grady grimaced, lowering his head. "Vince didn't plan on dating anybody until he got to college. Said he wanted to be in a better position to take care of somebody else. But I…kind of told him it was a good idea." His tone was rueful. "See, Alaina had this really hostile thing against the whole concept of faith. Something about a bad experience she had at a bible camp, or something. I figured if anybody could show it to her in a different light, it'd be Vince."

"Ah," Angie said, keeping her face as neutral as possible. She could already sense he was alluding to an emotional train wreck, and wondered if she was staring at its unwitting conductor. "I take it that didn't turn out very well."

Grady shook his head. "He fell for her after a while…started chauffeuring her around everywhere and doing whatever she wanted. He got set on making her happy, and he quit going to church. I don't know if she actually made him stop coming or what, but I know she was having a lot more of an effect on him than he was having on her. By then, I was busy with my own girlfriend issues, so I really wasn't looking out for him like I should have." His expression twisted with guilt.

"After we graduated, Alaina got accepted to a college a few hours away. I guess she started right away with summer classes, because she moved there just a week or two after graduation. Vince got a job in Birmingham, but he worked it out where he was driving to see her every weekend. It seemed like that was going to work fine for them. But then, out of the blue he gets this 'Dear John' email after she'd been down there just a couple of weeks—"

Angie winced. "She broke up with him in an email?"

Grady nodded. "I was here when he read it. Something about how they were growing up now, and should be free to go their separate ways. He tried to call her to figure out what was going on, but she blew him off. He had to find out from some mutual friends that she'd pretty much gone wild as soon as she got there—partying every night and going home with different guys," he went on, solemn in tone. "She told Vince they were through the day after she moved in with two guys she met at some frat party."

Angie's jaw tightened in mounting indignation. "So, she basically ripped out his heart and fed it to a wood chipper. No remorse." She heard the flatness in her own voice as she summed it up. Part of her found it odd how fast Grady's insights had moved her from being uncertain about Vince to protective of him.

"I don't know." Grady gave a slow, sad shake of his head. "But I remember she had this phrase she really liked: 'Never say you're sorry.' She went around and signed everybody's yearbook with it. So maybe that just became her life's motto."

"That's not exactly justification for being so…callous," Angie muttered in disdain. "Her parents wouldn't be just a little disappointed if they knew what she'd been up to?" she asked, hoping he might provide her with a reason for pity over animosity.

Grady snorted. "I don't think they'd ever believe it. Not that she'd be honest with them about any of it. She always said they didn't understand her—"

"Oh, boo hoo," Angie droned, rolling her eyes as she made the motions of playing an invisible violin.

Grady chuckled, but it didn't quite pass for humorous.

Angie frowned as something nagged at the back of her mind. "I think I remember Vince acting different online. It would have been…a little over a year ago? He came up with a couple of new evil villain concepts around then, and a lot of really dark plotlines." She wanted to kick herself for not making the connection until now.

I never thought to ask why.

Grady nodded. "It tore him up. He got depressed, and I ended up staying with him a lot. He had me really worried for a while," he confided. "I guess that's how he coped. He kept himself busy with college and his job—filled in any leftover time with the internet and gaming."

Angie stood and stepped up to the dresser. She remembered seeing one particular picture had been laid face down, behind a handful of ceramic dragon figurines and next to a childhood photo of Vince with his father in a fireman's uniform. She cast a glance over her shoulder again to make sure Vince was still asleep before she picked up the frame. "Is this…her?" she asked Grady, motioning with a tilt of her head to the prom portrait featuring Vince in a tux, poised genteelly while holding the arm of a tall, slender girl in a crimson gown.

Grady peered up at it and nodded. "Yeah." He then added offhandedly, "See why you remind me of her a little? I bet you can pull off a dress pretty well, too."

Angie studied the picture, struggling to ignore his attempted compliment. True, they both shared darker features and hair, but that was where any physical similarities diverged. Angie didn't consider herself to have the keenest eye for beauty, but she did have a decent grasp of symmetry — and this girl's face didn't have it. Her smile was lopsided, with a greater upturn to the left side that was emphasized by the framing of midnight curls she wore down over bony shoulders. There was a slight turn to her pronounced nose, and her eyes were deeply set — giving them a beady quality that struck Angie as sinister. She had to wonder if her perception of Alaina would be the same if she hadn't first heard of the wanton harm the girl had inflicted.

"No...I don't see it," Angie said at last, setting the frame back down onto its face before crouching back to Grady's level. *And I don't want to.* "Girls like her give all of us a bad name. It's probably a good thing I won't be meeting her," Angie added, surprised by the anger creeping into her voice. What had gotten into her? From what she'd been told, it wasn't as though the girl in question had claimed to uphold some value system that she'd subsequently violated. Common decency wasn't truly common, after all. For all Angie knew, Alaina's choices had trapped her in a bleak cycle of self-perpetuating misery.

Not that it should matter to me, she reminded herself.

"I think I'd pay to see you two duke it out," Grady said, with a halfhearted grin of amusement. He had a definite charm to him, Angie decided. But given a few hours to observe him, she'd begun to suspect that he was more of an affable yes-man than an independent thinker. While she couldn't fault him for it, she was rapidly becoming worked-up , and she would've preferred the company of someone who could keep her in check.

"It'd be a short catfight," Angie asserted with quiet confidence. She palmed the knuckles of her right hand, eliciting a low chorus of cracking from the joints before adding, "I'd promise to rearrange her nose, but I think that'd just be doing her a favor." She winced then, as her conscience gave her a sharp scolding.

Grady clamped a hand over his mouth to stifle his laughter. He looked off across the room then and froze, letting his hand fall away. "…Vince? You okay, man?"

Startled by the abrupt change in his demeanor, Angie followed Grady's gaze to the futon. Vince was now sitting up, glazed eyes fixed on the television screen near them that had long ago returned to the movie's menu display. If he'd heard Grady's question, he showed no sign of it. He couldn't have been like that for more than a few minutes, she was certain, but that fact didn't do anything to lessen the eeriness in his stare.

"Is he awake?" Angie asked Grady in alarm. She knew of people who would sleep-walk, but there was something disconcerting to her about the idea of sleep-sitting.

"I don't know." Grady got to his feet and crossed the room. He crouched down at Vince's feet, placing himself directly in his friend's line of sight. "Vince?"

Angie followed close behind, unnerved by the vacant manner in which Vince continued to stare through and past Grady. She would have been tempted to describe his state as catatonic, but she didn't want to jump to conclusions. It occurred to her then that his breathing seemed heavier than it should for someone at rest. While Grady tapped the top of his friend's foot, seeming at a loss, Angie eased herself onto the futon beside Vince. She noticed then his hands — clenched into fists at his sides — were shaking.

"Vincent." Angie spoke in a quiet, commanding tone. She touched the backs of two fingers to his forehead, finding his skin cool and clammy. That ruled out fever delirium. She didn't know a thing about his medical history, but she doubted this was some sort of seizure. Finding his closest hand, she wrapped hers around it. "Did you…have a nightmare?" she asked, more concerned about getting a response out of him than with making him feel childish.

"Not exactly." Vince's dispassionate voice came at a low mutter. He didn't move, and his eyes never deviated.

Grady jerked backward in alarm, lost his balance, and fell onto his backside. "Dude," he complained.

"Not dreams, just memories." Vince's head wilted forward.

Angie's stomach writhed in distress. "You heard what we were talking about?"

Vince gave an almost imperceptible nod, though he still didn't look at either of them. It was as though he'd been enshrouded in a cloud of despondence so thick, it was palpable. He was suffering. Angie recognized that much — as clearly as she recognized she was the cause of it.

"I'm so sorry. I didn't mean to—" She pried at his clenched fingers and worked her hand into his when they relented.

Oh God, what did I do?

"You're sorry?" Vince's expression remained as vapid as his tone. "My life is what's sorry. I shouldn't even be alive in the first place."

Grady pulled himself up to sit on the edge of the futon, worry creasing his brow. "What are you talking about? You shouldn't say stuff like that." His voice pitched with anxiety, and Angie guessed that Grady might be feeling nearly as responsible as she did.

Vince made a short, low sound that could have been taken for a laugh, if not for the fact that he was so completely void of his usual humor. "A while back my dad had a few too many, and he told me the reason he stayed with my mom was because of me. Because he was taught that when you knock somebody up, you're supposed to stick around."

"You know they say stuff they don't mean when they're tanked—" Grady interjected in a deliberate, careful tone.

"They weren't even going at it that day." Vince finally shifted his dull gaze to Grady for an instant before staring across the room again. "But…I already knew I was an accident. I've known since I was a kid—" His voice broke off for a long moment. "I was the reason they were always miserable. I overheard them a long time ago, going on about how they'd be better off split up, but they couldn't because of me. They sounded so...trapped. I remember thinking how selfish I was, when I'd pray every night for God to keep my parents together. And then I thought if I wasn't around, they wouldn't have to worry anymore. They might be sad at first, but then they could finally be happy." Vince's listless voice remained near a whisper, the retelling spilling out in a halting ramble. No one interrupted him.

A prickling sensation spread out across Angie's skin, beginning at the back of her neck. A part of her recognized this as her body's reaction to an unconscious suspicion — one which the rest of her mind hadn't quite caught up to. She squeezed Vince's hand in a feeble attempt at encouragement. Glancing at Grady in hopes of direction, she found only uncertainty in his furrowed brow. So she focused all of her attention on Vince's face as he spoke, straining to read something. Anything.

Vince continued on, "I found a broken bottle in the kitchen. I tried to cut my wrist with it, but it hurt too much. I chickened out." He twitched the hand that Angie held, and she tightened her grip. "I hid it. I told them I fell."

Another glance toward Grady told Angie he was shocked by his friend's confession. It didn't seem likely she would find much help from him. "How old were you?" she asked, softly.

Vince answered in the same detached tone, "Seven, I think. Maybe eight."

Angie swallowed hard, struggling to keep her emotions under control while enduring the sense that something had slithered into her chest and constricted around her heart. "You've never told anyone before?"

Vince shook his head, a slight and slow movement. "I didn't want to end up in a psych ward. I never tried again. I thought about it a couple of times…when things would get bad. When I didn't want to feel anymore." He turned his head halfway toward her, green eyes shifting the rest of the way. "I'm not crazy. I'm just—" He trailed off, his tired gaze revealing how drained he was on so many levels.

"You're in pain," Angie finished for him. She recognized the despair consuming him as she would have recognized a physical person. Like an old, tormenting enemy — she knew it well. But she also knew better than to whip out the 'I know how you feel' card.

What do I tell him? Please, give me something he needs to hear.

Vince looked away from her and lowered his head.

Angie lifted his hand with hers and clasped her other hand over the back of it. "You have plenty of reason to be," she said, adopting a tone she hoped was less analytical and more soothing. "But you can't keep stuffing this. You have to face it and release it somehow, or it's just going to keep eating you from the inside out." She paused. "Thank you—for telling us."

"Yeah—" Grady found his voice again. "And you're not an accident, you know. There's no such thing as accidents. Everything happens for a reason." He recited the adage with an air of authority.

Angie resisted the immediate urge to smack him. *Thank you, Captain Cliché'.*

She knew Grady meant well, but she had serious doubts about his effectiveness. She was reminded of another one of her mother's favorite sayings; "Well-meaning people are sometimes the most dangerous."

Vince's eyes narrowed as he looked to Grady. "Okay G, so tell me the -reason- my parents are alcoholics. Or the reason my ex-girlfriend turned into a lying skank. How about explaining why everybody uses me to fix their computers, but I still can't get a decent job in my field?" Vince demanded, bitterly. "Is that all just part of God's cosmic chess game?"

There's the anger.

Angie expected it to be seething somewhere under that unreadable facade he'd maintained. "You're not responsible for other people's decisions. Just yours," she said, evenly. "You're allowed to be angry. Heck, -I'm- angry for you. But hanging on to this is killing you, and you know it. Eventually, you're going to need to forgive people…and God—" She considered a brief moment before gently adding, "—and yourself. Or you're never going to have the peace of mind you need so badly."

"Peace? Who has peace?" Vince muttered, voice riddled with disregard.

"I do." Angie surprised herself with how immediate the answer came.

Now...how do I justify that without sounding nutty?

She had to try. Pausing, she searched her mind. "I don't always hang onto it very well, and I forget how important it is sometimes—but when nothing else makes sense, it does. It's worth having."

As she spoke, it occurred to her she was attempting to explain something that defied explanation. She knew she couldn't blame him for rejecting her claim. She'd only recently come to terms with the fact that certain things could never be done justice when recounted in words or read about in books. Some things had to be experienced in order to be understood.

Vince fell silent for a long while, closing his eyes and resting his head back against the futon. "Sounds nice," he said at last. "It must be easy if you have one of those 7th Heaven families. You don't know what it's like, trying to hide from all of this crap—trying to hold everything together. I wake up at night sometimes thinking the dark is finally going to suffocate me." The anger had receded, leaving his tone despondent.

"7th Heaven?" Angie controlled her tone. Now was not the time to be irritated. "Well, I know he's not talking about my family. How about yours?" She directed the question to Grady.

Grady threw up his hands and shook his head. He didn't try to contribute anything else, and for the time being, she was glad for it.

"Look, I don't know what it's like to be you...and I'm not going to pretend we didn't grow up in different worlds." Angie leveled her face closer to Vince's ear. "But I do know what it's like to be depressed. I dealt with that for years. I remember how it was, feeling like you're standing on the outside watching yourself— wondering why you feel the way you do. Like there's something heavy and horrible sitting on your shoulders, coloring the way you see things. I remember wondering why I couldn't snap myself out of it." The recollection poured out of her so easily, she didn't have to think about it. "I know what it's like to just want to feel -normal-, never mind happy."

Vince's eyes opened and he turned to look into Angie's with an intensity that made her draw her face back slightly in surprise. She waited for him to speak, but he didn't.

It frustrated her that she couldn't read his face, but at the same time, she was relieved that he wasn't showing any signs of belligerence. If she wasn't able to help him somehow, then at least she hadn't made things worse.

"Would you...let us pray for you?" Angie asked, her voice coming out more timorous than she'd intended. She wasn't in the habit of making such requests, but if there was ever an appropriate time for it, this was it. Her friend needed more salve for his soul than any amount of talking was going to accomplish. Still, a selfish part of her hoped he might refuse and spare her the anxiety of praying out loud.

"I think that'd be a good idea," Grady said. He moved to sit on one side of the futon and laid and encouraging hand on Vince's shoulder.

Vince looked at the hand, then sent his lackluster gaze scanning from Grady to Angie. "Sure. Whatever," he mumbled. His head lowered in a gesture that was more resigned than reverent.

Angie was still collecting her thoughts when Grady began to speak. She didn't mind his initiative in the least. He knew Vince better than she did, after all. Aside from that, she was grateful to have more time to reign in her self-consciousness.

Grady prayed aloud with an innate poise, able to articulate his petition on behalf of his friend with an almost polished clarity. In moments like these, Angie was particularly grateful for the assurance that God wasn't hung up on presentation skills. The list of requests was eventually punctuated with a somber "Amen," and Grady withdrew his hand from Vince's shoulder. He got up then and moved to sit on the other side of Angie. He clasped her arm as he settled, offering an supportive nod.

Angie took a deep breath, beginning with a quiet torrent of words that seemed to be waiting for release. She'd closed her eyes early on, not out of obligation, but to help her keep her nerve. Her mental focus drifted as she spoke — sometimes far away, and sometimes centering on Vince's warm hand, still held between her palms. The empathic strain in her chest began to dissipate. As she neared a sense of completion, she found she didn't have much recollection of her words. But regardless of what she'd said or how she'd said it, she was sure her intentions had been conveyed. To her, that was what mattered.

All that remained to fill the silence was the low pulse of electronic background music, flowing from the wall-mounted radio. When Angie opened her eyes, she realized Vince was dead asleep. He'd slumped to one side and his head now rested in her lap. His face had relaxed at last, leaving it boyish and tranquil. In that moment, she had the odd thought that he'd never looked more like himself.

Too bad it takes unconsciousness to achieve this.

Compelled by a gentleness she hadn't realized she had in her, she brushed the backs of her fingers along the hollow of his cheek. Vince didn't stir.

She turned her head to look at Grady and found him asleep on the other side of her, his legs bent at the knees and hanging off the end of the futon. Angie couldn't decide if this was evidence that it was incredibly late, or that she was incredibly boring. What -was- clear to her was that she was sandwiched between two handsome young men in a rather questionable position.

A tingling flush of apprehension crept up her neck. Technically, the predicament crossed a certain boundary line in her mind. She was fairly sure that her mother would "pitch a fit," if she understood the southern turn of phrase correctly. On the other hand, she was exhausted — and it seemed wrong to wake Vince after what she'd just put him through.

Coming to a tentative decision, Angie rested her head back against the futon and closed her eyes.

Chapter 23

July 21st,

Alabama The Beautiful

I arrived safely in Cropwell on Friday, but promptly got my butt lost. Fortunately, Vincent found me right away. He's turned out to be a really sweet guy. At first I was afraid we weren't going to get along. But then yesterday I spent most of the day hanging out with him and his best friend, Grady, and we discovered that my sense of humor blends pretty well with theirs. Grady spent the night at Vince's house, and I stayed up talking with him for a few hours after Vince fell asleep. He ended up telling me some of Vince's difficult history. Vince must have overheard at least some of it, we realized later.

I'm still not really sure what happened. Around 3 am Vince woke up, sat up, and started doing a zombie stare. Grady and I went to sit with him, and he finally told us what was wrong. As it turns out, he's been dealt more betrayal and neglect than most people would know how to cope with. It was almost like his past hurts from his ex-girlfriend and others were threatening to destroy him with bitterness. I think he's been hiding in his own darkness for a long time. We tried to talk him down, but I don't know how successful we were. He did let us pray for him, at least. I think it helped, but I think his freedom is still largely dependent on his will to attain it. I truly hope that he'll decide to release his pain soon.

It was a strange night I suppose, but I think some good came out of it. I can't explain it very well, I just feel like I've seen what Vince's soul is made of. Somewhere in there is a strong, brilliant, and compassionate person. Part of me is already sad that I'll have to leave on Tuesday. I know I can't take care of him, but I desperately want someone to be able to. He needs and deserves that much.

~Ang

Grady left mid-morning on Sunday. With Vince showing no signs of consciousness and his mother nowhere to be found, Angie kept herself occupied by rounding up food. Finding nothing in the refrigerator aside from milk, cheese, and copious amounts of beer, she dipped into the boxed-food supply from her car and made a pot of Fettuccini Alfredo.

Gathering her courage, she made up an extra plate and went to wake Vince. Still feeling responsible for causing her friend's emotional upheaval, she hoped sleep might have improved his outlook. But she couldn't be sure what condition he would be in.

Balancing two dishes along one arm, she eased open the door to his room. To her surprise she found Vince already awake and sitting at his computer, looking none the worse for wear. In spite of the odd sleeping conditions, whatever lacquer-like product he'd used on his hair had ensured that the spiky composition remained intact. What surprised her most was his demeanor.

"Afternoon," Vince greeted, with an easy smile. His expression was as collected as ever, but warmer and more transparent than she'd ever seen it. "Need a hand?"

"I'm good," Angie said, crossing the room before setting one of the plates on the desk in front of him. "Here, I made lunch." She moved to sit on the edge of the futon and placed the remaining dish in her lap, gauging Vince's reaction out of the corner of her eye. Budweiser whined with interest, creeping along the futon to lay at her hip. She ignored the dog's imploring gaze.

Vince pulled the Alfredo toward himself, coppery brows raised. "So that's what you were up to? I thought you were packing up to leave."

"Why?" Angie cut him a bemused look, watching as he forked a bite of noodles into his mouth. "I've got two more days left."

"Yeah, but after last night I wouldn't have blamed you if you wanted to get out of here sooner." His tone lowered, eyes trained on his plate.

Angie smiled to herself as she started in on her food. "Yeah, about that—" she began, catching a flash of worry in his eyes. She wanted to tell him the experience somehow had the opposite effect on her, but instead said, "Thanks for trusting me enough to be honest. I never meant for you to relive all of that."

Vince released a long breath. "I guess I had to deal with it eventually." He lifted one corner of his mouth in a wary half-smile before diverting his attention to eating.

"You don't have to deal with it alone," Angie said. "Everybody's damaged. It's just a question of how badly, and whether you're healing or still bleeding."

Vince gave her a skeptical look. "Is this where you tell me that God can snap His fingers and make it all better? Because it's not like I haven't asked. I don't know what else He wants from me."

Angie was relieved to sense simple frustration from him, rather than the overflow of anguish from the night before. "Have you ever tried thinking of God as a person instead of an all-powerful vending machine that never gives you the right amount of change? He has feelings too, you know." She put the proposal to him as more of a challenge than she'd intended. When he didn't respond right away, she tried to cover her frankness by voicing another question — one that had been nagging at her. "Vince…how did you end up so different from your parents?"

He gave a short laugh. "I get that one a lot. I used to think I had to be adopted—" He took another bite for a round of thoughtful chewing. "When I was a kid I tried to make them happy, but nothing worked. And obviously, nothing they were doing was working for them, either. So when I got older I decided if I handled most things the opposite of how they did, I'd be doing okay."

Angie was impressed, and she made no effort to conceal it. "That's not the conclusion most people would come to." She had been braced for the likelihood of offending him with one or both of her questions, but he didn't show any hint of enmity.

He seemed to study her for a long moment. "Look, I don't want you thinking that my parents are awful people. It's not like that," he said, leaning forward to stress his sincerity. "They mean well, and they love me. They've made a lot of sacrifices—"

"—and mistakes." Angie broke in, maintaining a careful tone. "You don't have to make excuses for them. I don't think they're awful," she reassured. "I probably don't have a lot of right to complain, but it's not like I had it perfect when I was growing up, either. My dad screwed up a lot when I was younger." Though she read doubt in Vince's face at her claim, she hesitated at going into detail. The last thing she wanted was to sound like she was competing for the title of Most Traumatic Childhood.

"What, did your dad smack you around or something?" Vince joked.

Unprepared for the question, however flippant, Angie stared back at him numbly. Before she could decide how or if she should answer, she saw his expression slacken and then shift in revelation.

"Whoa...wait. He -did- hit you?!" Vince's voice dropped, exuding both disbelief and anger.

Angie centered herself with a few slow breaths. "If you mean out of anger instead of discipline—then, yes. Sometimes." Seeing Vince's expression darken, she held up a hand in a staying motion. "It wasn't like we were regularly beaten. He just had a really bad temper," she explained. "Honestly, the screaming and belittling was probably worse on me than getting backhanded for no reason. My mom always said his father was so much worse, so he never had an example of how to be a decent dad..."

Angie mustered what she hoped was a calming smile, surprised by how upset Vince still looked. He hadn't said anything yet, but she could see his mind churning behind his gaze. "He's not like that anymore—not even close," she went on. "I forgave him a long time ago. That doesn't mean it didn't happen. It still affects me...and some of the things I don't like about myself. But I'm a lot better now than I used to be."

"You swear he doesn't hurt you anymore?" Vince eased forward in his chair, penetrating green eyes regarding her with a quality she was tempted to perceive as protective.

Angie nodded, forcing an uncomfortable laugh. "Don't worry about that. Even if he hadn't changed, I'm bigger than him now." As she watched, Vince's brows knit together into a perplexed expression. "What?" she wondered aloud. His gaze was so intent, she half expected he was trying to tell her she had food on her face.

"Your eyes—" he said, pausing, as though he couldn't decide how to deliver his thought. "Are you wearing contacts? They were brown before, and now they're hazel."

The question caught Angie off guard, and she blinked several times. "Oh. No, they just change sometimes when I'm thinking or upset." As it was an anomaly no one outside of her family had ever noticed, she readied a vague medical explanation.

Vince leaned forward for a closer look, showing no signs of the skepticism she expected. "Like a mood ring?"

"A little like that, but not so dramatic."

"I'm sorry." Vince formed a pained look of regret. "I didn't mean to upset you."

"You didn't." Angie smiled to reassure him. "You'd know. If I'm really upset, they turn green—almost your color."

"You should smile more," Vince said, contemplative in tone. "Maybe then they'd stay brown." Seeming to gain the sudden awareness of how close their faces were, he drew his back.

"I'll work on that," Angie said. Groping for a diversion, she leaned aside to examine a small stack of papers on the nearest corner of his desk. "What's UACT?" she asked, reading the first thing she saw.

"The University of Advancing Computer Technology," Vince replied. "That was my first choice of colleges to attend. I got accepted no problem, but even with loans I couldn't manage the tuition," he added, resignation in his voice. "The other problem was it's in Arizona, and my parents didn't like the idea of me being that far away."

"So, the Tech College in Birmingham was your second choice?"

Vince gave a somewhat aggravated sigh. "No. My second choice was an Art and Design college in Georgia. I thought my parents might be okay with me going there, since it's at least within driving distance. But they didn't think I could make it on my own."

"Maybe they just weren't ready to let go of you." Angie frowned. "You're smart and responsible. You would've made it."

"I like to think I would have." He smirked. "Being an only child isn't all it's cracked up to be."

"Are you at least getting the degree you wanted?"

"Close. I'm just not sure I can do what I want with it." Vince angled his computer monitor, allowing her to see the vibrant, three-dimensional image of a winged beast surrounded in flames. "That's the project I have due tomorrow."

Angie gaped, leaning forward again to take in the fantastical creature. Its guarded posture and curving wings reminded her of a gargoyle. The skin tone he'd chosen for it was a deep shade of plum, causing the lower half to make a seamless transition into shadows.

"Wow. That's -really- good," she said. His level of skill had taken her by surprise. "I bet you could do movie effects or something once you graduate."

"I wish." Vince laughed. Having finished his food, he pushed the plate away and reclined back in his chair. "Actually, I've always wanted to design video games." He winced after the admission and lamented, "It still sounds like a stupid little kid's dream when I say it out loud."

"No it doesn't." Angie shook her head. "Everybody needs to have a dream. It's not like mine sounds any more practical as a career."

Vince gave her a keen look of interest and drummed his fingers against the arm rests. "You've got one that's as much of a long-shot as mine?"

"I've always wanted to be a writer."

Vince maintained a doubtful look. "A lot of people make a living off of that."

"Yeah, but I want to write novels," she clarified. "Post-apocalyptic science fiction."

Vince broke into a humored smile. "Well that's...different."

"That's the problem." Angie shrugged, looking down as she finished her Alfredo.

"I could see you doing it, though." Vince spoke in earnest after an extended moment of thought. "You always wrote great stories online."

"I'd probably need to consult your expertise when it comes to evil villains," she deflected, unsure of how to take the compliment. "Don't you write at all? Outside of the online stuff, I mean."

"I used to, when I had time." Vince gave a hesitant nod. "I'm better with poems and essays, but I did write a short radio play a few months ago."

"Can I hear it?" Angie asked, straightening up.

Vince's eyes widened. "I'd…rather you didn't." He seemed to reconsider. "It's based on this really creepy dream I had about a clown, and it's got a lot better effect after dark."

"I can wait until dark." Angie crossed her arms, her curiosity heightened. "Do you have anything I could read right now?"

Vince cast an uncertain glance around his immediate workspace. "I think I've still got a poem from my English final project." He grabbed a three-ring binder from the shelf beside him and handed it to her. "If you want, you can bring it along for reading material. I thought we could drive into Birmingham and visit the art museum."

Angie resisted peeking into the binder, tucking it under her arm as she stood. "Sure," she said, relieved by the suggested change of scenery.

Vince headed for the door ahead of her, calling his dog to him with a soft whistle. "And since you made lunch, I'll buy dinner." He told Angie over his shoulder.

This time, she didn't feel inclined to argue with his sense of hospitality.

The hour long drive into Birmingham gave Angie ample time to look over Vince's work. At the front of the binder she located a five page poem titled 'The Quest,' and it didn't take her long to realize it was an epic.

Silence is the tool with which fear begins to rule,
A foreboding sense of restlessness, rippling like a pool.
It creeps along an empty place, in search of its next feast,
Inside the man whose twisted mind makes him like The Beast.

The poem wove on in four-line stanzas, depicting the medieval tale of three heroic friends in pursuit of an infamous creature. As the telling progressed in this rhythmic prose, the supposed glory of their mission became mired in trickery, deceit, and betrayal. The ending revealed a vicious cycle of tragedy, but Angie found it fitting rather than dismal. Behind that first poem she found a free verse piece brimming with the lament of a tortured artist.

"Don't read that one." Vince broke into her thoughts, casting her a disquieted glance from the driver's seat. "There's way too much teenage angst in there. I was feeling sorry for myself when I wrote it."

"It's good, though," Angie said, intrigued by his self-consciousness. As she looked out her window for the first time, she didn't recognize anything about the route they were taking. The recent rain had dissipated, leaving hazy shafts of sunlight piercing through the clouds to illuminate the two-lane road ahead. They were winding through dense forests, with the occasional farm breaking up the scenery. Hand-painted signs cropped up here and there advertising home-grown peaches and blueberries.

"Where are we?" she asked.

"I took the back roads," Vince said, hazarding only a glance her way. The irregularities of the road seemed to demand the bulk of his concentration. "I figured you might like the scenic route. It's a little faster."

"It's so pretty out here, " Angie said, catching a glimpse of a doe wading through the deeper shade along a roadside creek. The trees laced together and arched overhead, giving her the sense of traveling through a broad tunnel of vegetation. They passed a tiny country chapel that seemed to be a replica of others she'd noticed — down to the chastising platitude on the black-lettered sign and the promise of a Friday night revival service.

"So, what's with all of these little backwoods churches holding revival meetings?" she asked, looking aside to monitor Vince's response.

"Beats the heck out of me." He chuckled, genuine amusement reaching his eyes. "As far as I know, the only reason you'd revive anything would be if it were dead. And as often as they do it, I think they'd be better off pulling the plug."

Angie bent forward in laughter. "You might have a point there." She thought she detected relief in Vince's smile and guessed that he'd been concerned over offending her. It amazed her how different he seemed from the first two days of her visit. Though she wasn't sure how much of his aloofness was actual and how much was simply a misperception on her part, she was grateful for this new and comfortable familiarity between them.

Okay, so I'm actually glad I came to Alabama, she admitted to herself. *Didn't see that coming.*

~ ~ ~ ~ ~ ~ ~

After a leisurely afternoon at the art museum and dinner at a nearby deli, Vince received a call from Grady. On their drive back, they all met up at a scenic overlook and stood around watching the sun sink behind the foothills.

Angie found no shortage of entertainment in the back and forth between the two friends. Their topics ranged from the idea of visiting Minnesota in the fall, to the difference between the words "shank" and "shiv." From Vince she learned that a shank referred to an improvised weapon, and shiv was used to describe an action performed using a shank. While Grady seemed skeptical on the side of the two words being synonymous, he eventually conceded to Vince's advantage in the area of prison terminology.

Darkness set in, and Grady suggested they all meet for dinner the following evening. Before they left, he surprised Angie with a box a Krispy Kreme donuts and an album from one of the bands they'd discussed the night before. When she tried to refuse, he insisted he'd had an extra lying around. While she found this unlikely, she thanked him and headed back to Vince's car.

"That was nice of him," Angie said, opening the box of donuts and offering them out to Vince as he slid into the driver's seat beside her.

"Yeah. Nice," he commented in a remote tone, shaking his head at her offer.

Angie shrugged and helped herself to one of the pastries, wondering at her friend's apparent distraction as they plunged into the relative darkness of the back roads. "Something wrong?"

"No," Vince answered quickly, forming a faint smile before seeming to reconsider. "Well, my gum lost its flavor. But I think I'll recover."

Angie laughed. Instead of pushing him for a better explanation she opted to enjoy her sugary snack, contemplating their previous conversation. "So, what was it like growing up on the grounds of a prison?"

"A little unsettling, now that I look back on it." Vince chuckled. "Our house was right between camp thirteen and the gas chamber. But it's not like I knew any different at the time." He paused. "Except that I was lucky, because most kids didn't have inmates for friends."

She stared at him in shock. "You were friends with the inmates?"

"Just the ones that were allowed to work with my dad at the firehouse. They were the ones you could trust. Even though a few of them were technically murderers—"

"That didn't scare you at all?"

"Well, I didn't really know that back then." Vince smirked in reminiscence. "One of the guys, Big John, used to carry me around on his shoulders and play video games with me on the weekends. When I'd ask him what he was in for, he'd always tell me he got caught stealing pies off old ladies' window sills."

Angie polished off a third donut and gave him her full, intrigued attention. "Did you ever find out his real story?"

"Yeah. My dad told me after we moved here." He frowned, hesitating. "Somebody raped his daughter. Big John found the guy before the cops got around to it, and he beat the crap out of him. The guy ended up dying." Vince's eyes cut to her, as though he were weighing her reaction. "My dad never thought it was fair he had to do so much time for defending his daughter."

Angie's heart clenched. She took a few moments to process before asking, "Did his daughter come to visit him?"

He smiled at that. "All the time."

A comfortable silence settled as the drive wore on. Angie became entranced with watching the road as the headlights revealed the short hills and sharp curves ahead. Vince navigated them with deft skill, as though he'd long ago memorized every detail of every mile. She didn't have a clear view of the speedometer, but she felt sure they were going well over the posted limit. Between the rollercoaster-like effect and her narrow field of vision, the ride began to disagree with her.

Vince spoke up out of nowhere. "Grady was flirting with you. You know that, right?"

Angie rallied from the edge of wooziness and looked at him, unsure if what she read on his face was annoyance or dismay. "Was he?" She frowned. Part of her felt stupid for not recognizing the fact, but the rest of her was too distracted by her churning stomach. *Oh, please don't let me throw up in the car...* "So then, he actually meant it when he said he wanted to visit Minnesota sometime?"

"Yeah, probably." Vince flit his gaze toward her when the road allowed. "I think we both meant it." He seemed to struggle with his words before his expression shifted to one of concern. "…Are you feeling okay?"

"Not really," Angie answered, fumbling to open the window on her side. Sucking in a deep breath of cool night air, she found a sliver of relief. She felt Vince's hand on her shoulder.

"Was it dinner? Bad donuts?" He sounded alarmed.

Angie closed her eyes and fought the ripple of nausea that crept its way up her torso and into her throat. "Motion sickness," she replied, bracing her arms and hanging her head out into the wind. Somewhere amid her misery she sensed the car slow and felt Vince's hand on her back. She knew he was talking to her, but for several minutes she couldn't afford to divide her concentration. The steady hand between her shoulder blades was nearly as comforting as the fresh air. After a time, the balance tipped in her favor and the donuts stayed down.

Vince didn't remove his hand until he'd pulled into his driveway and parked. Before Angie could collect herself, he'd walked around to her door and helped her out. "I'm really sorry," he repeated, as she dimly recalled him doing numerous times.

Thankful to be on solid ground, Angie leaned against the car to steady herself. "It's okay—it's not so bad anymore." She formed a weak smile.

"I won't take those roads again," Vince said, guiding her by the arm once she'd pushed off from the car. He walked her into the middle of the half-acre front lawn and urged her to sit. Their presence did nothing to interrupt the constant, pitching drone of Cicadas in the nearby trees. The high vibrato of crickets and lower, distant bellow of frogs completed the nighttime cacophony.

Angie eased down and then flopped onto her back. The cushioning grass cooled her skin, while the stars overhead greeted her with unusual brilliance. "Wow," she breathed, pleased to have such a worthy distraction from her waning discomfort. "Not much light pollution out here, huh?"

"Yeah, that's one of the few perks." Vince chuckled, stretching out beside her. "My dad bought me a telescope when I was a kid. I wish I could remember more about it than just how to find the planets."

Contemplating, Angie stretched out a hand in front of her and pointed up at the first constellation she could easily identify. "That 'W' shape is Queen Cassiopeia." She traced the lines from point to point with her fingertip. "It's supposed to be her on her throne, but it leaves a lot to the imagination."

"The vain queen." Vince nodded when she glanced his way. "I remember something about that from Greek mythology."

"That's right." Angie nodded. With a degree of satisfaction, she motioned toward a kite-shaped constellation. "There, that one's yours. Draco." She followed along its winding tail with a sweeping finger.

"The Dragon." A smile came through in his voice. "So, where's the north star?"

"See Ursa Major…the Big Dipper?" Angie pointed to the star grouping, skimming upward as she drew along the handle.

"Yeah?"

"That's the easiest marker," she said. "Look to the cup part at the top corner, and then off in a straight line—you'll run into the handle of The Little Dipper. Its layout is reversed from the Big Dipper. See it?" She turned her head aside to follow his gaze as he tracked with her instructions.

Vince shifted closer until their shoulders touched, bringing his angle of sight in better alignment with hers. "Yeah, I see it," he said, lips quirking upward in recognition.

"It's right there," Angie said as she outlined the invisible connections. "The last one at the end of the handle."

Vince looked upward intently, nodding once before turning his face toward her. "So that's the one I follow, if I want to find you again?"

Angie gave a dismissive smirk to conceal her sudden trepidation. "I believe buying a plane ticket would be the easiest way." *He couldn't like me that much. Not after I almost got sick all over his car.* "But don't feel obligated. There isn't that much to see in Minnesota."

Vince made a thoughtful sound, but said nothing more.

Angie stared up at the glimmering starscape overhead until her thoughts settled and her eyes drifted closed. She didn't know how long she'd been dozing on the lawn before she felt a light, pleasant sensation moving along her skin. She opened her eyes to find Vince propped up on one elbow, smoothing his fingertips along her arm.

He smiled, lingering concern in his expression. "Feeling better?"

"Much." Angie fused her answer with a reassuring smile. She considered retracting her arm from his reach, but found herself curious over the soothing effect his touch was having on her. Instead, she pretended not to notice. "I might sleep out here tonight." She closed her eyes again.

"I suppose you can." Vince chuckled, his fingers brushed the inside of her elbow. "But I don't think our luck is going to keep holding out against the mosquitoes."

"I guess you're right." Angie sighed, though she was in no hurry to retreat to the house.

If he were gutsy enough, this wouldn't be a bad time to kiss me.

Where did that thought come from? She had little time to examine it before she sensed Vince shift his weight.

Warm breath grazed Angie's cheek just before she felt the tentative touch of lips to her own. Despite her passing thought, she hadn't expected this. Instead of her mind switching off in surprise, she was acutely aware of Vince. His kiss was gentle and timorous — almost novice. Though she knew sharing it could hurt him, in that moment, she feared she might cause him worse pain by rejecting the show of affection. Tentative, she returned the kiss.

Her acceptance ignited a mutual intensity she wasn't prepared for. Vince pressed closer, with a doting responsiveness that enveloped her in an inexplicable warmth. What she had meant to end quickly became a searching, drawn-out exchange of emotion. Vince surprised her again by being the one to break their connection.

Angie opened her eyes to find him staring down at her with a tense look of worry.

"Are you alright?" he whispered.

"I…think so." She forced herself to focus, unsure of what had startled him.

Without warning, Vince lowered his head and laid his ear against her chest. "Your heart—"

Only then did Angie realize her heart rate was so rapid, it felt as though the muscle was rebounding against her ribcage. Baffled by her own physical reaction, she sat up abruptly. "I'm fine. It just does that sometimes," she told him, neglecting to mention that the last time she could remember her heart beating this fast involved a double espresso and a strenuous Aikido practice.

What does that mean? Five minutes ago I wouldn't have thought of him as anything but a friend.

"Did I...scare you?" Vince eased himself back, brow creased with concern.

"No." Angie shook her head, mind buzzing with apprehension. She couldn't be sure if he'd gotten caught up in the stargazing, or if he'd truly begun to care about her. If anything scared her, it was the idea that she now had the power to hurt him.

Vince studied her face for a long moment, though she couldn't meet his gaze. "Has anyone ever kissed you like that before?" he asked, point blank.

"Yes," Angie answered without thinking. "Scott. The guy I stayed with in New York." She didn't expect the spark of disappointment she saw in his eyes as she spoke.

Vince eased back a little further from her. "Do you...love him?"

Angie looked down at her hands, weighing the question. "In a way." She glanced up in time to see Vince drop his chin and look away. "It depends on your definition. I love all of my friends." As she began to elaborate, she realized how evasive she sounded. "I'm not in-love with him, if that's what you mean."

Vince looked back at her again, his face more unreadable than it had been all day.

"I didn't go on this trip looking for a boyfriend," she added. "Look, I like you. There's a lot to like—" she said, hoping it wasn't too late to spare his feelings. "—but that can't happen again. I don't want to screw up our friendship. Besides, we live on opposite sides of the country."

"Yeah, I know it wouldn't make sense," Vince admitted with a hint of frustration. He regarded her for a long moment before his mouth softened into a rueful smile. "Why couldn't you have been the girl next door?"

It occurred to Angie that she'd been staring at him. She looked down, emitting a small laugh. "That would have been too easy." Satisfied they had come to an understanding, she took a steadying breath and got to her feet. "You know, you still owe me that radio play."

Vince picked himself up. "I guess I do."

When she turned and made her way back to the house, he followed without another word.

Chapter 24

Angie gripped the edge of the passenger seat, resisting the urge to comment on Vince's driving technique. In any other city she'd been in, the term "rush hour" was an oxymoron. Yet, the last time she'd glanced at his speedometer, it was sitting near 90 mph.

To Vince's credit, he was an adept driver and only seemed to be keeping up with the rest of the early morning traffic as they entered the outskirts of Birmingham. He was faithful in using his turn signal, and courteous in making room for anyone merging. That put him in the minority.

"Do people always drive like this?" she asked, after someone on a motorcycle took to the center line and raced past her window.

"Pretty much." Vince's answer was nonchalant, though he didn't take his eyes off the road. "It's nice for getting in on time, but when there's a wreck, it's really bad. I've sat at a dead stop for hours some days."

Angie forced herself to look more relaxed than she felt. She was confident he knew what he was doing, but she didn't have any reason to trust the rest of the commuters, who all seemed under the delusion that they were driving for NASCAR.

She stole a quick glance at Vince's intent profile again, remembering their kiss the night before. Thus far, he was acting like it hadn't happened. While he hadn't reverted back to complete aloofness, they'd hardly spoken since his alarm went off that morning. Part of her was relieved, but another part of her that thought perhaps she should bring it up. But talking about it could be interpreted as encouraging — and she couldn't risk doing that to him.

If he was keeping to himself, then he likely acknowledged that the whole thing had been a mistake. And while there was something dimly painful about that, she knew it was for the best. She just hoped that the remainder of her stay wouldn't be awkward for either of them.

Angie minded her surroundings as the car's transmission began to protest a steep mountain incline. Eighteen-wheelers fell into a sluggish line in the far right lane, unable to keep up under the strain. The climb lasted for well over a mile before they reached the crest and began a coasting descent.

The view into the valley was breathtaking in the morning light. Thick patches of forest spread out for miles in all directions, intermingled with the urban sprawl. Rather than merely carving out space for itself, the city appeared to have grown up conforming to the lay of the land. Beside the highway, Angie made out rock formations and sheets of earth that had sloughed downward in miniature mudslides. The bold, rust-red coloration of the stones and soil stood out — she was in the heart of the Alabama iron belt.

Vince glanced over and caught her stifling a yawn. "I can fix that."

"You can fix the fact that I had to get up at five-thirty in the morning?" Angie smirked. She'd never been an early riser, and Vince's lifestyle of minimal food and sleep was starting to take a toll on her.

"Absolutely," he said, veering the car down an exit ramp. "The culinary branch of my school has an awesome bakery, and I get a discount. It's just a few blocks from my office."

Angie sat up eagerly once they'd pulled into the parking lot of the Cullinard Bakery. The rich scent of coffee, cinnamon, and fresh bread invaded the car before they'd even opened the doors. Her stomach burbled in approval. She heard Vince laugh and looked over to find him watching her, eyes crinkled at the corners in amusement.

"I'm going to start feeding you better, I swear." He got out and walked around the car. By the time she'd unbuckled and fished her handbag off of the floorboard, he'd opened her door for her. She thanked him this time, while reminding herself not to become too partial to the custom.

Ten minutes later, Angie followed Vince into an office tower with a double mocha in one hand, her other arm loaded down with three enormous muffins. She'd polished off a blueberry scone in the car. Vince had insisted on buying her every pastry she'd shown the slightest interest in — apparently in an effort to make up for his sporadic eating patterns. As far as she was concerned, it was working.

The Alabama State government building was an unassuming, four-story concrete structure, poised at the top of one of the steepest foothills overlooking the valley. Angie hung back as she followed Vince inside, unsure of what to expect from his place of employment.

"Are you sure it's alright for me to be here?" she asked as they approached a small lobby where empty chairs lined the walls.

"Sure," Vince said, casting her a smile over his shoulder. "I cleared it with my bosses weeks ago. Besides, they have interns come in to observe all the time." He crossed the lobby to a Plexiglass-enclosed help desk. Behind it sat a squat, ungainly man who appeared to be in his late thirties. His thinning black hair was cut short and professional, well coordinated with a pale blue dress shirt and brown-and-blue striped tie. But Angie barely noticed the ensemble, thanks to the coke bottle glasses that stood out as his most prominent accessory.

"Hey, Owl." Vince greeted the man. "How was business this weekend?"

Owl gave a slow smile as he looked up from the switchboard. "Oh, not too bad. Got a nice tip from the wedding I told you about. I had a little trouble running things through my laptop, though. You think you could take a look at it for me later?" His articulation was precise, but his deep voice came out monotone. "Oh, hello there." He nodded once to Angie when he noticed her.

"I'll see what I can do. Bring it by on break," Vince said, motioning to Angie then in introduction. "Owl, this is Angeli—the friend from Minnesota I told you about. You mind letting her come and go if she needs to?"

"That's no problem." Owl nodded again to her. "Nice to meet you."

"Thank you." Angie smiled, giving the man a small wave. As Vince cut to the right, she followed him through a gray steel door into a maze of hallways and cubicles. Once the door had closed behind them she whispered, "His name is Owl?"

Vince chuckled. "No, it's Jerry. He's just capitalizing on his DJ persona. I guess it was his nickname back in the day, and he made the best of it. He's always had pretty bad vision." He motioned to his own glasses.

"Ah," she said, pausing at a hallway intersection to let a woman in a wheelchair go by.

As they rounded the corner, Angie noted a middle-aged man coming down the hall toward them. Tall and dark-skinned, the man approached while sweeping a thin white cane back and forth in front of his feet. His chin lifted as though he were looking upward, though his rounded sunglasses made it impossible to gauge their actual direction of focus. Wearing a faint, perpetual smile, he projected an uncanny confidence. The tip of his cane hovered just off of the floor, giving the walls an occasional tap as he walked.

"Good morning, Mr. Gill," Vince called out to announce their approach, coming to a halt just ahead of the man's cane.

"Well, good morning to you!" Gill exclaimed with vigor, stopping to angle himself in Vince's general direction. "And thank you again for your assistance last week. I was about ready to chunk that printer out the window! That's assuming the windows here open. Do they open? You know, I've never tried—" He rattled on in an easy, conversational tone. His jovial voice carried an edge of Alabama drawl to it, muddled with something that Angie guessed to be East Coast in origin.

"You're more than welcome." Vince laughed. "I brought a friend along to shadow me for the day. Mr. Gill, this is Angeli." He looked to Angie as he spoke, guiding the man's attention in her direction. He then explained for her benefit, "Mr. Gill is one of our guidance counselors."

"Angeli. Now there's a lovely name." Gill switched his cane to his left hand and extended his right out in offering. "Vincent mentioned you before, I believe. So glad you made it here safe and sound. Has this young man been treating you well?"

Angie handed her coffee off to Vince and grasped Gill's hand. "Thank you. Yes, sir," she answered, trying to keep up with his steady stream of chit-chat. The man's thick fingers flexed around her hand in a prolonged, assessing manner.

"Voice of an angel, and she's even willing to lie for you. How'd you ever get so lucky?" Gill took on a broad, teasing grin as he turned his face back in Vince's direction. He released Angie's hand and stacked it with the other around the handle of his cane.

Vince glanced at Angie before clearing his throat and changing the subject. "How was your birthday, Mr. Gill?"

"Oh, it was fine," Gill said. "A few of my friends took me to a gentleman's club."

Vince's copper-colored brows lofted in surprise. "...they took a blind man to a gentleman's club?"

"Yes, that bunch find themselves awfully hilarious at times," Gill replied. "I got the last laugh, though. I got us thrown out."

"And...how'd you manage that?"

"I asked the waitress if I could Braille her." Gill held up a hand and splayed his fingers, grinning wryly. "Her boss was fit to be tied. Evidently, they don't make exceptions on their 'no touching' policy. He came over and I got to arguing with him about how his establishment wasn't properly accommodating the differently-abled. The next thing I knew, some large fellah had me by the back of my belt and they hauled all of us out the door. I don't think they quite believed that I'm blind. Ha!" His voice jumped an octave at the last syllable and he rocked forward into an unbridled belly laugh.

Angie covered her mouth to suppress a giggle. She wasn't sure which she found funnier — the man's story, or the unusual sound of his laughter.

A grin crept across Vince's face and he shook his head. Before he could speak he was interrupted by a shrill, feminine voice coming from the cubical to his right.

"What's all this racket about? These are office hours, people!" A plump, diminutive woman appeared in the open "doorway" of the work space, hands planted on her hips. Her burgundy-dyed hair featured blunted bangs and was pinned back— teased to a comical height at the crown of her head. She pursed thin lips and cocked her head to one side as she surveyed Angie. "Who's she?"

Though the thirty-something woman couldn't have stood an inch over five feet, the abrasiveness of her voice was enough to make Angie want to shrink behind Vince.

"No one you need concern yourself with, Miss Deena," Gill piped up, angling himself in the woman's direction. "Say, aren't you in charge of the company picnic this year? As a concerned employee, I would like to know the precise origin and ingredients of the potato salad. I have an allergy, you see, and last year's recipe had my head swelling up like a Macy's Day balloon. Or so I'm told." He tapped the tip of his cane to the ground between his feet.

Vince signaled Angie with his eyes and eased around behind Gill, continuing down the hall while the brusque woman was distracted. "Thank you Mr. Gill," he said, almost under his breath.

Angie caught up to Vince in a few swift steps, concern gnawing at her stomach. "Is she one of your bosses?" she whispered.

"Deena? Nooo," he stressed, then gave a short laugh. "She's a secretary, like me. They just let her think she's in charge of a few things to keep her off everyone's back."

"So, Gill just took one for the team?"

"Yep. Now I owe him." Vince smirked, cutting into the farthest right cubicle as they reached the end of the sterile, blue-gray hallway. He moved behind a desk, facing the entrance to the small space, and nodded to a cushioned chair in the left corner. "You can sit there. I'm just sorry it's going to be boring."

Angie smiled, shaking her head as she found a place to unload her food near the designated chair. "I've got books with me," she said. "And so far, this place is shaping up to be interesting."

"If you say so." Vince gave her a thoughtful look before beginning to sort a tall stack of papers, going back and forth between them and his computer.

While he worked, Angie took the time to pick at a poppy seed muffin while she scanned the walls of his cubicle. Framed certificates and awards lined the back wall in neat rows, ranging from recognition for various honor societies, to a series of course completions in American Sign Language. The right wall featured a collage of photographs. Several she recognized to be of Vince's parents, all in a darkened setting with them holding microphones — karaoke, she supposed.

She spotted movement in her left peripheral vision as someone stepped into the cubical. Angie turned her head, and then had to consciously keep from staring at the miniature woman who stood smiling at her. If Angie had been standing, the top of the woman's head wouldn't have quite reached the level of her hip. Her face was soft, creased with age in a way that granted her a grandmotherly appeal. Blonde and silver-streaked hair was pinned into a tidy bun, and her deep brown eyes held an inviting warmth.

"You must be Angie." The woman extended a small, weathered hand out to her in greeting. Her voice came out airy and pleasant. "I'm Lydia. Vincent assists me with all of my sight-challenged clients."

Angie recovered from her fascinated stupor and grasped Lydia's hand. She couldn't recall ever having such a strong inclination to be careful with a handshake. "Pleased to meet you." She responded quickly, hoping the woman wouldn't think she was demeaning her.

Really? He couldn't have bothered mentioning that his boss happens to be a Little Person? She wondered to herself if the omission had been intentional on Vince's part, out of some perverse curiosity over how she might react. A quick glance his way told her otherwise.

Vince smiled to Lydia and held up a blue folder. "I'll have those medical requests finished for you before lunch."

"Thank you, that'll do just fine. I'll be busy with client meetings most of the morning anyway." Lydia turned her illuminating smile to Vince and then back to Angie. "You just let me know if you have any questions, Miss Angie. I should have time this afternoon if you'd like a tour."

"I'd like that very much. Thank you, ma'am." Angie nodded, distantly aware that Vince's manners were beginning to rub off on her. 'Sir' and 'Ma'am' had never been a part of her vocabulary when it came to interacting with her elders. Vince seemed to have been hardwired with more respectful terminology, along with a solid sense of chivalry.

Maybe it's just a southern thing, she mused.

"I'm Lydia's personal secretary," Vince said after the woman had stepped out and returned to her office. "Jim is my other boss, but he's over the entire unit. You'll meet him when he makes his rounds."

"You work with a pretty diverse bunch," Angie said. She found herself looking forward to whoever else she may be introduced to as the day went on.

Vince gave her an amused look. "That's pretty safe to say."

Over the next several hours, Angie tried to concentrate on reading. She picked out Deena's grating voice from time to time, thanks to the openness of the workspace arrangement. And every time she did, it seemed that the woman was making a point of badgering someone.

People came and went along the outer hallway, with a few stopping by to ask Vince computer-related questions. Some wanted his help with their work machines, and others were seeking advice on personal computers they either owned or planned to buy. Vince met every inquiry with a thorough and genial response.

As much as she didn't want to admit it, Angie was coming to respect the way Vince conducted himself. She caught herself watching him with some frequency, though she was careful not to let him notice. Eventually she gave up on her book, trading it for her journal in hopes of clearing her thoughts.

July 22nd,

I went with Vince this morning to his office job. Fortunately, his work isn't too strenuous. I get the impression that he ends up doing a lot of things around here that aren't in his job description. If he weren't as young as he is, I doubt people would be taking advantage of his helpfulness as much as they seem to.

I'm confused again today. And I guess I'm hoping that if I write it down, it'll help somehow. Last night, Vince kissed me. I'm still trying to process that. I know it was meant to express affection, but I feel badly. I didn't mean for him to become too attached to me; just like I didn't mean for it to happen with Scott. I wish I knew what's wrong with me. Now when I leave tomorrow, it'll be more like I'm abandoning Vince. He's been through so much...I don't want to be just one more person that hurts or abandons him. I have to try not to be stupid and pray that something works out for the better.

I always used to wish guys would like me and pay more attention to me. But now, I think it's more responsibility than I can handle...

"It's about lunch time." Vince spoke just loud enough to break her concentration. He smiled when she looked up at him. "Mom's coming to meet us. She doesn't think you should leave without experiencing some good southern barbeque."

Angie blinked, surprised by how quickly the time had passed. "Oh, okay. Sure." Vince stood up and she followed, stuffing her belongings into her handbag. While she'd thought she was resolved to keep her distance from his personal business, curiosity got the better of her.

"So, is all of this computer work you end up doing for people actually part of your job?" she asked.

Vince shook his head. "The IT department is on the top floor, and they're usually swamped. So I kind of unofficially take care of most things on this floor."

"Without being compensated for the kind of work you're doing?"

Vince rolled a shoulder. "I keep applying and taking the tests to compete for a computer tech position, but once they dock the affirmative action points, my scores don't get me anywhere."

She blinked at him in confusion. "Why would they take points away from your score?"

"Because...I'm a male," he said, sounding resigned to the predicament. "And because I'm technically considered "white." My grandma may have been Native American, but it isn't documented in any way that can help me."

Angie gaped at this. "That doesn't seem fair. You're smart and you know what you're doing—" she began, knowing her tone was aggravated but unable to temper it.

Vince held up a hand to stop her, "But these are state government jobs. They have to make a ratio quota." He gave a weak smile, lowering his voice to a hushed level. "It's okay—I've already accepted that I'll have to look at private companies if I'm going to move up in the world." He frowned then. "My parents won't be happy when I find something else. They think a government pension is the ticket to stability. But, this isn't what I want to be doing."

He motioned with his chin for her to follow as he ducked out of the cubicle and headed left down the hall.

A man wearing khaki pants and a yellow dress shirt was walking well ahead of them in the same direction, and Vince seemed to recognize him. But instead of calling to the man, he came to an abrupt halt and stomped his foot three times in quick succession. Angie stopped just short of running into his back, perplexed by his odd behavior.

The man ahead of them spun around, smiled, and began signing to Vince as he walked back toward them. He was of a fit medium build, sporting short, curly blond hair and a close-trimmed beard to match. She guessed him to be anywhere from his mid-thirties to forties. The signing continued back and forth between the two as Angie strained to discern something out of the silent, spirited conversation.

"Sorry," Vince looked to her and then motioned to the man. "This is Marshal. He's one of our deaf counselors."

Marshal signed "hello," and then spoke in a muted but articulate voice, "You must be Angie."

She recognized the rapid, one-handed spelling of her name. Nodding, she repeating the motions back to him at half speed. "That's me."

Marshal grinned at her fumbling effort. His face was every bit as animated as his hands when he asked, "Has Vince been boring you silly?" He didn't spell Vince's name, but rather seemed to use some shortened version of it that involved forming the letter V with two fingers, tapping them first to the back of his wrist and then to the middle of his forearm.

"Not at all." Angie shook her head, glancing to Vince and repeated the motion Marshal had made in reference to him. "What does this mean?" She attempted to ask both of them at once, making a point not to turn her face away from Marshal as she spoke.

Marshal nodded to Vince.

"It's my name," Vince said, chuckling. "But it's more like a personalized nickname that only a deaf person can give you once they get to know you. It's actually a modification of the sign for 'computer.'" Vince formed a C with one hand in demonstration, tapping it once to the back of his wrist, and then again halfway up his forearm.

"Oh...I get it." Angie smiled, charmed by the concept.

Marshal nodded, looking satisfied. "If you come back to visit again, I will have to give you your own name, too." He stared at her for a moment, as though he were trying to decide something.

"That'd be an honor," Angie said — and she meant it. Too bad she couldn't see herself ever returning to Alabama.

Marshal looked to Vince then and formed the letter A with both of his hands, tapping them to his shoulders and opening them into fluid, rolling motions out to either side of him. "What do you think?"

Vince formed a faint smile. "More fitting than she knows."

Marshal raised his pale brows and tapped his watch, directing to Vince, "I need to meet someone. Will you come by my office later? The Instant Messenger is acting up again."

"No problem," Vince said and signed back.

Marshal clapped him on the back and smiled once more to Angie before continuing down the hall.

Angie looked to Vince after Marshal's departure. "What did that last one mean?" she asked, repeating the sign Marshal had suggested.

Instead of answering her, Vince continued down the hall. Angie was forced to take a few jogging steps to catch up with him. He cast her a backward glance, hesitating. "That was the sign for angel."

"Oh." Unsettled, Angie decided it would be best for both of them if she changed the subject. "So, can Marshal hear at all?"

"Just low tones. He loves any music with a lot of bass," Vince answered. "I think he had partial hearing when he was born, so he's able to speak pretty clearly from the sounds he remembers."

"You're pretty good with the ASL," Angie said, though she tried not to betray the extent of her admiration.

"I've thought about studying to be an interpreter," he said, offhand. "Deaf culture is pretty interesting. I wish I could have taken you to one of the Silent Dinners, but they only hold them once a month. The timing didn't line up."

"What's a Silent Dinner?" Angie asked, falling back in step with him as they rounded a corner.

"Not as quiet of an experience as it sounds." He laughed. "It's sort of a club for deaf people, their families, and sign language students. They all pick a place to eat and sit around in a big group signing to each other the whole night. It's kind of a crash course in conversational ASL. The first one I attended, I kinda faked my way through it using the only three signs I could remember."

"Which signs?"

Vince smirked, dipping his chin in a look of vague embarrassment. He paused at the lobby door and signed each as he listed them to her. "What's up?, Whatever, and Bull$#&%."

Angie couldn't help but laugh. She found it particularly entertaining that the last sign involved the use of the pinky and index finger to form the distinctive shape of bull horns.

Vince laughed with her. "Yeah, I know. Real sophisticated."

As they moved into the lobby, Angie caught sight of Vince's mother hovering near the front entrance. She wasn't alone. Deena stood beside her, leaning in conspiratorially as they discussed something in low tones. While Marie appeared cheerful as ever, Deena had a more baleful cast to her pudgy features.

"I'll be right back, I forgot something," Vince told Angie just a few strides from their destination. When he turned and backtracked at a jog, she resisted the impulse to follow him.

Shuffling on toward Marie and Deena, she offered a pleasant smile for both women. "He'll be right back," she said. Angie was both confounded and relieved when Deena scowled, turned, and walked out the door without saying a word to her.

"Hey, girl!" Marie exclaimed with welcoming smile. "I've got us reservations at my favorite little place. Yer gonna love their cornbread cheese biscuits!"

Angie counted it as ironic that the thickest southern accent she'd encountered thus far belonged to someone who'd been transplanted from the Northeast. She found herself resisting the urge to mimic the woman's twang in responding. "That sounds great." Angie smiled to Marie and then gestured toward the glass exit door and Deena's retreating form. "Do you mind if I ask what that was about?"

Marie gave her a glazed look before seeming to catch up to the meaning behind the question. "Oh…oh! That was nothin'. Just sour ol' Miss Deena, stickin' her nose where it don't belong. If it were a pastime that paid, she'd be the richest person I know." She tossed her orange-red hair over one shoulder and laughed.

Angie frowned, staring past her out the door as she considered pressing for an answer she might regret. As it turned out, Marie didn't need much prompting.

"She was just askin' me about you," Marie divulged. "Where you came from, how long you're stayin', where you're stayin'—I just took her for curious at first."

Angie centered her focus on Vince's mother. "—but?"

"Well, after I told her you were stayin' with us, she wanted to know what room you were sleepin' in. You know…like she was fixin' ta uncover a scandal." Marie patted Angie's elbow in reassurance. "But don't you worry sweetie, I told her that wasn't any of her damn business." She gave another tittering laugh. "Shoot, it ain't none of my business either. If Vinny's door is closed, I give him his space."

Angie stiffened, feeling the uncomfortable flush of heat rising through her chest and up her neck. "It's not like that!" she blurted out before she could catch herself. She dropped her head along with her volume, hoping the woman wouldn't interpret anger. "And I think it - is- your business. It's your house." She glanced back up at Marie's face. Angie knew the woman meant well, but the implications of her statement were overwhelming. "You can come into his room any time you want while I'm here. In fact, please do."

"Alright, honey. Don't you let her get to you." Marie placed a hand on Angie's shoulder and gave it a warm squeeze.

"What's wrong?" Vince's concerned voice reached them as he came back through the lobby door.

Marie brightened. "Nothin' wrong, son. Deena was just bein' her unfriendly self again."

Angie looked to Vince, struggling to maintain a steady expression. He'd taken on a grimace at the news, and she decided to distract him from any deeper inquiries into the matter. "Sounds like she's a special kind of vile. You think if I threw some water at her, she might melt?"

Vince's mouth shifted, one corner tugging upward at her remark. "We're not that lucky."

~ ~ ~ ~ ~ ~ ~

Lydia gave the promised tour of the office building that afternoon.

On her way back to Vince's workspace, Angie had to edge her way around Gill, whose towering frame took up most of the cubicle entryway. She sat back down in her designated chair in time to overhear the tail-end of the man's contemplations on the idea of adopting a blind cat. Vince seemed to be listening to Gill and processing paperwork at the same time.

A boisterous voice carried down the hall. "Gill? You need ta get a move on. You've had somebody callin' about their screen reader."

Cut short mid-sentence, the blind man turned in the direction of the voice. "Is that so? I must have forgotten to check my messages—" He pivoted again and extended his cane as he set off in the other direction. "I'm on it!"

Moments later, Gill was replaced by an older, stately looking gentleman. His gray hair was neatly combed back and square-rimmed bifocals perched atop a hawkish nose, suggesting a seriousness about him that was contradicted by his mirthful expression. He wore a white dress shirt and teal tie over black slacks. His sizable paunch spilled forward over his belt, demanding he counterbalance with his shoulders thrown back and chest expanded. "Now, don't let Gill get away with chatting your ear off. He'd talk to a dead dog in the road." The man grumbled to no one in particular. Coming to a standstill, he noticed Angie sitting in the corner.

Vince set his papers to one side and gave the latest visitor a knowing smile. "Mr. Jim, this is Angeli. Angeli, this is Mr. Jim—the unit manager."

Angie sat up at attention and offered her hand. "Pleased to meet you, sir. And thank you for letting me be here for the day. I hope I haven't gotten in anyone's way."

Jim accepted her hand, shaking it only once. "Not at all! It's good for us to get more young faces in here. Keeps us old folk on our toes," he said. "So you're from Minnesota? You know, you don't have much of an accent." He sounded disappointed.

Angie cleared her throat and extended her vowels in an effort to humor him. "Yah, sure…you betchya?"

Jim tipped his head back in a hearty, resounding laugh. "She's a good sport. I like that." He directed the comment to Vince before looking back to Angie. "Gets pretty cold up there, doesn't it?"

Angie had begun to wonder how many people held the impression that her home state was a frigid, year-long winter wonderland. "Well for four or five months out of the year, yeah, it gets pretty cold. But it gets just as hot in the summer as it does here."

"You don't say." Jim gave a contemplative grunt. "Well, I've never been there myself. I suppose I've just got a picture of frostbite and ice-fishing in my head for some reason."

Angie smiled. It hadn't taken her long to decide she liked the man. "Probably for the same reason I associated the South with moonshine and rednecks. Media stereotypes are hard to replace until you see the real thing in person."

Jim leaned toward her and lowered his voice. "You haven't heard many car horns playin' Dixie since you've been here, have you?"

Angie chuckled, dropping her voice in a tone of reassurance. "Just once. But don't worry, I heard it more often in the parking lot of my high school."

Jim straightened up, exaggerating a relieved sigh. "Well good. That's one less person I need to apologize to for something I can't help." He broke into a beaming smile when he looked to Vince, as though he'd just shared a private joke. "How are you doin' on those reports, Wonder Boy?"

Vince seemed entertained by the back and forth, but he sobered quickly. "I'm keeping ahead of them so far. How are you holding up?"

"Oh, you know me—hangin' in there like a hair in a biscuit." Jim formed a determined fist in front of himself. "I've got an appointment with my cardiologist on Thursday. Assuming one of those surprise inspections don't agitate me into a heart attack before then."

Vince's smile grew. "Let's hope not. You'd be missed around here. Nobody takes flak from the higher-ups like you can."

Jim rumbled out a low, chuckling complaint, "I'm the flak-taker, am I? Well that's nice of you to point out, but it isn't much incentive to stick around. I've had about enough of this ol' body fallin' apart." He rocked side to side until he'd turned himself around and started back into the hallway, throwing a departing wave over his shoulder. "Carry on."

Vince shook his head, looking to Angie questioningly. "Feel like the guest star on a sitcom yet?"

"Something like that." Angie laughed. "I'm not bored, that's for sure."

She retrieved the book she had yet to make progress on and laid it open in her lap. When she glanced up, Vince was still watching her. His expression shifted from humorous to enigmatic. She expected him to look away, but he didn't. Opting to look down, she forced herself to appear as engrossed in the book as possible.

The work day came to a quick end, in Angie's mind at least. Before she knew it, Vince was packing up and she was following him out of the building. Sunlight warmed her face as they crossed the parking lot, and she realized she'd missed it. She had trouble imagining herself being confined to a windowless box, steeped in chilled, recycled air every day; forty hours a week.

A man with a salt-and-pepper goatee and sharp, pale features came toward them en route to the building. Standing just below average height, he was dressed down in a gray t-shirt and jeans. She wouldn't have noticed him, except that he raised a hand and paused to address them. "Hey, Vince!" His voice carried a nasal, Midwestern pitch. "Is this your girlfriend?"

The question caught Angie by surprise. As casual as the man had put it, it still seemed forward. Looking to Vince, she decided to leave the answering to him. She found herself intensely curious over how he would respond.

Vince missed half a beat in his reply, his gaze flickering to Angie's face and then back to the man. "Ah…no, Wayne. This is my friend, Angie. I'm pretty sure I mentioned she'd be visiting?"

"Oh! I remember." Wayne hooked a thumb into one of his belt loops and pointed at her with the other hand in a motion reminiscent of firing an imaginary gun. "From Minnesota, right?"

Angie mustered a polite smile and nodded. "That's right."

"Sorry, I guess you weren't quite what I was expecting," Wayne said, not bothering to explain what he meant before continuing. "Hey, I've seen that movie Fargo. It was pretty good. But do you folks really talk like that up there?"

Angie blinked, at a loss as to whether she should correct the man on his grasp of geography. Fortunately, Vince interjected for her.

"Fargo is in North Dakota, Wayne."

Wayne set his jaw forward in a look of confusion. "Oh. Well, I was close."

Vince nodded toward his car. "Sorry, but we need to run. My night classes are about to start. Good to see you." He waved in salute and motioned for Angie to follow.

She didn't need any encouragement to vacate the brief, yet awkward conversation. "Nice to meet you." She nodded to Wayne and all but sprinted for the passenger door of the Corsair.

Once the doors were closed, Vince gave her an apologetic smile. "Sorry about that. Wayne can be a little…odd."

"It's fine." Angie didn't feel in need of an explanation. She was more preoccupied with analyzing the way Vince had answered the man's initial question. A lingering contradiction left her mystified. She knew she would have been angry at the presumption if he'd said "yes." So, why was it she'd felt the bite of disappointment at his denial?

Vince glanced over his shoulder as he started the car and backed out. "I've got a little more time before class than I let on," he said. "Can I interest you in another mocha?"

Angie smiled, struggling to set aside her confusion. The thought of specialty coffee was a welcome distraction. "Oh, definitely. "

Chapter 25

Mocha in hand, Angie stepped out of Vince's car and
followed him through the crowded parking lot of his school.
They had passed the set of brick-faced buildings on their way
in that morning, but she hadn't recognized the place as a college. The
asphalt between the weathered buildings was veined with deep,
unfilled fissures and weeds growing unchecked. Short cement steps
led up to unmarked entrances. Several cars throughout the parking lot
contained loafing drivers, most sharing the booming bass of their
music selection with passersby.

The entrance they approached was crowded with at least a
dozen loitering students and faculty of varying ages. The grouping
shared the unifying effort of gulping down hasty lungfuls of cigarette
smoke. They parted just enough to allow Vince and Angie single-file
passage.

A dingy glass door opened into a compacted foyer, hallways
lined with offices and classrooms stretching to the left and right. The
dull blue carpet was thinning along obvious tread paths, and even the
silk plant near the elevator seemed ragged under the florescent lights.
Angie was beginning to see why Vince considered his education here
to be sub-par.

"Wow. Your school is kind of...ghetto," she said, continuing
her scan of the lobby. The next thing she knew, Vince caught her by
the crook of her elbow and towed her to an alcove beside the
elevator. Bewildered by the abruptness of his action, she didn't have
time to protest before he'd grasped her other arm and all but backed
her into the wall.

"You -can't- say stuff like that around here." His warning
came in a strained whisper.

Angie began an indignant objection, but stopped short when she read the genuine dread in his face. Her first inclination was to search the upper walls and ceilings for any recognizable form of surveillance. "What, do they do the Big Brother thing here?" she asked, concerned at once that she might have unwittingly gotten him into trouble.

"What? No." Vince shook his head. "It's not the school you need to worry about, it's…people. That's not a word you can just throw around without offending somebody."

Angie paused to process this before mouthing the word 'ghetto?,' in search of clarity.

He gave a curt nod.

Angie's jaw slackened in disbelief. Defensive, she whispered back, "But…where I'm from it's just common slang. We use it for describing anything run-down. I've looked it up, it was originally a Venetian term, and—"

"That doesn't matter," Vince interrupted, squeezing her arms just above the elbows to command her attention. "People aren't going to ask where you're from or what it's like there. They're not going to care that you don't know any better. They're going to jump straight to being pissed off." Seeming to realize he still had a hold on her, he let his hands slip down off her arms. His eyes searched hers, rapt with concern. "I just don't want you to get hurt. Please…be careful what you say."

Angie nodded, a belated sense of embarrassment creeping over her. "Sorry. I'll try," she promised.

Now let's see how long I can keep my big mouth muzzled.

Vince stepped back from her and then aside to hit the up button on the elevator. "Sorry about that," he said. Hands in his pockets, he looked as shamefaced as she felt.

Angie decided she was glad he'd cared enough to correct her. "Don't worry about it. Somebody needed to save me from myself." She gave him an appreciative smile, stepping onto the elevator when the doors slid open.

Angie glanced up from her corner of the white-walled classroom and checked the digital clock over the door. It had only taken her a few minutes to tune out the murmurings of the two dozen students around her. Intent on their computers and self-led in their work, no one had questioned her presence.

Overhearing her name, Angie's mind pulled back into focus. She sat up straighter in her chair. Several feet away, Vince was meeting with his pre-production editing group. Most of them were staring at her. Angie closed the book she'd been skimming and scanned over the young men until her questioning gaze landed on Vince. "Did I miss something?"

Vince started to answer but was cut short when a small, bushy-haired fellow across from him piped up, "You know some martial arts stuff, right? We want to put you in front of the green screen."

The lanky young man beside him reclined in his chair and slapped the back of bushy-haired-guy's shoulder. "Yeah, we'll have you beat up Jason here for about ten seconds and record the whole thing so we can import it into the game. Should look nice." The others nodded in agreement.

"Oh...okay. Sounds like fun." Angie shrugged, concealing her bewilderment. Her focus shifted back to Vince as everyone stood up and gathered their belongings. He offered an contrite smile, scooping up his laptop as he made his way over to her.

"Sorry to volunteer you like that...nobody else had a better idea." Vince cast her a sideways glance as he slid his laptop into its carrying bag. "It won't take long. We'll go meet Grady and eat somewhere after class is over." He slung the bag over his shoulder and turned to face her, a gauging expression tightening his features.

Angie tucked her book under one arm. "I don't mind, if it helps you with your class. It actually sounds interesting." She smiled, following the last of the group as they filtered out of the classroom and made their way down the hall. After some consideration, she added, "Just as long as you don't let them superimpose some sort of unflattering Battle Bikini onto me, I'm fine with this."

Vince chuckled. "Oh, don't worry about that—" He nudged her with an elbow, grinning boyishly. "I'll make sure it's -very-flattering."

Angie gave him the most offended look she could summon and sidestepped, aiming for the toes of his right foot. She hit her mark and Vince faked a limp for the next few paces, still smiling to himself.

As they walked, Angie scanned over the framed artwork that hung every few feet on either side of the hall. All of the pieces displayed graphic art done by present and former students. Some offered fantastical landscapes with abstracted scenery, while others featured bizarre machines and horrendous creatures. "Any of these yours?" she asked.

Vince shook his head. "Not yet. I haven't been around long enough to be noticed." They turned the corner into a narrow corridor which emptied into two small rooms. The one on the left was open and brightly lit, while the one to the right was dimmed — lined with computers and recording equipment. Vince made a quick gesture to the left doorway. "They'll set you up in there however they need you. I have to take care of things in the studio, quick."

Angie nodded, moving past him into the open room where the lanky, dark-headed young man she'd seen earlier was setting up a camera on one side. On the opposite wall a green screen hung from floor to ceiling, stretching unbroken to the floor and then out to cover several feet of the carpet.

Three more of Vince's classmates trickled in through the doorway. The camera man gestured for her to move back until she stood in front of the screen. A heavy-set young man hovered on one side and then the other, repositioning the lighting.

"Alright, now just do a little warm-up pose for us and then we'll send Jason in for you to take down," the camera man said while adjusting the camera angle. "He'll fake a punch, and you can take it from there."

Jason stepped in from the hall, casting the camera man a skeptical look that went unnoticed. He combed his fingers through the shaggy mass of his sandy-blond hair and gave Angie a nod. He then made a show of popping his fingers one at a time and bouncing from foot to foot. The students grouping near the doorway began to snicker. The camera man snapped his left hand into the air. "Ready? And...action!" He swept his hand back and pointed at Angie.

Angie took a deep breath and began a basic warm-up routine. She cupped both hands at her center with one curved over the other. From there, she made a wide arching motion with her right arm while taking a step in the same direction. Her foot came down as her arm straightened, and she held the position for a moment before drawing the arm and leg back into herself. She repeated the movement on her left side. Sliding her left foot behind the right foot to form a triangle of balance, she lifted her right hand and made a four-finger beckoning motion.

Jason took his cue and moved into camera view, rearing one fist back and widening his stance in an attempt to make his small frame appear more threatening.

"Try not to hurt him, he's fragile," came the mock-plea of an audience member. Jason shot an acrid look over his shoulder. Making a dramatic lunge forward, he threw a weak punch aimed at the center of Angie's chest.

Angie's arms were already extended in front of her, and so the action of deflecting Jason's fist with her left forearm required little effort. As she knocked his punch aside she kept the edge of her arm in contact with his wrist, sliding the blade of her palm down until she gripped the back of his hand. In a fluid motion she turned his palm upward, using her other hand to curl his fingers back toward himself. At the same time, she stepped forward.

With this force bending his pinky finger toward his elbow, Jason crumbled to his knees. His face twisted in pain. "Ow...ow...ow!" He clutched at his wrist with his free hand in an attempt to alleviate the strain. Angie gave his arm a leading tug to the left before releasing it. With his balance thrown, Jason flopped onto his side. He uttered one last punctuated "Ow!" and was rewarded with sympathetic noises from the onlookers.

"That should be enough," the camera man said, lifting the device from its tripod and handing it over to one of his classmates.

With that, the spectators all but disbanded, most of them moving across the hall into the other room. Jason picked himself up off of the floor and offered Angie a handshake. She accepted, somewhat apologetic.

"Sorry if that hurt."

Jason smirked. "Nah." He nodded to the camera man with his chin as he headed for the door. "Hope you made me look good, Brad!"

Angie side-stepped away from the green screen and rested her back against the wall. She considered escaping to the bathroom for a few minutes, but saw the tiny hallway she'd passed through was now choked with the overflow of students from the nearby studio.

"So, Aikido huh?" Brad said as he squeezed the legs of the tripod together and placed it in the windowsill behind him. He turned to face her, smoothing his hands down the rumpled front of his orange polo shirt. A thin-lipped smirk tightened across his face. "I had a guy teaching me Aikido once for a few weeks. I bet I could teach you a few things."

Angie was taken aback by a combination of disbelief and irritation. Was he actually challenging her? And what did he think he'd learned in a few weeks that she hadn't picked up in two years? Noting Brad's stance seemed to be preparing for action, her ego rose up to defend itself. "Well, I can appreciate the chance to learn new things," she said, pushing herself off from the wall with a quick flex of her shoulder blades.

Brad's gangly frame assumed a sparring posture, arms extended in front of him. "Come on, try to hit me," he said, appearing sure of himself.

Angie sighed. Every instinct she had warned her this scenario couldn't end well. "I'm not the best sparring partner, I should let you know—" She assumed a stance in front of him. Searching for any sign of Vince, she glanced around the room and past the door. No such luck. Spurred on by Brad's leering, Angie obliged him with a restrained right hook.

Brad blocked her fist with his left forearm, reaching with his right hand to clamp down on her wrist and yank her around in front of him. He followed the movement by pulling her forearm up behind her, pinning the back of her wrist behind her back. His movements were jerky and unpracticed, confirming Angie's initial impression of him as an amateur.

She permitted him to lead her by the arm at first as she studied his technique. Then, she began to counter his hold, rotating her shoulder while pivoting around to his right side. It was almost instinct. She'd spent many practices frustrating one of her black-belt instructors by finding ways to escape his holds. Her flexibility was well above average, and she'd always had trouble admitting defeat.

As Angie twisted out of his grasp, Brad reached around with his right arm and caught her neck in the crook of his elbow. He rolled the arm into his side, wrenching her into a firm headlock. Caught off guard, Angie strained to keep her balance as the sudden pull against her neck forced her cheek against his side.

All at once, she was acutely aware that he was wearing too much cologne. The movement of his ribs grated against her ear. "What are you doing?" She sputtered, reaching up to grasp at his forearm — which pressed too tightly against her throat. Her view was limited to the blue carpet and Brad's white sneakers.

Angie dropped her hips to regain leverage and turned her face toward Brad's elbow, trying to give herself enough slack to jerk out of his hold. The desire to break free overwhelmed her senses.

Brad's next move was as aggressive as it was outrageous. He pivoted, using his free hand to pin her nearest arm to her side while hoisting her into the air by her neck. He maintained the headlock even as her feet left the ground.

Shock had barely registered in her mind before Angie felt something in her neck pop, and a tingling sensation shot through her limbs. For the briefest, horrifying moment, she wondered if her neck was broken. She caught her dangling reflection in one of the window panels just as her peripheral vision began to fade to black. As conscious as she was of her own mortality, this was not one of the ways she'd ever imagined herself dying.

Oh God, please...not yet. Not like this.

A sudden, desperate need jarred Angie into the realization that her body was still responding. She raised her free hand and clawed at the offending limb that encircled her neck. Her pulse throbbed at her throat just below the spot where Brad's forearm constricted. She couldn't breathe. Her face felt tight and there was a deep, painful pressure building behind her eyes. Bright, iridescent flecks danced in the blackness that had begun to shroud her vision.

She had to make him put her down.

Disbelief took a backseat to survival as a hot surge of adrenaline filled her body. Her efforts at prying his arm loose were thwarted by her lack of leverage, and so, with what wits she had remaining, she threw her feet into the struggle. Her legs thrashed blindly at first, until she determined the location of Brad's closest knee and landed a solid toe-kick to the back of it. The leg buckled, and his balance went with it.

The moment she had her feet planted, Angie turned her head toward the toppling man and sucked in a breath. She took no pause. Feeling more than she was able to see, she wrenched his arm free with one hand and snapped her other arm out to catch his throat with the edge of her palm. She thrust her arm up and backward, clotheslining him. A dull *thud* sounded as Brad landed flat on his back. Just as it had faded, her vision was already returning from the center out.

Before he had a chance to try anything else, she wheeled around and dropped her weight into her right knee, which she landed in the middle of his sternum. Brad grunted as a rush of air was forced from his chest. The first thing her recovering eyes were able to focus on was the competitive sneer on his face. He was already reaching up to make a grab at her.

"STOP IT!" Angie roared, knocking his hands away. She sprang to her feet and back a few steps. "I'm done," she said, as Brad picked himself up off the floor and took a step toward her. Wary that he might ignore her warning, Angie took another step back and ducked behind the nearest object. Only then did she realize the object was a person — one of a half dozen students who'd spilled through the doorway during the tussle. She couldn't focus on any one of them to read their reactions. Had they seen the whole thing? Did they think it was just impromptu entertainment?

She picked up the murmur of someone behind her as she pushed past two more on her way through the door. "Hey, Brad…what the hell, man?"

Good, maybe they won't let him come after me.

She reached up and rubbed at her throat. Her pulse was racing, blood pounding through her momentarily deprived arteries. That triple shot mocha had been an unforeseen error on her part. Her sensitivity to caffeine had never meshed well with intense physical exertion. A giddy, light-headed sensation rolled over her as she stumbled out into the corridor between the rooms and collided with someone's chest. She tried to straighten up and met Vince's concerned gaze.

"Ang, what happ—"

Vince's inquiry was suspended as Angie crumpled in on herself, forcing him to catch her by the shoulders before her head had a sudden encounter with the floor.

While not completely out of touch with reality, the activity and voices around Angie seemed to whirl and run together for the next several minutes. When her senses convalesced, she found herself sitting in a chair in the corner of the darkened production room, a wall of computer monitors and blinking lights to her left. Vince was kneeling in front of her with one palm cupped around the back of her hand, insistently handing her a bottle of juice. His verdant gaze was both scrutinizing and disquieted.

"Hey…you feeling any better? Do you need me to take you to a hospital?"

Angie sat up straight, peering around the otherwise empty room before grasping the offered bottle and taking a slow sip. As she did so, a sharp twinge of pain shot through her head and neck. She handed the bottle back to him and reached to rub at the taut band of muscle to the right of her vertebrae. "Neck hurts," she said, giving her head a slow roll to either side to help her verify the pain's location. "It's just a muscle. No hospital." She looked past him then to see if she could make anything out in the filming room across the hall.

Vince squeezed her hand. "Think you're alright to walk to the car? You should lay down." His legs unfolded under him as he rose, maintaining a solid hold on her. The urging gesture became more of a steadying one after she nodded and eased herself out of the chair. Once she'd regained her footing, he reverted to a light hold on her arm as he led her out of the room and down the main hall. His other arm circled around her waist.

She was too dazed to mind.

Laying the front passenger seat back as far as it would go, Angie kept her eyes closed against the orange glow of the surrounding streetlights while she recounted the bizarre incident to Vince. He'd slid into the back seat and sat stooped over her, kneading his fingertips along the back of her neck as he listened. He was gaining ground on loosening the distressed muscles in her neck and shoulder. She eventually concluded with, "I don't know what kind of Mad Monkey Fu he thought he was doing, but that wasn't Aikido."

Vince's voice held agitation as he told her he'd often heard Brad talking about his hobby of amateur wrestling. Apparently, in certain downtown establishments, he'd been striving to build a reputation for himself with the aid of excessive amounts of spandex and body paint.

"He calls himself 'The Fly.' He's got a mask with bug eyes and everything."

Angie grumbled, "Somebody ought to get him a mask with donkey ears and you can call him 'The Jackass.'"

"I never would have thought he'd do something like that, though—" Vince's fingers ceased their soothing and drifted to hold either side of her face. He bent low and brushed his lips to her forehead. "I'm sorry. I shouldn't have left you in there alone."

Angie opened her eyes and stared up at him, warmth spreading through her at the tenderness she read in his upside-down face. She couldn't help but smile at the conviction in his tone. "Not your fault. I'm the one who let him bait me." As his face hovered over hers, she studied the worry lines creasing his brow. "I'll be okay. It could have been worse." She reached up to curl her fingers around one of his hands. She was sure now that she hadn't been mistaken — he cared about her. Too much. Enough that she knew it would cause him pain when it came time for her to leave the next day.

That was, assuming she would be in any condition to travel.

Vince's expression grew placated. "Will you be alright if I drive us to get some dinner? I think The Mill has a band playing tonight. Or…do you have a headache? I think I have some aspirin somewhere—" he said, delving into one of his cup holders between the front seat.

Angie chuckled. "I'll be fine. You already helped a lot." To demonstrate, she found the lever alongside the seat and eased it into an upright position. "Let's go eat," she said, hiding her smile as Vince relented his search and got out to return to the driver's seat.

Chapter 26

Five Points South formed the heart of downtown
Birmingham's entertainment district, an older section of brick-faced
storefronts and restaurants less than half a mile from the expansive
University. Vince found a curbside parking spot a block down from
the main intersection. A man approached the car and tapped on the
driver's side window, asking for a dollar.

Vince politely told him he didn't have any money. He
reached over and touched Angie's wrist, silently requesting she wait
while he watched the man move on.

"I never carry cash on me, so I don't have to lie," Vince said,
motioning to indicate that she could exit.

Angie found his sense of caution amusing, but she kept it to
herself as she slid out onto the sidewalk and stretched her still-tender
neck. Her attention was immediately captured by the broad display
window of the tattoo parlor to her left. Three long steps brought her
close enough to lay a palm against the glass as she peered in,
studying the plethora of designs on display.

"See one you like?" Vince chuckled behind her.

Something about his tone struck her as disbelieving, and that
was enough to cause her some small niggling of defiance. She tapped
the window with a finger and cast him an even smile. "No, but
there's one I've had in mind for a while. Is this is a good place?"

Vince's brows lifted and his jaw slackened in surprise. "Oh,
uh, I don't know."

Pleased to have broken out of his perception mold, Angie was
emboldened enough to pull open the door and let herself into the
shop.

The tattoo parlor was a narrow space, its walls painted off-
white and layered with pages of product examples. A long glass

counter stretched along the left wall displaying a selection of body piercing jewelry. Behind it stood a thin man with a braided, russet beard — looking much like an older version of the slouching, hoodie-clad youth clustered in the middle of the room. The threadbare carpet was a dingy shade of brown, likely to source of the musty smell which lingered beneath the sweeter tang of incense.

Relieved when no one looked their way, Angie drifted around a circular rack of T-shirts to a set of laminated flip posters. She leafed through for a short while before pausing at a section titled "Celtic."

"You're serious?" Vince had stood silently behind her for a time, but now sounded edgy. "Your parents aren't going to freak out when you come back inked?"

"I'm eighteen—they won't be thrilled, but it's my call now." Angie murmured in answer, tilting her head as she examined a trinity knot design. She absently traced a finger along the intricate pattern. "Relax, I'm not ready to commit just yet. I need more time to think about it." She dropped her hand and looked back over her shoulder at him. With a satisfied smile, she turned and headed for the door. She waited until he'd joined her on the sidewalk before adding, "Besides, if I get a tat, it'll be from a nice hygienic place that -doesn't- smell like pot."

Vince chuckled. "Noticed that, huh?"

"I'm not completely naive," she said, turning her gaze down the street to the corner. *Just somewhat naive.* "Was Grady going to meet us?"

Vince didn't seem as concerned about making his friend wait. "Yeah. He'll have a table saved." He motioned down the street and started walking.

Angie fell in step beside him as she took in the night life — such as it was on a Monday. College students made up the majority of the area's population, coming and going from various bars, clubs, and coffee shops. A small knot of people gathered at one of the five main intersection points beside a neglected fountain. There, a lone young man gave a break-dancing demonstration on a splayed piece of cardboard.

Distracted by the spectacle for a few moments, Angie's left foot slipped from the curb and she stumbled a step into the street. She caught the glow of headlights in her left peripheral vision, and then suddenly felt her body jerk back to the right.

Vince grunted as he caught her hand, and in one quick, controlled motion he pulled her around to the other side of him. She caught his wiry shoulder with her free hand to steady herself, surprised by both his strength and the sharpness of his reflexes. Righting herself as the car passed, she decided the error wouldn't have been enough to put her in the vehicle's path. About to work up annoyance over the unnecessary assistance, she caught the tense expression on Vince's face as he looked her over.

"You okay?"

Angie released his shoulder to touch her neck, feeling a twinge but not wanting to admit weakness. "Yeah." She knew his concern was genuine, if not on the hyper-vigilant side. He was still clutching her hand, though his grip slackened. "Sorry," she said, embarrassment catching up to her.

"How about you stay over here?" Vince stressed in a tone that held more calm than his expression. "I think you've had enough life-threatening excitement for today." He gave her hand a light squeeze, continuing to the crosswalk without releasing his hold.

Angie became immediately preoccupied with the public display of affection his would-be rescue had developed into. At first she felt childish. The idea of being some sort of damsel in distress was a reviling concept to her. And yet, she appreciated Vince's protective response. Perhaps it was simply what she should expect from the instincts of a firefighter. Or, maybe it was a convenient excuse for physical contact. Either way, there was undeniable warmth about his proximity that Angie was having trouble ignoring.

As they reached the front entrance to The Mill, Vince veered to the right, passing through the mouth of the waist-high iron fence that surrounded the outdoor seating. They found Grady lounging at a round table near the side door, and he waved them over.

"Hey guys!" Grady greeted with an affable smile, rising as they approached. He pulled out a chair and motioned for Angie to take it before he sank back down. "I didn't order yet. And, sorry, but I guess they don't bring in bands on Monday nights." He nudged the extra menus across the table and glanced between them, his gaze pausing on their clasped hands.

Just as Angie was beginning to feel self-conscious, Vince released her to her chair and grabbed a menu. "Thanks, G."

"So, what do you think of Birmingham?" Grady asked. His attention settled on Angie with affable expectation.

Angie held her finger on an artichoke dip appetizer she decided was reasonably priced, and she glanced up. "It's...different than I was expecting. I guess I hadn't gotten a very accurate feel for the South from what I've seen on TV."

That got a laugh out of Grady. "Well, it's hard to blame you. It seems like every time there's a tornado or something else worth reporting in this state, they go out and interview the biggest redneck they can find."

Angie smirked. "I'm trying to give it a blank slate in my mind. It deserves that much."

"Did you have any -good- impressions of the South before you came down here?" Grady asked.

"Krispy Kreme?" Angie laughed as the first thing that came to mind spilled out of her mouth. "—and Steel Magnolias," she added, in an attempt to redeem herself.

Vince flashed a grin. "I think you got the highlights right."

"So, how unbearably tedious was your day?" Grady inquired, his dark gaze darting to Vince as if to monitor for a reaction to the thinly-veiled taunt.

"Oh, it was anything but tedious." Angie glanced aside at Vince and caught him wincing behind his menu. "The Rehab office was really interesting. And class was—" She trailed off, at a loss for an appropriate adjective.

"Some idiot attacked her," Vince all but growled, dropping his menu flat onto the table in front of him.

Angie was surprised by the anger in his tone. She studied him in silence as he relayed the incident to his friend, gesturing sharply all the while. He'd maintained such calm through the ordeal, she thought he must have waited to fully process it. She took some comfort in the fact that she wasn't the only one who found the incident a little crazy.

"Whoa." Grady's response came hushed as he peered at Angie for a long moment. "Are you okay?"

Angie squirmed against the cold metal of the patio chair, feeling the focus of both young men on her. Before she could stop herself, she'd lifted a hand to cup the sore side of her neck. "I'm fine, really. No permanent damage." She waved off the attention and pretended to continue scanning the menu, hoping they would change the subject.

"You can tell how she really is by her eyes—they change color." Vince mentioned to Grady, with what Angie thought might be a hint of satisfaction over the privileged information. She glanced at him questioningly before her gaze slid to Grady to weigh his reaction.

"Yeah, my sister's do that," Grady said without skipping a beat. His eyes locked onto hers and he leaned forward in assessment. "They're brown now. She's happy," he added with a confident nod.

"Content." Angie corrected him without thinking. She glanced from Grady to Vince and then down at her menu again. She thought Vince looked somewhat perturbed with his friend's casual insight, but then decided she could be imagining it. Examining her snap response, she began to wonder if being content was as close to happy as she'd ever been — or could hope to be. Their waitress's arrival cut short her dreary introspection.

The evening went on with another hour of bantering between the three. Vince's levity returned as he took playful jabs at his friend, seemingly at every opportunity. Grady took it in stride, to such an extent that Angie began to conclude he had difficulty asserting himself. In the end she was the first to succumb to drowsiness, in spite of three refills on the sweet tea. Noting she'd begun to droop, the other two agreed it was time to part ways and begin the hour-long drive back to Cropwell. Angie didn't argue.

Walking back to the car, she monitored Vince out of the corner of her eye. At one point he seemed to reach for her hand, but stopped himself. He did, however, manage to usher her along while dutifully keeping himself between her and the street for the entire trek. When she began an unconscious drift toward the curb, he nudged her back into a straighter trajectory with his shoulder.

"I could swear you have some sort of a magnetic pull toward the most obvious source of danger," he joked, which earned him another puckish attempt by her at stomping on his foot. He dodged with skillful anticipation and an amused grin.

"My mom always said I like to keep my guardian angels on their toes," Angie said. She struggled to dampen her awareness of every fleeting instance his arm brushed against hers.

"Angels?" Vince probed, stressing the plural.

"Right. Obviously, I'm the kind of person who needs more than one of them." Angie laughed, meeting his intent gaze with a sidelong glance. She held his stare a moment longer than she'd intended before forcing her attention back to the sidewalk ahead.

"Maybe angels just aren't as good at looking after their own as they are the rest of us," Vince said, his voice a muted murmur.

If he'd meant for her to take him seriously, Angie didn't dare entertain it. She cut her eyes to him, shifting her weight to the side enough to deliver a teasing jab with her elbow. "That's a great line. How long have you been waiting to try that one out?"

Vince emitted a soft snicker, but didn't answer.

~ ~ ~ ~ ~ ~ ~

They arrived at Vince's house after 10pm. He had insisted Angie lay her seat back so she could rest during the hour-long return drive, which took the edge off of her weariness, but not enough to give her confidence in her condition. Her neck still bothered her, and there was no telling how it would feel the next morning. She decided to play it safe. While Vince took a shower, she set about calling her contacts and delaying her departure an extra day.

While her hosts in Atlanta didn't seem to mind the change, Scott had sounded annoyed. Considering it was the first time she'd spoken to him in several weeks, Angie was disappointed by his lack of consideration. When she suggested she could drive straight home and spare him the inconvenience, Scott became apologetic. Ultimately, they agreed she would arrive 24 hours later than originally planned.

Finding herself with leftover time as she waited for Vince to reemerge, Angie succumbed to snooping around the upstairs of his house. She told herself that as long as she didn't open any doors or drawers, it could only be considered browsing. That left her with the pictures on the walls and various mementos. She wasn't looking for anything in particular, just a better sense of understanding. It seemed like the safest way of gaining more insight into her friend's life without displaying a misleading degree of interest.

Despite his current build, Vince had been a chubby baby. The year-by-year progression of his development lined the hallways from within mismatched, wooden frames. She laughed to herself when she came across a picture of him at the age of four, kneeling in front of a rodeo-themed backdrop while dressed in jeans, western boots, and a cowboy hat. The next few showed him masked in freckles, wearing various baseball uniforms along with a proud smile. At what she guessed to be between the ages of ten and twelve, he'd worn braces. It was at about that same age she noticed his bright, boyish smile seemed to lose its gleam of authenticity. Whether that was due to the braces, or the onset of teenage angst, she couldn't speculate.

A small shelf along the kitchen wall held a family portrait, where a long-haired version of Vince's mother sat on a bench, holding an infant Vince in her lap. His father perched beside them with an arm around his wife. The picture beside it was a bit older, and it took a moment of study before Angie realized its significance. It had been taken in what looked like a garden in front of an old farm house. Vince's mother wore a summery blouse and tea-length blue skirt, cradling a bouquet of orchids in one arm as she leaned into Vince's father. The bearded man was clad in a crisp white dress shirt and had his arm hooked around her waist. A worn wooden sign over his left shoulder read: "Justice of the Peace." Their wedding photo.

Angie had the picture in her hands before she could stop herself. Did touching constitute snooping? If so, she'd already crossed the line. She glanced toward the bathroom door — which was still closed — and then flipped the frame over. She pried at the backing with her fingernail until it came free.

The scrawled writing on the back of the picture confirmed her suspicion. "Just Married," along with their names, the county, and the date. Angie committed it to memory and replaced the backing before setting the picture back on the shelf. It wasn't enough information, but it could be critical if what she suspected proved true.

Moving on to the living room, the most current picture of Vince she found was his high school graduation portrait. If not for the distinct vividness of his eyes, she might not have recognized him. In addition to sporting a scraggly attempt at a beard, his coopery hair was grown out straight, parted down the middle so it fell evenly to chin-level on either side of his slim face. His current clean-shaven look was a vast improvement, in her opinion. Hanging on the wall beside the frame were the gold, white, and blue honor cords he'd worn in the portrait. She didn't find the evidence of his academic record to be the least bit surprising.

The bathroom door opened. Startled, Angie began to dart out of Vince's eyeshot. She was too late.

"Like the hair?" he called out with a smirk. He'd thrown on a fresh white undershirt over his cargo pants, though for the first time since she'd arrived, he'd left his hair laying flat and free of gel. As he walked toward her he slipped his narrow-framed glasses back on.

"I can't say I'm a fan." Angie chuckled, looking from him to his old portrait. "I don't see how you kept it out of your eyes."

"I didn't." Vince laughed. "It used to drive my teachers crazy how I kept having to tuck it behind my ears. But I liked it for some reason. I kind of thought if it hid my eyes, it made me look more mysterious."

"Why'd you cut it if you liked it that way?"

"I tried out for a scholarship through the Auburn University fire department," he explained. "It was like boot camp with all of the physical testing and courses we had to run. It kept getting in my way, so I had it hacked off." He ran his palm over his head, and his hair fluffed in response.

"But you don't go to Auburn," she said, cautiously.

Vince shook his head. "They only gave out ten scholarships that year, and I came in eleventh in the testing. I was the best of the runner-ups. Not much of a consolation prize."

Angie winced. "I'm sorry."

I know how that feels.

Vince gave her an easy smile and shrugged. "It turned out okay. I'm getting done with school faster this way." His smile faded suddenly and Angie was startled when he lifted a hand to touch her chin, turning her face toward him. He brought his face closer to hers and she froze, perplexed by his actions and even more by the intense expression he wore. "Are those…bruises?" His voice registered obvious concern.

It dawned on her that he wasn't looking into her eyes, but just below them. She lifted a hand to touch her face, in case there might be some tactile sign of what he was referring to. "There's something on my face?" Self-consciousness replaced all previous thought and she pulled away from him, making a beeline for the bathroom mirror.

Angie hadn't looked at herself at all since getting ready in the morning. Rarely wearing makeup meant that she didn't have to worry about it smudging or requiring maintenance. But with that explanation excluded, she couldn't imagine what Vince could have confused for bruising. She hadn't been near any soot or—

"Oh." The exhaled word escaped her lips before she knew it had formed. There -was- bruising under her eyes. She leaned toward her reflection and wiped the pads of her index fingers at the tiny speckles of black and blue discoloration, though she knew the effort was useless.

"What's wrong?" Vince stood in the doorway, seeming hesitant to come any further. His brows were drawn together in worry, and his voice carried an underlying tension. "Did he...did Brad hit you?" Though leaning his shoulder into the door frame gave a casual cast to his posture, his hands tightened into fists at his sides.

"What? No—" Angie shook her head and looked back at her reflection. She lifted her chin and gave her neck a brief examination. No bruising there, at least. But then, she didn't expect there would be. Fingers left bruising. A forearm would have distributed the pressure. "It's just...what's the word?" She rolled her wrist as she pointed to herself, groping for the proper terminology. "Petechiae." She nodded once at the medical term. That sounded right.

"Petiki...what?" The controlled anger in Vince's voice cooled into confusion.

Angie lowered her head and slunk past him out of the bathroom, cutting left into his room. "It's bruising. But not the kind you're thinking of," she said, stepping onto the frame of the lower bunk to reach her overnight bag. She sat down with it on the edge of the futon, beside a sleeping Budweiser, and readied a less technical explanation while she rummaged through the bag. The dog emitted a disgruntled sound and hopped off the bed. "I thought he just cut off my airway when he had me in that head lock, but he must have pinched an artery, too. Those are little blood vessels under the skin that burst from too much pressure."

Vince crossed the room and sank down beside her while she hunted through her things. "You're saying...he tried to strangle you?" He spoke in a slow, deliberate voice.

"I'm not saying that's what he was going for." She shook her head. "It was just reckless and stupid. I never should have put myself in a position like that." Angie ended her search and sighed, turning up only an old eyeliner pencil and a small pot of lip gloss. Frustrated, she dropped the bag to the floor at her feet. "No cover stick. I guess I can't hide it."

Vince's weight shifted next to her and his hand settled on her shoulder, commanding her attention. Looking toward him, she turned to show as little of her face as possible. It was unreasonable, she knew, but part of her insisted on being embarrassed.

"He almost killed you, and you're worried about how it looks?" Vince's tone held a quiet sobriety. With his other hand he touched along her jaw and turned her face fully toward him. "I should have taken you to the hospital." His thumb slid over her cheekbone and brushed beneath her eye. "Does it hurt?"

"No hospital. I'm fine," Angie insisted. "Really. It doesn't hurt. I mean, the back of my neck is still sore, but my eyes don't—" Her voice caught in her throat when he brought his face closer.

Vince lowered his chin and his forehead came to rest against hers. He held himself there, eyes downcast and subdued. Angie, meanwhile, reminded herself to breathe. He smelled clean — a faint, simple mingling of bar soap and shaving cream. For some reason, she liked that.

"I'm really sorry," he said. "I wanted you to have some good memories of this place by the time you left. So far, I've dumped my problems on you, made you carsick, and, oh yeah, nearly got you killed." His self-directed sarcasm fell short of humorous.

Angie's distraction with his nearness was trumped by distress at his melancholy. She thought carefully before lifting a hand and laying it over the crook of his neck and shoulder. Her impulse was to touch his face, but she was still afraid of leading him on. Encouraging the wrong idea would only cause him more pain, and as far as she was concerned, he'd been hurt enough for one lifetime.

"Stop apologizing," she said. "It's not like I regret letting you talk me into coming here. Yeah, it's been a little weird at some points, but if I excel at anything its weirdness." She lightened her voice and smiled, willing his gaze to lift. "It'll make a great story one day."

Vince's eyes met hers with some reluctance, and he drew his face back several inches. His brow creased with skepticism.

Angie took a deep breath. If she couldn't convince him, she could at least redirect him. "Hey, random question—when is your birthday?"

It worked. After a brief flash of bewilderment lit his features, he answered, "The sixth of June."

Before he had a chance to ask why, she pressed him, "What year?" It occurred to her then that she didn't have a backup plan if she turned out to be wrong, and she immediately began praying she wasn't.

He told her the year, still looking mystified by her line of questioning. His hand fell away from her face and returned to him. Angie forced herself to ignore the sense of loss that accompanied his withdrawal.

"So that makes you nineteen—" She stated the obvious in an attempt to buy herself time to count months, though she was already excited.

"Uh-huh," he said, holding her in a blank stare. "What—"

She pressed onward at a nervous ramble, "I know it's none of my business and I shouldn't have been nosy, but I found your parent's wedding picture and the date was written on the back of it. Its August thirteenth." When his expression didn't change, she added the year.

Vince's jaw slackened and his gaze grew distant as he began to comprehend the direction of her thoughts.

"You weren't an accident," Angie said, putting her own elation on hold as she gauged him. "She couldn't have been pregnant when they got married. I mean, the dates are pretty close. You were probably a honeymoon baby. But they didn't get married because of you."

"All this time I was sure—" He looked away after a lengthy pause, and then back to her with sharpened focus. "I don't know why I didn't check the dates. I just thought it made sense."

Angie shook her head. "Not that it should matter. It's not like you're any more or less valuable as a person either way, it's just…I know it was bothering you. But you were all knotted up over believing something that wasn't even true in the first place. I just thought you should know."

Vince stared across his room for a moment, blinking rapidly. She wasn't sure if he was controlling an emotional response or simply processing the information.

"Thank you for being nosy—for caring." His voice came quiet and pensive as he took his glasses off with one hand and folded them, placing them on a shelf nearby.

Angie felt her pulse quicken, an instinctual reaction to sensing something her conscious mind couldn't pinpoint. When he turned back, he took her face in his hands.

She wasn't surprised when he kissed her, only by the enigmatic fervor she read in his gaze as he pulled her close. His lips met hers with sureness, separating this kiss from the one they'd shared the previous day. This was no nervous conveyance of simple affection or even brave curiosity. His mouth moved with hers in pliant warmth, and a keenness she wasn't sure how to interpret. She had to wonder if it was all a result of misplaced relief and gratitude. That seemed like the most reasonable conclusion, though it caused a tightening of regret to grip her chest.

Angie told herself she would end it quickly, for his sake. But when the kiss deepened, her rational mind seemed to retreat. His fingers caressed her cheeks and splayed to graze along her neck. Beyond that, she found it difficult to keep track of them. As her reeling senses attempted to derive an underlying meaning from the expression between them, only one word came to her mind.

Cherishing.

It was a sense she'd never encountered before — though granted, she had limited experience with this sort of thing. But she did feel certain there was a driving force at work that stood well apart from physical attraction. And something about that frightened her.

Vince shifted closer still, arms encircling her and bringing with them an enthralling sense of security. His fingers played along her spine, causing her to shiver. His lips began to surge against hers with what she vaguely recognized as a growing eagerness. Before she'd fully comprehended the progression, he'd eased his weight forward and lowered her onto her back. She knew she should stop him, but there was a part of her that didn't want to. And that part was more persuasive than she'd ever imagined.

His lips broke from hers only to roam along her jaw line, which failed to grant any reprieve from the confounding dizziness that overwhelmed her. His hands were roaming as well. The one that wasn't supporting him glided along her side before tugging at the hem of her shirt. Warm fingertips graced the skin of her belly, and a mental warning ran through her like an electrical shock. Her mind jolted from its haze back to clarity as she snapped a restraining hand around his wrist.

"Clothes stay on!" She blurted out the first coherent thing that came to her.

Vince looked as though he'd just stumbled out of the same hormonal miasma she'd been caught up in. He took in several deep breaths, nodding as his eyes searched hers. "I'm sorry. I shouldn't have—" His brows drew together in a pained expression, but he made no move to put any distance between them.

Stupid. Selfish.

Angie berated herself for letting things get out of hand so easily. Whatever she thought she'd interpreted amid their kiss, she was probably wrong. Like the typical gullible girl she'd never wanted to be, she was reading something into it that wasn't there. She wasn't aware of the iron grip she'd maintained on his wrist until Vince rotated his arm inward and bent his head, pressing a kiss to her knuckles. His eyes never left hers.

"Did I hurt you?"

"No." Angie shook her head.

Not physically.

But if she was risking the same emotional pain she'd been trying to keep him from, she knew she had no one to blame but herself. "I should go...and sleep." She glanced up to the top bunk and then back to his face. Separation would be the wisest thing, she knew, but she had no delusions about him acknowledging the fact.

"Let me rub your neck first," Vince requested. Then, as if he knew she was prepared to argue with him he added, "I don't want you to wake up in the morning and not be able to turn your head."

Angie considered his point for a moment before rolling herself away from him and onto her stomach. She turned her head, exposing the right side of her neck. "Okay." She had to wonder why she was finding it so difficult to be firm. It wasn't as though she felt sorry for him, of that much she was sure. If anything, she'd developed a solid sense of respect for him — not pity. Despite his youthful appearance, he was more of a man than most.

Perhaps his natural charisma truly made him that convincing. Or, maybe his personality had some sort of a moderating affect on hers. Either way, she didn't have much chance to ponder it further.

"Tell me what to do." Vince's request came in a earnest tone at her ear. His fingers settled against the back of her neck, awaiting instruction.

"Focus on the pads of your thumbs. Use medium pressure...small circles."

With one hand he brushed her hair back, while the other began to knead along the distressed muscles. Her soreness was acute at first, but the steady warmth of friction and circulation eased her into a more pliable state. His fingers gradually smoothed down along her neck, following the tension into her shoulder. He was a quick study, tuning in to her every twinge and working away at its source.

"Thank you," Angie said after several minutes had passed. Or at least, she thought it had been several minutes. Fatigue was catching up to her, affecting her perception of time. She considered blaming tiredness for her prior poor judgment while she was at it. At least Vince remained silent while he worked, even if it was a result of a new awkwardness between them. She didn't think she had enough will left for conversation.

Her eyelids fluttered with heaviness, and she allowed them to rest for just a moment.

Chapter 27

Angie awoke to the glare of sun in her eyes. Her dreams blurred together into a meaningless kaleidoscope of familiar images, leaving her to wonder if this was just a continuation of one of them.

She turned her head aside to shield her eyes from the offending streak of light. As her eyes refocused, an uneasy realization washed over her. She found herself curled on her side with her cheek pillowed soundly against Vince's chest. He was lying on his back with one arm cradling her shoulders and the other draped over her waist. She lifted her head slowly, testing the strain this put on her neck. When the shooting pain she anticipated didn't happen, she took a moment to examine the predicament she'd gotten herself into.

Vince's breathing came slow and even beside her. He was asleep, but Angie wasn't sure how deeply, and she doubted she'd be able to untangle herself without disturbing him. At her back she felt a slight stirring and an audible huff. Budweiser was apparently displeased with having to share his preferred sleeping space.

The sun sent bars of light streaming in through the parted slats of the window blinds beside the futon. She spotted an alarm clock on the window sill, but it was angled in such a way that she couldn't read it without moving.

"Good morning."

Angie's gaze snapped back to Vince's face at the whispered greeting. His eyes were open and he was regarding her with a hazy, placid expression. She was struck by the way a ray of light fell across his face and ignited their green depths to a state of brilliance. For the first time, she noticed that the inner ring of his irises were lined with gold flecks that radiated outward, reminding her of sunlight filtering through the leaves of a forest canopy. They were nothing short of captivating.

"Hi," she said, as all other words eluded her.

He lifted a hand to her face and brushed the backs of his fingers against her cheek. "How are you feeling?"

She smiled faintly at the touch and let the weight of her head settle back against his shoulder. "A lot better than I was last night."

Maybe better than I've ever felt.

As much as she didn't want to admit it, she liked this feeling — the warm security of being held. She understood the appeal of it now, as much as she understood the potential danger.

"You should have woke me up," she added.

"I tried." Vince's smile reached his eyes. "You were out like a light."

A sudden flurry of sound and activity from across the room shattered the stillness of the moment. Realization carried with it the hot surge of embarrassment, bringing a flush to Angie's skin.

Oh no. No no no...

"Vinny!? Did ya forget to set yer alarm?" Marie's high trill carried through the room as she came barging through the door. She didn't stop there. Her footfalls carried through the room as she approached. "Son, yer gonna to be late for work! Are ya sick?"

With nowhere to hide, Angie turned her head and buried her face in Vince's shoulder. Invisibility launched to the top of her list of desired superpowers.

"No, Mom," Vince intoned, patiently. "I'm taking the day off. Angie got hurt yesterday, and I don't want to drag her around with me again."

"Oh...well, bless her heart. I hope she's feelin' better." Marie's voice took on a pleasant trace of concern. "Just remember to call in. I'll see ya'll tonight, if it ain't too late. I've got karaoke with the girls again." The woman's footsteps receded into the background.

Angie waited for several seconds after she heard the door close before lifting her head. The extent of her mortification must have been plain on her face, as Vince's brows drew together in obvious worry.

"Are you okay?"

"No, I'm not okay," Angie answered, open with her aggravation. "Your mother just found me in your bed. You don't see how this must look?"

Vince's expression softened. "What does it matter? Nothing happened. She's not going to think anything of it—"

"Why, because it's normal for you to have cuddly slumber parties with girls?" she cut in, sardonic.

He shook his head. "That's not what I mean. That's just the way it works. She prides herself on staying out of my business and not asking questions. Even if she did think something was going on, it probably wouldn't bother her."

"Well it -should- bother her." Angie sighed, breaking her gaze away from his eyes to keep from staring into them for too long.

Vince caught the back of her hand and brought her palm to rest against the center of his chest. When he chuckled, the sound reverberated through her. "Sometimes I don't think you're from this planet."

"You don't have to stay home," she deflected. "I'm fine. I don't want to disrupt your routine."

"I've never had a more worthwhile reason to play hooky." He smiled at her with a fondness that made her stomach quiver. "Besides, I've worked for the state for over a year and never taken a day off. I can burn a vacation day without anyone missing me."

Angie couldn't think of an argument to that, and so she laid her head back against his shoulder, setting her eyes on the window. Some consistent portion of her thoughts reminded her she ought to be putting distance between them before she was any more unfair to him. Meanwhile, something else was nagging at her. The room was quiet. Distractingly quiet. It took her another second to figure out why that bothered her. She hadn't completely adapted to the constant background sound he required at night, but its absence still felt wrong.

"You didn't have the radio on. Did you get -any- sleep?" she asked, failing to strain the concern out of her voice.

"I don't think I've ever slept that well." Vince smiled as he answered, rubbing his thumb back and forth across her knuckles in an absent motion while staring up at the top bunk. His eyes were thoughtful, though his face had relaxed to a tranquil state. "Angeli...how would you define love?" He posed the question seemingly out of nowhere.

Angie felt a tightening of panic in her chest. She consciously forced her breathing to remain steady, even as she felt her heart rate speed up in betrayal. Her instincts blared a warning through her mind. She had every reason to suspect the conversation was about to go in a direction she'd never intended. And yet, the best she could come up with was a delay tactic.

"That depends on what kind of love you mean." She managed to hold a carefully intellectual tone, refraining from launching into a dissertation on the four separate Greek definitions that came to her mind. "Parental love, friendship love, romantic love—"

"Romantic love." Vince's voice held a calm decisiveness.

Angie swallowed hard, hoping he wouldn't notice. "Romantic love, I think, requires a degree of physical attraction, but devotion is needed to maintain it as an actual relationship. Physical attraction is a feeling you don't really have control over, but devotion is something that has to be chosen. So, ideally…I suppose it's passion combined with the commitment to value someone else completely above oneself," she said, daring to study his face.

Vince took his time considering her words before finally nodding to affirm he'd made sense of them. "Okay." His voice came subdued, and he turned his head aside to fix his eyes on hers. "Then, by your definition…I'm in love with you." He punctuated the revelation with a disarming smile.

Angie felt the entire surface of her skin begin to prickle, as though every one of her nerves had been pushed to their highest sensitivity. Guessing what was coming hadn't made it any easier for her to absorb.

No, no, no…how did I screw up this badly again?!

She commanded herself to remain still. He'd just made himself hopelessly vulnerable to her, and she would have to treat that fact with care if she was going to talk him out of it without crushing him. Never in her life had she so sincerely wished that tact didn't spend most of its time eluding her.

"Don't say that," she said, pleadingly. "You don't want to do this, Vince."

"I mean it." His face remained gentle despite his insistence. "I'm not telling you this to get something from you—I just wanted you to know. It's probably too soon to say that without sounding crazy or desperate, but I've had a lot of time to think about it. And I'm sure. I've never been this sure about anything."

"But, you know I have to leave soon." She opened her first argument. "And they say that long distance relationships never work out."

"Pfffft. 'They,'" he countered with a playful air. "'They' say a lot of things. And who are 'they', anyway?"

"You know what I mean," Angie said, building urgency. "You have work and school. You've barely got time to sleep as it is. And I still have the fall semester before I finish my degree. We can't be together. You'd be a lot better off finding a nice girl somewhere close by."

"I can call you every night on the commute back, and I'll fly up to see you." His response came with resolute ease. He'd thought this through — she had to give him credit. "We could make it work until you graduate."

"And then what?" she countered. "We keep indefinitely spending all of our money on airfare going back and forth? I come down here to stay? You move up there? You have to understand, I take this very seriously. I've never wanted to just date around or play with anybody's emotions. I can't let myself consider a relationship that wouldn't have marriage in mind as the ultimate goal." There, she'd dropped the 'M' word.

That should to do the trick. After all, weren't most young men hardwired to run away screaming at the mere mention of serious commitment?

Vince paused at length to contemplate, but otherwise appeared undaunted. "I'm okay with that. " He gave a faint smirk at reading her immediate skepticism. "It's not like I don't believe in marriage. I'm just...not really sure what it's supposed to look like. Almost everybody on my Dad's side of the family has been remarried two or three times—it's like a running joke. G's parents are still together...even though they fight all the time. But I figure, it doesn't have to be that way. Your parents are happy, right?"

Angie blinked, caught off guard. "Well, yeah, most of the time. I think it's just like anything else—if you want it to work, you have to do your homework and make an effort."

"Then, you can help me with my homework." Vince formed an amused smile. "If you decide I'm worth keeping around, I mean. I'm just asking you to give me a chance." He curled his hand around hers as he spoke, watching her with marked intensity. "Unless you already know you could never feel the same way about me. Tell me right now, and I'll accept that. I can be happy being your friend, and I won't bother you with this again."

Angie's heart sank in her chest under his expectant gaze. The most blatant way out of this was in sight, but there was one enormous problem. She would have to lie to him.

In the moments following his declaration, she'd let down her guard long enough to entertain the idea of being with him. Now, she was overwhelmed by the realization that she might be able to love him — truly and irrefutably — if she allowed herself to. While part of her was relieved she was capable of it after all, another part of her was petrified. As well intentioned as Vince might be, the situation would be difficult, if not impossible. She had to stand her ground, for both their sakes.

Oh, God...help me out of this.

Vince had begun to look more hopeful as her silence dragged on. So far, her debate skills had fallen short. She was going to have to do better. Angie knew what she would have to bring up — she'd just hoped that it wouldn't come to this. "Vince…how many girls have you been with?" she asked at last, forcing the words out one at a time. If her stomach were weaker, she would have felt ill. It wasn't that she was uncomfortable with personal questions, it was more the fact that she didn't want to hear the answer.

Vince's face went blank as he watched her struggle. "Just two. You, and the ex-girlfriend."

He answered faster than she expected. A glimmer of hope dared to materialize in the back of her mind, though her cynicism stepped on it. She had yet to clarify. "But her—" Angie paused. "Were you...sleeping with her? And I don't mean -next- to her."

His brows pulled into a furrow as the distinction she was making seemed to dawn on him. "Well…yeah. I thought we were always going to be together. We had plans—" He frowned as he reflected. "I was seventeen—I screwed up. I thought we were in love, but it turned out she was just using me to alleviate boredom. I shouldn't have let myself get so…attached." He cleared his throat, as though it would also clear the remaining pain. "But that doesn't have anything to do with you and me."

"Did you even know what love was?" Angie spit the question out before she'd thought about it. There was a coarseness to her voice that she didn't recognize, but she was too intent on studying him to analyze her own slip.

Vince flexed his jaw and broke eye contact for a moment. "No, I guess I didn't. I get that now. Back then, I just couldn't imagine that anybody else might want me." His doleful gaze shifted back to her face. "But that's just a bad memory now."

"It's a lot more than that." Angie looked away. "It's baggage." She closed her eyes as she sorted her thoughts, grateful that he waited in silence for her to continue. Her chest ached — the byproduct of a mental anguish she wasn't prepared for. This wasn't going to get any easier, no matter how much time he gave her. She forced herself to charge ahead, "I made a promise to myself, and to God, that I'd save myself for marriage—"

"And I respect you for that. I do," Vince broke in. "I didn't mean to push you last night."

"Maybe you can respect that now, but you'll resent it later." She shook her head, then forced herself to hold his gaze. "I know how this works—it's progressive. Self control just gets harder with time when you want to be close to somebody. It's never close enough." She managed to return to a more clinical tone. "And you know what you're missing. I don't."

"I'm not an animal, I can control myself," he protested. "And I'd -never- do anything to hurt you."

Angie slipped her hand from his grasp and cupped her palm to the side of his face. She held it there for a time before letting it slide to his shoulder. It pained her that he seemed so sincere. To make matters worse, she believed him. She couldn't imagine how anything short of honorable intentions could be causing him to persist, in spite of the requirements she'd laid before him. But even the best intentions could only carry so much weight before splintering.

"I'd always wonder if you were thinking about her." Angie's vocal control faltered as she choked out the final part of her argument. "I know how I am. I might not be a 'normal' kind of girl, but that doesn't mean I'm all secure in myself. I'd end up worrying about you comparing us in your head...if you think I'm prettier, smarter, funnier, a better kisser, a better—" She closed her eyes again rather than complete the thought.

Vince tightened his hold on her hand. "You are -so- much more than she was. In every way," he said, his eyes as intent as his voice. "There's no reason for you to worry."

"That doesn't change the fact that she was here first." Angie slipped her hand out of his grasp and reached up, touching the middle of his forehead with her index finger. "—and here." Hand hovering lower, she tapped the same finger to his chest directly over his heart. "Eventually, something I do or say will remind you of her and you'll get upset, and I won't know why. I don't think I can stand to be haunted like that."

Vince's verdant gaze recoiled. It seemed he'd finally been stunned out of any ready response. His expression went slack, and he turned to fix his gaze upward. The serenity that had been there just a short while ago was replaced by a warring torrent of emotion. "Is that really it, then? Did I give up my chance of being with you before I even met you?" His voice bordered on despondent, though Angie thought she still detected a determined set to his brow. "Couldn't you just…forgive me?"

His last question sent her mind reeling. "I can," she said at last, deflecting her gaze. *I'd have to.* "But you're not the one I'd have the hardest time forgiving. And forgiveness doesn't make consequences go away." What if his ex had given him an STD and he didn't realize it yet? The agonizing thought shot through her, settling in her stomach like a ball of lead. "I'm sorry. I just don't think I'm strong enough to work through all of that."

And that was the raw truth of it. She couldn't recall ever experiencing so much anger and grief on someone else's behalf — and he didn't even belong to her. How much worse would it be if she did have a right to it?

Angie sensed him shift position, turning onto his side until he faced her. His fingertips traced along her hairline, brushing behind her ear and then down her jaw until he'd lifted her chin. She had to look at him then.

"You are the strongest person I've ever met," Vince said, his eyes boring through every defense she'd erected between them. "Whatever you decide about me, you should know that."

Angie's throat tightened, and a stinging sensation formed behind her eyes. It took all her willpower to fight back the tears. She struggled to find something to tell him, but thoughts slipped from her mind like sand through her fingers.

He can't mean all of this.

Vince's expression grew troubled. "Your eyes look green," he said. Still holding her face he murmured a quiet plea, "Don't be upset, Angel."

Knowing she was close to losing control, Angie drew her head back and sat up. The change of position did nothing to alleviate the ache knotted low in her chest. In that instant, she wanted nothing more than to flee the strange upwelling of sorrow, longing, and fear. "I just need some air," she said, without looking Vince's way.

Angie pivoted to set her feet on the floor and laid a hand on Budweiser's head. "Come on, Bud. I'm borrowing you for a little bit." She fought to project a casual voice. The lounging animal tracked her movements, huffing to his feet when she made a beckoning sound. She was afraid at first that Vince would argue or follow her out, but he didn't.

As she reached the back door and clipped a leash onto Bud's collar, she couldn't decide if she was relieved or disappointed by his master's lack of pursuit.

~ ~ ~ ~ ~ ~ ~

Angie made it down the length of the driveway and back twice before it occurred to her that organizing her surroundings might help her to organize her mind. She then spent the next several hours doing her laundry and studying road maps in preparation for her departure.

All the while Vince went about his own routine, spending much of the time either mowing the lawn or at his computer. He sought Angie out periodically to check on her, though he kept a respectable distance and didn't hover. She would have been tempted to think he'd come to his senses, if not for the turmoil she detected behind his practiced smile. Her confusion continued to loom, in spite of her best efforts.

Toward the end of the afternoon she commandeered his dog again and set out to give herself a tour of the neighborhood. The crunching of gravel underfoot became a rhythmic sort of therapy to her conflicted mind.

"Just give me something—some sense that he's not what you had in mind," she said under her breath. Expecting the foreboding hesitation she'd had when considering a relationship with Scott, she was perplexed to be left without any impression at all. Logic told her that Vince should be an easy "no." But her emotions were clouded, even when he wasn't standing in front of her. Whatever it was she'd begun to feel for him, it was far more complex than attraction. "God, I don't know what I'm doing." She gave Budweiser's leash a light tug to direct them down another forested lane lined with dilapidated trailers. "I just want you to be happy with me," she continued praying. "And I don't want to cause Vince any more pain."

Angie wasn't certain how long she'd been walking and carrying on her seemingly one-sided conversation before she began to question her surroundings. By this time, her portly companion had lost his enthusiasm. Stopping to get her bearings, she used the setting sun to determine her direction and pulled together a mental map in her mind.

Great. Even on foot, I manage to get lost.

Budweiser seized the opportunity to lie down in the grass beside the road.

"Home, boy!" Angie said. The dog stared at her, pointed ears swiveling. Aside from that, he made no move. She sighed. "Well, it was worth a shot."

Catching sight of a familiar sign in the distance, she got Bud to his feet and turned her full focus to relocating Vince's house. Several minutes later they turned down a street she thought she recognized. Their progress was slowed by the dog's mulish attempts to sit in the middle of the road, which reduced him to cooperative equivalent of a thirty-pound doorstop.

"You're a disgrace to dog-kind." Angie grumbled, though all verbal persuasion had proven useless. "I am SO not carrying you."

The miniature pincher perked up to the sound of a distant whistle. He shot to his feet and set off at a gallop, pulling Angie along behind him. At the base of a low hill, their goal came into view. A lone figure paced back and forth in front of the house to their right. Relieved, she released the dog's leash, and the animal went bounding across the expansive yard to greet his master. Angie smiled to herself, watching the two wrestle while she followed the same path at a less exuberant pace. By the time she'd arrived, Vince had let Bud into the house and came walking back to meet her. The strained look on his face caught her unawares.

"Sorry to keep your dog out so long," she called to him. "I got a little turned around."

"How far did you go?" Vince asked, stress evident in his tone. "I've been walking the strip, and I didn't see you anywhere. I was about to start driving around—"

"I didn't mean to worry you." Angie stopped in front of him, studying the lines of anxiety that creased his brow and tightened around his eyes. She had to wonder how long he'd been distressed over her disappearance. "I needed to think. It helps when I'm walking."

"Could you at least stay close if you really have to do that?" He began to reach for her arm but seemed to think better of it, withdrawing his hand back to his side. "And take my phone with you. I don't know most of the people around here—I wouldn't call it a safe neighborhood."

"Well, that's why I took Bud with me."

Vince arched a brow. "Bud? Yeah, he'd be great protection...in the event that you were attacked by squirrels."

Angie held up a hand in pause. While his voice had relaxed, she noted an underlying air of drama to his hand gestures.

Why do I think it's so charming when he's being spazzy and sarcastic?

"Look, I know I got myself into a little trouble last night, but I'm a big girl. And I really am capable of taking care of myself. I'm not some delicate little waif." Offense reared its head as she spoke, and before she knew it, she'd started in on his chivalry. "I can open my own doors and pull out chairs for myself just fine, thank you. I've made it this far on my own and survived."

While she'd expected a snide and well deserved remark about her sense of self-preservation, Vince's thoughts appeared to shift elsewhere. With a profound expression she didn't understand, he took a tentative step into her personal space.

She didn't move.

"I know you can take care of yourself," he said, with absolute conviction. His vivid eyes probed hers. With the same underlying resolve, he lifted a hand and brushed her cheek with his fingertips. "I just think...you shouldn't -have- to."

There was nothing astounding about his choice of words. But the way he'd used them — the significance in the way he looked at her as he spoke — overwhelmed Angie in an instant. She finally understood. His attentive treatment of her had nothing to do with the presumption that she was weak, and everything to do with the conviction that she was valuable.

Before Angie had time to consider the impulse, she pitched herself forward, pressing her lips to his in a fierce conveyance of emotion.

Seeming almost as shocked by this as she was, Vince staggered back a half step as he caught a hold of her, arms circling her waist. He recovered quickly. Matching her intensity, he locked them into a lingering embrace. When it finally ended, it was at his initiative.

"Easy," Vince breathed, nuzzling his cheek against hers. "—shouldn't start something we can't finish."

Abashed by his astuteness, guilt circulated through Angie like ice water. She didn't know what had come over her. "You're right...I'm sorry." Choking out the words, she pulled away from him and turned.

"Wait—" He caught her hand, as if he knew she was about to fall to pieces before she'd realized it herself.

Angie pulled free and broke into a sprint. She didn't know where she was going — only that she needed to cry and didn't want anyone to see her. Within a few strides she felt arms encircle her waist and she doubled forward, a halfhearted attempt to escape. She only succeeded in throwing off Vince's anchoring balance, sending them both tumbling into the grass. He pressed her back to his chest as they landed, absorbing most of the fall with his shoulder.

"I'm sorry!" she cried, feeling her entire body shudder.

"Shhh." He whispered into her ear. "Is your neck okay?"

Angie nodded, unable to answer him until a round of sobbing had run its course.

"I don't...know why...I did that," she finally uttered between gasps, regaining some measure of control.

"Which one?" Vince asked. "The part where you kissed me, or the part where you ran away, bawling?"

She laughed at the unexpected wryness in his tone. "Both, I guess."

Vince gave a quiet chuckle, hugging her to him for a long moment before easing his hold. "You sure you have to leave tomorrow?"

Angie hesitated only a second before nodding. "Yeah, I'm sure. I caused everybody enough trouble delaying to tomorrow as it is." Certain that her expression would expose the extent of her reluctance, she was grateful she wasn't facing him.

"It's not fair." His voice dulled. "God sends me an angel, and then just...takes her away."

"Don't go blaming God," she sighed, rubbing at the tear stains and bits of grass that clung to her cheeks. "I messed up. You would have been better off if I'd just gone home instead of—"

"No, I wouldn't." Vince interrupted, his voice low with finality. "Meeting you is one of the best things that ever happened to me. Even if this is all the time I'll ever have with you."

Angie looked back over her shoulder to read the sincerity in his face, but her skepticism remained.

Vince seemed to struggle for words. "I've always felt like I have to put on different masks for people—be who they want me to be. With you, I don't have to think about it. I just...am. And somehow, you like me anyway."

"If that's true, how can I even be sure who you are?" she asked, reflecting on the coolness of his demeanor their first day together. She diverted her gaze to stare up at the dimming sky. "You've been acting so differently the last few days—"

"That's because the last few days, I've been myself," Vince said, tone lightening. "If I seemed different than when you first got here, it was because I was just...trying to impress you."

She turned her head and cut her eyes back toward him again, incredulous. "How was acting like an egocentric jerk supposed to impress me?"

"I don't know." He looked away, pausing at length. "When I first saw you at that gas station, I couldn't believe how beautiful you were in person. I freaked out." Vince gave an uneasy smile with the admission. "You remember how I left you up front and went to the bathroom?"

Angie stared at him in confusion. "Yes—" *He thinks I'm beautiful?*

She held onto his words, a bubbling sense of giddiness eroding her resolve. She couldn't remember ever feeling more feminine.

"Yeah, I actually went to go look in the mirror and give myself a pep talk." He emitted a weak chuckle. "I started out trying to be something I thought you would want. Aren't good girls supposed to like bad boys?"

Angie considered his presumption, reminded of Scott for a brief moment. "Well, not this girl." She smirked, not daring to look at Vince again. She couldn't let him see how much his honesty was affecting her. Part of her wanted to keep him...even if that part was so obviously short-sighted.

Make a clean break.

Vince cleared his throat, seeming to work up his nerve. "You still don't think you can give this...us...a chance?"

"I think," Angie began, buying herself time to choose her words. She had hurt him enough with her selfishness mixed signals — the least she could do now was have the mercy to uphold her decision. "When you truly care about someone, you want the best for them. Even if 'the best' doesn't include you."

At that, Vince was silent.

Chapter 28

July 24th,

I stayed up late last night talking with Vince. I know he needed sleep, but it was the first good chance I'd had to talk to him about the darkness that's been festering inside of him. I don't know how much of what I said got through to him, but I think he knows what he needs to do now.

He says that he's in love with me. It's like I'm experiencing deja vu. Some of the things he told me reminded me so much of things Scott told me: I make him happy, and he'd be willing to move so that he could be with me. ...I just don't understand why this is happening to me again.

It's so odd when I consider things. I know I was attracted to Scott, but I wonder now if that was more of a shallow, physical thing. Early on, I felt like it wouldn't work out between us. With Vince, I guess there must be some physical element...but so much of it is his personality and temperament. He's treated me with such care, and he's learned to read me so quickly. I really will miss him. And part of me hopes that he and Grady were serious about visiting someday.

I think... I -hope- Vince will be okay. Puppy love is easily gotten over. We've shared so much with each other now, though. I know it will hurt both of us when I leave today. I never expected he would open up so much, or that we would end up getting along so well. (Once he decided to be himself, anyway.)

I don't know what to think anymore. I doubt that I'm supposed to end up with Vince, but for some reason...I'm a lot less certain about that than I had been with Scott. I just don't get it. I never meant to cause so much trouble. I succeeded in getting close enough to understand, but the price seems too high. And I'm confused again.

God, help me.

~Ang

Vince stayed home from work for the second day in a row, and the last of Angie's time with him was spent talking. The afternoon was dwindling away, and Angie wanted to leave before she lost any more precious daylight. Vince seemed to pick up on her wavering state of mind, and offered to walk her out to her car.

"I'm going to head in to Birmingham and make it to my night class," he said, offering a rehearsed smile as he turned to her in the driveway. "You can follow me out as far as I-20, and then just head east. You can't miss Atlanta."

Angie returned the smile, "Thanks. For everything, I mean." Though she'd made up her mind that the best way for them to separate would be quickly — like the sharp but brief sting of pulling off a Band-aid — she found herself dawdling.

"Call me when you get there?" Vince requested, the right corner of his mouth twitching aside as the smile faltered.

"I will." Angie mustered a more reassuring smile. She closed the distance between them in a single step with the intention of hugging him, but surprised herself by kissing him instead. The action was innate and effortless. It would have taken more thought for her to stop herself than it did to sway forward and touch her lips to his.

Vince met her partway with a gentle, sure pressure. In his reply she sensed the poignant echo of regret before he grasped her shoulders and pulled back. Holding her at half arm's length, he averted his eyes, "We're making this harder than it already is."

Angie looked down and nodded. "I'm sorry."

Again.

His hands fell away as she stepped around him, retreating to her car.

Once she'd slid into the front seat, she waited for Vince to pull out of the drive and lead her back to the highway. Struggling to arrange her thoughts, she reviewed his last statement over and over. It struck her as oddly critical that he'd used the phrase "harder than it already is," rather than "harder than it needs to be." She pondered the significance of the subtle turn of phrase as she drove.

If it was worth anything, then it needed to be hard.

All too soon she noticed Vince had roll down his window and signal to ensure she wouldn't miss her entrance ramp. She honked once in reply and waved as their course diverged. Merging onto the highway heading east, she watched in her rear view mirror as the familiar white sedan entered the westbound lane.

A dull ache clutched at her heart. It felt wrong that they were traveling in opposite directions — as though it underscored the likelihood that their paths might never cross again.

~ ~ ~ ~ ~ ~ ~

She had been driving around Atlanta for two hours before Angie accepted she was lost. While she'd had a number of directionally challenged moments throughout her journey, this was the first time she'd misplaced herself in the middle of a large city.

Making matters worse, it was getting late and she'd been unable to locate an open venue where she could stop to call one of her previous hosts, Kalvin. Every gas station she passed either had inadequate lighting or at least one shady-looking man loitering close to the pay phone. She hadn't felt so uneasy with her situation since her long night in Lancaster.

The bright glow of a large drive-in restaurant called "The Varsity" eventually captured her attention. And it was there that Kalvin and one of his friends eventually found her.

When Angie saw the lanky pair approaching, she nearly ran to meet them. Her anxiety must have been plain on her face, as both young men were regarding her with worried expressions.

"You're way off course, lady," Kalvin said, bending to greet her with a hug.

"Yeah, well it doesn't help that half of the streets in this city have 'Peachtree' in their name." Angie said. She raised onto her toes to hug his neck in gratitude.

"Here, you might want to call Vincent." Kalvin held out his cell phone to her in offering. "When you didn't show up, we called to find out when you'd left. And...I may have said something a little accusing about him being the last one to see you alive." He gave a sheepish smile.

Angie laughed, if only to ease her own tension. "Aww, you made threats on my behalf?" She accepted the phone and reached up to ruffle Kalvin's thinning hair. Jeff, the slim, tow-headed young man beside him, grinned when she elbowed him. "You guys would have made great big brothers."

Jeff chuckled and motioned toward his car. "We'll get out of here when you're done. We can still make it to game night and get you something to eat."

"Sure," Angie said. As she wandered back into the entryway of the restaurant, she scrolled through Kalvin's phone until she found Vince's number. He picked up before the second ring.

"Hello?"

"Hey, it's me," Angie said, grateful to hear his voice.

"You're okay?!" Vince's tone pitched with relief.

"Yeah. I got lost."

"Well, I figured that much." It sounded as though he was attempting to cover something with humor.

"I know, I've got a bad track record." Angie sighed. "I couldn't find a safe place to call anybody from. Kal and Jeff found me, though."

"Good. They can keep you out of trouble," Vince said, voice gaining a tired quality. "I guess I should just head back home, then."

"What do you mean? Where are you?"

Vince hesitated. "I'm...about half an hour from Atlanta."

Guilt stirred together with gratitude, thickening into a lump that lodged in her throat. "You drove all the way back from Birmingham to come looking for me?"

"Well, yeah. You were missing."

"And how exactly did you think you were going to find me?" she asked, dumbfounded. The other end of the line was quiet for several seconds.

"I don't know," Vince said. "I thought maybe if your car had broken down partway there, I'd see it."

"And if I wasn't on the side of the highway?"

"Then I would have taken Atlanta one street at a time."

"That's crazy." Angie couldn't help but smile at his irrational determination. "I'm sorry I keep causing you problems. You must have left class early—"

"Just do me one more favor," Vince said. "Call me when you get to D.C. tomorrow. That -might- keep me from finishing off the ulcer I've been working on."

"I'll call," Angie vowed. "Just as soon as I get in."

"Thank you."

Angie felt an upwelling of tender emotion fill her chest. "Vincent?" She stopped herself just short of asking him to come into the city so she could see him one last time. The impulse was strangely powerful.

Wow, that would be incredibly selfish of me.

"Hmm?"

"Thanks—for coming after me." She took in a slow breath. "I'm sorry I wasted your time and gas money."

"Don't be," Vince answered, voice quieting. "You're worth it."

She could picture the sad smile she heard in his voice, and it pained her. "Get back home and get some sleep."

"I will. Good night, Angel."

"Good night."

~ ~ ~ ~ ~ ~ ~

It was nearing 10 PM the following evening when Angie completed her ten hour drive and pulled up to the curb in front of Scott's mother's house. The three-story home was one of the smaller structures in the well lit, affluent neighborhood. Made up of modern stonework and wood siding, the house sat behind an unimposing but well-tended lawn. She'd made a point of calling Scott when she was within an hour of the city, and he was waiting for her on the broad front stoop.

Toting her duffel bag across the yard, Angie approached with a twisting sense of anticipation. They'd spoken only once in the weeks since she'd left New York, and she hoped their mutual understanding was still intact.

"Sorry to interrupt your smoke break," she called out, teasing.

"You didn't." Scott stood from his partial crouch, scratching absently at the well-groomed patch of scruff along his chin. "Actually...I quit." He spread his arms at his sides, palms out.

"Seriously?" Angie's voice come out more astonished than pleased, and she amended it by giving him a quick hug. She took the opportunity to sniff at his collar, picking up only musky cologne mingled with sweat — void of even a trace of tobacco. Its absence seemed almost peculiar. "That's great! I'm proud of you." She smiled as she stepped back from him, concerned over promoting too much contact between them.

To her surprise, it was easy to let him go. The perplexing draw she recalled having toward him seemed...muted. He was just as handsome as ever, she decided. His broad shoulders and swarthy features still held all of their usual appeal. And yet, something about her perception of him had changed.

For his part, Scott was just as quick to release her and seek out his pockets with his hands. "Yeah, those first two weeks were pretty rough on me—and pretty much everybody around me. But it's been almost a month, so I guess I mastered my master." He looked pleased with himself. "I oughta last longer through my Kendo practices now."

"Maybe now your Sensei won't yell at you so much." Angie laughed, pulling her duffel bag around to hold in front of her. "So, is your mom going to let me sleep indoors? I'm just about dead on my feet."

"Right." Scott turned, crossing the inlaid stones of the porch to open the front door. "Come on in. Mom might still be up, but I dunno."

The entryway was sizable but not extravagant. Tasteful scenic paintings hung on the walls and flanked the grand, central wooden staircase. A darkened living room wrapped around to the left, and an office opened to the right. Scott led her straight ahead through a hallway that ran parallel to the stairway.

"My bedroom is up there, if you need something," Scott motioned toward the stairs. "I thought you could stay in my sister's old room across the hall, but mom didn't like that idea. She's giving you the spare room in the basement." He paused to tap a door to his left, just shy of the tiled eat-in kitchen.

"Smart lady." Angie chuckled, relieved at the deliberate separation. She moved to open the basement door, but Scott stopped her.

"You can head down in a minute—let me show you around." He took her bag and set it beside the door before leading her on a brief tour of the kitchen. Beyond the heavy oak dining table a set of white French doors opened onto an expansive deck, which jutted out over a level carpet of grass. Scott turned on the floodlights as they stepped out, illuminating a young tree poised in the middle of the back yard.

"Oh, a Weeping Willow," Angie noticed aloud. She walked out for a closer look, starting down the trio of steps. The tree stood less than twelve feet high, its spindly branches arched and drooped to form the silhouette of a lopsided umbrella.

"Yeah, I remember you like those." Scott answered from a few feet to her left, regarding her with an ambiguous smile. He looked like he was about to say something else when movement in the kitchen caught his attention. "There's Mom." He inclined his head toward the house and led the way back through the French doors.

Scott's mother hovered near the table as they entered. She wore a full-length lavender bathrobe, and her platinum-blonde hair was set with rows of curlers. The small, gaunt woman couldn't have stood quite five and a half feet, but her posture and movements suggested an enormous force of personality. Though her eyes were broad, blue, and lovely, the deep scowl she wore was enough to stop Angie cold.

"I thought you said she'd be here an hour ago." The woman addressed Scott in a curt tone before planting a fist on her hip and peering at Angie as though she already found her inadequate.

"I'm sorry," Angie spoke up, as apologetic as she could manage on short notice. "I got slowed down a little in North Carolina."

"So, Angeli...this is my mom. Cindy." Scott intervened, making exaggerated motions of introduction. "Mom, this is Angeli."

Cindy cut her eyes toward her son, pursing her lips in a look of irritation.

"It's good to finally meet you, ma'am." Angie said. She clasped her hands behind her back to keep from fidgeting under the woman's dissecting gaze. "Scott talks about you all the time."

"Ma'am?" The older woman gave a dry laugh. "So you did spend some time down south."

Angie looked to Scott in hopes of some clue as to how seriously she should take his mother. Scott looked uncomfortable, but didn't seem eager to speak up again. "Three weeks." Angie nodded, unsure of what else to say. It was taking all of her concentration not to stare at the brown pencil lines arching along the woman's forehead where eyebrows should have been.

"Well, I've got work tomorrow, so the sightseeing will just have to wait until the weekend," Cindy said, with an abrupt disregard. "I'm going to bed. You two keep the noise down, and don't do anything stupid." Pivoting in place like a tightly wound dancer, the woman headed back through the hallway.

Stunned by the less-than-pleasant first meeting, Angie waited until she heard footsteps receding up the staircase before turning to Scott. "You failed to mention that your mom already hates me," she hissed.

"She doesn't hate you—" Scott pinched his dark brows together in thought. "—she's just not the happiest person in the world. I told you, what my dad did really messed her up."

"And so—a decade later—she's taking it out on me?" Angie caught the stung look on Scott's face too late to soften her sarcasm.

"She'll warm up," he said, defensive. "Just give her a day or two."

Warm up, or thaw out?

Angie took pause and nodded, deciding she was overreacting. She eased her voice to something more temperate. "Sorry, I'm just tired." She moved over to the counter and picked up the telephone before turning back to him. "I'm just going to make a few calls to let people know I got here, and then I'm going to sleep. I'll see you in the morning, okay?"

"Sure," Scott said, barely concealing agitation. "G'night." He turned and slunk back into the hall, heading for the stairs.

Angie picked up the house phone and muttered under her breath, glancing upward at the night sky as she wandered onto the back deck. "So, I'm off to a great start here." She pulled a phone card out of her wallet and called her parents first, leaving a message.

She called Vince next, fulfilling her promise. His voice was glad but subdued when he picked up, and she learned he was in the middle of his commute home from Birmingham. Angie also discovered that, despite all sound reasoning, she was just as relieved to hear him as she had been the previous night. She deliberately kept their conversation brief, not admitting to him her concern that it may have been a mistake to visit D.C. — or more specifically, to see Scott again. Giving Vince any remaining reason to worry about her would only make it that much harder to sever their connection. She couldn't risk doing that to him.

Angie stared at the phone for a long while after she'd hung up, fighting an unsettling heaviness. More permeating than exhaustion, the feeling reminded her of the sucking pull of wet sand. It was as though both her body and soul were weighed down by some intangible force. The cause, she knew, was the realization that she may never hear Vince's voice again. Instead of the closure she'd been striving for, the finality of it left only a hollow sense of loss.

Making her way down to the stairs to the unadorned guest room, Angie flopped onto the daybed she found awaiting her. "It's for the best...isn't it?"

But she drowned in sleep before any semblance of an answer could come to her.

Chapter 29

July 28th,

   For the last two days I've tried to catch up on sleep, or as much as Scott would let me. We've mostly played chess, watched movies, and hung around the house while I help him write his college entrance essay. He's been getting bored easily and acting annoyed with me. Maybe that's mutual. We keep bickering about stupid little things.
   Scott's mother doesn't like me at all. I don't know what he told her about me, but I can't seem to get on her good side. I'd be tempted to say she doesn't have a good side at all, but she treats his other friends just fine when they come over to hang out.
   At least Scott's friends here are much nicer than the ones he has in New York. I've especially enjoyed the company of his friend Kristy. She's pretty talkative. We went on for hours the other day about video game plotlines and weird pets we had while growing up. I guess I've missed talking to another girl. Aside from Elsie, I mean. Sometimes I think Elsie doesn't count. (I think the deepest conversation I've been able to have with her all month was about her recently discovered allergy to cinnamon.)
   I'm feeling ready to head back to Minnesota, but I've still got a few days to kill. We're going to go see all of the major sights today, and maybe a couple of museums. I'm hoping this might be fun and educational.

Mileage Log: 5,603 mi

~Ang

The tour began at the Jefferson Memorial. While Angie had seen the domed, marble structure in pictures, nothing had prepared her for the grandeur of experiencing the monument in person. Scott's mother later dropped them off at the Lincoln Memorial, where they began the two-mile walk of the National Mall.

The heat of the cloudless mid-day caught up to them by the time they'd reached the east end of the Reflecting Pool, forcing them to seek refuge in the shade of the Washington Monument. There, they argued. Angie wanted to walk through the war memorials, and Scott was determined to press on toward the Capitol Building. When passing tourists with umbrellas mentioned the temperature had surpassed one hundred degrees, Angie finally relented to Scott's abbreviated plan.

They marched eastward along the grassy mall, passing up a number of the art galleries and museums lining either side. The squabbling between them continued, even as they ducked into the Air and Space Museum for a reprieve from the heat. It was after three o'clock when they finally reached their intended destination.

"Are you gonna take much longer?" Scott asked, arms crossed as he paced back and forth in the meager shade of the Ulysses S. Grant Memorial. "We still need to find the subway station."

Sitting beside the broad pool in front of the Capitol steps, Angie had found a measure of relief by dipping her hands into the water and blotting them against the back of her neck. "It's a stationary location, Scott—it's not going to hide from us." She couldn't recall him ever seeming so motivated. The timing of it was grating on her. "I'm sure there'll be signs."

Scott growled out something unintelligible in reply, setting his jaw as he stared up at the bronze statue nearby.

Angie pushed off from the low wall and took several steps backward, taking yet another picture. "I could have just come by myself, you know. I told you I didn't want to be a bother." She shot the remark in Scott's direction before striding off to the north side of the broad marble terrace. Scott followed, looking somewhat contrite as he came alongside her.

"It's not that you're bothering me," he said, arms locked across his chest. "My mom wanted us back in time to help get things ready for my going away party. She's pissed enough that I invited you to stay with us—we don't need to make it worse on her."

Angie's frustration boiled over into flat-out anger. "Why did you convince me to come to D.C. if you knew your mom didn't want me here?"

Scott lifted a hand to pinch the bridge of his nose, as though he were combating a headache. "I wanted you here, okay? I wanted to see you one last time." He hesitated. "And I didn't want to drive nine hundred miles by myself. I thought we could help each other out. Maybe I was being kinda selfish, but I mean, you're here now. Can't we just make the best of it?"

"I'm trying." Angie sighed, stuffing her camera back into her pocket. "So, what am I doing wrong? I've cleaned up after myself, stayed out of everyone's way, tried not to eat any of your food— What does your mom want from me?"

Scott pulled his shoulders up in a stiff shrug. "She just doesn't trust you or something. Maybe it's a personality thing." His sun-darkened brow furrowed as he pondered. "You should think about sucking up a little, you know? It's not like you're too good for that."

Angie frowned. Though she didn't like the sound of his suggestion, the relentless heat had drained the fight out of her. "We can go now," she said, motioning further north toward the street.

Allowing Scott to lead the search for the subway, Angie trudged along in a mental fog. While she'd spent time at the water fountain back at the museum, she wasn't sure it was enough to fend off the threat of dehydration. As much as she didn't want to admit it, the abridged tour of D.C. was likely for the best — she would have needed several days to do it justice, anyway. Her irritability eased with the realization.

As they progressed several stifling blocks, she struggled to commit her impression of the city to memory. The immaculate streets blurred together in her mind, along with the occasional sharp-dressed citizen. Compared to New York, there weren't many people out and about.

"You know your mom better than anybody." Angie restarted the conversation on a calmer note, glancing sidelong at Scott. "What do you think I should do?"

Scott seemed confident in the direction they were headed, though judging by his stooped shoulders and the sweat-matted bangs that had pulled free of his pony tail, the sun was getting to him as well. "She hates cooking," he said, pausing at a street corner to peer up at a sign. "You could make her dinner tomorrow night. She'd probably love that." He pointed across the street and then made a dash through the crosswalk.

Angie jogged to keep up with him, though the exertion made her temples throb. She was ready for the day to be over. "I can do that," she said, once the threat of traffic was behind her. "I'll see if she'll let me go with her tomorrow and help with the shopping. Does she like chicken?"

Scott had reached an outdoor access elevator that promised to lead to the underground station. "Who doesn't like chicken?" He cast an aggravated look over his shoulder.

"Well I don't know, I'm just asking!" Angie snapped back, exasperated. He kept punching the already glowing "down" button, and it took every ounce of her remaining self-control not to slap his hand away.

When the doors parted, an inviting rush of chilled air enveloped them. Angie lurched forward and made her way to the rear of the empty elevator, leaning her back flat against the cool wall. She closed her eyes and took in an appreciative breath. Amid her relief, she had only a vague awareness of the chime as the doors closed, and the shuffle of feet as Scott moved about.

Just as the elevator began to move, she was startled to sense Scott in front of her. And he wasn't just in her space, he was pressing against her, crushing her between his chest and the wall. The smell of sweat and aftershave burned her nose. Then his mouth was on hers, heated and demanding. Stunned, Angie tried to break away by pushing herself at an angle, but was stopped by the fact he'd braced his arms against the wall on either side of her. She attempted to voice her protest, only to have his tongue invade her mouth. Her mind swam with dread and confusion.

What is he doing?! Even more astonishing was the realization that she felt no desire to respond. Instead, Vince's face appeared in her mind. The memory of his imploring green eyes filled her with resolution.

Angie snapped her head to one side hard enough to sever their contact, catching Scott's face with her chin in the process. "Stop it!" Driven to put immediate distance between them, she dropped her weight, ducked out from under his arms, and retreated to the opposite side of the elevator. Scott remained propped with one arm against the wall, his other hand cupped over his mouth. He stared downward, dark brows pinched in a look of pain. She'd hurt him — likely in more ways than one.

Good. She clenched her fists at her sides.

"I'm sorry." Scott's voice came muffled from behind his hand. He turned toward her as the elevator came to a stop.

"You should be." Angie glowered at him, striding out when the doors parted. She scanned the cement floor of the underground hallway and started for the turnstiles she spotted ahead. "What happened to that 'just friends' thing? And why would you do that, after we've been on each other's nerves all day—?" She turned back to Scott.

"I know, I know...it was stupid." Scott dropped his hand. His lower lip had suffered a small split, which he began to chew at. He hung his head, avoiding any eye contact with her. "I wasn't thinking. You just looked so—" Without finishing the thought, he ambled past her toward the subway platform.

Angie's outrage dwindled as she watched him walk off. It was at least half her fault, she decided. She never should have come to D.C. In her effort to preserve a friendship, she'd failed to let enough time pass for both of them to see things clearly. And surely heat delirium could share some of the blame.

After all, kissing Scott had just made her feel like she was betraying someone who she had little chance of ever seeing again.

~ ~ ~ ~ ~ ~ ~

"There's a call for you." Scott's mother scowled as she carried the house phone into the living room.

It was well after dark, and Angie had been winding down with a book while Scott slept off a mild case of heat exhaustion on the nearby couch. Standing, she concealed her curiosity. She wasn't due to check in with anyone for several days. "Thank you, Cindy."

Angie smiled, willing the cantankerous woman to find her at least somewhat likable.

"Don't you go making any long distance calls on the house line," the smaller woman warned, handing off the device with a suspicious air. "I'll send you the bill if you do."

Angie held her smile, though it took all of her concentration. "Oh, don't worry. I shouldn't need to. I can just borrow Scott's cell if I do—" She cut herself off upon seeing a look of irritation flare across the woman's face. Angie pressed the receiver to the center of her chest and ducked her head as she walked to the back door, escaping onto the deck. Thick with humidity, the air outside was only moderately cooler than it had been earlier in the day. The distant rumble of thunder told her the condition of the sky before she glanced up.

"Hello?" She spoke into the phone, having nearly forgotten her curiosity. Enough of her mind was expecting Elsie to be on the other end that it caught her by surprised to hear a masculine tenor.

"Hey, Angel."

Angie's throat tightened. Vince's voice was strangely soothing, like the mental equivalent of ice on a fresh burn. She couldn't help but smile in relief. "Hey, you."

"I promised myself I wouldn't bother you," he began, sounding every bit as mollified as she felt. "But I had to know how you were doing."

"I'm doing okay." She eased across the deck and stepped down into the grass, dew dampening her bare feet. "Just tired and ready to leave. I wish I'd just gone straight home after Alabama." She found herself admitting more than she'd meant to.

"Is that Scott guy treating you alright?" Vince's tone shifted to concern.

"Yes." Angie reconsidered. "Kind of. We're not getting along so well. And I think his mother would like to set me on fire, given the opportunity and no threat of legal repercussions—" Her attempt at a joking didn't come out as convincing as she'd intended.

"You're leaving soon though, right?"

"I have just a few more days," she said, beginning an absent circling of the little willow tree in the middle of the lawn. "I should be back home by the fifth."

"Good." Vince sounded satisfied. "So, how soon should I start looking for plane tickets? Grady might tag along, but he knows to let us have time to talk if we need to."

Angie paused mid-step, struck by his resolve. "You...you're serious? You still want to visit Minnesota?"

"I want to see you again," he said, voice lowering in earnest. "I miss you. A lot."

"Vince—"

"Maybe it doesn't make sense, but I'm not the same as I was before I met you." He took in a steadying breath and went on. "I tried to leave you alone—I really did. I still will, if you tell me that's what you want. But I can't stop thinking about you. I don't even want to." He hesitated. "And not in a crazy stalker kind of way. I mean—I'm not obsessed or anything like that."

"I know." Angie chuckled, hoping to defuse his anxiousness. Before she could work up another dissuading argument, she remembered the sense of loyalty she'd felt for him earlier in the day. It mingled with Vince's potent sincerity and her elation over hearing his voice. Something in her faltered. "I miss you too."

"Would it be okay if I keep checking on you?"

Angie wrapped her free arm around herself, slowing her pacing as a closer peel of thunder sounded overhead. Looking up, she watched lightning flicker behind the clouds. "I wouldn't mind," she said. "I just don't want to take up a lot of your time. You don't get enough sleep as it is."

"I can't think of a better way to spend my time." His voice warmed. "Besides, sleep is for the weak."

"Sleep is healthy," she corrected. "And so is eating. You need to be doing more of both."

Vince laughed. "If it makes you happy, I'll work on it." His humored tone sobered after a pause. "My mom asked today if I took any pictures while you were here, and I realized I didn't. I really wish I had."

A spark of recollection jumped to the front of her mind. "Are you at home right now?" she asked.

"Yeah, I just got in. Why?"

"Go to your desk and lift up your keyboard."

Silence stretched out on the other end of the line, save for muffled hints of movement. "Oh wow," Vince breathed, indicating he'd found the picture Angie had left behind for him. The wallet-sized senior photo featured her in an elegant, powder-blue gown, which had served as a surprise last impression for her high school yearbook. She'd agonized over whether or not to leave him the picture. Now, hearing the smile in his voice, she was glad she did.

"I wish I'd gave you something to remember me by."

"Don't worry about it," Angie said. "I took a few pictures."

"I'll make up for it," Vince said, proceeding to change the subject before she had a chance to protest. "What's it like in D.C.?"

They continued with several minutes of effortless conversation before the encroaching thunderstorm arrived, chasing Angie back into the house. As he bid her goodnight, Vince promised to call again the following day. Angie caught herself hoping he meant every word he'd said.

Oh, God... I think I'm in trouble. If this is a bad idea, I need you to make it clear to me really soon.

~ ~ ~ ~ ~ ~ ~

Angeli was disoriented, that much she knew.

The forest around her was unfamiliar and lined with the long shadows of approaching dusk. The soft, loose soil beneath her feet was layered thick with decaying leaves that crackled in objection to her every movement. She was losing her footing, becoming more alarmed as she slid back toward the darkened ravine behind her.

On instinct she flailed her arms out, desperate to catch hold of one of the trees. Her left palm slapped a thick trunk only to have the bark break away in her clawed hand. Her right hand caught a more spindly tree, which shuddered under her weight as she jerked to a halt. With a violent *crack* the rotted roots gave way, bringing the towering shaft hurtling down on top of her.

Angie yelped. It was the first sound she'd managed to form in her throat, aside from the panicky breathing that drowned out everything else.

Throwing her full weight to one side, she lunged headlong into the hillside. The musty scent of rotting leaves overtook her. The breeze from the fallen tree raised the hairs of her arm as it slapped against ground and began a slide into the depths of the narrow valley. Wasting no time or momentum, she grappled with the earth. The cool soil shifted under her, peeling away from the hill in a sheet with the effect of a small avalanche.

Angie didn't know how deep the ravine went, or what may lie at the bottom. Craning her neck to look behind her, she could only make out blurry shapes and shadows. Imminent danger was too thick for her to process how or why she'd ended up in this predicament. She splayed her limbs, praying one of them would encounter a sturdy object she might be able to cling to.

Her right hand caught something solid and her entire body wrenched to a stop. The surge of dirt and leaves continued around and under her for several moments, distracting her from comprehending that she hadn't so much grabbed onto something, but had instead been caught. A strong, warm force flexed around her wrist and she jerked her face back up to see the hand it belonged to.

Her strained gaze followed upward and she was stunned to recognize Vincent's face, set in a look of determination. With one arm latched around a tree trunk, his feet were planted against an upraised root. He'd extended himself fully in catching her in this state of suspension.

"Reach!" he instructed.

Angie grasped his forearm with her free hand and pulled her knees under her until she'd wedged the toes of her shoes into the ground. She unfolded her legs and stretched herself upward as he hoisted her up. He kept his anchoring arm in place and wrapped the other around her waist, pulling her back against him as he leaned into the tree.

Angie grasped a handful of his shirt and turned her face into his shoulder, catching her breath. Disjointed questions formed in her mind as she closed her eyes, willing the situation to make sense. Vince's breath came short and sharp as he kissed her temple.

"It's okay," he whispered. His embrace tightened and he dropped his chin to nuzzle his smooth jaw against her cheek.

Angie didn't understand, but at least she was safe. Lifting her head she scanned Vince's face, which was set with lines of concern. It occurred to her then that the light filtering through the surrounding trees was growing brighter. Dawn was approaching. Not that this minor revelation clarified anything. In the fog of her thoughts, she struggled to verbalize a question. She was interrupted by a sudden shift in his expression.

"Come with me." He kept his voice low and urgent. His arm slid from around her waist to grasp her hand.

Then, he was moving. Sure-footed and calculating, he guided
her along behind him as he followed the protruding root lines in a
path running parallel with the ravine. She followed without
hesitation.

The misty daylight that shone over the top of the hill
continued to grow brighter. She faltered often, forcing Vince to brace
himself and correct her balance. The crest of the hill to her left
seemed much closer as the incline lessened. To her right, she could
finally see that a dry creek bed made up the floor of the ravine — a
sheer drop of ten or twelve feet from where it cut into the earth.

The erratic patterns of their labored breathing mingled with
the soft thrashings of their feet through the long dead foliage.
Somewhere in the recesses of her mind, it occurred to her that these
were the only sounds to be heard. If it was dawn, shouldn't there be
birds, or at the very least, the occasional scolding squirrel? Her
confusion deepened.

Vince came to an abrupt halt, and Angie ran into his back.
Vince swayed forward while still managing to hold his ground. He
tightened his hold and pulled her around to his side, releasing her
then so she was braced against the low V of a thick tree trunk. She
followed his attention to the top of the hill. The silhouette of a person
was moving toward them — male, judging by the stature.

"Stay here. I'll find you," Vince said, turning away before she
could protest.

"But why? Who—" Angie choked out, watching as he placed
himself between her and the backlit figure that was now charging
down the incline.

Vince shifted forward, stance widening as he lowered himself
in preparation for the inevitable impact.

A dull *thud* resounded through the trees as the attacker
careened into him. The grappled pair spun in mid-fall before hitting
the ground, their heads barely missing the tree where Angie stood.
Locked together they rolled down the incline, churning up debris and
grunting in exertion.

Angie's mind caught up to the sudden violence. "NO!" She
reached out, too late to snatch at Vince's clothing or otherwise slow
them down. She gripped the tree trunk with one arm and swung
herself around it to track them.

Near the lip of the drop-off, Vince's back slammed into a
rotting stump, bringing them to a stunning halt. The assailant took

immediate advantage, coming to his knees swinging. He'd landed several brutal punches before Angie went skidding after them and leaped onto the man's back. Screaming in some mixture of rage and fear, she threw her weight to wrench him off Vince. Her back hit the ground, knocking all breath from her lungs as the attacker landed on top of her.

Dazed, she fought for air as the speckled forest canopy filled her vision. It was soon blotted out by the ominous figure who was already getting back up. His face turned toward her as he shook off her rubbery hold and stood. Shock surged through Angie's uncooperative body.

It was Vince. She recognized every detail of his lean form in an instant. How could she have made such a mistake? She turned her head aside to identify the figure he'd been pummeling, and her bewilderment was compounded. The young man lying against the stump, who'd begun to rise, was also Vince.

She couldn't be getting enough oxygen.

Angie's wild gaze darted back and forth between the two. Their clothing was identical — black cargos and a faded beige t-shirt bearing the emblem of a coiled dragon. Their copper hair gleamed in the growing streams of daylight. The intense look of malice was mirrored in both sets of emerald eyes as they stood, squaring off once more.

As Angie recovered enough to sit up, the violence resumed without explanation. The Vince near the tree stump lunged first, landing a solid punch to the gut of the assailant closest to her. The latter doubled over, but managed to hook an arm around the first aggressor's neck and drag him down. Then they were entangled again, in what Angie suspected was a death match. Neither one of them was holding anything back. By the time she'd drug herself to her feet, both of their faces were bloodied.

Angie staggered, first forward and then back several steps. Her impulse to break up the embattled pair was stayed by one nagging thought: *This can't be happening!*

Yet, her pulse hammering away in her ears felt real. As did the familiar tingle of adrenaline, and her mounting sense of desperation.

"Stop! Please—" she began to scream. One of the badly beaten figures slammed his knee into the chest of the other as he got enough clearance to stand, and then took off running down into the lowest point of the ravine. The other Vince gave chase, compounding the refrain of scraping leaves and snapping twigs in their wake. As she watched, the pursuer snatched up a club-like piece of tree branch without breaking stride. Angie didn't have the impression she could affect the outcome of this epic act of self-destruction, but she couldn't watch it unfold.

One of them would die, she was sure of it. But which one? And was there a difference between them? Better still, why was this happening in the first place? As vivid as this all felt, her sense of reason seemed adrift. The identical opponents disappeared into the shadowy recesses of the valley, where she heard their struggle resume.

At first, Angie had only a dim awareness that she was running. Not toward them, but away. The idea that they were killing each other, while bizarre, was more than she could handle. She plunged on through the forest, staggering between trees and bounding over rotted logs as fast as her faltering traction would allow. She fell often, her lungs burning with the strain. The spaces between trees grew larger, and the landscape gradually flattened. She had no idea how far she'd gone before her final tumble.

Angie slipped into listless apathy as her toe caught a protruding tree root and she pitched forward, her cheek planting first as she rolled. She came to a rest on her side atop a bed of moss. Her spun, and she closed her eyes against the dizziness. Her stomach threatened to heave.

When her senses gradually returned, her skin had chilled, making her aware of the perspiration gathering along her brow and down her neck to the small of her back. A light breeze alerted her to the damp streams tracing down her cheeks. She shivered. Anguish pressed a low cry from deep in her chest. Vince was gone. And however surreal the circumstances, the loss was devastating.

When Angie opened her eyes again, the arrangement of shadows around her had changed. She had either fallen asleep or lost all grasp on the passage of time. It took her several moments to realize her attention had been roused by the rustling of leaves from somewhere behind her. While her heart sped up in alarm, she resisted the desire to look for its cause. Holding still went against every fight-or-flight impulse she had, but it was necessary to identify the origin of the sound. It came again, steady in approach and too heavy to be a bird or rodent.

Angie held her breath.

A hand cupped her shoulder and she jumped, twisting to strike out. The form kneeling over her caught her wrists, then released them as recognition stopped her. Vince's battered face hovered over her. Amid the marks and swelling that marred his features, he wore a drawn look of concern. She wasn't able to study the extent of his injuries for long, as he quickly turned her away from him.

"I'll be okay," he said, answering before she could ask. "I'm sorry." He sank onto his side and embraced her fully, holding her back to his chest and setting his chin on her shoulder.

Angie took slow breaths to calm her heartbeat. She didn't know what she should be feeling. Fear came to mind, but her body didn't seem interested in the logic. She couldn't help but feel safe with him — whichever "him" this was. He'd obviously been the winner of the fight, which begged the question she finally whispered, "What happened? What did you—"

"I had to." Vince spoke softly. His hold became a comforting embrace. "I had to protect you."

Angie's bewilderment remained, but the weight of her misery had been lifted. Exhaustion crept in to take its place. Combined with the security of being held, her mind was coaxed toward sleep. Though she resisted, her eyes fluttered closed.

When a burst of will let her force them open again, she was met with darkness. The bed of moss beneath her now felt suspiciously like an actual bed, the frame creaking as she sat up and groped her hands over the blankets. Her thoughts regained familiar clarity as she reached back and found an empty pillow behind her.

She'd been dreaming. Of course — some part of her had known that all along.

Angie's dreams had always been peculiar things. She rarely remembered more than a few indistinct thoughts or images upon waking. Fantastical and nonsensical, they often involved things like flying unaided over a vast landscape or observing a herd of technicolor rhinoceroses. She thought of her dreams as mental screensavers — their lack of profoundness seemed reason enough for her conscious mind to forgo any long-term storage.

This dream was different. The images and sensations remained etched in her memory, as clear as any real event. She wouldn't be able to forget, even if she wanted to.

What did that mean?

Her eyes strained to make out objects in the basement guest room. Absently, she reached up to touch her face and found her cheeks still damp with tears.

She'd been crying in her sleep.

Chapter 30

At the end of an uneventful day, Angie finally made some progress with Scott's mother. The woman had begun speaking to her with calm civility, and even smiled at her once. Angie's upbeat mood was further elated that evening when, true to his word, Vince called.

Before she knew it, two hours had gone by while she paced around the darkened back yard. When a natural lull entered their conversation, her thoughts turned to her bizarre dream from the night before.

"You don't happen to have a twin brother, do you?" she asked, offhanded.

"Not that I'm aware of," Vince laughed. "Why do you ask?"

"Oh no reason. I just had a weird dream last night."

"And there were two of me in this dream? Now, I could see me having a dream like that about you—"

"Neither of you were very happy about it," she recalled, cutting short his playful speculation.

"So, they were fighting?" Vince sounded fascinated. "Like...a good twin versus evil twin sort of thing? Who won?"

"I don't know. I couldn't tell them apart before or after." Angie said, hesitating. "More than fighting—I think one of them died."

Vince was quiet for a short while. "What do you think it meant?" His tone had grown intent.

Caught off guard by his seriousness, Angie forced a chuckle. "I don't know that it means anything. I just thought it was strange. No reason to read into it—"

"I need to tell you something," Vince said, taking a long pause as he seemed to collect his thoughts. "I had just started seeing someone before you came to visit — a girl I knew through some friends at college. I'd only taken her out on one date, but I really liked her. Or at least, I thought I did at the time." He paused. "She wouldn't have been good for me...I know that. I guess I'd just gotten so numb and lonely, I forgot what actually matters."

Angie's stomach clenched and she braced herself mentally, unsure of where he was going with his confession. "Why are you telling me this?"

"Because I can't look at her the same anymore. I haven't been looking at any girls the way I used to." He gave a faint laugh. "I was trying to explain this to Grady today, and he thought there must be something wrong with me. But I don't think that's it. I think there's finally something -right- with me."

"You're not going to see her again?" Angie asked, dwelling on Vince's assertion.

"No."

"Because of me?" Angie knew she should be flattered, but part of her was still clung to guilt.

"Yes." Vince's voice took on a serene quality. "I told you, I'm not the same person anymore. I've been seeing things differently. I've even been seeing God differently. It's like I was looking at everything through the end of a cardboard tube, and you came up and knocked it out of my hand."

"I'm...sorry?"

Well, I never claimed to be subtle.

"No, I'm glad." His tone was tinged with humor. "It was a stupid tube, anyway." With a pause he seemed to sober. "Can I ask you to do something for me?"

"What is it?"

"I've been thinking...if we're going to keep talking like this, we should just spare ourselves a lot of trouble and misunderstanding," Vince began. "I wanted to know if you'd agree to an absolute honesty policy between us."

Angie considered for a short while. "How would that be different? I haven't been keeping anything from you."

"I know," Vince said. "I just think it could help both of us, since we only have our voices to go by. I need to know you'll tell me what you're thinking and when you're upset, since I can't see your eyes."

"Okay, I'll try." Suspecting his request was a prelude to something, she eased herself down to sit on the steps of the back deck. "You should have noticed by now—I don't usually have trouble speaking my mind."

"Yeah, I'm counting on that." She heard a smile in his voice before he took a breath. "You know how I feel about you. That hasn't changed. If anything, it's gotten stronger," he said. "But I don't know how you feel about me. Before I buy a plane ticket, I'd like to know where we stand."

Angie felt her pulse quicken as she sorted through a jumble of thoughts. "That's fair. It's just... a little hard to explain." She stalled. "I've never been able to talk with any of my friends the way I can with you. And I think I understand what you were saying—about seeing things differently. I haven't been looking at guys the same way, either. I honestly don't know what that means," she said, feeling the sudden need to try one more time to dissuade him. "Is there some way I can convince you this isn't worth it?"

"Nothing short of telling me to go away." Hopeful humor carried in his tone.

Angie smiled, feeling her cautious heart swell over his determination. Before she could order her thoughts any further, the floodlight behind her switched on. Squinting, she looked over her shoulder as the back door swung open and a silhouette filled her vision.

"You're still on the phone?" Scott's lowered voice came tinged with agitation.

"Hang on a minute." Angie murmured into the receiver before pressing it to the inside of her shoulder. She stood and turned to face her host. "Yeah, I'm sorry. Did your mom need to use it?"

"She just went to bed," he said, lifting his chin. "You talkin' to that Alabama guy again?"

"Vince."

"Right, whatever." Scott crossed his arms.

As Angie's eyes adjusted to the glare of the overhead light, she made out the disdain in his face. Defensive anger coursed through her and she tightened her grip on the phone. "What's the matter with you?"

"Nothing," Scott said, brushing past her. He cleared the deck steps in a short leap and began striding through the back yard.

"Where are you going?" Angie called out.

"For a walk!" he barked. "I need a cigarette."

She lifted the phone to her cheek, sighing. "I need to go. I think Scott's throwing a tantrum, and it's my fault."

"I'll call you tomorrow," Vince said. "Just be careful, okay? I don't trust him, and I don't want you getting hurt—"

"The only person that's hurt is him," she assured, crossing the deck and stepping through the door that had been left standing open. "Don't worry. I'll talk to you tomorrow, Vincent."

"Goodnight, Angel."

"Goodnight."

She set the phone on the kitchen counter before bolting back out the door. With any luck, she could catch up to Scott before he did something stupid.

Angie trailed Scott for several blocks through his darkened neighborhood. He looked back at her only once, making no attempt at conversation as he avoided sidewalks and skulked along fences. She hung back several paces, deciding it was best to give him his space. Eventually they cut through a hedge line and came out behind a convenience store. There, she waited outside until Scott emerged with a pack of cigarettes. She stood by in silence as he settled cross-legged in a patch of grass, lighting the first stick.

"So that Vince guy...is he in love with you too?" Scott spoke up at last, his tone flat.

"He seems to think so." Angie answered, matter-of-fact. She glanced at his profile to gauge his reaction, but he didn't appear to have one. He took a series of long drags, releasing the smoke through his nose and parted lips.

"And—?"

"And, what?"

Scott turned his face toward her, apathy replaced by a haggard expression. "How do you feel about him?"

"I'm not sure," Angie answered, sinking down into the grass nearby. *And that's the truth.* "I care about him, and he's treated me well. I'm just...confused. Nothing new there."

"Huh." Scott snorted. He turned the cigarette around and offered it out to her.

"You know I don't smoke." She shook her head, drawing her knees up close to her chest.

"He's doing what I wanted to do the whole time you were gone." Scott took another series of long pulls, flicking the ashes off to one side. "I wanted to call you, but I didn't. Because you told me not to, and I -respected- that. I thought you were right about feelings wearing off and everything, but as soon as I saw you again—" His strong features crumpled in a tortured look. "—it all came back."

"I'm sorry, Scott." Angie looked away, the cold fingers of remorse squeezing at her chest. "I shouldn't have come here. I wanted us to still be friends. I just didn't realize what that would do to you."

"We can be friends!" Scott insisted, shaking another cigarette out of the pack. He pressed the glowing stump of the first stick to the end of the new one until it began to smolder. "We have to at least be friends. I can't completely lose you."

Angie grew increasingly distressed at his misery. "Obviously, I'm not doing you any good right now. I'll leave in the morning—"

"No," he snapped. "Everything's already set for the trip. I want to be there to look out for you. I should have been there the first time you left." He inhaled and held the smoke-laden breath, his stormy gaze flashing her way with renewed fervor. "I didn't tell you before, but I did like you said while you were in New York. I talked to God about you—even asked his permission to be with you. I thought it couldn't hurt, you know? I didn't expect an answer. But, I sorta got one—"

"What do you mean?" Angie studied Scott's face, wondering why he was pulling the faith card. She couldn't be sure, but he seemed too uneasy to be making it up.

"I'm not crazy—it wasn't like I heard voices or something," Scott said, without looking away. "I just got this question in my head out of nowhere. It was asking if I'd take care of you, protect you, and stay with you no matter what. I said I would—" The sharp edge to his voice eased as he hesitated. "And all I got back was: 'we'll see.'"

Convinced that he at least believed what he was saying, Angie was quiet for a time while she considered. "We'll see?" *Now that's cryptic.*

Scott shrugged. "That's the impression I got in my head. Not that it helped." He puffed away as he took to staring out at the hedge line. "I can't change how I feel. I've tried. I guess it's true what they say... you can't control what the heart wants."

"Maybe not," Angie said, with some reluctance. "But you can control your actions." She gestured to the pack of cigarettes beside him.

Scott blew streams of smoke from his nose in a dull laugh. "This is my last pack. Once it's gone, I'm done." He used a pinky finger to draw an invisible X along the left side of his chest. "Cross my heart, and hope to commit Seppuku."

She frowned. "Don't you think promising ritual suicide is a little melodramatic?"

"So I'm feeling a little dramatic right now." He scowled. "The girl I love doesn't love me back. I think I'm allowed."

"And what do you know about love, Scott?" Angie demanded. Her eyes stung from an acerbic blending of anger and regret.

"I know you make me happy." His voice thickened with frustration. "I know I've never felt as good as I do when I'm with you. And I know I could take care of you, if you let me."

"I don't think that's enough." The thought struck Angie with force, and so she wasn't surprised when it came out of her mouth in the same instant.

"Then what -is- enough for you?"

"I don't know." She turned her face away to hide the tears she couldn't hold back any longer. "I've been wondering that myself."

"For somebody who knows a lot, you don't seem to know anything important." Scott muttered and then frowned. "Sorry. That didn't come out right."

Angie heard a dry chuckle escape her. "No, you're right. At least we can agree on something."

July 30th,

I had my chance to suck up to Scott's mother last night. I made us dinner; grilled chicken over angel hair pasta. Fortunately, she really seemed to like it. I think I may have worked my way into her good graces at last. Now if only I could stay there.

I spent part of the evening talking to Vince. He wanted to know how I feel about him before he actually makes the trek to Minnesota. I think that's reasonable...I just couldn't quite answer him. I don't know what to do. Part of me still thinks that this will wear off and Vince will find someone more practical to be with. Maybe I'm just being cynical. There's another part of me that so wants to believe him. I have this feeling that somehow a lot is riding on Vince and his true degree of determination. It's just hard for me to believe that I could possibly be worth all this trouble I've caused him. I think I'm scared. I wish God would just tell me what I should do.

Vince and I didn't get to finish talking. Scott came outside, got angry, and stormed off to buy cigarettes. I didn't try to stop him, it was his choice. I ended up following him and watching him chain smoke for a few hours. We talked. I cried. He kept offering me a cig, for some reason. He told me again that he's in love with me. (Thinking about it now actually makes me mad. I don't know how he can claim to love me and then act the way he's been acting.) We talked until the sun came up, and at one point, he told me he'd quit smoking and drinking and clean up for my sake. That just seems so immature. It was like he was blackmailing me with his health. I feel so awful for hurting Scott, but at the same time, the whole experience reassured me that I'm not supposed to be with him. At least I'm sure about *something* now.

I only got to nap for a few hours this morning before Scott woke me up to apologize for his behavior. Evidently, trying to record things in his journal gave him some new perspective. We're back on the same page about staying 'just friends.'

~Ang

~ ~ ~ ~ ~ ~ ~

"Are you sure you're okay?" Vince asked for the third time since discovering how little sleep Angie was running on. She'd attempted to gloss over her explanation of the night before, but he'd

used their newly-instated honesty policy to extract most of the
details.

"I'm fine—stop worrying." Angie said, shifting the phone to
her other ear. She'd lost count of how many times she'd circled the
miniature willow tree while they talked. The grass laid flat along the
path she'd been pacing.

"I can't help it." Vince sighed. "You're twelve hours away
and sleep deprived, on top of being manipulated by that son of a—"

"It's mostly my fault. I shouldn't have gotten myself into this
mess."

"You're letting him off too easy."

"At least it's straightened out now." Angie eased down to sit
at the base of the tree, tracing her fingers down along one of its
slender, drooping limbs.

"Don't be so sure." Vince sounded wary. "You're hard to
give up. I should know." He hesitated before adding, "I don't think
you should spend any more time alone with him."

Angie smiled to herself over Vince's caution. "That won't be
an issue. He's spending all of his time with his friends now. They're
even staying over every night until we leave."

Vince seemed to consider this at length. "Okay."

"So you're going to stop worrying?"

"I didn't say that."

She feigned a sigh. "Well, I'm a little worried about you, too.
Don't you have work in the morning?"

"It's morning now," he pointed out.

Angie frowned. "I should probably let you go, then." But it
was the last thing she wanted to do.

"I'd rather pass out listening to your voice." Vince's tone
eased into weary humor. "Just know that if I start snoring, it's not a
sign of how interesting I find you."

She chuckled. "Seriously, we both need to catch up on sleep."

"Yeah," he agreed, begrudgingly.

"Call me tomorrow?"

"Of course." His voice warmed. "But before you go, I have a
question." He paused. "I'm not trying to pressure you—I just have to
know for sure. Is what we have a friendship...or a relationship?"

Angie laid herself back in the grass and stared up through the
willow branches at the night sky, taking a steadying breath. Her heart
rate shot up as though she'd just run a mile.

Time to make a big-girl decision, she mused. *Please, let it be the right one.*

"I've given that a lot of thought," she began, offering her reasoning as it came to her. "I don't know if we could make it work, Vince. I'm scared we're too young to be this serious. I'm scared of both of us getting hurt." Her eyes tracked from star to star as she made the admission. "I'm scared of a lot of things, and I hate that. It was part of the reason I went on this trip in the first place. I don't want to keep running away from things just because I'm afraid of failing," she went on, calm realization settling over her.

"There's so much I don't know, I think it's been distracting me from what I do know. I know you have a good heart, an amazing mind, and the potential to do great things. I know I respect so many things about you. And...I like who I am when I'm around you." She felt a smile forming on her face as she gathered her courage. "I guess what I'm trying to say is—if you're still sure about this—then I suppose we can give it a try."

The other end of the line was silent for so long, Angie began to wonder if her rambling had put him to sleep. She cupped the receiver closer to her lips. "Vincent?"

Vince spoke at last, voice faltering. "Is that...were you trying to say no?"

Angie suppressed a surprised laugh. "I was -trying- to say yes!" she stressed, laughing. "You really are tired, huh?"

"Yeah, I guess I am." He released a quiet chuckle, along with the breath he'd been holding. "And maybe just too used to bad news."

She sensed an innate gentling to her tone, "I'm sorry, I know I made this hard on you." A thought occurred to her then, and a nervous laugh spilled out as she added, "You know I'm still not going to sleep with you, right?"

"I can deal with that." His answer came quick and sober. "Sex isn't love."

His sincerity stunned her. Closing her eyes against the stinging threat of tears, she whispered, "I just don't understand why you would put yourself through all of this."

"Because, you're worth it." Vince said, with an air of simple certainty. "I don't know if I'm what's best for you...but I want to be. I want to make you happy."

Angie considered his words at length before a question surfaced. "Why does...my happiness matter?"

Vince answered in a pensive tone. "I have this feeling that, if you're happy, it would make God happy. And if I could have a hand in making -both- of you happy—" She heard the smile in his voice. "That just seems like the best thing in the world to me."

He paused then, and his confidence seemed to waver. "Think that's weird?"

"I think...your heart is in the right place." Angie smiled to herself, going over and over his words in her mind. "But now that that's settled, will you be able to get some sleep?"

"My chances have never looked better," Vince said, voice heavy with contentment. "Goodnight, Angel." Without hesitating he added, "I love you."

Angie caught herself just short of returning the sentiment. *Too soon.*

She wanted to — the desire strained at her heart like an unfulfilled need. But her mind told her she'd delved far enough into the unknown for one night. Instead, she closed her eyes and whispered, "Goodnight...my Vincent."

Chapter 31

On the morning of the final leg of Angie's trip, she emerged from the basement early to bid farewell to Scott's friends. She found them all together in the kitchen. Scott and his best friend, Andre, were engrossed in an animated discussion about Samurai swords, while Kristy sat at the table picking at a bowl of cereal. The girl's round, mousy features lit up at the sight of Angie.

"Hey lady! I was afraid I wouldn't get to say goodbye," Kristy said. Behind oval-rimmed glasses, blue-green eyes held the warmth of a tropical lagoon. Her short, ash-brown hair was mussed, as though she'd run her fingers through it and nothing more. Angie had enjoyed her conversations with the talkative girl. She'd even considered exchanging contact information so they could keep in touch, but concern over forging additional connections to Scott gave her cause to reconsider.

"You poor thing. How long have you been drowning in testosterone?" Angie offered a wry smile as she sat across from the girl, acknowledging the other two with a nod.

"Like, half an hour." Kristy rolled her eyes. "Seriously, I think I'm turning Japanese." She produced a school yearbook from the backpack she'd brought with her, laying it open to a particular page and turning it around for Angie to see. "You know how I was telling you about Darrel? That's him! I forgot I had this with me." She tapped a neon-green fingernail over the photo of a strapping young man wearing a blue letter jacket.

Angie gave the picture a quick study. "Ah, yep. Easy on the eyes." She nodded, humoring the girl's apparent fixation. In their conversation the previous day, Kristy had carried on about Darrel for almost an hour, going so far as to ask opinions on different combinations of his last name with hers. While Angie suspected the infatuation might be one-sided, she wasn't about to squash her new friend's girlish enthusiasm.

"He's perfect." Kristy hugged the book to her chest. "Did I tell you we're going to the same college this fall? He even told me we should pick some of the same classes so we can study together. That has to be a good sign, right?"

"That sounds...promising," Angie said, feeling unqualified to be making any sort of assessment. She heard Scott and Andre snickering, and wondered why the tone of their conversation had changed. In her peripheral vision she caught the guys looking at them. Kristy didn't seem to notice.

Angie steered the conversation to college, a subject that gave her more assurance in her own first-hand knowledge. After several minutes there was a knock at the door, announcing Kristy's ride had arrived. Andre and Scott continued their hushed exchange as she left, smothering their laughter when Angie gave them a curious look. Andre went home shortly thereafter, and Angie followed them both to the front door.

"What was so funny?" she asked the moment the door closed behind Andre.

Scott smirked to himself as he walked past her through the foyer, shaking his head. "It's just an inside joke. You wouldn't get it."

Angie didn't know whether to take his words as a challenge, or as a confirmation that the 'joke' was about her. "Try me."

"Nah, it's not your kind of humor." He kept walking, moving into the dining area where he set about packing up his laptop. Angie trailed after him, annoyed by his sudden elusiveness.

"Is it about me?"

"Nope." Scott shook his head, grimacing under her insistent stare. "It's just something with Kristy, that's all."

"What about her?"

"It's nothing."

"Just tell me, I feel left out." Angie folded her arms and tapped her foot.

"She's just kinda crazy, that's all." Scott shrugged, slipping the computer into his backpack. He chuckled then as if he'd remembered something amusing. "She thinks Darrel actually likes her. We've all been buddies with Darrel since elementary school, and trust me, he's not into girls like her. We tried telling her that for years, but she wouldn't listen—just kept doing his homework for him and living her little fantasy."

Angie allowed confusion to cloud her expression as she stood by, awaiting the punch line.

"It's funnier if you've been around here a while." Scott cleared his throat. "Kristy was always the smartest one in our group. Best grades, full scholarship, voted most likely to succeed…but when it comes to Darrel, she's a total moron." His ironic smirk returning. "Andre was just saying he saw them at a party and figured out they're 'friends with benefits' now. Darrel's getting all the perks with none of the hassle, and Kristy's all off in lala-land thinking it's going somewhere."

Angie gaped at him, stomach seizing. "That's not funny, Scott. That's awful."

He forced a sharp exhale, casting her an exasperated look. "See, I knew you'd be like this."

"Like what?" She sputtered, still in shock over his callousness. "She's a nice girl with low self-esteem. Do you have any idea what it might do to her when she realizes that guy is just using her?"

Scott threw up his hands. "Hey, she brought it on herself. It's not like we didn't warn her."

"How can you be so concerned about your friend Tessa's drinking, but think Kristy's issue is so entertaining?" Angie wondered between clenched teeth.

"Because it's not the same thing!" Scott's dark brows knit in mounting anger. "I'm friends with Kristy -and- Darrel. I don't get involved with stuff like that."

"So what, are you going to not get involved when she ends up heartbroken?" Angie demanded. She couldn't help the intensity of her voice. She'd been witness to the destructive consequences of too many relationships gone wrong, which made Scott's insensitivity to the concept all the more appalling to her. "What if she gets depressed or wants to hurt herself over it? Or worse—"

"You're making a big deal out of nothing," Scott accused, nostrils flaring as he took a step toward her. "Don't stand there judging me like I'm a shi**y friend or something. You're just too damn wholesome to accept reality, you know that? Just like Kristy—off in your own little world where you think you know everything."

Angie stood her ground, stunned that she hadn't detected this side of Scott before. Repulsion flooded her mind and soured her stomach. How had she ever found him attractive?

I'm such an idiot.

Unable to think of any response that wouldn't provoke him further, she stayed quiet.

"I'm a good person!" Scott bellowed, his full mouth twitching into a snarl. "So maybe I'm not perfect, but at least I do more good stuff than bad. That should be enough for anybody." He took another step forward and pointed at her face. "I don't need all of your God and forgiveness crap. I'm done with it!"

Feeling as though she'd been verbally slapped, Angie looked away and stared out the French doors into the sunny backyard. She was determined not to become emotional. Crossing her arms, she waited, reduced to the responsiveness of a stone. Scott finally turned, stomped off through the hall and up the stairs.

Taking several moments to collect herself, Angie headed down to the guest room to finish collecting her things and loading her car. Whether Scott was still in the mood to caravan with her or not, she was leaving.

By the time Scott came out to pack his car, his anger was replaced by sullen remorse. Angie did her best to ignore him as they readied their vehicles side by side in the driveway. While she was checking her tire pressure, he brought her a cheese danish. Supposing it was a peace offering, she accepted the pastry but refused to break her silence.

Scott hovered nearby, head down and hands in his pockets. If he'd been working up the gumption to apologize, he was cut short when his mother came out the front door with a wallet in hand.

"Missing something?" Cindy held up the item, penciled brows quirked in a skeptical look.

Scott patted his back pocket and grumbled, walking over to take his wallet from her. "I woulda figured it out."

"Uh-huh." Cindy huffed, stepping up to peer in through the widows of his blue sports car. "You can use my card for gas, but that's all. No junk food. If I find one empty bag of chips, so help me—"

"Got it," Scott mumbled.

"I put the cards for your grandmother in your backpack," Cindy continued, her thin arms fluttering at her sides. "Remember to stretch your legs every few hours. And don't you dare speed. Call me every night—call me if you get tired—call me if you get lost." Her pallid face pinched in a concerned look that she shrouded in irritability. She rattled off a checklist of supplies — Scott nodding his assent after every item.

"I think we're good to go, Mom." Scott wrapped the diminutive woman in a hug, setting his chin on her head. "Don't be all worried, okay?"

Against her will, Angie felt a tiny bit of empathy return as she watched the exchange. "Yeah, no worries. I'll look out for him," she said, offering her hand to Cindy for a parting shake.

The woman gave Angie's hand a long look as she took a step back from her son, her expression growing cold. "He can look out for himself just fine."

"Right." Angie withdrew her hand, attempting a tight smile. If she'd had a tail, she would have tucked it. *That's what I get for breaking her baby's heart.*

Ducking into her car, she waited for Scott to pull out of the drive.

August 3rd,

On the Road Again

So, Vince and I are official now. Every night I talk to him, I'm more hopeful that he's got permanency potential. It's amazing to me how well he's managed to walk this thin line between not trying hard enough…and stalking. I know that sounds odd, but I don't know how else to explain it. Guys like Don and Zak might have liked me, but they didn't care enough to prove it. I know Scott really liked me, obviously. But even if there hadn't been problems with the way our personalities mesh, he was just too forceful about it. Vince is different; in the best way possible. I finally called Mom yesterday and told her about him. She didn't sound as skeptical as I was expecting. I think she considers the long-distance thing to be a worthy test; one he'll either pass or fail.

Today Scott and I got a later start leaving than I would have hoped, but we were on the road by 11 AM. We took turns driving lead. It was a long eleven hours, but it felt a little easier to be following someone while I drive.

We made it into Indiana after dark and looked for a place to stay. I'd originally planned on sleeping in the car, but Scott wasn't keen on the idea. So we found a Holiday Inn, only to be told that all of the hotels within a 100 mile radius of Indianapolis are booked due to the Brickyard 400 race. The man behind the counter felt sorry for us and offered to check with a local Bed and Breakfast. It's been so ridiculously hot and humid today...I don't think he wanted us sleeping in our cars either. While he was making calls, someone canceled a room. We reserved it right away, though it was pretty expensive. Scott told me he had permission to use his Dad's credit card for this sort of thing. He said his dad is touring Italy and wouldn't notice anyway.

We went out to find something other than snack food, and Scott apologized for the big argument we had before we left. He told me he didn't mean what he'd said...he was just trying to hurt me. (I already suspected that much.) But then he asked if I thought there might still be any chance for 'us.' I told him no, and he took that pretty hard. He broke down and cried, actually. I told him we should just get some sleep and he'd feel better in the morning. I couldn't bring myself to tell him about Vince.

As for sleeping accommodations... they didn't have any rollaways left, so we have to share a king-sized bed. Granted the thing dwells in two zip codes at once, but considering how awkward things have been, I wanted to have more assured separation. Scott agreed to sleep on top of the covers on his side and I'm sleeping under them on my side.

Scott seems so dejected. I just hope he can start to see things differently, or I don't know if we can save this friendship.

Mileage Log: 6,175 mi

~Ang

~ ~ ~ ~ ~ ~ ~

This time, Angeli knew she was dreaming.

The foreboding forest felt familiar, though a starless twilight made it difficult for her to make out anything aside from looming shapes. She waded through crackling layers of dead leaves, groping her way from tree to tree. A rustling sound launched her heart into a rapid tempo. She froze in place, fighting the instinct to flee.

This isn't real, she reminded herself, craning her head back to search through the murky shadows. Though she couldn't make out anything threatening, her taut muscles refused to let down their guard. As she struggled to collect her wits and will herself into less eerie surroundings, the sound came again.

"Vince?" Angie whispered, turning as she steadied herself against the nearest tree trunk. Under her hand the rough surface rippled and came alive. An unforgiving force encircled her wrist and jerked her off balance. She thrashed against it as she fell onto her back, yanking her arm free only to sense the other one had been seized.

The shadows themselves were attacking her, flowing like ink and converging into an amorphous mass. She kicked and twisted, but her attempts to scramble backward were nullified by the pressing weight of the entity. Blackness enveloped her, blotting out her remaining vision. It clung to her limbs like tar and pressed her down with a suffocating heaviness.

A perplexingly warm, almost pleasurable sensation began to fill her. *I'm dying*, she concluded somewhere in the back of her panic-stricken mind. She felt and heard something tear near her shoulder. For a split second, she thought her arm was being ripped from her body. And then her sense of reality came flooding back.

Angie knew she was awake now, but her body told her she was still in danger. Sensing motion around her only compounded her confusion. She couldn't move. The coarse, tearing noise came again and she realized at once it was the sound of her shirt, ripping. Her eyes snapped open. Scott was on top of her, panting, heated lips on her skin. A dizzying shock of understanding lanced through her brain. Suddenly, death didn't seem so terrible.

"Stop," she rasped, straining to draw up her arms and push him away. They remained pinned at her sides. "Stop it—" she tried again, but her words were stifled by his mouth crushing against hers. Angie twisted against his weight. He was strong, and she had no leverage. Despair began to mingle with her overwhelmed senses, and she heard herself whimper. Something in her mind suggested she give up and lay still.

The thought settled for a moment, and then ignited her anger.

NO! She channeled her focus into her arms, wrenching them with all of her remaining strength. Her right arm found freedom and she made the most of it, whipping her face to one side while she lashed out with a clenched fist, catching her assailant in the throat.

"GET OFF!"

Scott grunted, clutching at his neck as he was hurled onto the floor. He rolled onto his back, coughing hoarsely.

Angie sat up and snatched the blankets around. She turned on the lamp beside the bed, clutching at its base as the closest thing she had to a weapon. "What the hell is wrong with you?" she demanded, in a shrill voice she didn't recognize. Her muscles ached from resistance, and her soul ached from betrayal.

Scott held up a hand and squinted against the light, continuing to cough and sputter. He rolled further away until he'd braced himself against the wall. When he looked up at her from behind his tangle of long, wild hair, she saw a flash of something carnal. Fear cooled her outrage. For an instant, she fought the impulse to hurl the lamp at him and bolt for the door. He looked down and then back up, and the feral look was gone.

"I'm...sorry." He groaned, stretching out his neck as he continued to hold his throat. "What happened?"

"What happened?!" Angie repeated, incredulous. She glanced down at her torn shirt, grateful she had slept in her street clothes. It was then she realized that her hands were shaking. "You—" she clenched her teeth. "You...hurt me. You tried to—"

"I didn't mean to." Scott gave her a bewildered look.

"How could you not mean to?" she shot back.

"I dunno." Scott groomed his dark bangs back from his face with one hand, shifting until he'd reclined himself into the corner of the room. "I musta done it in my sleep. I'm really sorry, okay?"

"No. NOT okay." Angie pulled the top blanket with her as she stood. It dawned on her then that he was wearing only boxers and a sleeveless undershirt, and she struggled to recall his state of dress when they'd turned in for the night. Hadn't they both been fully clothed? Her memory refused to cooperate.

Darting around the foot of the bed, she retrieved her overnight bag from the low dresser. The clock told her it was 4 AM. She was exhausted, but she knew she wouldn't be getting any more sleep.

"Oh, come on, don't leave!" Scott pleaded.

Angie fished a fresh T-shirt out of her bag. Her thoughts were in such disarray, she wasn't aware of how badly she wanted to flee the room until he asked her not to. But where could she go? The idea of staying in her car until dawn unnerved her, but so did the thought of staying anywhere near Scott. Though her senses had been pushed to a heightened state of alertness, she knew she was too tired to continue the trip straight through — never mind the fact that the maps were in Scott's car.

Stupid, stupid, stupid. The accusing mantra echoed through her mind.

She turned to face him and snapped, "You don't touch me. Never again."

"I won't." He raised his hands in surrender, face crumpling into a pained look of regret. "I don't know what happened, Angie...I swear. I'm sorry."

She regarded Scott at a distance. Guilt began to worm its way into her cluttered mind. How much of this was her fault? She'd put herself in a compromising situation, after all. There were those that would say she was asking for something like this to happen. She tried to imagine explaining it to Vince, and jolt of dread shot through her. What would he think of her now?

"We should get some more sleep, you know?" Scott said, rubbing his eyes with his palms as he slid down from the wall to lay flat. "I'll just...stay on the floor. Okay?"

Angie said nothing. Moving to the bathroom, she closed herself in and locked the door. She sank to the cold floor and dropped her head into her hands. Was it possible he'd attacked her in his sleep? It would be so much easier if she believed him. And somehow, less painful than the only alternative.

She shuddered. All Angie could be sure of was that she'd never felt more trapped — or more in need of a shower.

Chapter 32

Angie accepted a plate of cookies from her elderly hostess before escaping to the living room of the archaic farmhouse. Agitated over how nonchalant Scott's behavior had been since their arrival, she left him in the kitchen chatting with his grandmother. After the long day's drive, involving incessant tension and repeatedly getting lost in rural Wisconsin, she was eager to wind down with her journal.

Her thoughts were still a jumble. Travel had been a numbing and welcome distraction, but being in the same room with Scott again seemed to trigger a torrent of anxiety. With him so close by, Angie had cut short all of her check-in calls. That included her call to Vince.

The sound of his voice had caused her a forceful upwelling of emotion, nearly bringing her to tears before she could regain control. Vince seemed to realize something was wrong. He'd learned to read her voice too well for her to hide it. She'd made reassuring excuses, promising to tell him everything the following night once she made it back to Minnesota. Before hanging up, he mentioned a present would be waiting for her at home. "Nothing extravagant—just something to remind you where my heart is," he'd said.

Now, settling down onto the far side of a plastic-covered chartreuse sofa, she let herself wonder about Vince's gift. It brought her some measure of comfort to think about him. But at the same time, a sense of trepidation had taken hold. As they'd said goodnight, Vince had again said 'I love you,' just as he had the last several nights — persevering despite her continued lack of reciprocation. She couldn't imagine how much her omitted words must be hurting him.

But once she told him what had happened, would he regret having been so vulnerable with her? Would he still even want her?

Angie opened her journal, hoping to sort her thoughts onto paper. She wrote two sentences about the day's travel and then stopped, rereading them over and over. Knowing it wasn't what she'd set out to write about, she erased everything.

How do I even start?

She held the mechanical pencil hovering over the first line, dimly aware that her hand was trembling. Whatever had happened the night before...was it even something she wanted a written record of? Every time she tried to review it, her mind bounced to something else. Anything else. To her, it seemed every bit as reflexive as it would be to jerk her hand away from a hot surface.

Angie had no idea how long she'd been staring at the same blank page before Scott's grandmother came hobbling in to collect her plate. She looked up and forced a smile of appreciation for the sturdy old woman. "Thank you."

Scott crossed the room and slumped into a chair in the corner, cracking open his own journal without sparing Angie a glance.

"Well, it's past my bedtime." Scott's grandmother announced. "I'll be up with the sun. You two sleep in as long as you like." Her leathery face crinkled with warmth.

Angie forced herself to hold a smile as she nodded and thanked the woman again. She felt herself abruptly consumed with the awareness that she would be left alone with Scott. Anxiety knotted in her stomach, but she convinced the rest of her to remain still.

Though he told his grandmother goodnight, Scott seemed to be ignoring Angie with the same determination she'd been using to avoid him. She forced herself to stare into her open journal for several more minutes, sketching a picture in one corner after she'd resigned herself to the fact that she wouldn't be accomplishing much else. Just as she considered retreating to the guest room, Scott spoke up in a low voice.

"I don't know what to do, sis." He spoke in a defeated tone without looking up, apparently reciting from something in his journal. "Me and Angie had a fight last night. A big one."

She looked up and stared across the room at him, dumbfounded.

A fight? Is that what he's calling it?

"There's no chance for us now. I know that," he read on in lament. "If you ask me, romance is a pretty sucky thing to happen to a friendship. But I dunno—maybe friendships need to go through hard stuff like this to prove what they're really made of."

Angie couldn't decide if she was more angered or baffled by his words. He was only partially making sense. Was Scott intentionally editing his own version of events, or was his memory that distorted? Some small piece of her mind wavered then, suggesting that her own recollection could be faulty. Even now, her impressions from the previous night lingered more like an obscure nightmare than lucid reality.

But surely he was trying to manipulate her by reading this out loud.

"She never talks anymore. I can't tell what she's thinking." Scott paused, but he wasn't finished. "So what are we now? Maybe we're still friends. I don't even know if I'm supposed to call her my ex, or what."

Angie stood up, fury trumping confusion in an instant. "To be your ex, I would have had to agree to the whole girlfriend thing in the first place," she said in a steady, definite voice. "Which I didn't."

Scott looked up at last, mouth twisting at the corners. His hazel eyes narrowed into a tempestuous glare. "So what, making out doesn't count for anything? Cuz I'm pretty sure you liked that as much as I did."

Taken aback by his accusatory tone, Angie's spine went rigid. Humiliation burned like bile at the back of her throat.

He thinks I deserved it.

Rather than speak another word, she fled — through the kitchen and down the hall to the tiny spare bedroom that was hers for the night.

She locked the door behind her and pressed her back against it, slowing the rapid breathing that accompanied her sudden upheaval of emotion. *So stupid*, her mind condemned her. She decided then that she would depart right away in the morning, only saying goodbye to Scott's grandmother if possible. If he caught her leaving and tried to guilt her into a parting hug, he would just have to be disappointed. The mere thought of him touching her again made her stomach churn.

Lightheaded, Angie turned out the light and eased forward to the foot of the bed. She bent and crawled to the middle, laying herself flat over the patchwork quilt.

After all this, I'm still just a gullible little girl.

If she'd been so wrong about trusting Scott, what else was she wrong about? Steeped in a fog of despair, Angie found herself second-guessing the road trip, Vince, and even the conviction of her life holding any purpose. In that moment, she'd never been as disappointed in anything as she was in herself.

~ ~ ~ ~ ~ ~ ~

If Angie dreamt at all that night, the memory of it eluded her. It seemed as though she'd been adrift only a few moments before being startled awake to a fear so raw, she had to clamp a hand over her mouth to keep from screaming.

She sat up, heart pounding. The guest room was dark, but she knew where she was. A shadow broke the shaft of light that spilled in from narrow gap between the door and the floor. Keenly aware of the sound that had shocked her into consciousness, she tuned in to the faint scrape and click of the locked doorknob being tested. The shadow shifted away and she heard the door to the nearby bathroom open and close.

Aware she'd been holding her breath, Angie leaned forward over her lap and sucked in a gasping gulp of air. She lifted her hands and held her head between them, rocking forward and back. *You're overreacting,* she told herself. No one was trying to get into her room. For all she knew, it was only Scott's grandmother wandering the halls. The logic should have reassured her, but she couldn't shake the sensation of an invisible clamp squeezing at her ribcage.

Desperate to find a position to ease her strain, she managed to stretch herself out onto her hands and knees. No longer surreal, images from the night before came tearing through her brain. She felt her skin chill as sweat broke out along her brow and down her spine.

A dull pain clawed at her chest. "Oh…God," she choked, a whispered plea for help.

Coherent thought scattered in all directions. Was this what a heart attack felt like? No, that didn't make sense. She grasped at mental fragments until she'd pieced together a more plausible explanation — she was losing her mind. The idea sat better with her than an untimely death, but just barely.

Before she'd had time to mourn her sanity, the intensity of her distress began to recede. Like an ebbing tide, tension pulled back from her in steady waves. Her lungs relished their restored freedom.

Limbs heavy and quivering, Angie sat on the edge of the bed for a long moment as she regained her bearings.

Normalcy seemed far more hesitant to return than it had been to flee. There was no clock to tell her how much real time the episode had consumed, but she knew by the sounds coming from the bathroom that it hadn't lasted long. It was as though she'd spent a minute in Hell, and it had felt like an eternity.

A prickling urgency lingered. She stood up as soon as she felt able and went to the door, reassuring herself that it was still locked. Pawing along the wall, she located a wooden desk chair near the corner of the room. She moved it over, setting the slatted back against the door. However paranoid she thought it was, she needed the additional line of defense — her peace of mind demanded it.

As she made her way back to the bed and crawled under the quilt, Angie heard the rattle of the bathroom door. She froze. A lesser form of the same mindless, instinctive fear gripped her once again. Her elbows locked under her, sending a trembling tension through her arms and shoulders.

The door opened and closed. Footfalls faded into another part of the house. Silence returned, leaving nothing to distract from her frayed nerves and tormented spirit. While she may not have misplaced her mind for long, it hadn't returned to her unscathed. She recognized then that she'd become what every well-meaning road trip naysayer had feared — a victim of circumstance. A statistic.

Angie buried her face in her pillow and sobbed.

Chapter 33

"Hey, these aren't bad," Elsie said, flipping through a stack of Angie's freshly developed photos. "For coming from disposable cameras, I mean." The willowy girl had draped herself backward over the arm of the living room sofa, hanging her upper body upside down while she examined the evidence of the road trip.

"Thanks, I think." Angie answered from a worn armchair nearby. Arriving home only hours earlier, she'd first dropped off her cameras and had a brief conversation with her mother. She'd then attempted a fitful nap, which Elsie had mercifully interrupted with her arrival. Angie still felt tired and unsettled, but she was grateful for the company.

"Aww, what a dork." Elsie crooned, holding up a picture of Scott. In it, he was seated in a meditative position on top of his pool table, glowering at the camera. "I can't wait until he gets here. We need to come up with stuff to do while he's around. I had an idea the other day, but we're going to need twenty pounds of fireworks and a porta-potty."

"That sounds…messy and illegal," Angie said, darting her gaze away from Scott's photo while forcing an amused smirk for her friend's sake. A dull sense of astonishment descended over her as she considered how much her perspective had changed in the weeks since she'd taken that picture.

Elsie gave an exaggerated sigh. "That's what my dad said. Blah blah blah…something about a burn permit…blah blah…the bail money is coming out of my college fund." She flicked her wrist in a dismissive wave and perked up with renewed gusto. "Hey, how about driving us all to The Mall of America instead?"

Angie squirmed in her chair. "You might have to handle that yourself. Your cousin and I weren't really getting along by the end there," she replied.

Understatement of the century.

"Couldn't you just play nice...for me?" Elsie whined in disappointment, grabbing up another stack of pictures to flip through. "Come on, you guys were getting along great over the phone. It can't be -that- different."

"It is, trust me." Angie swallowed to ease the tight sensation gripping her throat. She wanted to tell her friend what had happened in Indiana — just as she'd wanted to tell her mother, but she hadn't found the words or the courage to do so. The need to tell someone had been gnawing at her all afternoon. But two things held her back like a tether: Embarrassment, and the overriding fear of being blamed.

Now, seeing Elsie's eager anticipation over having her cousin in town, she had another reason to hesitate. The timing felt wrong. If she told her friend at all, it would have to be after Scott came and went. That left only one person she could talk to.

"So, is this the one you decided to keep?" Elsie asked. She paused her shuffling to hold out a picture of Grady.

"Nope." Angie reached for the remaining stack and picked up the next image — a shot of Vince with his dog huddled beside him. She flipped it over to offer Elsie a long look, but then brought it in close to her own eyes to study the photo of the young man who'd chased her with such determination. A wistful smile touched her lips.

"Wow, he must have a stellar personality," Elsie said.

"Hey—"

"Don't go taking it wrong!" The other girl righted herself on the couch arm and held up a finger. "It's nothing against him or anything. He just...looks like the kind of guy -I- would date. So I figure something about him must have really won you over." Her pale eyes held a rare sincerity as she spoke.

Angie considered before nodding. "I gave him every reason to give up on me, and he wouldn't."

"Oh good, so he's as stubborn as you are." Elsie arranged her expression into a lopsided grin. "You think that'll be enough?"

"There's a lot more to it than that." Angie got up from the chair and crossed the living room, plucking a padded envelope from atop a stack of mail on the kitchen counter. She returned to the chair and withdrew a small felt box along with a folded piece of paper. While she busied herself with the box, she handed Elsie the accompanying note to read.

My Angel,
    I was feeling guilty about sending you home with nothing to remind you of your experiences here, save for a few pictures. Enclosed, you will find a box that holds something very precious. It is a symbol of love and a reminder that with you always are two who will carry you in the hard times, love you in the trying times, and comfort you in the sad times. You should know that you have made a great impact on my life, introducing God to me in ways I have never accepted him. This is something I will be eternally thankful for. Because of you, I know what happiness feels like. I don't quite understand how it is that you found me or how I found you. But I don't want to question it.
    When all else fails, I hope that you will remember that I will always be there for you... and so will God. And I hope you will never forget you can talk with me about anything that troubles you. I will do everything in my power to make you happy, Angel. It's the least I can do to repay you for the happiness you've brought me.
    Love always,
    Vincent

    "Aww," Elsie said. She handed the note back with a teasing look on her face. "Do you have a mint or something? I think I just threw up a little."
    Angie pulled off one of her flip-flops and poised herself threateningly.
    Elsie squawked, holding her hands up in defense of her face. "I'm kidding!" She tipped over then, falling sidelong onto the couch cushions. Scrambling into an upright position, she bounced once playfully and held out an upturned palm in request. "Okay, okay. Let's see it."

Angie held up the delicate gold chain she'd just finished securing around her neck, allowing a simple cross pendant to dangle between her fingers.

Elsie leaned forward, peering at the necklace. "It's...petite."

"It's perfect," Angie insisted.

"Sure." Elsie snickered. "Man, you both got it bad." She sobered, drawing her legs up under her. "You sure this is such a good idea? He does live on the other side of the country."

"I know it'll be tough." Angie leaned back in the plush chair, caressing the pendant between her thumb and forefinger. "I think I'll know for sure if we can make it work after tonight," she added, her mind drifting back into anxiety. As much as she longed to talk to Vince, she felt sure what she had to tell him could make or break their fledgling relationship. He would either believe her, or he would finally have a reason to change his mind. Unable to forgive her own poor judgment, she couldn't see herself blaming him for the latter.

"You're not going to end up moving to Dixieland, are you?" Elsie looked at her with some mixture of worry and disbelief.

Angie glanced to the other girl and formed a half smile. "I will if I need to."

"Ugh," Elsie's nose crinkled in mock-disdain. "When did you turn into a romantic idealist?"

Angie chuckled. "Maybe I always have been. I just needed a good enough reason to admit it."

The phone rang in the kitchen and Angie rocked to her feet, sensing herself divided between eagerness and apprehension. She looked over her shoulder once she'd gotten halfway to the kitchen. "If that's him, you might want to head on home. We can do more catching up later."

"Oh, I see how it is." Elsie crossed her arms, wearing an offended look.

Angie wasn't sure how seriously to take her friend, but as she fetched the phone, she decided not to think about it. She doubted her ability to deal with more than one endangered relationship at a time.

~ ~ ~ ~ ~ ~ ~

"Alright, I'm home now," Vince said. His claim was corroborated by the sound of a car door closing in the background. "Will you please just tell me what's wrong?"

Angie paced the floor of her bedroom, staring down at the path she'd worn in the deep blue carpet as she held the phone to her ear. She had put off anything but light conversation until she was sure that Vince was no longer driving. It was one less thing for her to worry about. "I will. Tell me when you get to your room."

"I'm there now," he said, on the heels of a short pause. He sounded nearly as uneasy as she felt.

"Just...sit down and listen, okay?" she said. "I promise I'll try to tell you everything, but you have to let me get it out."

Please, let him believe me.

"I'm sitting."

Taking her own direction, Angie eased across her bed and sat with her back pressed to the wall as she began to fill in the gaps of the previous two days. She started with the argument on the morning she and Scott had left D.C., tediously explaining the reasoning behind the stop near Indianapolis and the shared hotel room. Vince made a throaty sound on occasion, but didn't interrupt her telling.

When she finally made it to the part about waking up to being assaulted, her breath became quick and shallow. Resurfacing panic fluttered along the fringe of her mind. The description of the event poured out of her, faltering partway through. Before she could recollect herself to continue, Vince interjected.

"He raped you!?!" The roiling anger in his tone reverberated through the phone's receiver.

Angie was stunned to hear the word she hadn't allowed herself to form. That one awful word, her mind had refused to accept until that moment. "No." She heard herself murmur in a detached voice. "But...almost. I suppose." She wondered if Scott's lack of success meant she should feel any less violated. "I hit him—really hard." She went on, conveying the remaining details of that night.

Vince's breath came low and ragged on the other end of the line. "You...didn't call the police?"

A crushing sensation engulfed Angie's heart. She'd confided everything in him, and now she was going to lose him. Naivety had never cost her so dearly. "Maybe I should have. I don't know." Her eyes stung. She didn't bother to stop the tears from flowing. "He told me he did it in his sleep."

"Bull$&*%!" Vince roared. "He knew exactly what he was trying to get away with."

"You're probably right." Angie cringed, though she sensed his hostility was directed toward Scott alone. "But if I reported him, it would just be my word against his. They wouldn't believe me after I put myself in that kind of...situation. They'd think—"

"It's not your fault." Vince broke in, tone softening.

"But, at least part of it is!" she cried, pulling her knees up until she could set her weary forehead against them. "He was my friend...I should have known better. I should have known -him- better. I never meant to hurt him or lead him on—" She gasped, losing control of her voice.

"Angel," Vince's voice came again, gentle and commanding. "There's no excuse for it. He tried to take what didn't belong to him. You can't hold yourself responsible for that."

Angie paused, thankful for his willingness to overlook her idiocy. She didn't feel remotely deserving of it. "I just...I feel like I failed. I should have set a better example. I should have done so many things differently," she said, shame clawing its way into her chest. Part of her knew her distress wasn't rational — but it was there, regardless. "What if...he goes off to college and hurts another girl because I made him so frustrated?" she choked out.

"Stop. Listen to me," Vince said, his tone slow and purposeful. "Please...please don't cry, babe. You didn't fail at anything—Scott did. He should have protected you. Even if that meant protecting you from himself." Vince paused and then emphasized, "He failed—not you."

"I'm sorry," Angie whispered, biting her knee to muffle a sob. The conviction in Vince's voice resonated with her as much as the words themselves. Together, they seemed to cut through the weighty veil of guilt. She felt both liberated, and somehow shielded by what he was trying to convey. It rang like truth.

How did he know to tell me that? she wondered in amazement. *How could he know that's exactly what I needed?*

"You have nothing to be sorry for," Vince said. "I'm sorry. I'm so sorry I wasn't there with you. I would have killed him." His voice grew dangerously definite.

Angie believed him. Every word.

"Then, I'm glad you weren't there. You'd be in prison right now," she said, dragging in a steadying breath. As she tuned in to his breathing to gauge his emotional state, she heard the rapid clicking of a keyboard somewhere in the background. "What are you doing?"

"I'm looking up plane tickets," Vince answered, factual in tone. "I can be there before Scott gets into town. If he tries to so much as get near you again, I'm taking a baseball bat to his kneecaps."

"That's really not necessary," Angie protested, unsure whether she should be flattered or appalled. Her heart was leaning toward flattered. "He'll be with Elsie the whole time. And besides, I don't want you flying up here all bent on violence. When you do come up...I want it to be so you can meet my parents." Even as she said it, she realized how much she meant it.

Vince fell silent at length. "You want me to meet them?" He sounded caught off-guard.

"Of course I do." Angie wiped at her damp cheeks with her free palm, feeling herself lighten. "But I want you to plan it out so you don't get yourself in trouble at work or school. And you might want to wait a couple of weeks, that way we can work around my last semester and space out our visits," she said, deliberating aloud. "We could alternate. I'll save up some money and fly down over Thanksgiving—"

"You're smiling," Vince said, his voice regaining much of its usual calm and warmth.

"Yes." She closed her eyes, picturing his face and the pleased expression she knew he wore. A calm sense of assurance settled over her. "I think we can make this work, if you're still up for it."

The silence on Vince's end extended long enough to cause her concern. When he spoke again, it was with great care. "No matter the time, no matter the place, I'll always be there for you. I'll be waiting. Even though I'm 20 hours away—I don't care if I'm 200 hours away. My heart and soul are there with you. So just keep smiling, babe." His words came rhythmic and laden with certainty. "I love you."

Angie felt the overspill of tears return, but this time for a very different reason. She left them untouched to slide down her face and fall against her knees. "Vince?"

"Yeah, Angel?"

"I love you, too."

Epilogue

October 2nd,

It's been almost two months since my expedition into the real world came to an end. Looking back on it, I'm not sure I accomplished what I set out to do. Bad things happened. Amazing things happened. I hurt, and I healed. For a little while I was brave. I didn't find myself all at once or anything so simple, but I did find a few pieces of me along the way…jagged, mixed-up pieces that are starting to fit together and form a shape I hadn't expected. I also found a few things I didn't know I was looking for. And ultimately, I think I've decided how I'm going to start the next chapter in my life.

It's amazing how much has changed in just a few months. I'm stronger now; and so is my faith. Hopefully I'm a little wiser too, but that's up for debate. I still don't know what I want to do with myself career-wise, but I think I'm finally okay with that. What I do isn't who I am; I've figured that much out at least. As for 'finding myself'…well, I suspect that's something I'll be doing for the rest of my life. And I'm okay with that too. I may not know exactly where I'm going, but I'm pretty sure I've found a traveling companion for the rest of my life's journey. Okay, so maybe 'found' isn't quite the right word for it. He kind of…followed me home.

I'm sitting at the airport right now, waiting for Vince's plane to de-board. If I were any more excited someone would probably have to call security on me. Suffice it to say, we're doing well in spite of the distance. Most nights we talk for hours and end up falling asleep on the phone. Yeah, we're that sappy. I guess it's strange I've gotten to know someone and their personality so completely without being able to see them in person. But in a way, I think we have a huge advantage. We've already discussed everything that's remotely important to us and hashed out our differences in perspective and background; all without the distractions that most couples face. It hasn't been easy and we've still got a long way to go…but it's been more than worth it.

So, it looks like the end of my first big adventure is turning into the beginning of a new one. The plot of my life is still being written. And fortunately, I'm just a co-author. I'm pretty sure it's more interesting this way.

Mileage Log Total: 6,832 mi.

Bonus Tally: 1 awesome boyfriend, a dash of personal growth, and one heck of a story to tell one day.

~Ang

Road Kill Records

Deer 卄卄卄卄卄

Deer 卄卄卄卄卄

Armadillo? IIII

rabbit 三卄卄

squirrel 三卄卄卄

Coyote II

coon 卄卄卄卄卄卄

possum = 卄

porcupine II

mouse 卄卄卄卄卄卄卄

Acknowledgments

Innumerable thanks to God for keeping me alive, giving me purpose, and loving me in spite of myself.

Thanks also to my RWA sisters (the HOD, MCRW, and Southern Magic chapters) for the years of encouragement, critiquing, and camaraderie.

I want to thank Katherine "Kitten" DeVoe and Patience Holloway, my sprightly sisters in spirit. You've helped me walk this path in more ways than I could imagine.

Many thanks to Courtney Wichtendahl, for your OCD-induced excellence and most especially for your friendship over the years.

Thank you to the illustrious C.J. Redwine, for your query-ninja skills, relentless support, and all-around awesomeness.

Thanks to very my first critique partner, Elizabeth Vershowske. To Ian Cavanaugh, for your invaluable insights and analysis, to Michelle Gullixon for the honest feedback and unwavering loyalty, to Robin Roberts for being my "extra mommy." Thank you to my "name dude" John Denart for the unsolicited belief in me, to Danielle Barnum for her phenomenal photography skills, and to Mollie Fischer--my courageous butt-double.

Thanks to my precious and precocious beta-readers: Anna, Kelly, Lana, and Tatya.

Also, a big thank you to my parents--for bringing me into this world and fostering the conviction that I could somehow affect it for the better.

I'd like to thank all of my most enduring friends who choose to overlook my daydreaming, glazed looks, and sudden impulse to suspend conversation so I can write down a thought before it's lost to the void of my ADD-addled mind.

Book Club Discussion Questions

1. How would you describe your personal experience with this book? Were you engaged immediately, or did it take you a while to "get into it?"

2. Describe the main character, Angeli — personality, motivations, self-perception.

3. Does Angeli change by the end of the book? Does she grow or mature?

4. Why might the author have chosen to tell her story the way she did?

5. What main ideas/themes does the author explore?

6. Are any of the events in the book relevant to your own life?

7. Was there a specific passage, quote, or scene that elicited a strong reaction from you — good or bad? Share the passage and its effect.

8. Did you find the ending satisfying? Why, or why not?

9. If you could ask the author a question, what would you ask? Have you read other books by this author? If so, how does this book compare? If not, does this book inspire you to read others?

10. Has this book broadened your perspective in any way? Have you learned something new, or been exposed to a different way of looking at something?

11. Do you feel this book truly belongs in the nonfiction genre?

12. Compare this book to other memoirs you've read. Is it similar to any of them? What do you think will be your lasting impression of the book?

About The Author

Angela N. Blount is a Minnesota native, transplanted to the deep South--where she currently resides with her understanding husband, their two children, and a set of identity-confused cats. She is a former book reviewer for RT Book Reviews, a memoirist, freelance editor, sporadic poet, and webcomic artist.

In her spare time, Angela enjoys reading, coffee shop loitering, questionable attempts at horticulture, and all things geeky.

Find out more about Angela and her latest projects here:
http://www.angelanblount.com/

Facebook: https://www.facebook.com/AngelaNBlount
Twitter: https://twitter.com/Perilous1

Made in the USA
Lexington, KY
12 November 2013